Bing
and
Billie
and
Frank
and
Ella
and
Judy
and
Barbra

DAN CALLAHAN

CHICAGO
REVIEW
PRESS

Published by Chicago Review Press Incorporated
814 North Franklin Street
Chicago, Illinois 60610
ISBN 978-1-64160-922-7

Library of Congress Control Number: 2023936693

Typesetting: Jonathan Hahn

Printed in the United States of America
5 4 3 2 1

In Memory of Ms. Hazel Thomas and
my grandmother Mary Mikula

"My music is coming back, Danny, you wait and see."

Contents

Introduction

The Democracy of American Music

BY THE EARLY twentieth century the songwriters of what was known as Tin Pan Alley had sheet music of their songs readily available to the general public at ten cents a copy. A young Irving Berlin got his start as a song plugger, demonstrating and pitching new songs in saloons and music stores, and George Gershwin and Jerome Kern were also pitching songs and making music spread as far and wide as possible. Lillian Hardin Armstrong worked as a song plugger and promoted her own songs like "Just for a Thrill" and the career of her husband Louis, who apprenticed with the cornetist, bandleader, and songwriter Joe "King" Oliver, one of the pioneers of a new kind of music called jazz.

Music began to be everywhere in America in the 1910s and early 1920s, played at home with extended family gathered around the piano, in barrooms and later in speakeasies, and then on record and on the radio, on the street, coming from windows, listened to through the day and at night, rousing people to action, making happy people even happier and sad people even sadder. This was both a heightening of life and a heightening of possibility, that great American lure that says, "You can change your life," or even, "Life might change."

Music was now open in some form to everyone in America. Blues, opera, classical, operetta, popular, novelty songs, songs about love, songs about mother love, songs to sell war, songs to escape with. There was "Let Me Call You Sweetheart," "Alexander's Ragtime Band," "I'm Always Chasing Rainbows," "Look for the Silver Lining," "Down Hearted Blues,"

"The Donkey Serenade," "I Cried for You," "Nobody Knows You When You're Down and Out," and "Fascinating Rhythm." You might work all day and then go to your bedroom and listen to the broadcasts on the radio from famous ballrooms in populous cities. You could be there. The music from the radio and on records meant that nobody needed to be entirely alone now. People could dream. They could reminisce. They could cry their heart out, and it would be a good cry.

And they could get up and dance, for the new American music of the 1910s and 1920s, first ragtime and then jazz and swing, was the music of celebration and liberation. There were dance crazes like the Castle walk and the foxtrot, and beyond this were the shimmy, the Charleston, and the Lindy Hop, and a deliverance from corsets for women. This was an age of fast-paced or hot music that even came to be known as the Jazz Age, and it ran on bootleg liquor, nerve, and dance bands of some kind at schools and grand ballrooms where men and women could meet, take a turn around the floor, and experiment.

Pleasure-loving flappers could cart around a phonograph and a few of their favorite records. In the movie *Sadie Thompson* (1928), a hypocritical reformer named Davidson (Lionel Barrymore) is driven to heights of judgmental fury whenever Gloria Swanson's Sadie plays her jazz records over and over again. The "bad girl" heroines of 1920s and early 1930s movies always seem to have a phonograph and a few hot records to aggravate the puritanical men and women around them, and it is clear they get a kick out of this, as if they are saying, "Ain't nothing you can do about it, dearie."

Once that window to music for everyone was opened, it could never be closed again, not by moralizing or classism or racism or sexism. This book is about that window being opened even further, and the fight for freedom and equality that it eventually led to. It is also about the way a human singing voice can be a directly amorous spur to the deepest of desires and fantasies, and how it can be a bond of friendship or fellowship, and how it can ascend to the highest form of all-seeing and objective art. The sound of the right singing voice can reach out slowly and touch us, and it can feel like fingers gently caressing our flesh. Can this be? *Yes*, the voice says. *Yes, it can, and it will, and it is.*

1

Bing: Out of Nowhere

THE STORY BEGINS with a voice on the radio. The voice is low, rough even, a baritone—urgent, throbbing, and sexy. Those who only know the later Bing Crosby might be taken aback by his vocal for "Out of Nowhere," which he recorded on March 30, 1931. He is not playing it safe here, as he increasingly did by the early 1940s. This record has a feeling of "It's now or never," and he's betting everything on it. Crosby had been a singer with the Paul Whiteman Orchestra as one of the Rhythm Boys, with his partners Harry Barris and Al Rinker, but he was going out on his own now, out on a limb.

He begins "Out of Nowhere" softly, intimately, singing sweet some-things directly into our ear, as if he's making his pitch at a crowded party and has taken each of us into some corner of it. The voice on this record is trying to observe some modicum of propriety, but youthful ardor and copious amounts of liquor have their way and Crosby is soon singing full out, like one of his idols, the Irish tenor John McCormack. But then, about two minutes into the song, he decides to pull way back on the volume, and the effect he gets from this pulling back is enough to make anyone weak in the knees from hearing it.

Crosby is singing at full tilt again by the end of the song, which has a lyric by Edward Heyman, who wrote the words to "Body and Soul." Technically he's using dynamics, controlling the volume of his voice so that when he decides to sing softly after singing full out it cannot help but be felt as a plea—and a winning strategy. He uses a lot more vibrato as a young man than he will in the future, and he also uses his early trademark: a mordent, a slight fluctuation between notes.

Crosby is both laying himself bare here and asserting his own power and command. It took guts to sing "Out of Nowhere" the way he did. He was done fooling around. Crosby was throwing his hat into the ring now, and he changed and transformed American popular music with his hip, intimate style of singing.

When he recorded "Out of Nowhere" for Brunswick Records, Crosby was singing with the Gus Arnheim band at the Cocoanut Grove in Hollywood, and he was making important contacts while also drinking and carousing, sometimes with his friend Louis Armstrong, who was also playing in that area at Frank Sebastian's Cotton Club. "Every night between their outfit and our outfit, we used to *Burn up* the air, *every* night," said Louis. "Yea—Bing & Gus Arnheim & Co would broadcast first every night and leave the ether wave sizzling hot. Just right for us when we would burst on in there from the Cotton Club. Oh, it was lots of fun. The same listeners would catch both programs before going to bed."

When their respective bands were done broadcasting, Louis and Bing would get together to jam. "After Bing—the band—Mr. Arnheim and the boys would finish work at the Grove, they would haul ashes over to the Cotton Club where we would be playing and swing with us, until Home Sweet Home was played," Louis said.

Louis captures the Bing look of this time: "Sometimes he would come over wearing his sharp uniform, the one I admired so much. It was a *hard* hitting blue with white buttons, which made him look (to me) like a young Captain on some high powered yacht." Lots of women had Bing's attention then, but he was most focused on one beautiful singer who would become his first wife. "That's when he and Dixie Lee were CANOEING," said Louis.

Louis and Bing idolized each other, and their mutual admiration society lasted all the rest of their lives. In this period, early in 1931, when Bing's records were making him into a star, they were close enough that Bing asked Louis and his band to come to the train station to serenade Dixie Lee after she got back from shooting a movie on the East Coast. "Oh—Daddy Bing—Harry Barris and Al Rinker—they gave me all sorts of inducements, etc. to just go down to the station and sorta toot a few hot ones as she hit the ground from the train," Louis said, but he had amorous plans of his own for that evening and had to decline.

Music as a means of seduction was something that Bing was making use of in life and also on the air in 1931. In January he had recorded one of his first hits, "I Surrender Dear," which has an intricate and expressive arrangement with a Gershwin flavor to it. Bing is singing here of a Frank Sinatra–Ava Gardner–type relationship where fighting is the spice that keeps things lively, but the couple has reached an impasse and stopped speaking, and so Bing is surrendering, with a mordent on "dear." He is making himself appealingly vulnerable but not abject, as Sinatra so often did in his own vocals, for the persona that Bing created is far too proud for that. He is almost never lovelorn on record. The early Bing, more than anything, is out for pleasure.

The scapegrace Bing revealed on the song "One More Time," which he recorded in between "I Surrender Dear" and "Out of Nowhere," might come as a real shocker to those who only know the older man and his Christmas specials. After over a minute of swinging intro, Bing comes in with "Oh my pretty baby one more time . . . ba bum . . . just one more time!" That "ba-bum" in between phrases shows the kind of rhythmic inventiveness that he was capable of in this period, which gave his vocals such an exciting feeling of recklessness. "You can spend my dough, you can drink my gin, you can snap the lock if you'll let me in!" he promises.

Bing conquered America musically in 1931, and his other records included "At Your Command," with just a Harry Barris piano accompaniment for his impassioned and emotional vocal, and "I Apologize." He was winning over a female audience with these tunes in 1931 and strategizing so that he could win the men later. When he made this first decisive impact, Bing was a dream man on the radio, an undressed sound. He apologizes, he surrenders, he's at your command. Bing's ardent vocals promised fun and a little trouble, and an intensity that left a crooner like Rudy Vallée, with his thin, prim, ghostly voice, in the dust.

That the visual he could offer didn't quite match the sexual urgency of the voice was something that Bing was well aware of, which is why he so often looks sheepish in his early 1930s movies. When he sings

"Out of Nowhere" in *Confessions of a Co-Ed* (1931), a Sylvia Sidney vehicle at Paramount, his hair looks strange, for he had started losing it very early in life and didn't have convincing hairpieces yet. His face is apprehensive, but he is still calm enough to break off singing his great make-out song to say hello after being greeted by Phillips Holmes, who is dancing by with Sidney.

Bing had been educated by Jesuits, so he was trained to cast a cold eye on life, and it was this essential coolness that set him apart. It made him hip enough to know that Louis Armstrong was a musical genius and the foundation for a new way of singing, and it also kept him steady for decades when so many others faltered. He became increasingly removed, held back, and suburban, but he started out in 1931 as a naked voice on the radio, and that voice is still very winning and very seductive, like a first boyfriend with bad-boy tendencies who drives you crazy but always has you coming back for more.

2

Bing: Just One More Chance

BING'S FATHER WAS known around Spokane, Washington, as "Happy Harry," and he wasn't a guy who let work or responsibilities stand in the way of a good time; he was something like the free-spirited characters Bing often played in his 1930s movies like *Pennies from Heaven* (1936). Bing's strict and forbidding Irish mother Kate was the disciplinarian of the household, and she had to be, for Harry made little money and she had seven children to bring up. At one point Happy Harry bought a phonograph with money that might have been intended for groceries, but this was a music-loving family, so Kate didn't stay angry for long.

There were several versions of how Bing got his unusual name, but the true story is that the young Harry Lillis Crosby Jr., born in 1903, loved a local paper called the *Bingville Bugle* and especially a comic feature in it called *Bingo from Bingville*. A friend and neighbor named Valentine Hobart started calling him "Bingo from Bingville," and this eventually got shortened to "Bing."

At Gonzaga High School, where he received his Jesuit education, Bing took lessons in elocution, and he was someone who delighted in words for their own sake, which became one of the most distinctive features of his persona, particularly on the radio. He had a near-photographic memory, was an expert all-around athlete, and was also an altar boy in the Catholic Church. Even in the most dissipated days of his youth, Bing always tried to make it to Sunday mass. He could be diffident, but deep down Bing was ambitious, and this came out in a poem he wrote while in school where he dreamed of being an adored and indolent king surrounded by wealth.

The Crosby family enthused to John McCormack and Caruso records at home, but Bing was most impressed by seeing Al Jolson live at a Spokane theater where he was working as a property boy one summer. Jolson came from a Jewish family; his father was a rabbi and a cantor in a synagogue, and so his style of singing out came from that tradition. But when he was still in his teens, Jolson started performing his shows in blackface, a grotesque holdover from the minstrel era of the nineteenth century. He was billed at that time as "The World's Greatest Entertainer," and he was wowing Spokane in his smash-hit musical *Robinson Crusoe, Jr.*, in which he played a resourceful chauffeur named Gus, a character Jolson had assumed in several earlier shows. Jolson's voice sounds both corny and studied on records, and in surviving footage from 1926 where he sings some of his hits while wearing blackface, his fake-intimate, cajoling style is odious.

The popularity of blackface in the early twentieth century cannot be ignored, although too often it is written out of the history of some of America's most beloved performers. "Any form of history that gets suppressed or repressed or erased out, it comes back to haunt," said critic Margo Jefferson. "Some of this came out of a genuine fascination with the music, the songs, the dances, the performance styles of Black people. . . . You can be fascinated, you can be excited, but you can always feel superior."

Bing was riveted as he watched Jolson seize the stage, rushing around and ad-libbing lines and even song lyrics. Seeing Jolson excited Bing about the possibilities of performing, but the influence of Jolson vocally only comes out in some of his early recordings. The decisive influence on him in the 1920s would be a real Black man, not an imitation: the fabled Louis. Yet the influence of Jolson as a performer would prove hard to shake off for Bing.

Bing and his friend Al Rinker played the drums for a band called the Musicaladers, and they performed at high school dances and also entertained between movies at the Clemmer Theatre. Bing was a few years older than Rinker, and he soon asserted himself after looking askance one day at the way Rinker was being bossy with the other band members. "After one rehearsal Bing came over to me and said, 'You'd better not talk that way to me or I'll give you a punch in the nose,'" Rinker remembered.

Bing and Rinker would often spend all day listening to the latest records at a store in town called Russ Bailey's House of Music. "We practically lived there," Bing said, remembering the impressions made by recordings of the Mound City Blue Blowers, the Original Memphis Five, and the Original Dixieland Jazz Band. But the most important order of business for Bing and Al was to listen to certain Paul Whiteman records over and over again until they had learned the arrangements by ear. Rinker said that they would buy one record after memorizing twelve others.

Bing drank and partied heavily at this time, and he and the band gladly accepted a gig at a shady dive called the Pekin Café. "I was able to allay some of my mother's doubts about the restaurant's respectability by pointing to its most respectable financial rewards," Bing said.

Though he went to college at Gonzaga University, Bing didn't get a degree. In October of 1925, Bing and Al Rinker set off for California, where Rinker's sister Mildred Bailey was living. Happy Harry wished them well, as did Kate, who had been unhappy about Bing quitting school. Harry later said that both he and Kate knew their son had some talent, so they didn't stand in his way when he went off on his own to sing with Rinker and make his fortune.

Mildred Bailey was a vocalist herself and had known Bing in Spokane, where she sang in speakeasies, and to her he was something of a delinquent. "Bing was always a fella to get into trouble," she said in 1941. "I expect he spent every Saturday night of his life in jail."

Bailey was a small woman, barely five feet tall, with a bright, sharp, intimate voice and a sure sense of rhythm. Both she and Rinker were of Native American heritage, and she introduced Bing to some new sounds on record, particularly Ethel Waters and Bessie Smith, getting him out of the white-guy jazz pocket he had settled into at Russ Bailey's House of Music. A hip lady who always kept her eyes and especially her ears open, Bailey also told Bing when he reached Los Angeles with her brother that if he was serious about singing he had to listen to Louis Armstrong.

Louis was playing with the Fletcher Henderson Orchestra, and in November of 1925 he started making records with his own group, the Hot Five. His strong-willed wife Lil got him to quit the Henderson band to go out on his own, and she was one of the Hot Five herself, on piano. She had him billed as "The World's Greatest Trumpet Player," much to his chagrin, but he was that and much more. Maybe you had to be there for Al Jolson, the so-called world's greatest entertainer of his time, even if that's looking and sounding increasingly unlikely. But the legend of Louis, dead now for fifty years, is always expanding and ascending.

Louis told the story later that he started to scat, a New Orleans term for wordless vocalizing, on the song "Heebie Jeebies" because he dropped the lyrics and didn't want to spoil the take, and this song sold somewhere in the vicinity of forty thousand copies. Musicians like cornetist Bix Beiderbecke, who was of German heritage, listened to Louis's records over and over again, laughing at his audacity and sense of fun. Speaking of his audience, Louis once said, "They know I'm there in the cause of happiness."

Bing in this period was there for the cause of youthful hedonism, and he sometimes got so drunk that he fell off the platform where he was singing. If a heckler gave him a hard time, he was ready to jump off the bandstand and follow the guy outside. He did not have many serious girlfriends. When years later he met the young nephew of one girl that he had seen steadily in this period named Dorothy Bresnan, Bing wrote a charming note to her in remembrance of their romance. To pick up the slack at this time, he was an ardent customer of ladies of the evening.

Inspired by Louis, Bing and Al were doing jazzy numbers and even scatting, a novelty on the vaudeville circuit. The bandleader Paul Whiteman was similarly inspired by Louis, Duke Ellington, and Fletcher Henderson. After listening to these musicians intensively and talking to them, Whiteman concluded that the best jazz musicians were African American, but when Whiteman tried to hire Black players for his band, his management told him he would lose all his bookings in the South. He was also told that the Black players would be forced to accept separate accommodations and dining rooms, and so Whiteman compromised and hired Black arrangers for his music.

Whiteman's manager Jimmy Gillespie saw Bing and Al perform in late 1926 and spoke of them enthusiastically to Whiteman, who immediately hired them. Bing and Al soon left with the Whiteman band on a tour of the Midwest that took them to Chicago, where Whiteman brought Bing to hear Louis at the Sunset Café, which was run by Joe Glaser, an associate of Al Capone who would eventually become Louis's manager.

Bing was delighted by Louis's trumpet playing and singing, but he also loved his comic inventiveness, especially a routine Louis had worked up where he put on a frock coat and dark glasses and played a character called the Reverend Satchelmouth. This character stayed with Bing. "I'm proud to acknowledge my debt to the Reverend Satchelmouth," he said in 1950. "He is the beginning and the end of music in America. And long may he reign."

Bing and Al were doing fairly well on the tour, but they laid an egg when they played at the Paramount Theatre in New York in February of 1927, one of those unaccountable show business things having to do with audiences and what works for some and doesn't work for others. Young Bing was unfazed, set on his course of good times and golf wherever he could play it.

He had begun making records with the Whiteman band and took a solo vocal on the southern ditty "Muddy Water" in March of 1927. His slightly hoarse voice really stands out on "Changes," which features a hot solo from Bix Beiderbecke, for as his definitive biographer Gary Giddins has observed, Bing was a baritone in a world of tenors. By April, Harry Barris joined their act and they rejoined Whiteman as the Rhythm Boys.

The musical *Show Boat* opened at the end of 1927 and was an immediate success. Bing recorded two of the Jerome Kern and Oscar Hammerstein songs from that landmark show in 1928: "Make Believe," fetchingly if hoarsely, and "Ol' Man River," inadequately. Jules Bledsoe, who played the role of Joe in this original production because Paul Robeson was unavailable, sings "Ol' Man River" in a very dramatic and dynamic way, hurling out words and notes as if they were challenges filled with rage and pride. By contrast, Bing sings his "Ol' Man River" to a fast and blithe Whiteman foxtrot arrangement for dancing that totally disregards the lyrics of the song. Aside from this, his low notes are not fully supported here. Blame it on his youth.

Robeson also recorded "Ol' Man River" with Whiteman's band in 1928, and the fast tempo doesn't allow him to do everything he could with his signature song. Bing returned to "Ol' Man River" again on record in 1945 and sang it in his mature and distant style, and this at least has the benefit of a clearly objective point of view, and pained respect for the lyrics. But then he mistakenly sang it again as a fast rhythm number in an anniversary special that aired in 1977, the year he died. Blame it on his age.

Louis spoke very highly of a record that Bing made with Beiderbecke in early 1928 called "From Monday On," and Bing spoke admiringly of Beiderbecke, who died young in 1931, for the rest of his life. Bing brings a distinct jazz flavor to "You Took Advantage of Me," a Rodgers and Hart tune he recorded in April of 1928, playing with the melody on certain syllables in a way that feels liberatingly sexy. Once he had that jazz feeling, Bing was nearly incapable of singing a number straight. He plays with time on his 1929 record "Louise," a catchy song introduced by Maurice Chevalier, taking the tempo faster than you expect it, which gives it a sense of danger.

The Rhythm Boys were on tour in late 1928 and stopped in Chicago, where Bing made sure to see Louis again, and Louis went to see Bing play at the Sunset Café. Marijuana was legal then, and they both partook of it with regularity; pot was a way of life for Louis, who did a song about it called "Muggles." Speaking of how marijuana got him through and how it inspired friendships, Louis said it "makes you forget all the bad things that happen to a Negro. It makes you feel wanted, and when you're with another tea smoker it makes you feel a special kinship."

During an interview with Barbara Walters at the end of his life, Bing startled his TV audience when he went from saying that he would never speak to his daughter Mary Frances again if she lived with a man without benefit of matrimony to saying that he thought marijuana should be legalized. When he was angry at his son Gary for drinking too much, Bing once told him that he should smoke pot instead. Louis was as anti-alcohol as he was pro-pot.

Louis wrote in later years about the excitement over Bing's singing in the jazz community: "There were just as many colored people 'buying air,' raving over Bing's recordings, as much as anybody else. The chicks (gals) were justa swooning and screaming when Bing would sing."

The women were crazy for him, but the men who were serious about music were taking notice too. "I remember the first time a friend of mine in Chicago, he came to my house and said, 'Man, there's a little cat comin' up singin',' you got to dig him!'" Louis remembered. "And that was my boy, Papa Bing."

Louis started doing Bing-like mordents sometimes as a kind of tribute when he sang, which can be heard on late-1920s records like "When You're Smiling," and Bing could growl like Louis, most notably on his 1931 recording of "I Found a Million Dollar Baby (in a Five and Ten Cent Store)." They inspired each other while still remaining their own singular entities, and they changed over time, which Louis noted. "Bing's voice has a mellow quality that only Bing's got," Louis said to *Time* magazine in 1955. "It's like gold being poured out of a cup."

The late 1920s was a period of experimentation for Bing. He would husband his vocal resources in later years, but it becomes apparent just how much voice he had on "Great Day," recorded in late 1929, where he has the kind of confident, rounded tones of a semi-operatic baritone. He could likely have handled operetta roles, at least, if he had wanted to, and he would get around to Victor Herbert in the 1930s.

The Rhythm Boys played the Palace Theatre in New York, the top gig for anyone in vaudeville, and Bing had a near miss at this time. After a forty-eight-hour bender that found him waking up in a strange hotel room, Bing went to the bathroom just in time to miss being sprayed by machine gun fire from the front door. The other men inside were wounded but not killed, and Bing stayed in the bathroom "for what seemed hours" until a cop came up, whereupon Bing learned that he was in the hideout of "Machine Gun Jack" McGurn, a Capone mobster who had cut the throat of singer Joe E. Lewis.

The Rhythm Boys traveled to California to appear with Whiteman in the lavish color feature *King of Jazz* (1930) at Universal. Bing sings solo under the credits, selling the charms of music from a symphony grand by Schubert or Brahms to a popular band or a "uke 'neath the palms."

This mix of the old and the new would be borne out by this oddball and certainly overproduced film. "Ah, tell it," cries Bing as encouragement when the Rhythm Boys do a number, his problem hair mitigated by his blue eyes and playful physicality. Bing's jazzy modernity here is set off by John Boles, who sings "It Happened in Monterey" with pompous declamations and rolled *r*'s.

Boles took over a number that Bing was supposed to sing in *King of Jazz* called "Song of the Dawn" after Bing got arrested for drunk driving. "He practically drove through the lobby of the Roosevelt Hotel in Hollywood," said singer Bobbe Brox, who eventually married the songwriter Jimmy Van Heusen. Jimmy Gillespie bailed Bing out of jail, and he arrived in court the following week fresh from the golf course, snazzily but slightly eccentrically attired in his usual motley of colors and patterns. (Bing was color-blind.)

The judge asked him if he had heard about Prohibition, and Bing said something sassy in response, either "Only remotely" or "Yes, but nobody pays much attention to it," which was his preferred line of dialogue for this story when he told it as an older man. Bing was sentenced to sixty days, and it was only after much behind-the-scenes maneuvering that he was allowed to continue filming *King of Jazz* under police escort.

Determined to appear in the movies, Bing had made some screen tests but was turned down by Fox because of the way his ears stuck out. The best he could do at this point was an appearance with the Rhythm Boys in a short called *Two Plus Fours* (1930), a film that is notable for the way Bing stands up for a very sympathetic older Jewish character and a moment where he waves his hand and cries, "Oh, hush!" in a nance way that shows how hip and in the know he was. He then made a brief appearance singing during a "whoopee!" party scene in Edmund Goulding's *Reaching for the Moon* (1930), a vehicle for Douglas Fairbanks.

In September of 1930, Bing married Dixie Lee, who as a singer at that time was somewhat better known than he was, and this was a key step in his move to settle down and become the king he had dreamed of being in school. The following year, when he was making his first huge

Bing began his film career with a series of shorts for Mack Sennett.

impact as a solo artist on records, Bing began appearing in a series of short films for comedy director Mack Sennett, starting with *I Surrender Dear*, which was named for his star-making hit song. He is playing a version of himself here, singing "I Surrender Dear" at the Cocoanut Grove, and this movie makes comic hay out of the fact that a lot of Bing's audience didn't know what he looked like yet; he was just a very seductive voice on the radio in this crucial transitional period.

This early screen Bing is a cutup and a scamp, and he's a camp, too, ironically calling a jealous butch guy a "pansy." He pantomimes to his own recording of "Out of Nowhere" and he's very good at being silly, which does match an aspect of his radio voice image: the unreliable but fun good-time guy. His rough speaking voice is just as sexy as his singing voice, and all of these things serve to distract us from possible stumbling blocks like his hair problem, his ears, and his round waistline, which spoke to a less visually attractive aspect of his hedonism.

Bing is followed by adoring women in his next Sennett short, *One More Chance* (1931), where he sings one of his many hit songs from that year, "Wrap Your Troubles in Dreams," and the title tune "Just One More Chance," which he does in a very jazzy and rhythmic freewheeling Louis fashion to a girl at a table in a club.

Billboard Girl (1932) is a short that pushes Bing the Camp to his outer limits. His character is selling magazines in order to go to college, and he is engaged to a girl named Mary (Marjorie Kane). Mary's naughty brother Freddie (James Eagles) pretends to be his sister over the phone with Bing, and they make kissing sounds at each other. "Don't queer it!" Freddie says to his friends as he tries to finish this phone call. The none-too-masculine Freddie gets into female drag and pretends to be Mary again so that Bing can pitch some woo to him, and Bing nearly kisses him, all of which suggests that horny nances must have liked Bing as much as so many of the women in America did.

He had his own show now on the radio too, so Bing was everywhere in 1931, conquering all aspects of mass media, goofing around on-screen, crooning and seducing over the airwaves and on record, and providing comfort during the worst years of the Depression. His theme song on the radio, "Where the Blue of the Night (Meets the Gold of the Day)," is meant to soothe listeners and ready them for sleep, where troubles could be wrapped in dreams like a warm blanket.

But this early Bing could also provoke, and the way he often does that is with his daring sense of time. Listen to the way he somehow slips in the phrase "Cuz I'll never stand for that" on the song "I'm Gonna Get You," and the breakneck way he ends it with a super-fast decrescendo on the words "Wait'll you see what I'm going to do to you, babe!" Bing's rhythmic inventiveness signaled then and still signals, "We don't need to follow the rules." And of course playing hide-and-seek with the beat of a song and filling it with as many extra notes as possible has a very sexy effect.

Bing signed with Paramount Pictures, partly because he had befriended Gary Cooper and that was Cooper's studio. He played a version of himself in his first feature for Paramount, *The Big Broadcast* (1932), which collects a lineup of radio stars of that time like Kate Smith, George Burns and Gracie Allen, and the dynamic Boswell Sisters, plus Cab Calloway and the Mills Brothers, with whom Bing had a number-one hit in "Dinah," one of his most delightful early records. He starts it slow, but once the Mills Brothers take the song up with a fast tempo a little over a minute in, Bing offers up a scat break and then slips in hip encouraging phrases as the brothers come back in: "Sell it!" and "Snag it!" and "Ah, tell it!"

Frank Tuttle, the director of *The Big Broadcast* and several of Bing's subsequent 1930s movies, introduced him to screenwriter John Bright, who was raising money to defend nine young Black men falsely accused of rape down in Scottsboro, Alabama. Bright remembered Bing responding, "Nine colored boys in the South accused of rape. They didn't do it. How much do you want?" He wrote out a check to Bright for $1,000. In the 1930s Bing leaned left and was progressive by instinct.

Bing is attacked by a mob of female fans at the start of *The Big Broadcast*, so his face is covered in lipstick kisses as he does a bit of "I Surrender Dear" on the air. He is late for his show, which plays on Bing's own reputation at this time for unreliability. A blonde secretary who is in love with him calls him "everybody's type," and he looks better than he ever has here with a full toupee and his ears pinned back.

The Bing in this movie is all over the place emotionally, even considering suicide fairly seriously. "You sing into a little hole, year after year, and then you die!" he says, and this isn't really played for comedy. The 1932 Bing is a heavy drinker and a moody romantic who might fall so deeply in love with a woman that his heart will get broken and never mend. He speaks the lyrics to "Here Lies Love" before starting to sing them, which emphasizes his sincerity as a singer and the way he made singing as intimate as whispered conversation. The words of a lyric are just as important to Bing as the music, and sometimes more so.

The vocal trouble that had caused some raspiness during his Whiteman days had started to vanish or come under his control. A node had been discovered on his vocal cords, but doctors advised against having it operated on, and this accounts for some of the pleasingly virile roughness of his tone in this period.

Bing scatted on several other of his 1932 records like "Sweet Georgia Brown" and "Some of These Days," Sophie Tucker's signature song, which Bing made his scapegrace, near-ne'er-do-well own. But this was the same year he recorded a pained acknowledgment of the Depression,

"Brother, Can You Spare a Dime?" This story song is early Bing at his most engaged, with just a hint of distance to make it universal.

The Bing-ian subtext of "Brother, Can You Spare a Dime?" is that if you do what people tell you to do, they'll use you and toss you aside on the trash. Go to war, and what was that for? The character he is playing in this song is named Al, and nobody can even remember his name now that he's down and out. Bing's Al is angry, yet he can't let go of his nostalgia for the past either. This is a very complicated song, and Bing explores every facet of it, ending on a surge in volume and full voice that dies off just slightly at the end—the perfect choice. Bing had made it to the top of his profession in 1932, and now he was tasked with speaking for everyone.

3

Billie's Blues

SADIE FAGAN MET Clarence Holiday at a dance or a carnival when she was nineteen years old, and she never got over him. Sadie had his child, born Eleanora Fagan, on April 7, 1915, in Philadelphia, after being kicked out of her Baltimore home by her parents for getting pregnant. A man named Frank DeViese is listed as the father on Eleanora's birth certificate, but he was likely just a friend whose name was put down as a formality. It is almost certain that Clarence was Eleanora's father.

Clarence was a musician and played the banjo, and he was off touring when Eleanora was born. Sadie brought Eleanora back to Baltimore to live with her half sister Eva Miller, but Eleanora had almost no supervision as a young girl. There is a photo of her at age two where she stands in a white dress with a white flower on her head, and the look on her face is adult, scarred, demanding. This is a face that already does not like what it sees of life.

Eleanora felt that the haughty Fagans had rejected her mother and her, and this feeling of rejection went deep. When some of her mother's side of the family came to see her sing in later years, she was heard to say, "As far as I'm concerned, all the Fagans are dead." When they got up to leave in a huff, one of the women cried over her shoulder, "*You're* the one who's dead, girl." This story comes from Eleanora's uncle Johnny, Sadie's brother, who later said how much he enjoyed his niece singing "I Cover the Waterfront" in later years, for it was redolent of her rough seaport upbringing in Baltimore.

A photo of Billie Holiday at age two.
Courtesy of Wikimedia Commons

At age nine, Eleanora was brought before juvenile court for playing hooky and was sent to reform school at the House of the Good Shepherd, where she was called Madge, as if to let her be reborn. Eleanora/Madge was remembered as a sullen child, "always down in the dumps, very seldom had anything to do with nobody else," said Christine Scott, who worked at the school. But Scott remembered that little Madge's face brightened up when she was told that she was going to be baptized. "She was grinning from ear to ear, you could almost see her back teeth," said Scott. "She was just light as a feather . . . she was so tickled."

Eleanora was paroled and moved with Sadie to the bottom of the Point, the wrong side of the tracks in Baltimore. Sadie got them electricity and gas and they opened a restaurant, the kind of venture Sadie tended to enjoy the most. Sadie had her proper Fagan side, but she was also capable of running after a man with a pistol, whereas her young daughter was all bad girl and rebel, at least on the outside.

Eleanora's friend Ethel Moore operated a good-time house in the neighborhood, and so Eleanora started making use of that as a money-making opportunity from a very early age, stealing men's wallets from their pants. She was tall already, a "big noble-looking girl," according to Wee Wee Hill, the man that Sadie once went after with a gun, and she wanted fast money. In her ghostwritten 1956 autobiography *Lady Sings the Blues*, she describes washing steps outside houses for cash, but her friends of this time didn't remember her scrubbing steps much. Sadie sometimes worked as a maid, and Eleanora had nothing but scorn for that kind of work for herself.

At Alice Dean's sporting house, Eleanora listened to blues records on what they called the graphophone, she listened to Florence Mills and Mamie Smith and Bessie Smith, and she loved the low powerful sound that Bessie had. Eleanora was singing in the streets right from the start. A man from this time named Freddie remembered her singing along to the records he would put on. "Eleanora always like the sad ones," he said.

"She was getting a meal, missing a meal, catching a trick or two," said her friend Pony Kane. Some of the adults around her tried to get her to be a "good girl," but she went about her business getting herself a bad name regardless. Wee Wee Hill said of Eleanora, "You know the kind of people that say, 'I'm gonna get cussed out anyways, so what's the difference? What the hell?' Well, Eleanora just went out and done what she felt like doing 'cause she was just don't care-ish."

On Christmas Eve 1926, Sadie and Wee Wee walked in on a forty-year-old man named Wilbur Rich attempting to rape the eleven-year-old Eleanora. Rich was arrested and received a custodial sentence of just three months, and Eleanora was sent back to the House of the Good Shepherd, where she was held until February of 1927.

Eleanora had to prove her toughness physically time and again at Good Shepherd, where fights between the girls happened regularly. When Eleanora got out she was on her own, unsupervised at age twelve, drinking and smoking reefer and out for a good time. Pony Kane described how Eleanora would be outside on the streets, feeling high and feeling good, and would come out with the worst words she knew just for attention: "You motherfucker, cocksucker, kiss my ass, kiss my ass," she would say, getting up in men's faces until they chased her and beat her. "She must have liked the men beating on her," said Pony. "The fellas that was crazy for her, she didn't have no time for, and the ones that have somebody else was the ones she wanted."

In the midst of all this outward chaos and perversity, the proud and sensitive interior Eleanora found a new way of expressing herself. "I heard a record Louis Armstrong made called the 'West End Blues,'" she said. "And he doesn't say any words, and I thought, this is wonderful! And I liked the feeling he got from it. . . . Sometimes the record would make me so sad I'd cry up a storm. Other times the same damn record would make me so happy."

Sadie was living in Harlem while her daughter was roaming the streets and drinking and living by her wits in Baltimore, and finally Eleanora was sent to join her mother in early 1929. They lived in a brothel run by Florence Williams at 151 West 140th Street, and it wasn't long before they were both arrested on May 2, 1929. Sadie was released from a workhouse in July, and Eleanora was released from Welfare Island in October.

In 1930 Sadie and Eleanora lived in Brooklyn, but then they moved back to Harlem. Eleanora was making the rounds of the nightclubs and singing, doing songs like "Honeysuckle Rose" and "How Am I to Know" and "My Fate Is in Your Hands." She would sometimes see her father Clarence, who was playing guitar for Fletcher Henderson; he was known then for his sense of time. "He was just a rhythm man, he had that left foot going, stomping, yes he did, he had all that going, and he was swinging!" said drummer Jimmy Crawford of Clarence.

It was proposed at one point that Eleanora might move in with Clarence and his wife Fanny, who described the girl as "a fat thing with big titties" when she first met her. Though Fanny liked Eleanora, she felt that this tough young teenager was too uncontrollable to live with, and Fanny couldn't stand Sadie, who made trouble as often as possible for the easygoing Clarence, chasing after him and causing scenes and looking for attention from him any way she could get it.

Singer Mae Barnes said that Eleanora was covering a lot of Louis Armstrong tunes at the various clubs. "She was doing everything that Louis Armstrong was doing," said Barnes. "She knew his records backwards, every one of them . . . she wasn't imitating his style, she was using all his numbers. She always had this deep voice . . . she could do it just like him, because she had this heavy voice, this gravelly tone, even when she had her own style. . . . 'I Surrender Dear.' She'd slide, and do the Louis run as if he'd do it on the trumpet." Barnes also remembered Eleanora singing "Them There Eyes," which stayed in her repertoire for the rest of her life.

It was at this time that Eleanora changed her name to Billie and took her father's last name for her own stage name; she tried out Halliday for a while but then settled on Holiday. She said later that she chose the first name because she admired the beautiful movie star Billie Dove, but she might also have been thinking of her friend Billie Haywood, a comedienne and singer.

Barnes and Billie worked together at the Nest on 133rd Street in Harlem, a bar where the singers would sometimes take the tips off the tables with their vaginas. "That's the kind of club it was," Barnes said, but she said that Billie "wasn't that type" and took the tips with her hand. Billie, Barnes, and Haywood would finish singing around seven or eight o'clock in the morning, and then they'd head to the gin mills until noon and go to people's apartments and smoke reefers and go to bed at four or five in the evening and then sleep so they could get to work singing again at two in the morning.

"We used to try to drink 24 hours a day," said Barnes, who held a clear picture of Billie "raising Cain" in the streets with her friends at the break of dawn, talking loud and hollering and laughing, when a cop asked them to quiet down. "They wouldn't keep quiet and got louder," Barnes said, "and they wanted to lock them up, so they were screaming, 'I don't believe it, take me!' and they refused to go and sat down in the middle of the street and refused to get into the patrol wagon . . . so they had to bring around a police car." They were booked for disorderly conduct but let go right away.

At sixteen Billie met a pianist named Bobby Henderson, a gentle man who loved and understood her. "The only man I think she ever loved in her life," said Barnes. Henderson only learned that Billie had been sixteen at the time she knew him when he read her memoirs in the 1950s, for she seemed much older. "She was the kind of woman that you would admire," Henderson said. "You would say she was statuesque."

"The thing that I found out about Billie was not to arouse her temper," Henderson said. "Now, she had a lot of patience, the people that she worked with, and the people that she knew. But if some guy insulted her, you had it." Billie trusted Henderson enough to let her guard down with him, and at those times "she was like a little girl . . . as if nothing bad had ever happened in her life—to hear her laugh—she laughed from the soles of her feet to the top of her head, plus some."

"I used to love to watch Billie eat," Henderson said. "She was very dainty, and Billie was what could you say, a full-bodied woman, and she was very graceful in everything she did. She was very clean, very neat . . . the way she handled a fork, the way she did eat . . . we'd be in a restaurant, and we'd be eating. And somebody would say to me, 'What's the matter with you?' I'd say, 'Nothing.' But deep in my mind I'm saying, 'You do things in a beautiful way.'"

Henderson took Billie home to meet his mother, who was very supportive of his career, and Billie took Henderson to meet Sadie. He observed their stormy relationship from a distance, trying to steer clear when they would start screaming at each other seemingly out of the blue.

"I didn't know enough about their business to have any feelings about what they were arguing about," Henderson said. "This was something I never understood and I never interfered with. A couple of times I'd say, 'Billie, don't holler at your mother like that,' or 'Don't argue so loud.' And I tried to say, 'Sadie,' I'd try to make an excuse, but I couldn't say anything. I made up my mind: keep your mouth shut, 'cause you don't know what they're *really* arguing about."

Wealthy jazz aficionado John Hammond saw Billie singing in a club around this time and was very impressed by her. Hammond said that Sadie sometimes worked for Mildred Bailey, and that Bailey liked to complain to Billie about her mother's poor housekeeping: "This was Mildred's way of getting back at Billie because Billie was so good—she couldn't stand it. Mildred told this to me among other people."

Clara Winston, who ran a food-and-drink club in Harlem on 142nd Street, said that Sadie used to run along behind Billie, crying her name,

"Billie! Billie! Billie!" just like a little baby or a little bird. Sadie lived vicariously through Billie, and she behaved sometimes more like a neglected little sister than a mother. The two women lived together a lot of the time, bound to each other by ties that other people couldn't understand.

Billie was singing at a short-lived club run by the singer Monette Moore when Hammond saw her, and he knew right away how good she was and wrote her up in a British magazine called *Melody Maker*. Hammond took people to see Billie wherever she performed in Harlem, oftentimes in brownstones. She would go from table to table and sing the same chorus of a song over and over again, forty or more times, collecting tips and building excitement each time she sang it. Hammond remembered Billie singing an early effort from lyricist Johnny Mercer called "Wouldja for a Big Red Apple?" He loved everything about her phrasing and her regal beauty, and he knew Billie was the find of a lifetime.

Hammond brought clarinetist Benny Goodman to see her, and he also brought the great British actor Charles Laughton, who got friendly with both Billie and Sadie, who seems to have helped him find some gentleman friends and quite a lot of marijuana. Pleased with her efforts on his behalf, Laughton wrote them a check so large that Billie was afraid to cash it until several years later, when she was in desperate need of money and decided to try the Laughton check, and she was surprised and relieved when it went through.

On November 27, 1933, Hammond made sure that eighteen-year-old Billie was squeezed in to record with Benny Goodman at the end of a Columbia session with the cantankerous, theatrical, and competitive Broadway star Ethel Waters, who disliked Billie right away and later said that when Billie sang she "sounded like her feet hurt."

Billie's first recorded song was a ditty called "Your Mother's Son-in-Law," in which she references Jules Bledsoe, the star of *Show Boat*: "You don't have to sing like Bledsoe / You can tell the world I said so!" she chirps, in a key that is much too high for her, which Billie found comic when she talked about this initial record later in life. She sounds eager to please, sticks to the beat, and uses a bit of vibrato on certain words and even a dying fall at the end of the tune, which would become one of her early trademarks.

On her second record with Goodman, "Riffin' the Scotch," another song with Johnny Mercer lyrics, she does a mordent on the word "fire," which shows how much Bing-ness had infiltrated popular music by 1933. "She was quite a pretty girl," Mercer said. "But there was something about her—not just the torchy quality of her voice—that made you want to help her."

4

Frank in Hoboken

FRANK SINATRA HAD a chip on his shoulder about many things, including the way he had been born in December of 1915: "They just kind of ripped me out and tossed me aside," he said. Forceps had been used, and so there were major scars on the left side of his face and a near-deformed left ear. Add to this a bad case of acne as a kid, and Frank often felt disfigured. To compensate, he applied pancake makeup to the worst areas on his face, and he had a fetish for cleanliness and neatness, often taking several showers daily.

Frank once said that there were only two people in his life that he had ever been afraid of: the bandleader Tommy Dorsey and his formidable mother Dolly, who campaigned for women's suffrage. Dolly had a flair for the dramatic, once chaining herself to a building during a protest in 1920, and she was known around Hoboken, New Jersey, as an all-around fixer and political operator for the Democratic Party; if there was any problem of any kind in her neighborhood, you called on Dolly. She worked as a midwife, and she provided abortions for girls in trouble, which sometimes got her arrested. Her husband Marty was the quiet type, a fireman who lived in his wife's lively shadow.

Young Frank was somewhat spoiled or entitled, wearing fine clothes and even playing with dolls, but he had a "What did I do this time?" relationship with Dolly, who would hit him at the least provocation and sometimes with no provocation. She once threw a shoe at him and called him a bum because he had a photo of Bing Crosby on his wall, and she could not have been happy about his copying his idol Bing in everything. Teenage Frank tried to smoke a pipe like Bing and wore a yachting cap, rigging himself up in the kind of Bing costume that had so impressed Louis Armstrong.

Frank would sing sometimes on top of a player piano for tips at a tavern his parents ran in Hoboken, so he was a saloon singer from the start. He was expelled from high school, where he had arranged bands for school dances, and he also dropped out of business school. Dolly got him a job as a delivery boy at the *Jersey Observer* newspaper, but that didn't last, and neither did a job she found him as a riveter, for Frank was clearly more interested in performing at social clubs around town and on local radio. He was developing a lifelong bad habit of reacting with anger whenever he was caught not doing what he should have been doing, and anger and resentment would always be Frank's go-to emotions whenever guilt or remorse might have been called for instead.

Dolly was a shrewd woman, and eventually she could see the writing on the wall. Though she loudly disparaged the idea that he could become a singer like Bing, she later bought Frank a microphone to replace the megaphone he had been using, and she also paid for orchestrations so that he could sing a few of Bing's tunes.

Young Frank and his steady girlfriend Nancy Barbato saw his idol sing live in Jersey City in 1933, and in later years Frank said that while in New Jersey Bing had been arrested and jailed in Hoboken, a not unlikely story given Bing's penchant for drink and disorderly conduct in this period. Bing was being held in a cell below street level with windows, and a skinny young Frank supposedly got down on his stomach and told the older performer how much he loved his singing. He wanted to be a singer himself, he said, and he asked Bing for advice, but Bing was so loaded that he yelled at the young Frank to go away.

5

Ella: You're Going to Hear from Me

A very young Ella Fitzgerald would tell her friends, "Someday you're going to see me in the headlines, I'm going to be famous," and they'd laugh and say, "Oh, yeah, sure!" Ella was skinny in grade school, but she could fight if she had to. She was a happy, upbeat child, always dancing in the streets and dancing outside school, where she was a good student. "She always knew she was going to be someone someday because she kept on saying, 'I want to do something, I want to make something of myself,'" said her friend Charles Gulliver, with whom she often went to the Savoy Ballroom in Harlem to pick up the latest dance steps.

Ella was born on April 25, 1917, in Virginia to Temperance "Tempie" Henry and William Fitzgerald, who lived there with their baby for a few years. By the early 1920s, Tempie was in a relationship with a Portuguese man named Joseph Da Silva, and she went to live with him and Ella in Yonkers, New York. Ella's half sister Frances, with whom she was very close, was born there in 1923, and by 1925 they were living in a racially mixed area of Yonkers with many Italian residents.

Ella's friend Annette Miller remembered how much Ella loved Louis Armstrong's records and how she imitated him singing "Ain't Misbehavin'" for their friends. Young Ella also loved Bing Crosby's records, but she idolized Connee Boswell, whose rhythm numbers with her sisters had the most intricate harmonies. "My mother brought home one of her records, and I fell in love with it," Ella said in 1988. "I tried so hard to sound just like her." But Ella wanted to be a dancer at this point in her life, and she would do a dance act in little clubs with Charles Gulliver.

Tempie died at age thirty-eight in 1932, when Ella was fifteen. She said later in life that Tempie died after getting hit by a car while trying to save a child, but her friends didn't remember that. Ella continued dancing with Gulliver after Tempie's death, and she was having problems with her stepfather Joe Da Silva, who didn't want her going out late and punished her for it. "He wasn't taking good care of her," Gulliver said, and people began to talk about the situation. Finally Ella's aunt Virginia took Ella in to live with her own family in Harlem.

While living with Virginia, Ella became very close with her cousin Georgiana, who later became her full-time traveling companion and wardrobe specialist, and she would return to Yonkers sometimes to see Frances and her friends. Joe Da Silva died, after which Frances also came to live with Virginia.

What followed were two bad years for teenage Ella, years that went from bad to much worse. Having lost her mother Tempie, she found herself competing for the affection of her aunt Virginia, and she didn't react well to this. She dropped out of school and began making extra money any way she could: performing in the street, running numbers, and even working as a sort of lookout for a brothel.

Ella was finally sent to an orphanage in the Bronx and then to a reform school in Hudson, New York, and this reform school was segregated, with a cruel male staff. Thomas Tunney, who was the last superintendent of the school, learned that Ella had firmly rejected overtures to return as an honored guest. "She hated the place," Tunney said. "She had been held in the basement of one of the cottages and all but tortured."

E. M. O'Rourke, who taught English at the school, remembered Ella as a fine student. "I can even visualize her handwriting—she was a perfectionist," said O'Rourke. Ella didn't sing in the choir, which was all white, but Beulah Crank, who was a housemother at the school, remembered Ella singing at a church service. "That girl sang her heart out," said Crank.

6

Baby Gumm

FRANK GUMM HAD a beautiful tenor singing voice. He played in vaudeville and managed theaters in Cloquet, Minnesota, but he had to leave town abruptly because he was gay and his advances to young men made him unwelcome. "He was accused of being a pervert and he had to skip town and get out fast," said his singing partner Maude Ayres.

Frank met bossy, managing Ethel Milne, herself a performer who played piano and did sound effects for silent pictures, and they came close to marrying before he suddenly went off for a few months on a vaudeville tour. Ethel waited for him, and when Frank came back they were married; they settled in Grand Rapids, Michigan.

Ethel had two daughters, Mary Jane and Dorothy, and when she got pregnant a third time, both she and Frank thought seriously of trying to get her an abortion because they felt that three children would be too many. But they were dissuaded because of the difficulties involved, and so Frances Gumm was born on June 10, 1922.

For the rest of her life, these first years in Grand Rapids would be viewed as a kind of lost Eden by Frances, who was pampered by her lavishly affectionate father and known as Baby. At the age of two and a half, Baby Gumm made her show business debut onstage with her family, singing "Jingle Bells" over and over again, and loving the audience response so much that she finally had to be carried off. Ethel kept a portable stage with her so that Baby Gumm could get up and tap-dance for anyone who wanted a show.

Ethel confided to the wife of their friend Marc Rabinowitz that she had no sexual life with Frank, who started hitting on two of the ushers of the theater he managed. When the ushers complained, the Gumm family had to leave Grand Rapids. They drove out to California in 1926, and Frank got them a tour of MGM Studios by flagging down handsome cowboy star Fred Thomson, the husband of screenwriter Frances Marion. The family settled again in dusty Lancaster, California, where Frank got a new theater to manage.

At age six, the highly confident Baby Gumm supposedly drove an audience into an uproar with her rendition of "I'll Get By," and Ethel could see what she had in this little girl, even if she still had her singing in an act with her two sisters. In surviving recordings and film footage, Baby Gumm will shout, "Yes, yes!" as punctuation, but in the film short *Bubbles* (1930) she seems nervous and not too polished.

In the winter and spring of 1932, Baby Gumm was asked to sing at the Cocoanut Grove in Hollywood, where Bing had made his name the year before. "I'm going to be a movie star," Baby told people in Lancaster, where she sometimes lost friends because of Ethel's domineering control of her.

Her father Frank was crazy about Baby and Baby was crazy about him, but Ethel generally saw Baby as an asset to be exploited rather than a child to be loved, and she worked to instill fear in her. Ethel was giving Baby pep pills and sleeping tablets at this point, when Baby was just nine years old, a damning piece of information confirmed by two sources: tap-dancing star Ann Miller, whose mother knew Ethel, and Gumm family friend Dorothy Walsh Morrison.

Frank was still sexually harassing ushers, and he was connecting with contemptuous local high school boys in Lancaster while Ethel took up with a man named Will Gilmore. Baby once walked in on Ethel with Gilmore, and she developed a strong hatred of this man. When stories about her father sometimes got back to her as an adult, she would call them "a ghastly, dirty lie" that had likely originated with Gilmore, the bad father figure to Frank's good father figure.

The Andrews Sisters were as startled and touched by Baby's very mature singing voice as everybody else was when they heard this prodigy perform, and so the sisters secured her first big break in a stage show with entertainer George Jessel, who gave the sisters a new last name, Garland. Baby Garland's life was a round of performances and auditions, many of which were unpleasant and frightening, but she had those pills her mother had given her to fortify her.

7

Diana's Dream

IDA ROSEN CHANGED her name to Diana because she felt it was prettier and more glamorous. Diana's father was a cantor, and she herself had a light soprano voice and thought about going on the stage. "When I was 17, I registered with my best girlfriend to sing in the Metropolitan Opera Chorus," Diana said. "But we attended rehearsal only once. It brought us home too late and worried our parents. So both of us girls gave it up and put it out of our minds." Yet Diana would still perform around the house, and when she looked in the mirror, she liked what she saw.

In a TV interview from the early 1980s, when she was an older woman, Diana merrily says that she used to have "a nice shape," and there is an urge to be seen somewhere inside her, an urge to perform. As a young woman she had often sung the very romantic "One Kiss" from *The New Moon*, a Sigmund Romberg operetta that premiered in 1927, when Diana was nineteen years old. This was music that was also popular in the late 1920s and the 1930s, a sort of gorging on very tasty melodies.

Diana married the academic Emanuel Streisand in 1930, but what she saw in the mirror and what she heard when she sang "One Kiss" stayed in the back of her mind.

8

Bing at the Top

ON THE RADIO, on records, and in movies, Bing Crosby was omnipresent in 1933 in America, the voice that everybody heard somewhere or somehow. Yet with success came some calculated doubts. He was convincingly lovelorn on record, for one of the only times, on "I Don't Stand a Ghost of a Chance with You," for which he has a writing credit. This is the sort of torch song that Billie Holiday and Frank Sinatra would later make their own, but while they would wallow in the emotions of unrequited love, Bing is sad but slightly above it all, and prepared to scat his despair, which lightens it. That's what listeners needed and loved him for during the Depression.

Bing would record "I've Got the World on a String" in 1933, and Frank's later version of that song is more memorable, for with Frank you get higher highs and lower lows, but Bing's sexy reading of this tune has that slightly otherworldly positivity that made him a phenomenon in his lifetime—an untouchable, a fact of life. He was steady, and he would never be counted out; he was built to endure because he always held something back. People would argue over Frank in the 1940s and 1950s and beyond. But practically everyone was won over by Bing and what he came to represent as an American male in the 1930s.

He recorded two songs from the hit movie *42nd Street* (1933), "You're Getting to Be a Habit with Me" and "Young and Healthy," in which he brags that he is full of vitamin A and does a brief scat excursion that quotes from the Gershwin tune "Lady Be Good," the vehicle for one of

Ella Fitzgerald's later scat masterpieces. Bing's "Young and Healthy" was backed by Guy Lombardo and His Royal Canadians—pure corn—but it might be remembered that Louis Armstrong himself liked Lombardo's music, or saw its place as a kind of contrast.

"Prosperity is just around the crooner," Bing promises in *Sing, Bing, Sing* (1933), another short for Mack Sennett in which nance character actor Franklin Pangborn spanks him with a paddle. In the short *Please* (1933), Bing tells a singing mechanic that he sounds "like John McCormack," one of his own idols, and says that he'll sing that Crosby guy right off the radio. "They're getting wise to him anyway," Bing says, modestly pretending to be a flash in the pan, which paradoxically ensures his superstar status. He sings "I Don't Stand a Ghost of a Chance with You" in this short subject with a solemn, reflective face, giving nothing away with the visual, which only enhances his vocal.

Somehow living up to his vocals visually while retaining the requisite air of universality and mystery would be Bing's chief challenge and problem as a movie star in the 1930s. In his next feature for Paramount, *College Humor* (1933), Bing plays a professor of drama who teaches his students to croon "in a sexy tone" if they want to win their heart's desire, for the sweet nothings of his "ba-ba-ba-boos" are meant to get women in the mood for love. In a scene toward the end of this movie, he tells off the dean rather forcefully, a clue that there might be more to Bing than the rather bland, slightly apprehensive face he chose to show the camera.

Bing had grown very close to Eddie Lang, who played rhythm guitar for him. He had gotten Lang a job in *College Humor*, but Lang was suffering from chronic laryngitis, which made him worry that he wouldn't be ready for a movie part. Bing suggested that Lang should have his tonsils taken out, and doctors assured Lang that it was a simple operation. Lang went into the hospital, and his wife Kitty stayed by his side.

Shortly after the operation, Lang hemorrhaged and died. Bing rushed to the hospital, where he sank to his knees, sobbed, and put his head in Kitty's lap, saying, "Kitty, he was my best friend." He carried guilt for Lang's death for the rest of his life, and some people observed that he never really got as close to anyone as he had been with Lang ever again. Bing made certain that Kitty was taken care of, and he went forward with his thriving life and career, but he retreated and became more aloof, focusing intently on his many opportunities for work. Loyal to his family, Bing sent for his parents Kate and Harry and set them up in a house, and he had several of his brothers working for him at various times.

Paramount asked Bing to fill out a publicity questionnaire, in which he revealed that he admired Debussy and Ravel but not Beethoven or Wagner. In a publicity form for his radio show, Bing said that he was "pretty socialistic" and that he really didn't "think anyone is entitled to or should have more than they need to live comfortably." He left a little money for some crew members who went on strike in the summer of 1933.

For the movies Bing wore a corset and had lifts in his shoes. He also had padding in his shoulders, he had his ears pinned back, and he wore a lush hairpiece on his head, all of which led his *College Humor* costar Jack Oakie to joke on the set that he was "the robot of romance."

The Paramount lot, like RKO, was a movie studio where it sometimes felt like nobody was minding the store, and so it was often a fun and creative place to be. Paramount contract players included some of the most attractive performers in town: Bing's friend Gary Cooper, for whom he named his first son Gary in June of 1933, Carole Lombard, Cary Grant, and Marlene Dietrich, with whom Bing listened to Richard Tauber records.

He taught people to croon again in *Too Much Harmony* (1933), and then he went to MGM to be a leading man for Marion Davies in *Going Hollywood* (1933), where his semi-camp version of the torrid "Temptation" is the apotheosis of ardent early Bing—a heavy drinker led by his emotions, his voice rising, the volume surging, surging, as he rolls out that beautiful sound with vibrato to make it extra beautiful and emotional. This is all more effective on the record, for his cute woebegone look in the film can't live up to the intensity of his voice.

Bing laid it on the line vocally in all of his 1933 recordings, with tenor throbbing to go with the baritone groaning (it was Tommy Dorsey who first called Bing the Groaner from Tacoma). He gives his all to the morbid "Blue Prelude," which features lyrics by a young Gordon Jenkins, and the outright suicidal "Black Moonlight," bending himself to the

Bing ardently sings the song "Temptation" in *Going Hollywood* (1933).

bluesy words but still keeping his reserve, and then he was the king of make-out music for the number-one hit "Shadow Waltz," which offers one of his jaunty whistling interludes.

His use of dynamics is at its most expressive on the very pretty "Thanks," a song of gratitude for a love affair, and he even does a falsetto note at the end of "My Love." Bing recorded two of his first cowboy songs in 1933, "The Last Round-Up" and "Home on the Range," which showed that he wanted everyone, the sophisticates in the city and the hicks in the sticks.

Bing did three movies for Paramount in 1934, starting with the all-star *We're Not Dressing*, where he played opposite the challenging Carole Lombard, resplendent in a white satin gown as a rich girl who tangles with Bing's sailor, who turns out to be a college boy and architect with a job waiting for him in New York. Bing dominates here, even with a young Ethel Merman on board, but his character is supposed to be tougher and more Clark Gable-ish at times than Bing can manage.

Lombard was engaged to singer Russ Columbo, a crooner who was briefly thought of as a rival for Bing. Columbo sings directly through his nose, but his voice has a sexy quality, particularly on his hit song "Prisoner of Love," that might have carried him further along if he hadn't died after an accident involving a gun in September of 1934.

Bing looks cowed and intimidated by the manic Miriam Hopkins in *She Loves Me Not*, for she offers about as physically hyperactive a star performance as can be imagined. Already known for her shameless upstaging, Hopkins does a particularly crazed dance in one scene for a seated Bing and even sticks her behind directly in his face, and she keeps him so flustered that he registers poorly with her when he registers at all.

As if aware of this problem, *She Loves Me Not* eventually separates them and lets Bing vocalize with Kitty Carlisle, and he goes from sheepish to magnetic in a flash once he starts in on the grand "Love in Bloom," which was later Jack Benny's theme song on the radio and was so associated with Benny's comic persona that it became unthinkable for anyone to ever sing it straight again.

"I was a serious singer, I had studied seriously," said Carlisle, "and I was impressed by his technique, his effortlessness, the fact that his voice was so much bigger and more available for, really, operatic roles than you saw in the movies." She also noticed that Bing didn't quite look right for films, that his face and especially his body didn't match his voice, but *She Loves Me Not* was the picture where he finally refused to have his ears pinned back, which had caused him all kinds of pain and trouble. And throughout his movie career Bing would wear a hat in a scene if at all possible rather than don his toupee.

Bing was teamed with Carlisle again for *Here Is My Heart*, which features his hit "June in January" under the credits. His extended falsetto note at the end of "With Every Breath I Take" gets Carlisle in the mood for a kiss, and he used such ultra-high notes again on 1934 records like "Two Cigarettes in the Dark," a song about betrayal. Bing had so many voices to choose from in this period that he could handle the rangiest material given to him.

Bing's wife Dixie discovered that she was pregnant again soon after their son Gary was born, and this time she gave birth to twin boys in July of 1934. On the surface this was a happy period in their lives, a time when Bing was at the top of his profession and was coming home to what publicity would insist was the perfect family, and so it was, for a time. But Dixie's sons were taken care of by nurses, and Bing was so often working that Dixie grew bored waiting for him and started drinking more than she should have.

Dixie had given Bing an ultimatum about his own drinking at the start of their marriage, even threatening to leave him if he didn't get it under control, and so he did; he was able to have a drink or two now without going on a bender. During their courtship, Dixie had labored to keep up with Bing's drinking, and she found it a solace that she couldn't give up once her own career as a singer and actress evaporated. She appeared in two movies in 1935, including *Love in Bloom*, which capitalized on her husband's hit song, and that marked the end of her professional life. Dixie was shy and insecure and even became nervous about public appearances, which she increasingly avoided.

The traditionalist music producer Jack Kapp had signed Bing to Decca Records at this point, and Kapp steered him steadily away from the jazzier approach to singing that he had favored in his Whiteman and Cocoanut Grove days. A sign was up at Kapp's Decca offices that read, WHERE'S THE MELODY? Stray too far from the melody, or toy around with it, and Kapp would not be happy.

Nothing jazzy would be countenanced for Bing's next picture. Richard Rodgers and Lorenz Hart provided him with some of their best songs for *Mississippi* (1935), a film set in the old South in which Bing played opposite W. C. Fields and placidly let the great man steal every scene he was in. Fields gets his laughs, but Bing is in perhaps the best voice of his life for this movie, and he lets it ring out at top volume on "Down by the River," which he ends with full-throated high notes, and "It's Easy to Remember," one of the most heartbroken torch songs ever written, which he sings with impassioned precision.

Bing has a sure instinct for the architecture of the greatest songs, and he goes about building his version of "It's Easy to Remember" with exciting thoroughness and authority. When he finishes, the whole song stands like a building: kitchen, hallways, library, bedroom, den, backyard, nothing is left out, and nothing feels more American. Bing recorded his first Christmas songs in 1935, including "Silent Night" with some ethereal high notes, laying the groundwork for his enduring image as the voice of the holidays.

"The Touch of Your Lips," which he recorded in 1936, is a very intimate ballad by Ray Noble, and Bing embraces the full sensuality of the lyrics, using vibrato to make the song sound prettier, lusher, stronger. Bing uses almost as much insistent vibrato as Judy Garland later would on the cowboy song "Empty Saddles," and a strongly placed falsetto note too, deployed at just the right moment on the word "lonely."

He introduced "I Wished on the Moon" in *The Big Broadcast of 1936* (1935) against a stylized backdrop. When it came time to record the song for Decca, Bing was feeling tired and thought his voice was hoarse, so he said that he would only do one chorus of the song, as in the old Whiteman days, and this led to an argument with Jack Kapp, but they eventually did it Bing's way. Compared to the extreme beauty of his voice on the songs he had been recording at this time, he does sound held back on this one, but Bing could always get a lot out of restraint of any kind.

He did a bowdlerized movie version of the Cole Porter show *Anything Goes* (1936) with Ethel Merman, which is notable mainly for their duet on "You're the Top," and this shows how gracefully Bing can perform with and handle strong personalities, and it also shows off his still-vibrant rhythmic inventiveness with lyrics. He played opposite the beautiful, haughty, ill-fated Frances Farmer in *Rhythm on the Range* (1936), in which he really lets himself go physically to dance with Martha Raye on the very catchy Johnny Mercer tune "I'm an Old Cowhand." Bing coasts along phlegmatically in so many of his 1930s movies, and then suddenly he will do some kind of wild physical business to signal that he is not as unexceptional or representative as he appears to be.

Bing was loaned to Columbia to do *Pennies from Heaven* (1936), which gave him another Depression theme song. This was his most characteristic and suggestive role of this time, a vagabond and troubadour who carries a thirteenth-century lute to strum on as he moves as freely as possible through life. Bing's Larry Poole takes up with a problem child named Patsy (Edith Fellows), and we are allowed to see all the displaced people living in the out-of-doors all around them.

Bing's Larry sings the great soothing title song to Patsy during a thunderstorm, putting a little catch in his voice on the word "showers" so that the reassurance of the tune comes from a place that knows and acknowledges great trouble. With his ability to navigate very low notes and very high notes, Bing had one of the few singing voices of his time that could musically express the intent of the lyrics of "Pennies from Heaven," which says that there are no happy highs in life without the lows of difficulties and sadness.

"All females are troublemakers, they slow you down," Larry tells Patsy, but Bing doesn't sound like he means it. A similar playing against the material is at work during Louis Armstrong's appearance in *Pennies from Heaven*, in which he has been given a comedy bit that is supposed to revolve around his difficulty with math. Louis kills the embarrassment of this routine by looking very sly, like a trickster of some kind, a tactic that defangs it.

Bing had pushed hard to get Louis into this film at Columbia, and Louis blows Bing away as a screen presence, but Bing was always happy to bask in the authority of a Louis or a W. C. Fields or an Ethel Merman. Louis should have been the star of *Pennies from Heaven*, not Bing, or they should at least have been equal partners, as Bing later was in his series of films with Bob Hope. That they were not is a sadness and an injustice and a loss, but it should be remembered that Louis appearing at all in this movie was a sort of victory for both him and for Bing in 1936.

When he sings "I'm an Old Cowhand" in *Rhythm on the Range*, Bing cries, "They don't call me Elmer, they call me Satch!" in a call-out to his friend and inspiration, the Reverend Satchelmouth, who hopefully got a kick out of the reference.

9

Billie and Ella

WHEN BILLIE RETURNED to Columbia to record in 1935, she did so with a song that Bing had introduced, "I Wished on the Moon," with Teddy Wilson and a small group of musicians. She takes her time with the lyrics . . . weighting . . . each . . . word . . . yet lifting them up too, and the effect is one of heaviness and lightness at the same time, with that sense of rapture that the young Billie was so good at catching.

"What a Little Moonlight Can Do" is a trivial tune taken at a super-fast pace that Billie made into one of her classic songs with the help of a hotter-than-hot Roy Eldridge trumpet solo at the end. Her voice here is earthy, rough, authoritative, unmistakable, a voice that comes out of a specific milieu, the Harlem of the Daisy Chain, a notorious house where sexuality was explored unconstrained, and Reefer Mae's, where pot was smoked and good times had. The way Billie near-snarls the words "I love you" has a sting that speaks of experience, but her "oo oo" sounds speak of pleasures that might make that sting worth it.

Billie is twenty years old now, and she sounds ten years old and a wised-up sixty by turns. On "Miss Brown to You," which had been done as a Black production number in *The Big Broadcast of 1936* with Bing, she is euphoric and encouraging: "Yes, yes," she says at one point, and then "Knock it down" to Teddy Wilson, who is tinkling his ivories in his own unmistakable way. "Even Mr. Crosby Bings it," she sings on "Eeny Meeny Miney Mo," a Johnny Mercer lyric that turns Bing's name into a verb.

Billie appeared in a short film in 1935 that was released by Bing's studio, Paramount: *Symphony in Black: A Rhapsody of Negro Life*, which featured Duke Ellington and his band. We first see her leaning against a wall here, stoic, dignified, betrayed. When she confronts her boyfriend and his new girlfriend, he knocks her to the ground, and Billie begins singing about her man walking out on her while still on the sidewalk, eventually picking herself up and standing and leaning again, her eyes closed as she sings, "I've got those lost my man blues," lip-synching very tentatively. The Billie in this movie is more like the later beaten-down Billie of her Verve 1950s period than the musical genius spreading her wings and emerging on her first recordings.

The early recordings from Billie in the mid-1930s are ever fresh, and what is most distinctive about her on these initial platters is her sense of play and deconstruction, and the lethal humor that could turn any sentiment or melody around or on its head. She is as above it all as Bing is—objective but in an enormously different, more humorously modern way. When she sings the line "Life begins when Cupid wins" on "Life Begins When You're in Love," she seems to be saying, "Oh, does it?" underneath.

The dying fall in pitch that she used as a signature is most expressively deployed on "It's Like Reaching for the Moon," where she keens the line "You're so far above me" in a luxuriantly painful tone. There is a masochism in her persona already that insists on enjoying pain if pain is to be your lot, a radical viewpoint still often misunderstood or ignored by people trying to deal with the implications of Billie's art. As Angela Davis notes in her book *Blues Legacies and Black Feminism*, there is an investigation "throughout her body of work between pain and pleasure, love and death, destruction and the vision of a new order."

Billie had a hit with her over-all-that "I Cried for You," and "Did I Remember?" benefits from her "I actually mean nothing I am singing here" irony and an Artie Shaw clarinet solo. "Summertime" from Gershwin's *Porgy and Bess* is Billie in an evil mood, backed by drums—the Billie that you cross at your peril. She pounds home the beat here almost contemptuously, for her usual style is to stay behind the beat and let it wait for her to stroll up to it.

She recorded three songs from Bing's movie *Pennies from Heaven*, including "One, Two, Button Your Shoe" (his version is hip, hers is far hipper) and "Let's Call a Heart a Heart," which doesn't suit Bing at all but which he gives his full rolling baritone voice anyway while Billie swats it away by lagging behind the beat and toying with the melody, emphasizing certain syllables and bringing up her tone at the very end. Her version of "Pennies from Heaven" is both elated and teasing, the exact opposite of Bing's stern and comforting version, as if to say, "You know those clouds don't contain pennies from heaven!" But this knowledge of how wretched life is seems to *exhilarate* Billie, maybe because seeing it so clearly and in such a multileveled way is its own kind of triumph and brings its own kind of pleasure. She goes beyond the specific to the general, where there is joy for her; she would linger in the specifics later. This voice says, "How lucky I am to be able to express in such an all-seeing way just how unlucky we are."

Billie sang her share of cut-rate tunes at this time, and she makes all of them worth a listen or three because of her youthful inventiveness and audacity, but she was lucky in that some of the very best songs ever written were new then and available to be sung, like Cole Porter's "Easy to Love," which premiered in the movie *Born to Dance* (1936). Her recording of this song brings up a commercial problem for the Billie of this time. She was a jazz singer, and her instinct was to deconstruct "Easy to Love" and come up with her own very different variation of its Porter melody, which would have been fine if she'd been doing it in 1956, but it was a new song then, and the music industry at large wanted songs done as written.

She sticks somewhat dutifully to the Jerome Kern melody of "The Way You Look Tonight," but the lesser-known "That's Life I Guess" is a perfect early Billie song, with that "I guess" in the lyric signaling her quizzical sort of hope. She is euphoric again on "I Can't Give You Anything but Love, Baby," an older song that she gives some of her sarcastic accents, with Lester Young's tenor saxophone behind her, intimate as whispered speech, ghostly and intense—a star sound, just as hers is. Billie and Lester loved each other, but like brother and sister. She was drawn to tough guys, and Lester was soft and eccentric. But their love affair as musicians was deeper and more important and more lasting than any of her other love affairs.

As Billie began to really establish herself, the young Ella Fitzgerald was homeless on the streets of Harlem in the fall of 1934, unable to return to her aunt's place, with no guarantee of food or shelter of any kind. This must have been a frightening time for the former good student and happy camper as she performed on the street for tips and entered contests. Being the daughter of Sadie Fagan had its disadvantages, but at least Billie always had a place to lay her head at night.

Ella entered an amateur talent contest at the Apollo Theater as a dancer, because she still considered herself a dancer then, but at the Monday-night audition on November 19, 1934, she discovered that a snazzy dance act called the Edwards Sisters was going to perform, and so she decided to switch and enter the contest as a singer.

When she walked out on the stage of the Apollo that Wednesday night, the emcee Ralph Cooper noted later that Ella was "jumpy and unnerved." The Edwards Sisters had professional costumes, whereas Ella was wearing cast-off clothes and workman's boots, and it was visibly clear that she had literally come in off the streets. Her voice cracked when she started to sing "The Object of My Affection" in the manner of her idol Connee Boswell, and the audience began to rumble. There was even some booing, according to a young dancer named Norma Miller, who was there that night and interviewed for a 2020 documentary on Ella.

Aware that Ella was losing them, Cooper stopped her and allowed her to compose herself. When she started the song again, Ella won everyone over, and she sealed the deal with her delivery of the song "Judy." Improbably, she won the contest, which brought with it a week-long run at the theater.

But that week never materialized. Billie started a run at the Apollo on November 23 with her adoring boyfriend Bobby Henderson on piano, and the management never got around to giving Ella her chance, and the reason for this was clear to singer Charles Linton, who said Ella was viewed as a street person. Her hair was disheveled, her clothes were dirty, and she herself was dirty because she was unable to bathe. "I was promised a week at the Apollo, but that never came through," Ella said later to the writer Joe Smith. When an impressed Benny Carter brought Ella in to audition for Fletcher Henderson, his reaction was the same: she was a homeless person and looked bad, and he couldn't use her.

Ella was booed off the stage of the Lafayette Theatre, but she won first prize again at the Harlem Opera House, which did book her for a week in early 1935. Billie also played at the Harlem Opera House in this period, and Ella went over between shows to catch her backstage. "I did something then, and I still don't know if it was the right thing to do—I asked for her autograph," Ella said.

Billie had made the rounds of clubs for years already, and she was known by lots of people because she liked to hang out and have a good time, but musicians hadn't seen or heard of Ella before. She'd been in school and had a home life before her mother's death and the series of events that led her to the brutal reform school and then life out on the streets. Ella would never be one to party and live it up like Billie did. A large part of her always remained studious.

On a snowy day in 1935, the homeless Ella asked bandleader Chick Webb for his autograph, and this was her first encounter with him. Webb had spent a long time climbing to the top of his profession, and he was ready now to go as commercial as possible. One day Webb asked his singer Charles Linton to find him a girl singer, and Linton asked an Italian chorus-girl friend of his if she knew of anyone right for the job, whereupon she raved about this girl who had won a talent contest at the Apollo, sang out on 125th Street every day, and had no place to live. Linton told his friend to find Ella and bring her to him, which she did several days later.

Linton asked Ella to sing for him, and she shyly sang "Judy" all the way through, with a slightly hoarse voice. Linton brought her up to meet Webb, who took a fast look at young Ella and joked to Linton, "Look at him, he's robbing the cradle!" When Linton asked Webb to listen to Ella sing, Webb was not happy and pulled Linton behind a door: "You're not putting that on my bandstand," Webb whispered. "No, no, no. Out!" A talent agent for the Savoy Ballroom came in, and Webb said to him, "Look what Charles wants to put on my bandstand," and the agent had a similar reaction: "No, no. Out!"

According to Linton, he stood up for Ella and said that he would quit the band unless they listened to her sing, and the agent, whose name was Buchanan, said that she would get two weeks at the Savoy. If the public liked her, they would keep her.

Linton made sure that Ella finally had a place to stay, in a room above his on 122nd Street at Seventh Avenue, and a place to eat, at the Hollywood Restaurant. He himself was unable to explain in later years why he vouched for her so strongly and played good Samaritan with her, but he gave credit to his friend. "If it hadn't been for the Italian girl, we wouldn't have any Ella because she wasn't in any condition to accept any job anyplace," Linton said.

After much deliberation and asking for the opinions of others, Webb finally decided to add Ella to his band, and the Moe Gale Agency got her a room at the Braddock Hotel. At the Savoy, various people took her in hand. A woman named Helen, who worked there, used to take Ella into the restroom and comb her hair to make it look nice.

A young writer named George T. Simon went to review Webb's band for *Metronome* in May of 1935, and he gave Ella a good write-up in June, remembering as an older man that she was still doing some dance moves at this point. "I was so knocked out by her," Simon said, "not only by the way she sang but the spirit and the way she would lead the band by throwing kicks on the side of the bandstand . . . I remember she had very thin legs." In his review he wrote, "Miss Fitzgerald should go places," and this so excited Ella that whenever she saw Simon in the audience at her shows in later years, she would always introduce him and make him take a bow.

Ella was singing a large repertoire of songs with the Webb band in 1935, and already her student-like instinct was to catalog them. According to band member Teddy McRae, Ella would write the lyrics to songs down on index cards that she brought with her. In her years as a mature performer Ella would carry a book where she kept all the songs she loved or liked or that intrigued her or that she wanted to try at some point, and it was a book that overflowed with songs of all kinds. She could sight-read music, and she picked up any type of tune very quickly.

In her first recordings with the band from 1935, Ella has a some-what nasal voice, small and somehow cramped, but her talent is there in nucleus form, and this is evident especially in her sense of rhythm. Ella respects the beat and is getting ready to run marathon races with it, whereas Billie, just two years older, scorns the beat, ignores it, or slaps it around.

Ella's music is a music of joy and renewal, and her way of looking at life couldn't be more different from Billie's. The third song Ella recorded with Webb is called "I'll Chase the Blues Away," and she makes good on that promise; she is never going to wallow in sadness like Billie. "Change your woe into a vo-de-ho," Ella advises on "Vote for Mr. Rhythm." This is a persona she kept up for all the other novelty songs she did with Webb's band, and it was a persona that had its limits. She is absurdly unsuited to torch songs like "My Last Affair," sounding as if she has no experience with these feelings, and this was a problem that would have to be finessed over time.

Ella did some engagements at the Apollo with the Webb band, and George T. Simon raved about her and her promise again in *Metronome* in January of 1936. In March of 1936 Ella recorded with Teddy Wilson while Billie was out of town singing with the Jimmie Lunceford orchestra. According to jazz critic Dan Morgenstern, Wilson said that he preferred Ella's singing to Billie's at this time and also said that Billie copied Louis Armstrong too much, which means that one of Billie's key musical collaborators didn't really understand or like what she was doing. Yet Ella's singing on "All My Life" with Wilson could be said to copy Billie in everything but mood and intention. Ella was a fan enough of Billie to ask for her autograph, and her attitude toward her would always be one of shy adulation that kept its distance.

Billie's own feelings about Ella were standoffish to hostile at this time, but curious. Charles Linton remembered Billie coming into the Savoy Ballroom with "a big coat on, and she would walk and look, just a look. What I figured was that she was surprised to see Ella with Chick Webb's band." Linton also remembered Billie saying, "A great band like that with Ella, that bitch," and turn around and walk out, so it sounds like Billie checked in on Ella more than once.

It should be stressed that Billie's use of the word "bitch" was all-purpose and used to refer to most females, including herself. Did Billie remember Ella as the homeless girl who had asked for her autograph? Her feelings about this young singer had to be complicated because everything was complicated with Billie, in her life and in her art. Billie's early aversion to Ella might have had something to do with the ragged way Ella looked at first, especially given the extensive testimony from others who reacted negatively to Ella based solely on her grungy street surface when she was waiting for her break.

But there was also an innocence about Ella's voice and manner that could not have sat well with Billie, who was wised-up in ways that most people will never be able to comprehend. This innocence that Ella had was something that Billie had either lost very early or never had to begin with.

Ella wanted above all to please her audience, whereas Billie held herself aloof from it. Ella reaches out to us, but we have to come to Billie on her terms and no others. And so it is worth considering what Billie might have been experiencing and settling with herself when she walked into the Savoy in her big coat for protection and took a look at Ella and then walked right back out again.

10

The Hoboken Four

FRANK STARTED TAKING elocution lessons from a vocal coach named John Quinlan, which partly accounts for his fine diction and the rather fancy mid-Atlantic *a*'s he used later as a professional singer. His mother Dolly helped get him a gig singing with a group called the Three Flashes, and together they became the Hoboken Four. The leader of that group, Fred Tamburro, said later that they only took Frank because he had a car and could drive them around.

The Hoboken Four entered a contest for a radio show called the *Major Bowes Amateur Hour*, on which they sang "Shine," a rhythm number, which was never Frank's forte. "I'm Frank," a young Frank tells the host. "We're looking for a job, so how about it?" This is the first recorded instance of Frank's clunky anti-charm, which is so total that sometimes it even seems charming. "Everyone that's ever heard us likes us," he goes on. "We think we're pretty good." They won the contest.

Frank had started out rather meekly with this group, hanging around them like they were gods, begging them for a chance, but as they toured around he increasingly took the lead. He made a short movie that has not survived in which he wore blackface, and he also appeared in blackface for a minstrel show put on by his father's fire department.

It was at some point in this mid-1930s period that Frank first saw Billie sing at a club. Her phrasing, her distant grandeur, and her emotional depth made Billie another idol for Frank, and her influence on his singing eventually went much further and deeper than what he took from Bing. Frank would never swing like Billie and Bing did, but Billie's way of looking at life and her slow way of weighting each syllable of each word for emphasis and impact had a long-lasting effect on his own instinct for drama in music.

11

Judy Swings

BABY GUMM BECAME Judy Garland in 1935, and she chose her first name because of the Hoagy Carmichael song "Judy," the same song that Ella had sung the night she won the contest at the Apollo Theater. The teenage Judy Garland would get up on a piano and sing torch songs in her deep, rich, mature singing voice. W. E. Oliver, a critic for the *Los Angeles Evening Herald and Express*, compared the young Judy to Sarah Bernhardt. This was a prodigy, and the people who knew started to talk her up.

Her father Frank had been asked to leave Lancaster, California, because of his relations with some high school jocks in town, and the family moved to Los Angeles, where Judy got an audition for the biggest and most prestigious movie studio, Metro-Goldwyn-Mayer. For this all-important chance, she sang "Zing! Went the Strings of My Heart" and the Jewish song "Eyli, Eyli (My God, My God)" for studio chief Louis B. Mayer, who was all verklempt at her emotion, and she was signed to a contract.

In October of 1935 Judy appeared on the *Shell Chateau* radio program, and she tells Wallace Beery that her mother taught her how to sing. "I want to be a singer, Mr. Beery . . . and I'd like to act, too!" she says, very cutely. Judy then sings a number called "Broadway Rhythm" and does a scat interlude—acceptably from a rhythm standpoint—with a kind of frenzied eagerness that would become a trademark.

Judy's swinging in this period was part of her showmanship and overall exuberance rather than something that was important or integral to her, as it was to Ella. And Judy would always be too easily carried away as a singer to care too much about the kind of measured phrasing that the young Frank was so drawn to with Billie.

In mid-November 1935, Judy's father Frank was hospitalized with meningitis as Judy prepared to go on the *Shell Chateau* program again. She sang "Zing! Went the Strings of My Heart" on that show, and Frank listened to it in his hospital bed. He died the following morning. Judy said later in life that his death was the worst thing that ever happened to her, a loss that she never got over.

But there was little time to mourn. She was singing on the radio a lot and doing anything to get noticed at MGM, and they finally put her in a short film called *Every Sunday* (1936) with soprano Deanna Durbin. We first see these two young singers applauding at the end of a classical music concert, and they are both beaming, but Judy is beaming with just that little something extra.

Judy is very in-the-moment in *Every Sunday* and present and heightened; she knows that this is her big chance and she is taking it. She blows Durbin's trilling away with her vibrant belt and her modern swing rhythms, and the director Felix Feist even does a dolly shot in to her as she sings, as if to say a star is being born here. Judy proves that she can really swing in this first movie, though few wanted her to past a certain point in her career.

Durbin went to Universal, where she became a top star in *Three Smart Girls* (1936), while Judy was loaned out to Fox to be ninth-billed as a hillbilly in the college musical *Pigskin Parade*, which stars femme Jack Haley, her future Tin Man, butch Patsy Kelly, and a bespectacled Elisha Cook Jr. as a student communist agitator.

"I'm Sairy Dodd and I can sing, you want to hear me?" Judy asks forty-one minutes into *Pigskin Parade*. She is barefoot and wearing pigtails, and she has a character going: extreme, quick to anger, open mouthed. Judy's Sairy keeps asking people if they want to hear her sing, and she finally gets to for a production number called "The Balboa," a rousing song that allows her to steal the movie, followed by two other numbers that come

Judy in the college musical *Pigskin Parade* (1936).

practically back-to-back. There was a stupendous wall of sound somehow emerging from this small fourteen-year-old girl, and people took notice.

This freakishly mature voice rang out on the radio, where she sang "Stompin' at the Savoy" with Bing's bandleader brother Bob and did a Bing-like mordent on the word "joy," her volume surging louder and louder. This is a sound that will not be ignored, and it is filled with energy, ambition, and need.

12

Sweet Leilani and Mexicali Rose

BING MADE AN excursion to Hawaii in life, on film, and on record, and it took some doing to get the rights to sing one of his biggest hits, "Sweet Leilani." Bing and Dixie had vacationed in Hawaii in the late summer of 1936, where they stayed at a hotel that had an orchestra conducted by Harry Owens. Bing was very taken with a song the band played that had been written to celebrate the birth of Owens's daughter Leilani, and he kept asking for it to be played, five or six times throughout the evening.

Bing called Owens the next day and said he wanted to sing "Sweet Leilani" in his new movie *Waikiki Wedding* (1937), but Owens felt that this song was too personal to him and his family and asked Bing to listen to some other songs he had written. Bing did so, and he liked them all and later recorded them, but he loved "Sweet Leilani" best and felt that he just had to sing it. A solution was proposed: Bing said that all royalties for "Sweet Leilani" would go into a trust fund for Leilani herself and any future children that Owens might have, and to this Owens agreed.

"Sweet Leilani" starts not with Bing's voice but the voice of tenor Lani McIntyre, who sings the song in a high register for over a minute of the three-minute track before Bing comes in himself. As Gary Giddins describes "Sweet Leilani" in his magisterial Crosby biography, "It was like wandering through a strange city and suddenly meeting an old friend."

Bing returned to the town of Spokane, Washington, to receive an honorary doctorate in October of 1937, and his brothers Larry and Ted got to work putting together a talent contest and invited some Crosby colleagues and friends to attend, including Connee Boswell, with whom Bing had recorded "Bob White," another hit song. Ted thought that Louis Armstrong would be attending, and Ted wrote to Larry, "One thing—how about accommodations for Louis Armstrong. How do you handle that?" Giddins thinks that Louis may have been pulled from the lineup because it was too awkward for the Crosby brothers to put Louis in a separate hotel.

We don't know if Bing was aware of Louis being excluded from his return to Spokane, but he was very aware and very angry that Louis's role was entirely cut from his movie *Doctor Rhythm* (1938). Louis was supposed to have two musical numbers in this picture and also some scenes with dialogue with Bing, but when he showed up to shoot, his role had been reduced to one production number in which director Frank Tuttle shot Louis in front of a racially integrated band. This was the likely reason that Louis's appearance in the film was entirely cut, the studio bowing to pressures from southern exhibitors.

There is a photo of Louis and Bing on the set of *Doctor Rhythm* in which Louis is looking at Bing with great adoration. But the friendship they had solidified in the Cocoanut Grove days of 1931, which was based on how much they inspired each other as performers and musicians, was limited professionally by the racism of the time, and these professional limits were reflected by personal limits. Bing and Dixie were still doing some entertaining at this point, and one of their parties in 1938 was a full-scale minstrel show, with minstrel costumes and a blackface number between Johnny Mercer and Joe Venuti for a close. Louis was never invited to Bing's house after Bing married Dixie. Past 1939, the Crosbys more or less stopped socializing because of problems with Dixie's drinking, but Pops and Papa Bing were separated now by a gulf that could not be bridged.

When Bing sang "Basin Street Blues" with Ella's idol Connee Boswell, they imagine a "heaven on earth" where "all the light and the dark folks meet," what Billie referred to once as the "one happy family" she sometimes but too rarely experienced in integrated nightclubs. The only way that could be accomplished most of the time in the 1930s in America was on records.

Bing's unfortunate liking for minstrel shows turns up in *Sing, You Sinners* (1938), where he does a kind of minstrel character in a beard when he sings "Small Fry," but he does not actually darken his face for this song, as if someone had told him not to go all the way with it. Bing plays a semi-unsympathetic guy in this picture, a man who drunkenly makes a pass at the girlfriend of his brother (Fred MacMurray), but this is smoothed over by his winningly conversational way with a song, which comes as naturally to him as talking. He does a scat break on one song here, and he scats delightfully with the shameless comic Martha Raye in *Double or Nothing* (1937), just one of the flurry of fluff movies with which he ended the 1930s.

One day in 1938, Bing needed to come up with a song for his radio show, and a secretary told him, "I heard my mother humming a pretty song." This song turned out to be "Mexicali Rose," which had lyrics by Helen Stone and a melody by the bandleader Jack Tenney, who wrote it in 1923 when he was working in a border town. Gene Autry sang it in the mid-'30s, in a bland, loping-along way that made it sound like just another cowboy tune. Crosby sang it for four months on the radio before he recorded it for Decca, which perhaps begins to explain why he was able to work out the ideal way to do it.

Bing's "Mexicali Rose" is a pop vocal masterpiece, maybe the best track he ever recorded next to "Out of Nowhere" from 1931. His sense of the architecture of a song is at its peak, and what he achieves here is only possible because he is able to travel up and especially down his vocal scale with such ease and authority, starting out in a middle range, going up somewhat high with a kind of strangled mordent on "crying," and then moving way, way down to the basement on "sunny day" with connected and resonant low notes that are as solid as concrete.

This is a song about an interracial love affair, and Bing is playing the part of a man who is leaving his Mexican lover and reassuring her that someday he will come back to her. Will he actually return to Mexicali Rose? Probably not, but Bing is at a midway point in his persona, still within hailing distance of irresponsible and sexy 1931 Cocoanut Grove Bing but within sight of the conservative icon of the 1940s and beyond, and so "Mexicali Rose" is tantalizingly suspended between these two ways of being, which accounts for its ambiguity. It is the sort of record meant to be bought and played over and over again, for it only gains in strength each time it is listened to back-to-back, its perfection growing more and more unaccountable with each listen.

Bing had a number-one hit that year with "I've Got a Pocketful of Dreams," another song meant to act as a balm to Depression-wearied listeners. It plays on his sense of being the carefree troubadour who somehow doesn't need money, and he playfully bends a note on the word "me" at the end just to send home the free-spirited message. Bing's spontaneous, low little cry of "Stop it!" at the end of his 1938 recording of Benny Goodman's "Don't Be That Way" is one of his sexiest and most winning moments on record.

He still has his high notes on a fervent 1938 performance of "My Reverie," a very pretty adaptation of a Debussy piece, but close listening reveals that something starts to happen to his voice in 1939, when he recorded a very large number of songs—likely too many. Bing's recordings in 1939 have a blander accompaniment, and his ardency and intensity start to drain away, partly to protect his voice from overuse.

He treaded water now with some derivative songs and some oldies like "My Melancholy Baby" and even "Ah! Sweet Mystery of Life," which he had refused before because he didn't think his "casual" voice was appropriate for such operetta material. He gets through it just fine, though he might really have let loose with more sound if he had tried it in 1934 or 1935. Jack Kapp was masterminding Bing's choice of material by 1939, and Bing adapted, feeling his high notes going and deciding to shore up his low notes and make really low bass notes a specialty that could carry him through the rest of his career.

From 1931 to 1938, everything Bing touched vocally turned to gold and delight. He sang some great songs, but what is really notable is how many good and of-interest songs he recorded in this period, a treasure chest for anyone looking for fresh material from this era to listen to or revive for performance. It is a shame for Bing's legacy that most of his radio shows of the 1930s, when he was in his finest voice, were lost in a fire, so that we can't hear now so much of the best of him in this medium, which was so essential to his unparalleled success.

By 1939 Bing had fully capitulated to Kapp's "let's do any kind of music" idea, and so he did everything from hymns to Hawaiian songs to what were then considered standards, and this is also when he started singing with the Andrews Sisters, a mixed blessing certainly, though with a certain camp value, at least at first: their record of "Ciribiribin" from 1939 is wonderful nonsense, with some rhythmic playfulness from Bing. But when he starts yodeling with them on "Yodelin' Jive," it becomes clear that this Kapp-ordered "I'll sing any type of music" persona is going to be too reliant on novelty and stunts.

Bing's recording of "I Cried for You" is very remote, especially compared to Billie's version, but he did do one really first-rate track at the end of the 1930s: "What's New?" His increasing distance from emotion makes this song touching because Bing in any era is never too hurt by love, but that doesn't mean there isn't some deeper hurt that he is carefully hiding, which gives a torch song like this a restrained sort of drama far removed from the suicidal depths that Billie and Frank would plumb with it.

13

Billie Swings Her Way and Ella Finds a Hit

BILLIE SIGNED WITH the crude and mob-connected manager Joe Glaser, who handled Louis, and Glaser told her to lose weight. She had penciled-on eyebrows at this point, 1930s style, because she accidentally cut off half an eyebrow while she was trimming it. Billie was singing on what became known as "the Street" in Manhattan, Fifty-Second Street between Fifth and Sixth Avenues, and she was not happy when she was told not to mix with the customers at a club called the Famous Door.

Billie also had trouble connecting to the noisy crowd at the Famous Door, and she had trouble again when she played a gig in Chicago at the Grand Terrace. She would not and could not adapt her style to please any audience, as Louis or Ella might have. Billie had her own way of singing, and the audience would just have to adapt to it.

Billie got fired from the Grand Terrace gig and somehow got back to New York. Glaser told her that she should speed up her tempo on songs if she wanted more success, but she refused. If an audience member requested a song, Billie might sing it when she was good and ready, or she might not.

Billie and Sadie moved to Ninety-Ninth Street and Central Park West, and Billie set her mother up with a restaurant where there was a party atmosphere and lots of handouts. According to their friend Babs Gonzales, they fed a lot of the city for years, or anyone with a sob story, and Lester

Young moved in with them for a time, which made both women happy. Billie started calling him Prez, for "President," and she sometimes called him Daddy; he nicknamed her Lady. Her love life was robust, and she had a liking for pretty men and sometimes pretty women.

Teddy Wilson saw how joyful Billie was at this time. "She enjoyed singing so much," he said. "She was bubbling at those recording dates. Very nice and cheerful person." Her sheer exuberance comes through even on a song like "Why Was I Born?" with Lester Young backing her. "What can I hope for?" she asks, "*I* wish I knew!" She hits that second "I" with such a hopeful twist, making the note ring out piercingly and sweetly, and she uses vibrato for expressive purposes here just to make the song prettier, a practice she would later limit.

In March of 1937, Billie received word that her father Clarence had died of pneumonia, and Billie said that "it wasn't the pneumonia that killed him, it was Dallas, Texas," because he couldn't find a veterans hospital that would take him in. Sadie insisted on taking a car of her own to his funeral, separate from Clarence's wife Fanny and a girlfriend named Atlanta who had had two children by Clarence. Sadie didn't arrive until it was all over. She would tearfully tell anyone who would listen that Clarence had been the love of her life.

This was the time when Billie was knocking out one major single after another. She puts all of her emotion into "They Can't Take That Away from Me," weighting each word and socking over the lowest notes on "tea" and "off key" and "three" with defiance. Bing's low notes are very solid and supported largely because of technique but also due to his wide vocal range, but Billie puts over her own low notes through strength of will, as an interpretive flourish, and she ends the song on a near Jolson-esque effect for the word "me," in her own small and enclosed tone. No one ever sang this great song better or with clearer images, all of which call up more desire than regret, as if the entirety of this love affair is coming back to her through memory. Her skill here is very mature, but the persona she is putting across is youthful and heedless.

Billie was defining all kinds of great songs when they were new by turning them on their head and using them to express all her complex feelings about life and possibility. On "Easy Living," Billie sounds like she's been through it all, and she has, yet here she is, triumphant and relaxed about it, high and down at the same time, with a sense of surrender and wonder even, but also the kind of authority and very nasty humor that says, "OK, baby."

Billie was a person who was so radically in the moment, in her music and in her life, that she could say one thing one minute and say the opposite thing twenty minutes later, and both would be true because she was always moving on. You could say that was because she was broken, and she was, but it was also a way of keeping possibility open, and it was the wellspring of her creativity. Nothing would ever be settled or closed, and if that meant chaos, so be it.

She does "Things Are Looking Up," one of her favorite songs at this time according to her friend Greer Johnson, in a very sad way that totally goes against the words, but her first "My Man" is fast and jaunty. She kids "When You're Smiling," as Judy later does, but her "You Go to My Head" is downbeat and obsessive. Billie sometimes uses Bing-like mordents, as so many singers did in the 1930s under his influence, but she does them in such a subtle way that they are nearly imperceptible.

Billie started singing with the Count Basie band, and the musicians loved and respected her, but in Detroit, Michigan, at the Fox Theatre, the management ordered Billie to put on blackface to make her skin darker to match the other band members. "When I came out on stage, I laughed," said trumpet player Harry Edison. "It was funny to me, and then she turned around and called me a motherfucker." This shameful incident was only one of the worst that Billie increasingly had to deal with as she made her living as a singer on the road.

Back in New York, Billie was such a hit at the Apollo with the Basie band that they practically wouldn't let her off the stage. There is a surviving live recording of Billie singing "Swing! Brother, Swing!" from the Savoy with the Basie band in the summer of 1937 that captures all her early fighting spirit and joy and hedonism, especially on the line "Raring to go, and there ain't nobody gonna hold me down!"

Ella was recording now with Chick Webb's band, and she also recorded with Benny Goodman, who wanted her for his outfit. She had a brief affair with Goodman's Italian saxophonist Vido Musso and took a leave of absence from the Webb band in December of 1936 for reasons that remain unclear.

When Ella returned, she showed her ambition when she wanted a ballad that her benefactor Charles Linton was singing; according to Linton, she threw a tantrum with tears to get it, and he gave it to her. "When she came up she was tough, yes she was," insisted band member Ram Ramirez. Linton said that Ella was highly conscious of her appearance now and would constantly think that people were laughing at her whenever she got looked at in a crowd or on the subway.

Ella was recording novelty song earworms with Webb like "The Dipsy Doodle," and John Hammond, who was promoting Billie, criticized Webb in *DownBeat* magazine for selling out for commercial success with Ella, though he allowed that Ella was a great "personality" and clearly was going places.

Toward the end of 1937, Ella was having a serious love affair with Jo Jones, the drummer in the Count Basie band, even moving to the Woodside Hotel to be close to him. On January 16, 1938, there was a battle of the bands at the Savoy Ballroom: Count Basie versus Chick Webb, Billie versus Ella, and so on this night they were directly competing with each other, and Ella's boyfriend was playing for Billie.

There was record attendance at the Savoy that night, and hundreds of people were turned away from the box office. Ella sang a swing version of "Loch Lomond," a Scottish folk song that she did on television many years later in the 1960s, and it was irresistible then—catchy, cheerful, and filled with her need to give joy—so this likely came across even in 1938. "When Ella sang she had the whole crowd rocking with her," reported *DownBeat* magazine. And she was at a technical disadvantage, for Count Basie wrote in his memoirs that there was something wrong with Ella's microphone at their main bandstand.

What did Billie sing that night? "My Man," about as heavy a torch song as there is, but *DownBeat* reported that the crowd was "thrilled" by it, even though many of them had come to dance. The Basie band was popular with the dancers, partly because of a misunderstanding that had caused a rift between Chick Webb and a small but flashy group of Lindy Hop dancers that included Norma Miller, who wrote about this historic night in her memoirs and said that Webb told them not to dance when he played. But Webb consistently drew applause on his drums.

A highlight of the evening was when Duke Ellington was persuaded to play a little piano and the Basie band joined him. Based on the press afterward, this was an evening when there was good feeling all around, and there was no real winner in the competition between the bands and between the singers because there didn't need to be. The crowd didn't feel the urge to choose between Ella and Billie and their very different styles and points of view. They enjoyed both of them equally. But when the ballots were tabulated, Ella and Chick Webb had won, even though some elements of the evening had been working against them.

Ella recorded a song called "You Can't Be Mine" before Billie did, in May 1938, and her pitch is wobbly here. She is also fairly detached from the words, whereas Billie is a far-reaching explorer of language, the fancier and more elaborate the better. This is early Ella, the Ella that Billie scorned, and Billie, only two years older, is singing Ella under the table at this time, both technically and in terms of emotional investment. Her "You Can't Be Mine," recorded in September of 1938, has that peculiar playful sadness that was Billie's own.

But Ella had a major hit when she also recorded "A-Tisket, A-Tasket" in May of 1938, which knocked Bing off the number-one spot on the hit parade and stayed there a while. "That was Ella's own thing," said band member Teddy McRae. "It was her own idea. That was her thing that she would sing up in Yonkers. . . . that's a nursery rhyme. . . . We had nothing to do with that. We called Van Alexander to put it down on paper for her, and Van made the arrangements."

Bob Stephens, a recording engineer at Decca, didn't want to record Ella's nursery rhyme song, but Webb packed up his drums in protest and insisted that they do it, and this record brought Ella to national attention. "A-Tisket, A-Tasket" was everywhere in 1938, to a Bing-like degree. Bing's wife Dixie listened to this Ella record over and over again, and when her rambunctious sons broke it, she went right out and bought another one.

In September of 1938, Ella and Webb set an attendance record at the Paramount Theatre in midtown Manhattan, and Webb knew that it was

Ella and her sweet search for her basket that had put his band on top. But she was inexperienced, and when Webb let Ella choose the songs for their program they didn't go down as well with the audience according to band member Beverly Peer, and so they went back to Webb's set list.

Moving on from Jo Jones, Ella enjoyed her success and the subsequent attention from handsome men who swarmed around her, one of whom was a son of President Franklin D. Roosevelt; he sent his car and chauffeur to take her home every night when she played in Boston. Ella did some nightclubbing with Charles Linton in this period, and he remembered her in the morning after a night of fun with her "shoes hanging across her shoulders, and as we were walking down the street, she was walking barefoot. She was cute, you know."

Ella recorded a sequel to her hit called "I Found My Yellow Basket" in late 1938, and it was also a success. The young schoolgirl who had told her friends that they were going to see her in the headlines was savvy about what press attention could do for her. When a journalist in Baltimore named Billy Rose saw her talking to the musician Haywood Henry, Ella told Rose that the ring she had on was from Henry, and it got written up that they were engaged. Ella sent Henry a telegram afterward asking if it was all right with him and if he minded the publicity, and he wrote back that he was fine with it.

But outside forces were starting to work against her rise to stardom. Ella and Webb were playing what was supposed to be an indefinite engagement at the Park Central Hotel in New York, but that gig ended abruptly after the *New York Age* reported that they were having trouble with "race prejudice" and that some "cheap, jealous Nordics are supposed to have functioned an ouster." Their manager Moe Gale said they would "fight to a finish," but he was unable to save the booking, and they soon were off on a series of one-nighters.

Webb's health was in decline, and he told his band members that if anything happened to him they needed to take care of Ella. The band played the Park Central again after Webb got out of the hospital, but he died on June 16, 1939, and his poor health had certainly not been helped by all those one-nighters when they might have stayed in their plush New York gig. At his funeral in Baltimore, Ella got up and sang

"My Buddy." She took control of the band, and within two weeks they were recording again and went back out on the road.

Billie had endured the road herself with the Count Basie band, and there are conflicting stories about why she either left the band or was fired in early 1938 after the battle of the bands at the Savoy, but it seems like John Hammond somehow screwed things up for her. According to Jo Jones, Hammond wanted her to be a blues singer, like Bessie Smith, and she wasn't about to limit herself in that way or stay in the past. Once again, Billie had a professional setback because she refused to let people tell her what to sing or how to sing it.

Billie then joined the Artie Shaw band in March of 1938 but only recorded one tune with him in July of that year, "Any Old Time," and had no end of trouble trying to be a part of his white orchestra. After a nasty incident in Kentucky where Billie was insulted by a racist audience member, Shaw finally hired Helen Forrest to sing for him too. There are also conflicting reports about Billie's reaction to that, partly because she felt different things at different times when she talked about her life.

Billie accepted many indignities when she toured with Shaw in the South, but what she couldn't take was prejudice in New York. When they played at the Lincoln Hotel in Manhattan in October, Billie was asked to use the freight elevator because the management didn't want their guests to see her in the lobby. She was also shut out of radio broadcasts from the hotel, and Shaw was unable to pass up this chance for his band. So Billie finally quit in December of 1938, almost totally demoralized by this experience.

She had been singing at Café Society, a racially integrated night-club in downtown Manhattan in Sheridan Square, and this gig became increasingly important now for Billie. She was living apart from Sadie at this point, and Sadie was doing cleaning work in office buildings. Sadie would sometimes come down to Café Society and ask the owner Barney Josephson to try to casually mention to Billie that her mother could use a few bucks.

Billie was having a fairly serious affair then with John Hammond's second cousin Louise Crane, a society woman who would later become the lover of the great poet Elizabeth Bishop, who wrote a poem for Lady.

"I think I had Billie Holiday in mind," Bishop said. "I put in a couple of big words just because she sang big words well."

At Café Society, Billie was by and large treasured and respected. The room was quiet when she sang, and if it wasn't the waiters would efficiently ask the noisy patrons to leave. There was one time that Josephson remembered when the crowd was too noisy, and so Billie finally turned around, picked up her gown, and showed them her ass. When Josephson scolded her afterward, Billie said, "Fuck 'em." Josephson said she took her work very seriously and would not tolerate sloppy or casual playing from her musicians, who revered her.

Abel Meeropol, a left-wing high school teacher and poet, had written an anti-lynching protest song called "Strange Fruit," and he brought it to Billie to sing at Café Society. Her immediate reaction was that the audience would hate it. She was not a crowd pleaser by nature, but this song was very extreme, so she took a moment to think it over after Meeropol left the club, but this did not take her long at all. Frankie Newton's band finished their set, and she told him, "Some guy's brought me a hell of a damn song that I'm going to do."

Both Josephson and songwriter Arthur Herzog said that they thought Billie didn't fully understand the song at first, but neither seems to have considered that she did understand but was somewhat stunned by it and had to work through some complicated emotions and calculations before she put herself fully out there with it. "My recollection is that the song didn't have much punch at first, when she sang it, and suddenly the impact of it hit her," Herzog remembered.

When Billie finally decided to do the song full out, tears ran down her face, and the audience was with her. She sang "Strange Fruit" at the end of each of her three sets of the night at Café Society, leaving the stage afterward and not coming back even for a bow no matter how much applause she got. Josephson told the waiters that they were not to serve drinks or take orders during this song, and the whole club would come to a standstill as Billie stood in front of them in a pin spot, unmoving, not touching the microphone, singing about the "gallant" South, the bulging eyes, the twisted mouth, and burning flesh. Sometimes audience members would walk out, but not often. When she sang it up at the

Apollo, the song was followed by a heavy silence and then the sound of almost two thousand people sighing.

Billie recorded "Strange Fruit" for Commodore, a small label run by Milt Gabler that took chances that Decca or Columbia would not. Billie went to Gabler on her own and asked him to record it for her because she said Columbia was afraid to. So she did four tunes for Gabler, including Jerome Kern and Otto Harbach's "Yesterdays," a great Billie song with its grand statements about "sequestered days" and "then sooth" and so forth. The more elaborate the wording of a lyric and the larger the perspective, the more emotional and particular Billie could make it with her piercing little voice.

The voice on this record and on "Strange Fruit" is a totally different voice from the one she started out with in the mid-1930s. Billie has almost entirely done away with vibrato now because she wants the notes to reach us more directly and wound us more deeply. Gabler asked her for a blues tune, and she obliged him with "Fine and Mellow," which went on the other side of the "Strange Fruit" disc and was a jukebox hit, according to Gabler.

Billie was close friends with Irene Wilson, who had been married to Teddy Wilson, and Wilson played her a melody she had written that Billie loved so much that she brought it to Arthur Herzog and asked him to write lyrics for it. The result was "Some Other Spring," one of the ultimate "I'm going to go into every possible detail of this sadness" Billie songs. A love affair has left her so desolate that the sun shining around her does nothing for her. Deep in her heart, it's cold as ice.

Herzog really outdid himself here, rhyming "worn" and "torn" and "mourn" in a way that feels opulent, chilly, and inevitable. This is the opposite of renewal. "Some Other Spring" is a flowery, pitilessly evocative song that says that wallowing in loss can be as pleasurable in its way as reaching for or experiencing love again, and Billie's voice presses insistently on the wound, on the dead flowers, especially on the last "spring," as if she does not want the pain to fade. The pain is important. It has to be made to mean something.

Billie had tears in her eyes when she first heard Carmen McRae sing "Some Other Spring" at Herzog's apartment. She said in her memoirs that when she brought the song to Benny Goodman, he told her that it was very beautiful but that it was too beautiful and that it wouldn't sell, and it didn't sell then. By 1939 Billie was defining herself with "Strange Fruit," the ultimate protest song, and "Some Other Spring," an outright art song. These were not choices that could lead to the success and popularity of Ella looking for her yellow basket. But they started to leave a mark for a legacy.

14

Band Canary Frank

FRANK WAS STILL paying his dues and singing as a single now at a roadhouse in Englewood Cliffs, New Jersey, and he was dating Nancy Barbato but seeing several other women, including Antoinette Della Penta Francke, a married woman who confronted Frank one night and got into a physical fight with Nancy, who did not back down. In retaliation, Francke had Frank arrested on an archaic charge of "seduction" on December 22, 1938, which is when his now-famous mug shot was taken. Frank never looked more beautiful than in this mug shot, wounded and ethereal and chagrined.

Dolly got involved and Francke fought with her and then had Frank arrested again, for adultery this time, but of course these frivolous charges didn't stick. Dolly was arrested for performing abortions, and so the Sinatras were always making the papers at this point, a prelude to a lifetime of headlines.

Frank's nerves were getting the better of him as a performer. He screwed up an audition for Tommy Dorsey, and he choked when he had the opportunity to sing one of his favorite songs, "Night and Day," for its composer Cole Porter. But his luck started to change after he was heard on the radio by Louise Tobin, the wife of trumpet player and bandleader Harry James, who went to see him sing and then signed him.

James suggested that he change his name to Frankie Satin, but this didn't get far. "You want the singer, you take the name," Frank said. As Frank Sinatra with the Harry James Orchestra, he won over a following of young girls nearly right away. "It was real, it was not a gimmick," said singer Connie Haines.

In August of 1939 Frank recorded "All or Nothing at All" with Harry James, and he sounds a bit self-conscious and green at first, like Ella often does in this period, and the word "nothing" is a difficult word to sing for any vocalist. But there is a rare tenderness to the way he sings "No, no," and he does a huge surging high note for the finish that comes as a shock, as if he's hurling himself off a cliff vocally. This is the sound of a voice that wants to be noticed, and it is much riskier and more insistent than Bing's would ever be.

This recording would not make its real impact until it was rereleased in 1943, but it signals who we are dealing with here. Frank sang "All or Nothing at All" all through his life. The big high note at the end is far more assured and carefully prepared for on his album *Sinatra & Strings* (1962), and as an older man in concert he would end it softly, which works just as well. But the way he first did that "all" at the end of this song is the most touching because it is so youthfully raw.

He left James in late 1939 and joined the Tommy Dorsey Orchestra. Even at this time, Frank had a small entourage, for he always needed a group of guys around him. Jo Stafford, who was singing with the Dorsey band, was very impressed by him. "I sure knew this was something," said Stafford. "Everybody up until then was sounding like Crosby, but this was a whole new sound."

15

Judy and Mickey and the Rainbow

JUDY WAS STILL finding her way as a performer. On the radio she sang Irving Berlin ballads like "How Deep Is the Ocean?" which she dedicated to her stage mother Ethel, and "Always," and at age fourteen she didn't have the experience to sing mature love songs like those. Judy was a giggler in this period and filled with energy and joy, and so her "Always" is immature. She does a gasping intake of breath in between "there" and "always" at one point, and she's too excitable and show-offy to really take care with phrasing.

MGM put her on Dexedrine, a combination of Benzedrine and phenobarbital. When Judy couldn't sleep, Ethel gave her a sleeping pill, but then Judy was unable to get up quickly, so Ethel took her off the pills entirely for a time, according to Gerold Frank's lengthy 1975 biography.

She was given a special spot in *The Broadway Melody of 1938* (1937) to sing "Dear Mr. Gable" to a photograph of Clark Gable, a routine that she had wowed everybody with, including Gable himself, at a studio function. At age fifteen Judy was without any inhibitions at all, and she already had the ability to let her guard down and immerse herself in each moment like a 1950s method actor would have. Her emotional intensity kills the corniness of this song and also makes it a little frightening.

That sock-it-to-'em trouper Sophie Tucker plays Judy's mother in this movie, and it is said that Judy's character was "born in a dressing room, raised in a wardrobe trunk." Soph does her signature "Some of These Days" and a bit of "Happy Days Are Here Again," and she urges her screen daughter to "sing loud!" Judy is like a sponge in her scenes here, and vibrating with responsiveness, and she even serves up some hip, edgy camp humor when dealing with Barnett Parker, a very flamboyant English character actor. She looks drawn to Parker, as if she knows he is her sort of person.

Judy was top-billed with Mickey Rooney in *Thoroughbreds Don't Cry* (1937) as a plucky character named Cricket West. "I'm going to be a great singer, and I'm going to be a great actress too!" she cries, putting on a "grand lady" act that includes some Garbo mimicry, a sequence that shows that fifteen-year-old Judy somehow has the camp sensibility of a middle-aged gay guy. There is a curious extended scene here where Rooney keeps pulling down the pants of an English boy (Ronald Sinclair) to give him an alcohol rub while Judy is kept outside the door.

"Benny Goodman's here to stay!" Judy insists in *Everybody Sing* (1938), and she also insists on swinging some jazz with a girl chorus in the opening scene. This picture makes it clear that MGM was beginning to categorize Judy in a way that was insultingly specific. She is called a "poor little ugly duckling" by her mother (Billie Burke), who then says, "Mother loves you anyway!" But at least they allow Judy a close-up to sneer at Burke, and at least Burke's character is supposed to be foolish.

Judy is given another role model like Sophie Tucker here in the commanding Ziegfeld stage star Fanny Brice, who plays a maid and is a virtuoso of funny faces, a hint that comedy could have become a large part of Judy's persona if she had wanted it to. Even if she hadn't possessed her huge singing voice, Judy could have focused on her instinct for mocking, disruptive, sophisticated humor, which runs through her like a jolt.

Judy sits on the stage to do a ballad called "Down on Melody Farm," which she brings to a rousing conclusion, but then she is given a scene where she wears blackface and pretends to be a sort of character called Opal Pearl Washington. She does a song in this getup and then does a Big Scene with tears with the blackface still on, and this makes the tears more painful, but not in the way that was intended. This blackface scene seems to go on forever, and it ruins the movie.

Judy was boy crazy from an early age, and she had lots of hectic teenage romances, but her main focus by early 1939 was the older Artie

Shaw, with whom she was madly in love. Shaw loved Judy like a little sister, and he was touched by her enthusiasm for his music and her knowledge of what he was trying to do. She confided in him all of her insecurities about her looks and even her singing voice, the one thing that seemed so much in her favor. "I've got this vibrato," she told Shaw. "I can't control it." She would say that she wasn't a really good singer and could never have sung with his band like Billie or Helen Forrest did. At this young age, Judy was aware of her musical limits.

Billie had a very small voice and Judy had a big voice, but Billie thought like a musician and Judy was a singing star who would get too carried away with her own emotions to stay within any musical structure or play around with it as a jazz singer would. Like her movie characters, Judy wanted to be truly great, like Billie. But in *Everybody Sing* she had been complicit in creating a grotesque caricature of an African American singer while two real African American female singers were making their own shot at musical greatness and dealing with the fallout of such offensive mockery.

Judy was being cast by MGM in the mold of a top performer like Al Jolson, who sang out and drove audiences into a frenzy, but taking on his tradition of performing in blackface was an enormous mistake, an attempt to pull her back into the past when her best instincts were modern, sophisticated, ironic.

In the oppressively wholesome *Love Finds Andy Hardy* (1938), one of a commercially lucrative series starring Mickey Rooney, Judy plays girl next door Betsy Booth. "I sing, you know," she says, quietly this time, as if she's aware that it's a running gag now. Judy is blessed and cursed with a deep camp awareness that makes her see the absurdity and doubleness of everything, and she was all too aware that Rooney himself was crazy for the pretty, sexy, and confident Lana Turner, who is in this movie with them, and that he had no time for her very needy soulfulness.

"No glamour, no glamour at all," Betsy laments of herself, singing a song about being in between age-wise and wanting to be older. Judy is sixteen here, but the studio has cast her as much younger, so that Betsy is twelve or thereabouts and longing to be sixteen, while Judy herself is sixteen and more than ready for Mickey to notice her.

She does a slow and sweet "Zing! Went the Strings of My Heart" for her widowed mother (Mary Astor) in *Listen, Darling* (1938), where the lack of a father figure in the story leads Judy into some raw emotional places. When it came to dramatic scenes with tears, Judy could be a little overeager and needed to be restrained somewhat by sympathetic direction, which she doesn't quite get here. Judy's early MGM movies weren't directed so much as produced, unlike Bing's Paramount movies, which at least had a capable visual stylist in Frank Tuttle.

There is a touching moment in *Listen, Darling* where her character comforts her little brother, and this shows that Judy is at her very best on-screen when asked to care for or look after someone else because this takes the pressure off her own deep despair. At one point in this movie, Judy weeps and says, "I just wish I'd never been born," and she's awfully young to be so fully feeling a line like that. In many of her MGM movies as a teenager, her emotionalism is condescended to as cute, but not in this scene.

These small movies were all a buildup to *The Wizard of Oz* (1939), an über-classic that can handle many different interpretations, for it is both conservative and radical, and it has something in it that can please everyone. Like her other early MGM movies, it was produced rather than directed, even though two major directors did pitch in and help out. George Cukor created Judy's look for the role of Dorothy, taking a blonde wig off her head and heavy makeup off her face and urging her to make her performance a bit less stylized and more natural, and King Vidor directed the sepia scenes set in Kansas. The score by Harold Arlen and Yip Harburg contains what would become Judy's signature song, "Over the Rainbow," which she sings yearningly just six minutes or so into the film, in the Vidor section.

Dorothy's Auntie Em (Clara Blandick) says that her niece is always getting herself into a fret, and Judy's Dorothy is very much a dramatizing teenager—open mouthed, credulous, and easily shocked by everything she sees when a hurricane takes her to the Technicolor land of Oz. The editing can be a little choppy in spots, as if scenes have been hastily cut, but there is a beautiful overhead shot of Judy's Dorothy as she skips down the yellow brick road with assurance, a reminder that Judy is often at her most commanding when she is moving or dancing.

Dorothy soon finds herself a ragtag group of fey men in Oz who all need something, a "dandy-lion" (Bert Lahr) who wants courage or the nerve to fight back, a tin man (Jack Haley) who wants to be able to love, and a scarecrow (Ray Bolger) who longs to be able to think things through. Judy's Dorothy has all of these qualities already herself. She is always fighting back and standing up for herself, and what is most touching about this legendary movie is that this fighting doesn't always come naturally to Dorothy. She is very vulnerable. When she cries, it is with luxurious abandon, so much so that she seems to enjoy crying. Judy was the ultimate drama queen, and anything dramatic had her full attention in life and on the screen.

Dorothy finally destroys the Wicked Witch of the West (Margaret Hamilton) by throwing water on the Scarecrow after the Witch has set him on fire, and so it is her active protecting of her friend that vanquishes the "beautiful wickedness" of the Witch's malevolence. Yes, this girl goes back home to Kansas in the end and says there is no place like it, but Judy's Dorothy has lasted because she is a very believable fighter against evil who does not back down no matter how upset she gets, and the appeal of this image is evergreen.

Judy would tell funny and exaggerated stories about the making of *The Wizard of Oz*, but she understood what it meant to people. She loved mocking or camping everything, but she would never mock Dorothy or *The Wizard of Oz* because they were too important. When she was doing her television show in the 1960s, Judy even used the word "sacred" in relation to this movie and "Over the Rainbow" when she was speaking of it to her collaborator Mel Tormé. She knew Dorothy was her passport to immortality, and she wasn't above exploiting this to get out of her worst jams later on in life. Judy could get exasperated sometimes at the image this movie gave her as "Dorothy adorable," but she accepted it most of the time, and at her best with some gratitude. Whether she ever understood what this movie eventually meant for gay liberation is an open question, but if ever anybody threw the first brick at Stonewall it was Judy's Dorothy Gale when she stood up for her friend the Scarecrow.

Judy was given a special juvenile Academy Award for *The Wizard of Oz*, and it seems strange now that they wouldn't let her compete for the real thing, but that year's rough competition included Vivien Leigh in *Gone with the Wind* and Bette Davis in *Dark Victory*, so at least her performance got its own special Munchkin Oscar.

MGM teamed her again with Mickey Rooney for *Babes in Arms* (1939), which had been a Rodgers and Hart show on Broadway. In their first scene Mickey and Judy swing "Good Morning" irresistibly, with Rooney crying, "Sell it, Ma, sell it" to Judy in a very Bing-like way as they bubble over with exuberance. But *Babes in Arms* becomes an increasingly disturbing experience, at least partly due to its director Busby Berkeley, who became Judy's chief tormentor on the MGM lot.

Berkeley's production number set to the title song plays out like a fascist rally, with people carrying torches, and there's a startling moment when the girls start to sing Ella's "A-Tisket, A-Tasket" and then toss some baskets into a large fire. Things get far worse with a minstrel number where Judy once again performs in blackface and disgraces herself, this time with Mickey. Reviving old show business traditions was a large part of Judy's image always, and minstrelsy nostalgia was a hellish wing of that image in 1939.

"I might be pretty good-looking myself when I get out of this ugly duckling stage," Judy says here, and this obsession with her looks in her MGM movies has begun to feel neurotic and unnecessary. The whole thing winds up with a number called "God's Country," which can only be interpreted as a song in favor of appeasement of the growing fascist threat.

So *Babes in Arms*, which was a huge hit financially for MGM, starts out well with that swinging "Good Morning" but turns into a nightmare on many levels once it gets going. Berkeley exposed the ugliness and hate lying just under the surface of that MGM gloss, and the very impressionable and undefended Judy was taking all that hate in like poison.

16

Bing: Minstrelsy and Father O'Malley

THE START OF a new decade for Bing meant the start of a new partnership on-screen with Bob Hope in *Road to Singapore* (1940), where Bing plays the heir to a fortune who is against desk work and says to Hope, "If the world was run right, only women would get married." This first *Road* movie is fairly straightforward, establishing only that Bing and Bob will do a patty-cake routine to distract their enemies before coming in swinging with the punches.

Bing is unfazed by the consummate unfunniness of Swedish dialect comic El Brendel and the trilling of pint-sized soprano Gloria Jean in *If I Had My Way* (1940), but he bestirs himself to do some broad comic faces at times, as if he knows he has to work harder for us with such costars. He was then teamed with Mary Martin in the excellent and overlooked *Rhythm on the River* (1940), which has a story cowritten by Billy Wilder and tackles a music world problem: credit grabbing. Basil Rathbone plays a famous songwriter whose tunes are actually composed by Bing and others on his payroll, which includes Martin and piano-playing wisecracker Oscar Levant.

Martin's character writes "Only Forever," which became a number-one hit song for Bing that year and spoke to his eternal quality as an "I am everywhere at once" American icon. Martin urges his character to show his songs to publishers under his own name, but when he does so a music publisher thinks that he is just imitating the work of Rathbone's successful and corrupt composer, and Bing brings an uncommon edge to this rather upsetting extended scene of humiliation. The desperation he shows here gets balanced by a sequence in which he sings the title song in a pawnshop and does some drumming, one of those moments in Bing's movies when he stops being Mr. Everyman and reveals himself to be a magical person who is deeply in touch with music and rhythm.

Bing's own arranger John Scott Trotter appears as himself in *Rhythm on the River*. Trotter was not known for either musical excellence or experimentation, and Trotter is present in a scene where William Frawley's music bigwig talks about how he hates "hot" swing bands ruining the melodies of songs, a clue as to why Billie was becoming a cult singer and Bing's predilection for jazz was getting sidelined by 1940.

Bing had two more number-one hits that year, "Sierra Sue" and "Trade Winds," both of which are assured and modestly paradisiacal. Frank's recording of "Trade Winds" from 1940 with a high thin voice is apprentice work next to the Groaner's easy mastery and relaxed access to bass notes. Bing's voice is very close to a narcotic high on "Trade Winds," almost completely detached from reality, and it seems to say good riddance to it.

Bing got on the *Road to Zanzibar* (1941) with Hope, and this is an improvement on the first picture in that they know that "fast and loud" is the way to go, and they also have their first meta moment when Bing and Bob are unable to finish their patty-cake routine before a guy punches them and Hope remarks, "They must have seen the picture." Of far more interest that year was the fascinating *Birth of the Blues* (1941), a story about how jazz and swing music were born out of Black musical traditions in New Orleans.

Music is seen as something that could dissolve the barriers between races in America in *Birth of the Blues*, if only stuffy and prejudiced white people would allow it to. In a prologue we see Bing's character as a boy told not to play "that vulgar darkie music" by his racist father, and he gets called "low white trash" when he grows up and plays swing music on clarinet. Black prisoners are seen in jail clapping along to white cornetist Brian Donlevy as he plays hot jazz in his own prison cell.

Eddie "Rochester" Anderson, who was famed as a comic sidekick on Jack Benny's radio program, is given a substantial role here, and in his best scene he poetically tries to explain how to vocalize with soul to Mary Martin, who wants to "sing like the colored folks." Toward the end of *Birth of the Blues*, the main characters are menaced by gangsters, and Anderson's character gets hurt. As the wounded Anderson lies in bed, Bing sings just a bit of "St. Louis Blues" for him before letting an operatic Black singer (Ruby Elzy) take over, and the expression on his face here looks unusually stirred and even guilt stricken.

"That ain't mine, that's gonna be everybody's music," Bing says at the close of this neglected film, which ends with a visual roll call of the jazz musicians of the day, starting with Duke Ellington and Louis Armstrong and moving on to Benny Goodman, George Gershwin, and Paul Whiteman, Bing's first boss. The order is telling, even if no one would be likely to include Whiteman anymore, and Goodman has his place, but not alongside Louis or Duke.

Bing's finest recording from that year was "Dolores," an ideal song for him with rich, surprising lyrics by Frank Loesser where Bing sounds teasing and ardent as he insists he doesn't want "Marie or Emily or Doris" but only his Dolores. The vocal group the Merry Macs provide some tension and explosive release in the background, especially when they cry about Dolores's "lips like wine!"

"Dolores" is one of the sexiest platters Bing ever put his voice to, and one of the most dramatic. It signaled that the 1931 Bing of the Cocoanut Grove and "Out of Nowhere" was still there somewhere underneath, but there is a vocal change in that his own "lips like wine" sounds restrained, and in the 1930s it might not have been. Frank's version of "Dolores" is nasal and straight-ahead, on the beat and simplistic, but it is noticeable that he has a larger range of sound to choose from than Bing has by 1941. Yet Bing still has his masterful control of dynamics and sound placement on another song with a Frank Loesser lyric, "I Don't Want to Walk Without You," which played on jukeboxes irresistibly in 1942.

Bing also made his most famous recording in 1942, Irving Berlin's "White Christmas," which became for him what "Over the Rainbow" was for Judy: something sacred, a balm to all. Bing's voice on "White

Christmas" is the voice of nostalgia, the voice that yearns for a peace that was in the past and can be again in the future, whereas Judy's "Over the Rainbow" yearns for a place that doesn't exist yet, or exists only in fantasy—a key difference.

Berlin wrote "White Christmas" for *Holiday Inn* (1942), in which Bing costarred with Fred Astaire, and the perpetually anxious Berlin performed his songs for the picture in Bing's dressing room. "I sang several melodies and Bing nodded quiet approval," Berlin said. "But when I did 'White Christmas' he came to life and said, 'Irving, you won't have to worry about that one.'" Yet Berlin songs never sounded like themselves until they were arranged and orchestrated, and Paramount arranger Walter Scharf remembered reassuring Bing that "White Christmas" would turn out well, which made Bing say, "I *hope* so" while rolling his eyes, a rare moment of doubt for him.

Holiday Inn is notable for that perennial Christmas song, a fabulous dance with firecrackers for Fred, and an extremely misguided number where Bing comes out in blackface and white beard and sings about the greatness of Abraham Lincoln. This character Bing is doing is much like the one he did for a number in *Sing, You Sinners* from 1938, where he played a similar part but did not darken his face.

There is a section of this song called "Abraham" where the Black character actress Louise Beavers speaks to her children about Lincoln, but it is spoiled by the offensively stereotyped outfit on leading lady Marjorie Reynolds, which is similar to what Judy wears in *Everybody Sing*. Before they go on, Reynolds says to Bing that she had hoped to be "pretty" onstage with him, which only compounds the offense.

Bing revived his double act with Bob Hope for *Road to Morocco* (1942), which is the first *Road* movie that fully embraces the meta nature of their series with its theme song, in which they sing that they'll meet up with their regular leading lady Dorothy Lamour before long. Bing had another hit here with "Moonlight Becomes You," a pretty, disposable tune, empty calories, that ends on a rather high note for him, for 1942, that he manages to sustain. The boys accidentally kiss at one point, but this isn't of any interest because two more heterosexual men than Bing and Bob never existed. Their super-fast delivery of ever-lame one-liners allows Hope to ask Bing at one point if he's "making reefers" as Bing rolls cigarettes, a question that somehow got past the censors.

Things were not running as smoothly in Bing's personal life, which is why he liked to keep his schedule as busy as it was. Dixie had given birth to a fourth son in 1938, and these four Crosby boys got into trouble a lot. Their father was often absent, and their mother was in her room drinking.

Alcohol consumption, which Bing himself had managed to control or tame by the early 1930s, overtook his unhappy wife and made for trouble elsewhere. Lyricist Johnny Mercer, who idolized Bing and wrote some of his best songs for him, was about as bad a drunk as ever lived; liquor would transform him. According to Mercer's wife Ginger, Mercer made a drunken pass at Dixie at a party, and though Bing continued to sing Mercer's songs, they never socialized again after that.

It was at some point in 1942 that Bing and Dixie had a fight during which Dixie said some things to Bing that he could not forgive. Bing did not specify in a letter to his brother just what Dixie had said to him, but it was so bad from his point of view that from that point on he didn't fully love her anymore. Their marriage was basically over, but he felt that he couldn't divorce her because of his Catholic faith.

This impossible situation was only exacerbated that year when their house burned down because of faulty light bulbs that turned their Christmas tree into a torch. When Bing was reached by phone and told what had happened, he took a beat and said, "Did they save my tuxedo?" The unfazed man he played on-screen had also become a part of his own off-screen character. Bing could be cold, and he was unable to express his feelings to his loved ones and gave them the silent treatment when displeased, but he could also be as cool as that when told he had lost everything.

Rumors ran around Hollywood that Dixie's drinking had something to do with the fire, and this cruel lie eventually found its way into a movie called *Smash-Up: The Story of a Woman* (1947), in which Susan Hayward plays an alcoholic ex-singer character based on Dixie who burns down a house due to drunken carelessness. Bing was unhappy about this movie and thought of suing, but he was advised that he would only bring more attention to it if he did, and so he let the matter drop. *Smash-Up* spread a false story about Dixie, but it did capture aspects of her stymied, inactive, very unhappy life, especially when Hayward's character says, "Did you ever spend day after day, night after night staring at your hands? I have."

If *Holiday Inn* is still a TV perennial, *Dixie* (1943), a Technicolor biopic of songwriter and blackface performer Daniel Decatur Emmett, has been banished to limbo, or a circle of cinematic hell that very few will want to visit. It begins pleasantly enough with Bing singing his sleepy hit song "Sunday, Monday, or Always" to a girl, and when Bing's Emmett sees a group of African American men on a riverboat, he sings "Swing Low, Sweet Chariot" to them. He then gets into a fight that gives him a black eye, and he's set to go on and perform, so Dorothy Lamour suggests that he darken the rest of his face to go with the black eye.

We then descend into a full-scale and full-color re-creation of a min-strel show with rows of men in blackface wearing outlandish costumes and Bing himself in blackface topped by cones of kinky hair. "Such poor taste," says a society matron in the audience (Norma Varden) as she watches a lavish minstrel show toward the end of this movie, and she's right of course, but in *Dixie* she is meant to be one of the snooty whites from *Birth of the Blues* who are prejudiced against Black culture, which is represented here by the most insulting stereotypes. This white matron is soon laughing at the lame jokes coming from the stage, though we have seen actual African American men open the doors to the theater where this show is playing, and they look miserable.

Birth of the Blues still plays well, whereas *Dixie* is unwatchable. Why did Bing want to make this all-out tribute to minstrelsy in 1943? Was he still that boy in Spokane thrilled by the stage authority of Al Jolson in blackface? Or was the impulse for racial unity in *Birth of the Blues* the same impulse that led him to *Dixie*, just horribly mistaken and distorted? Daniel Decatur Emmett wrote the Southern anthem "Dixie," which Bing sings in full blackface at the end of *Dixie*, a sequence that ranks as a particular low point for the medium of film. Unlike Judy, who had little say about her own appearances in blackface at conservative MGM, big star Bing decided to do this movie, and his legacy has to live with the consequences.

Bing as Father O'Malley in *Going My Way* (1944).

From this rock-bottom level, Bing traveled back up into the open air on the radio for Gordon Jenkins's "San Fernando Valley," a number-one hit in 1944 that crowned him as the future king of suburbia. "I'm for-gettin' my sins, yes yes" he says with offhand grace as descending violins remind him of the past he is escaping from. Like many of the best Bing tracks, "San Fernando Valley" is a convincing depiction of paradise.

He had another number-one that year with "I'll Be Seeing You," the ultimate wartime song of that era, which he handles with manly care and sighing sensitivity, and with particular attention paid to making us really see the images he speaks of: that small café, the park across the way, the children's carousel, the chestnut trees, the wishing well.

Bing won an Academy Award for best actor for Leo McCarey's *Going My Way* (1944), in which he played a hip priest named Father O'Malley. This was the height of his film career, and he later said that he had won the Oscar partly because so many talented men were off fighting in the war then. Bing won over Charles Boyer's villainous husband in *Gaslight* and Cary Grant's working-class antihero in *None but the Lonely Heart*, and he was right to be modest about his win. He barely does anything in *Going My Way*, a movie in which very little happens, a creative comedown for McCarey from the heights of his best 1930s work.

Bing looks great in *Going My Way*, far better than he did ten years earlier, tanned and slimmed down and alight with the splendor of his own success. Since he first hit in 1931, Bing had experienced no period of professional struggle or failure and only seemed to travel up higher and higher in public estimation. He was a soothing figure in wartime now as he had been a soothing figure during the Depression, and that should not be underestimated. But becoming the very public face of the Catholic clergy in *Going My Way* made it even harder for Bing to contemplate getting a badly needed divorce from Dixie.

Bing's Father O'Malley deals with the cutest and most harmless juvenile delinquents you would ever want to meet, and he teaches a girl to sing with emotion, and with his signature mordents. The whole picture seems designed to put people to sleep, and to that end Bing even sings a lullaby, "Too-Ra-Loo-Ra-Loo-Ral," for those in the audience who might still be awake.

He also sings "Swinging on a Star," another number-one hit for him on the radio, with lyrics that were inspired by a fight he had with his oldest son, Gary. The very unhappy Gary had a tendency to gain weight, as Bing himself often did, and Bing felt that mocking him would get him to slim down, but this only made Gary more miserable and resentful. Bing's mother Kate had used corporal punishment on her children, and so Bing followed suit, relentlessly and coldly. He had trouble with all of his sons but particularly with Gary, who was the Christina Crawford to Bing's Joan Crawford in that Gary wanted to be Bing and Bing himself saw all his own faults in Gary, and so the struggle between them got to be ugly.

Also ugly was Bing's final screen performance in blackface in *Here Come the Waves* (1944), in which he introduces Johnny Mercer's "Ac-Cent-Tchu-Ate the Positive" while doing his "Negro characterization" in white beard. Of all Bing's blackface appearances, this one is perhaps the most harmful because he is introducing a classic song that is rooted in Black church culture but he is twisting and exploiting those roots cluelessly. This is such a Louis Armstrong sort of song that what it really needs is Louis himself to introduce it, but Louis was kept from us in the movies, and these blackface appearances from Bing were a repellent substitute that epitomize the brutal racism of this era.

Bing is playing a version of himself in *Here Come the Waves*, and an audience of girls scream for him when he sings the Harold Arlen and Johnny Mercer song "That Old Black Magic" onstage. A shriek from the girls goes up when he does one of his mordents, and then he bends a note and actually groans the word "I" for them, and so it feels here like Bing is both competing with the young Frank, who was driving some bobby-soxers into a frenzy at this point, and sending him up.

Even though his character is color-blind, as Bing himself was, the army eventually takes him, and this cannot be seen as anything but a dig at Frank, who was 4-F and did not fight in the war, whereas Bing took on long tours of duty and sang for the troops in dangerous places, sometimes doing five one-hour shows a day and making sure to sing "White Christmas" as a balm at every one of them. This is the first time that Bing acknowledges that he is in direct competition with Frank, and he was not about to go down without a fight to the finish.

17

Billie and Ella Travel Light

WHEN CHICK WEBB's band played the Roseland Ballroom at the end of a long tour in December of 1939, there was conflict among its members about Ella's role now as bandleader. "After Chick died, I had charge of the band for a while, but I was young," Ella said. "A bit later there was a lot of resentment." The band was offered to Benny Carter, but he said that it would need to be his band with Ella as a featured singer, and her manager Moe Gale wanted Ella to keep her name on the outfit, so Teddy McRae took over.

Ella's band traveled to Baltimore in early 1940 to play a benefit for a Chick Webb Memorial Recreation Fund at a large stadium, and Billie traveled back to her hometown to be on the bill with Ella along with several other acts, including the dancing Nicholas Brothers. They raised nearly $10,000 for the fund in Webb's name.

Billie's first encounter with Frank happened when they were both playing in Chicago at this time. "I told him he didn't phrase right," Billie said to the columnist Earl Wilson. "He should bend certain notes. He says, 'Lady, you're not commercial.'" Much as Frank admired Billie from the start, he also knew that her way of singing was not going to get him on the hit parade.

Back in New York, Billie started to become unreliable at her standing gig at Café Society, perhaps because she had been used to singing for many years in a more informal way at Harlem clubs where it didn't matter as much when you went on and when you stopped singing. When she just didn't show up for her new October engagement in 1940, Barney Josephson canceled her contract.

On record Billie reconstituted the melody of Cole Porter's "Night and Day" and made it gloomier and more plaintive, with no release, focusing on the obsessiveness of the song and emphasizing what a narrow grind such an obsession can be. She was drawn again to another elaborately sad tune by her friend Irene Wilson, "Ghost of Yesterday," and she did the equally sad "Tell Me More," which sees love as a kind of drug, and which she has a writing credit on.

Her version of the Vincent Youmans song "Time on My Hands" seems to come out of a narcotic haze, for Billie was always pushing for altered states, an expanded consciousness, more pain, but intensified joy, too, in these early years. She moves forward creatively as if she wants to get away with something and come out the other side of reality and wind up finally in some far-off room, with maybe a bed and a man.

In 1940 Billie was still capable of exultant happiness, and she expresses this memorably on "I Hear Music," a Frank Loesser and Burton Lane song where music is everywhere and all her senses are alive and vibrating and she is taking everything in and her favorite melody is "you my angel . . . phoning me." She does one of her dying falls in pitch at one point on "melody," but this is an unusual track from Billie because of the way she outright belts the last word "song" in her own piercing childlike way. Billie had a technically small voice, and she wasn't a belter, but she's in such a good mood for "I Hear Music" that she flings this final note out as loud and vibrant as she can get it. It was Frank Loesser who stimulated Bing to be at his best at this time, and he did the same for Billie.

Billie and her mother Sadie were living together again, and Ruby Helena, an entertainer who stayed with them at this time, felt that they often related to each other as sisters, telling each other everything. Sadie was very possessive, needing to know where Billie was all the time and insisting on phone calls so that she knew where her daughter was every night, and Billie was already in her midtwenties at this point.

Helena said that Billie would often bring white girls back to the apartment and became known as Mister Holiday and William, and Helena felt this shift to pursuing the company of mostly women was at least in part because Sadie was constantly talking about how bad men were and how Clarence had deserted them. Underneath all of this, Helena felt that there was a deep fear in Sadie that Billie would desert her.

Sadie had made her way back into Billie's life again, and their behavior didn't make sense to people who observed it. "Billie's attitude toward her was alternately tender and very abrupt, a disturbing thing to watch, really," said Billie's friend Greer Johnson. "Billie was often very impatient with her, and I felt like I could not understand what their relationship was."

When Billie was seeing saxophonist Ben Webster and he beat her up, Sadie defended her daughter, running down the stairs of their apartment and hitting Webster with an umbrella, which made Billie laugh. The relationship with Webster fizzled, and then Sadie was very unhappy that Billie took up seriously with a very good-looking musician named Jimmy Monroe, who did his best to charm Sadie.

Billie had been happily smoking reefer for a while now, but Monroe was a smoker of opium, and Billie started smoking opium now too, just to try it, even though its effect didn't suit her. Monroe started taking money from Billie, which really got Sadie mad, and Sadie took Billie to court for nonsupport.

After Sadie came to her and asked for money for an after-hours place, Billie said, "God bless the child that's got his own," and from that came one of her most famous songs, "God Bless the Child," cowritten with Arthur Herzog, which she recorded in 1941. In her memoir, Billie changed this story around and said that she was the one who came to Sadie and asked for money, an attempt to make her mother look better.

She recorded another signature song in 1941, "Gloomy Sunday," and it really is a little much when it comes to wallowing in misery, the mood of her Irene Wilson and Arthur Herzog songs taken a step too far, a suicide song in which she sings, "In death I'm caressing you."

In August of 1941, Billie married Jimmy Monroe, in defiance of Sadie, who couldn't stand him. Shortly after the marriage they traveled out to Los Angeles so that Billie could sing in a West Coast version of Café Society, which lasted only a few weeks. Billie was very pleased when it was reported in the papers that Ginger Rogers said she wished she had Billie's beautiful mouth, which had a carved look to it, like a statue.

Billie went back out to California to sing in May of 1942 at the Trouville Club with her soulmate Lester Young, whose slang term for the police was "Bob Crosby," Bing's brother, as in "Bob Crosby is in the house." One night they were all drinking and having fun at Billie's place after the show when one of her musicians, Leo Watson, started to cause trouble; he was talking too loud and making people uncomfortable. Billie told her husband to take care of it, but Monroe was a little guy and Watson was a large fellow.

Billie continued to talk and laugh and dance around, but when she got close to Watson she slammed some of her best records over his head and then grabbed him and picked him up and said, "Open the door," and once the door was open she threw this big guy clear across the hall. Unfazed, Billie put on another record and continued to have her good time, and Watson was meek with her for the rest of the gig. Billie could be emotionally vulnerable, but in a situation like this she was physically powerful and decisive, her own bouncer. If you insulted her or made a nuisance of yourself, Billie was more than capable of administering a beatdown to even the largest and toughest men.

Trouble came in different forms. In Billie's memoir, she tells of a time she played at a club in the San Fernando Valley when a racist white man in the audience started heckling her after she sang "Strange Fruit." This happened for two shows, and after the second show Bob Hope and Judy rushed up to Billie to say how sorry they were about what was happening, and Hope said that he would take care of this guy.

When Billie started her third set and the guy still kept yelling at her, Hope jumped up on the stage with Billie and traded insults with the heckler for five minutes until he finally shut up. If this is true, and it might be, it counts as one of Hope's finest hours, and with Judy there in support, and the story does ring true Judy-wise because she was always drawn to any dramatic situation.

Paul Whiteman asked for Billie to record the tune "Trav'lin' Light" with him, which became another signature song for her; the lyrics were by Johnny Mercer. In order to avoid conflict with her Columbia contract, she was billed as Lady Day for this Capitol record, which was the last tune she recorded before a musicians' union ban started in late July of

1942. The musicians' strike is why Bing's "Sunday, Monday, or Always" is backed by only a vocal choir.

Billie's drug use and drinking increased dramatically. She didn't start shooting up heroin until late 1942 and early 1943, and she was using it in congress with many other narcotics. "She could consume more stimulants than any ten men and still perform," said bass player John Simmons. "She would smoke opium when we got home from work at night, and she'd light up a joint, and she had a ten-pound candy box full of pills—she'd grab a fistful of them—all kinds of pills—and chase it with a big tumbler of ale. And she would drink scotch behind that. *And* she would go in the bathroom and fix. She could barely whisper. . . . Anybody else would have been dead in six months doing what she did . . . anything to get high she was for."

But her feeling for music remained strong. She had befriended Greer Johnson, a gay white southern man, at one of her club dates in 1943, zeroing in on him in that hypnotic way she had when she wanted someone to be one of her people. He took her to meet the harpsichordist Ralph Kirkpatrick, who in turn introduced Billie to Bach's Partitas, which he either played for her himself or took Billie to hear the pianist Wanda Landowska play them in concert. Kirkpatrick supposedly said that Billie's face reflected every detail of the music as she drank all of it in.

Billie used Johnson as an escort sometimes, as when she wanted to attend a Katherine Dunham dance performance. "I want to know what the Negroes are doing, baby, would you take me?" she asked him. Johnson was living with the writer Elizabeth Hardwick, who later wrote about Billie and Sadie in her autobiographical novel *Sleepless Nights* (1979), and together they made some awkward attempts to socialize with Billie. There were barriers up between them, as there were with Bing and Louis, but they wanted to break through them.

In 1944 Billie began recording again, this time for Commodore, and she had simplified her style, using long wounding notes with practically no vibrato on "My Old Flame" and "I Cover the Waterfront," which became another of her songs that she did again and again. Her "I'll Be Seeing You" from this year is one of her greatest recordings, taken at an ultra-slow pace, with each word so weighted that when she goes down in pitch on "wishing well" it feels like she is taking us to some level past consciousness, like she wants us all to pass out with her.

Bing's "I'll Be Seeing You" is authoritative and expressive, but Billie's version is on a whole other level of artistry. No one was expressing pain as deeply and as openly as she was in music, and with such technical control; her last long drawn-out "you" with no vibrato is like a lance drawn from a scabbard, and it is the opposite of pretty or comforting. Bing's essential service in his music was comfort. Billie's way was to shine a light on such detailed hurt that there is a measure of exhilaration in how far she goes with it and how clearly she presents it to us.

Dealing with racists and hecklers in the clubs could get wearying, but Billie had grown up in the Point in Baltimore and could handle plenty. Frank supposedly floored a heckler for her one night, but she could take care of herself. Thelma Carpenter told a story about a time when two sailors standing at the bar of a club Billie was playing at started putting out cigarettes on her coat. Carpenter pointed this out, and Billie pouted and asked them to step outside.

"She gave me that coat to hold," Carpenter said. "And I want to tell you, she'd laid them flat. . . . When the cops came, she got very feminine, and she says, 'They *attacked* me!' And the cops cracked up. Two sailors laying out on the street, and she says, they *attacked* her. She put on her coat and went back into the club."

Billie's singing was fully matured, but Ella was still learning in the early 1940s. When she recorded "My Man" in 1941 for Decca, Ella was very shy of the lyrics, as if she were afraid of the feelings described in the song, but her cheerful novelty tunes charted and she was commercially successful in a way that Billie was not. Milt Gabler pointed out that all the young kids liked to dance to Ella's songs, whereas most of Billie's songs could never be dance hits.

Ella was seeing a man at this time named Benny Kornegay, and he traveled with her and her band; when he borrowed money from promoters, she paid them back. They married on December 26, 1941, but this was not reported in the music press because Ella's manager Moe Gale was concerned about how much of Ella's money Kornegay was spending, and Gale was having her new husband investigated.

It turned out that Kornegay had a criminal record for drug charges and had served time. Gale sought an annulment for Ella based on Kornegay's supposed criminal intent, which was granted in mid-1942, and Ella's press office released a statement saying that the judge had told her, "You go back to singing 'A-Tisket, A-Tasket' and leave the boys alone." So her management and the judiciary treated Ella like a naive child who had been duped, and she eventually accepted this and moved on, but it must have been deeply embarrassing for her.

In later years Ella couldn't even seem to remember Kornegay's name when asked about this first marriage, as if she had blocked the whole thing out. Certainly Ella still somehow had her sheltered side, but she was tough and practical too, and her career would always come first with her. Whatever the situation was with Kornegay, her management did not like him, and so she set this attempt at a personal life aside.

This instinct of hers to move on and forward extended to some of her professional contacts as well. Charles Linton, the singer with the Chick Webb band who had supposedly put himself on the line to get the homeless Ella that all-important first gig, said that by the start of the 1940s she refused to say hello to him.

Some of what Linton had to say in later years about his role in Ella's career sounds a little unlikely, or at least as if he is leaving some things out in order to present himself in the most flattering possible light. Ella may have had other reasons for breaking off contact with him, but we don't have her side of this particular story.

Ella made her film debut in an Abbott and Costello comedy for Universal called *Ride 'Em Cowboy* (1942), in which she emerges from the back of a bus to sing her mega-hit "A-Tisket, A-Tasket" and a second number called "Rockin' 'n' Reelin'," which she leads after being seen in the background of a club serving drinks. This second number is a precious glimpse of what Ella was like as a young performer—slim and filled with infectious energy, ready to dance as much as to sing—but it's dispiriting in that she goes right back to serving punch after delivering just one verse of her song from a stage.

What remained of Webb's band broke up in July of 1942, and Ella went out on her own. The musicians' union strike meant that she could only record, as Bing did, with a vocal chorus, and her popularity began to slip a bit, though she had a hit with "Cow-Cow Boogie" with the Ink Spots in 1944. Her vocal range was starting to expand a bit, but Moe Gale was booking her with amateur-level pickup bands on tour, and the future of her career looked uncertain.

18

Frank: The Voice

TOMMY DORSEY TOLD Frank, "There's only one singer, and his name is Crosby. The lyrics mean everything to him, and they should to you too." Frank would speak the lyrics of a song out loud before he sang them so that they would have a quality of speech, but Puccini was his favorite composer and his musical instincts were far grander than Bing's. He started to get called "the Voice" when he worked with the Dorsey band in the early 1940s because the intimate quality of his delivery revealed or unveiled words, and nobody could do a big finish to a song quite like Frank.

The record that made him a star was "I'll Never Smile Again," in which he was backed by the vocal group the Pied Pipers. Jo Stafford was part of the Pied Pipers, and she had some shrewd things to say about Frank and how Frank related to Bing. "Frank really loved music, and I think he loved singing," said Stafford, who had one of the purest tones of her time. "But Crosby, it was more like he did it for a living. He liked music well enough. But he was a much colder person than Frank. Frank was a warm Italian boy. Crosby was not a warm Irishman."

What Frank really learned to prize in the Dorsey band was breath control. He would marvel at how Dorsey could play on and on without seeming to take a breath, and he wanted to be able to do that himself. Stafford said that it had to do with having a large enough rib cage to take a really deep breath. "You can sing a note and use half as much breath as most people do," she said. "I think that if you want to learn to do that, you can. Frank certainly could. I could. Tommy also."

Frank had a feeling that he would die young, and all he cared about was his career and reaching the very top, where Bing was, and beyond. He was in Manhattan when his first daughter Nancy was born, but he didn't make the short trip over to New Jersey to be there for the birth.

When Frank went out to Hollywood to do "I'll Never Smile Again" in the movie *Las Vegas Nights* (1941), Bing visited the set, sans toupee but beautifully dressed, and everything came to a halt so that he could be welcomed. Here was the biggest star in America, and he made everybody smile and look alert.

Bing smoked his pipe on the sidelines as he carefully watched Frank do his number, and after it was finished, he strolled over to Dorsey to say, "Very good, Tommy." And then Bing looked over at Frank and said to the bandleader, "I think you've got something there," in that casual baritone-bass speaking voice. Bing then approached Frank directly to shake his hand and say, "Real nice, Frank. You're going to go far."

Frank was in the land of his dreams now, and there were beautiful women everywhere. It was also at this point that Frank first met Ava Gardner, who was a starlet then at MGM, Judy's studio, just one more great beauty to make Judy feel insecure.

Frank had palled around with gangsters since he was a kid, and when he wanted to get out of his contract with Tommy Dorsey and go out on his own, pressure was put to bear on Dorsey to make this happen by Frank's mobster godfather Willie Moretti. Some stories have it that Moretti held a gun to Dorsey's head, and this is entirely possible. Frank signed another contract saying that he would pay Dorsey part of his earnings, but he had no intention of doing that.

Frank was very frustrated with the musicians' union strike, but "All or Nothing at All," the record he made with Harry James in 1939, was rereleased in 1943, and this reissue was a smash hit for him. In *Reveille with Beverly* (1943) Frank sings "Night and Day" to a group of female musicians and makes it seem as if he is indeed capable of thinking of all of them night and day, for he had that kind of appetite. Frank's early image was waifish and vulnerable in a way that broadcast to women "please take care of me," but there were signs already that he was a wolf in sheep's clothing.

Frank did actually have screaming-girl bobby-soxer fans at his live shows, but they were disorganized. Frank's manager George Evans paid select girls to sit in certain sections of the theater and lead the other screamers at specific points in the songs, a very clever idea that ensured that Frank's show at the Paramount Theatre in early 1943 became a phenomenon. Calls of "Frankie!" carried the hormonal rush of female desire for a fragile-seeming man who needed mothering and encouragement to reach his full intense love potential. It was a trick, and it did the trick.

Evans played Pygmalion with Frank's wife Nancy and improved her wardrobe and grooming, and Frank found himself drawn to her again in the midst of his already epic womanizing, and Nancy got pregnant again, but Frank spent little time at home with her in Jersey.

Frank's entourage started calling him "the Monster," for anger was Frank's go-to emotion for everything. He got angry when he was scared, he got angry when he was ashamed, and he got angry when he felt slighted, which was often. The Irish in Hoboken had looked down on the Italians like Frank and his family, which is one of many reasons why he wanted to please and befriend the half-Irish Bing.

"From now on, I'll listen to Crosby!" he is told by a disgruntled female fan in *Higher and Higher* (1943), in which Frank struggles to play a version of himself on-screen. He is awkward here and not certain whether he should be natural or try to act, and so he'll think about acting or mugging for a moment and then just drop it, which is hopeless. This early Frank is would-be ethereal, and that is emphasized in the conclusion of this movie, where he is seen singing in front of heavenly clouds.

Frank was classified 4-F by the military in late 1943 due to a punctured eardrum, his low weight (119 pounds), and "emotional instability," and this made him the most hated man among soldiers overseas, who thought that Frank was enjoying the company of their girlfriends while they were off fighting. Bing was doing several of his wartime tours at this time, but Frank was too intent on his career to do more than tour briefly for the soldiers, and this caused much negative publicity for him.

Frank plays himself in *Higher and Higher* (1943).

Back in Hollywood, Louis B. Mayer saw Frank singing "Ol' Man River" at a benefit for a Jewish old-age home, and afterward the sentimental old mogul tearfully said, "I want that boy." Frank's management got him a plush MGM contract, and with that Frank purchased a spacious house in the San Fernando Valley that was not far from Bing's residence.

There is a live recording of Frank doing the song "San Fernando Valley" after Bing did his definitive version, but Frank is far too volatile and restless to make a tune like that work. Frank was the opposite of laid back. He couldn't sing that he would "never more roam" and make it convincing, or that he would forget his sins.

19

Judy: The Girl Next Door

JUDY PLAYED LOVELORN Betsy Booth again in *Andy Hardy Meets Debutante* (1940) and sang "I'm Nobody's Baby" with a lengthy verse, and all she got in the end for her trouble was a kiss on the cheek from Mickey's Andy. MGM next teamed her with Mickey for *Strike Up the Band* (1940), where the Mick says that Gershwin is just as good as Beethoven or Bach, and he's American! Such jingoism was the order of the day at MGM.

The Paul Whiteman Orchestra appears in *Strike Up the Band*, and it sounds pretty corny by 1940. "Rhythm can either excite the worst in us . . . or bring out the best," says Bing's old boss to Mickey here, a strange moment where the white face of jazz music of yesteryear feels the need to offer reassurance from the increasingly conservative MGM under Louis B. Mayer.

Busby Berkeley staged a conga number in *Strike Up the Band* where Judy looks overstimulated to the state of frenzy. Berkeley always wanted more animation from her, yelling "Eyes! Eyes!" at her because he wanted her eyes to sparkle for his camera, and she winds up looking demented in some shots, which is entirely Berkeley's fault.

"Who's been feeding you vitamins?" Judy asks a hyped-up Mickey at one point in *Strike Up the Band*, but Rooney downplayed MGM giving them pills in later years, gently but firmly correcting some of Judy's more flagrant exaggerations. "They had us working days and nights on end," Judy said in a piece for *McCall's* magazine. "They'd give us pep-up pills to keep us on our feet long after we were exhausted. Then they'd take us to the studio hospital and knock us cold with sleeping pills—Mickey sprawled out on one bed and me on another. Then after four hours they'd wake us up and give us the pep-up pills again so we could work another 72 hours in a row." Rooney denied all of this as an older man.

It was on *Strike Up the Band* that Judy's mother Ethel started to become concerned, in her own blunt way, about how hard MGM was working her daughter. Ethel told the studio that she wanted the teenage Judy to work only eight hours a day, and this got her banned from entering the MGM lot for a few months.

Judy got her own small-scale showcase movie that year, *Little Nellie Kelly*, which was based on a George M. Cohan show. She plays a dual role here, employing a light Irish brogue in the first half of the picture before doing her only on-screen death scene midway through, and then coming back as the daughter of this first character. It was a very modest film, but Judy is fresh and excitable in it, and always tempted to be a little overemotional.

There was more drama off-screen than on for Judy in this period, especially when she went into floods of tears and dramatics after finding out that her beloved Artie Shaw had married blonde beauty Lana Turner, in whom she had confided her feelings about Shaw. Judy told the singer Margaret Whiting that she wanted to kill herself when she heard about their marriage.

When Shaw asked Judy afterward why she didn't visit him anymore, Judy told him, "Lana's nice, but talking to her is like talking to a beautiful vase." This was Judy's acerbic queen side, which she could use as a weapon whenever she felt slighted, which was often.

Judy liked musicians and she liked witty men, and so she pursued the older Oscar Levant relentlessly for a while. Levant, who was also a pill popper, later quipped, "If we had married, she would have given birth to a sleeping pill." She had a very romantic affair with Johnny Mercer, who was so in love with Judy that he wrote one of his best songs with her in mind, "I Remember You." But she never sang it herself on record.

Judy stood up to both MGM and Ethel to marry the older musician David Rose in 1941, but her feeling of breaking free from their control was short-lived after she found out that she was pregnant and was ordered to get an abortion. Rose was a quiet type and Judy liked to go out and nightclub, so they were temperamentally unsuited from the start and began drifting apart almost from the beginning.

On-screen Judy was still Betsy Booth in *Life Begins for Andy Hardy* (1941), and Betsy has turned into a chatterbox here. "I've lost six pounds!" she tells Mickey's Andy. "It was mostly baby fat anyway." Judy wears her hair up and gets to look older and prettier in streamlined '40s clothes instead of the awful puffed-sleeves outfits they had been putting her in. And she gets to be funny too: "My mother bought me an evening dress that simply has no visible means of support!" she cries, revealing that sharp campy edge of hers again after so many pictures where it had been smothered.

But then in *Ziegfeld Girl* (1941) she was starred opposite Lana Turner and Hedy Lamarr, maybe the greatest female beauty of that time, in a movie where beauty is looked on as a woman's only value. Judy plays a girl who is doing a corny vaudeville act with her father (Charles Winninger), and at one point he shows her how to "sell" a song, a good demonstration of what Bing had broken away from in the early 1930s.

Judy does this number in the "beating a song to death" style that Winninger insists on, which looks a lot like what her parents Ethel and Frank were likely up to onstage in their youth. Setting this old-fashioned way of performing aside, she then sings "I'm Always Chasing Rainbows" slowly and with feeling, and with two Bing-like mordents to bring home just how important Bing was in changing the way performers delivered songs.

At the beginning of *Babes on Broadway* (1941), another teaming with Rooney, Judy does a comic crying scene where her aspiring performer character acts upset over losing a bit part. She has the wit to parody her own "insecurity" here, and there is a telling moment where Rooney tells her she's just acting and enjoying her own distress. Rooney asks her to sing and Judy says, "How do you know I can?" Mickey tells Judy he knows she can sing because she sings when she talks, she sings when she walks, and her eyes are "singing right now," and truer words were never said about Judy.

Her hair looks particularly beautiful in this picture, longer and more mature in styling, and she has the natural grace of a woodland creature, like Rima in *Green Mansions*, which might have made an apt musical for her. She sings "How About You?" and does a mordent on "you," and when Rooney joins her they even mordent it up together, Bing's influence on popular singing still holding steady.

Katharine Cornell and John Barrymore are the touchstones for Mickey and Judy in this one, for they always reverence the show business past. Judy briefly plays Sarah Bernhardt here, and Mickey does a Carmen Miranda impersonation that once seen is never quite forgotten. A young Ava Gardner first met Rooney, she said, when he was dressed as Carmen Miranda on the set of *Babes on Broadway*, a scarifying prospect. Yet Gardner wound up marrying Rooney in 1942 because he pursued her relentlessly and he was king of the MGM lot then while she was just a starlet who wanted to be noticed.

Babes on Broadway plays pretty well until the very end, when Mickey and Judy both sing, "How about a minstrel show, does that appeal to you?" to which the answer has to be a resounding "No!" But they do one anyway, and blackface Judy sings "Waiting for the Robert E. Lee." This is the last time Judy made up like this for a number, and it is a reminder that a Black woman could not have been a lead in movies of this time, even with a super-human singing voice. Black performers like Lena Horne and Louis were relegated to isolated numbers that could be cut for distribution in the gallant South.

Judy had certainly paid her dues at this point, and MGM gave her a movie where she alone was billed above the title, *For Me and My Gal* (1942), and a new partner, Gene Kelly. Judy was twenty years old now and ready to take on more adult roles. In the first scene of *For Me and My Gal*, she wrinkles her nose and sneers at Kelly's attempts to flirt with her, and her hard mockery with Kelly comes as a relief after the monotony of all those movies with Mickey where she pines for him and he doesn't seem to notice. This is the first film where some anger and resentment can be felt in Judy, and this allows her to be more human and dimensional on-screen than she had been previously.

But *For Me and My Gal* once again pits her against a glamorous soprano and includes a section where she is unrequitedly in love with Kelly, a continuation of her old MGM routine mitigated only by their delightful song and dance to the title number and her capering through "After You've Gone." Both of these songs became Judy's songs. There was a longing for domesticity in "For Me and My Gal" and a longing for revenge after love in "After You've Gone," and she always gave herself to both of these themes wholeheartedly, and then some.

One person who saw Judy in *For Me and My Gal* and fell in love with her was Tyrone Power, the male equivalent to Hedy Lamarr in the beauty department, and when they met he embarked on an intense love affair with Judy that must have done much to shore up her bruised ego. But this affair led to a devastating hurt for her.

Judy had befriended a woman named Betty Asher, who worked at MGM as her publicist. She even lived with Asher for a time and considered her a solid and trusted friend, but Asher was really just a spy for the studio, reporting back to Mayer and others about her activities. The studio was not happy about Judy's affair with Power, who worked at Twentieth Century Fox and was married to the French actress Annabella. And so when Power went away to fight in World War II, the Iago-like Asher cruelly fed Judy untrue stories about Power reading her love letters to fellow soldiers to mock her, and Judy believed it. When Power returned, he took up with the omnipresent Lana Turner, who always seemed to be there to take the men Judy was in love with.

Her work rate continued to be strenuous. She played another stage-struck kid in *Presenting Lily Mars* (1943), doing Lady Macbeth's sleep-walking scene and camping it up for showman Van Heflin. Her singing voice has a new strength here as she swings with Bing's brother Bob and his orchestra, and her last number features Tommy Dorsey and his trombone.

Girl Crazy (1943) was her final teaming with Rooney, an adaptation of the hit Gershwin show on which she finally broke down under the pressure of being directed by Busby Berkeley, who belittled her and bullied her until she could no longer function. This was the beginning of Judy not wanting to come to the set on time because she so hated the pressure of what might happen to her when she got there. She missed seventeen days on this picture because she just didn't want to be on a set with Berkeley.

Judy in the MGM vehicle *Presenting Lily Mars* (1943).

On-screen it is Rooney who pursues Judy this time, and she keeps laughing at him, and her laughing fits have an uncomfortable hysterical edge. She sings "But Not for Me" in the heaviest torch song way, without irony or humor, and she does "Embraceable You" in a rather high key to a whole bunch of guys, a number that is similar to Frank's singing of "Night and Day" to a group of women in *Reveille with Beverly*.

This link to Frank is emphasized when Tommy Dorsey and his band show up and attempt to swing "Fascinating Rhythm" in *Girl Crazy* but can't seem to find the rhythm or the beat. Bing, Billie, and Ella all knew where the beat was and could toy around with it jazz-wise any way they liked, whereas Frank and Judy were show singers who never had a strong sense of what rhythm could do for a song.

Judy now became involved with a man who would be of crucial importance to her. Joseph L. Mankiewicz was an influential person on the MGM lot, a writer, a producer, a wit, and a ladies' man. He was drawn to the young Judy, and she was drawn to him, and they began an affair that started to influence the way she was thinking about her life and work. Mankiewicz was in psychoanalysis, and he brought Judy to a therapist named Ernst Simmel to discuss the problems she was having.

This was not taken well by either her mother Ethel or Louis B. Mayer, who called Mankiewicz on the carpet and confronted him about the affair. Judy had been rebelling more and more against Ethel's control of her life, and at a second meeting between Mankiewicz and Mayer, Ethel was present and eventually screamed at Mankiewicz, "So! My daughter's crazy!"

There was a prejudice against any kind of therapy then, but there was likely some fear, too, in Ethel's response. She could not have helped noticing how Judy's emotionalism and need for attention affected the people around her. Judy had told both Tyrone Power and Mankiewicz that she was pregnant with their babies even though she wasn't.

Mankiewicz was right that Judy needed help, and he sacrificed his career at MGM to get her the help she needed, finally leaving the studio and signing with Fox because of this fight with Mayer over Judy. But Judy saw her therapist as one more authority figure to rebel against, and she began to invent stories for him of mistreatment, one of her worst habits. Still, Mankiewicz had tried to help her, and he held a key place in her heart. In the 1950s, when she saw him at parties, Judy liked to sing "The Man That Got Away" directly to Mankiewicz.

Judy did not want to do *Meet Me in St. Louis* (1944) when the script was sent to her, and Louis B. Mayer even agreed that it might not be right. Director Vincente Minnelli had not been able to relate a clear plot to Mayer, for what Minnelli had in mind was a dream of the past focused on a family living amid fin de siècle abundance with a slight art nouveau perversion of setting.

In her first days on the set, Judy started to camp the material, but Minnelli urged her to take it seriously, and she settled down, especially when she saw what pains he was taking to make her look beautiful. Minnelli sets her in a doorframe to sing "The Boy Next Door," and this frame is surrounded by green plants, which emphasizes Judy's woodland creature quality. She uses her abundant, textured vibrato here to linger over notes sensually in a way that Billie had begun to scorn in her own work, caressing the quivering words as her Esther Smith pines for the boy who lives next door (Tom Drake). When Judy's Esther reaches the end of this song, Minnelli has her pull a white lace curtain in front of her face, a Josef von Sternberg touch that elevates Judy to the level of a movie goddess.

Meet Me in St. Louis is the second great film Judy made at MGM, and it is a mysterious picture, wrapped up in set design and the sense that the Smith family is capable of ignoring any problem. Judy mimicked Minnelli's dithering indecisiveness on the set to appreciative crew members, but what got on the screen was complete and suggestive, a classic, both comforting and disturbing.

Judy was having great trouble now getting to the set on time, and it began to annoy Mary Astor, who was playing her mother again. In her memoir *A Life on Film*, Astor described confronting Judy about her lateness and telling her that she was no trouper. Judy tried to laugh about it, but then she grabbed Astor's hand and said, "I don't *sleep*, Mom!" Astor brushed it off and told her she wasn't so damn special to keep everyone waiting all the time, but Judy was starting to break down. She would get "jittery and weepy with fatigue," Astor wrote, and they had her recording at night and doing too much, and so sometimes Judy was like an overworked toy that could not function.

Judy was interested in the actor who played the boy next door himself, Tom Drake, and she pursued him, but he was gay, and when they tried to go to bed together he couldn't perform. Not understanding the real reason behind this, Judy took this failure as a personal affront, as if she weren't attractive enough, and she distanced herself from Drake on the set. "There was never a harsh word between them, but Judy shut him out after that, which made Tom awfully unhappy," said assistant director Al Jennings.

Minnelli himself had shown up on the MGM lot wearing makeup in the early 1940s, and he had a steady lover in New York named Lester Gaba. Word was getting around that Minnelli had slept with several male actors, but when this got back to Judy she refused to believe it. "It's not that at all, it's just his artistic flair!" she cried, hopefully.

20

Barbara and the Mirror

IDA ROSEN HAD changed her name to Diana Rosen before meeting
Emanuel Streisand, a high school teacher and scholar. They married in
1930, and they had a son named Sheldon in 1935. Their second child,
Barbara, was born in Brooklyn on April 24, 1942.

Emanuel, known as Manny, had been in a serious car accident, and
in August of 1943 he died following an epileptic seizure. He was only in
his midthirties, and his death came as a shock to a heartbroken Diana,
who moved back in with her parents with her two young children.

The young Barbara missed her father and his warm presence. Diana
was not a demonstrably affectionate person, and neither were Diana's
parents. At age two, Barbara would stare into a mirror and put on her
mother's lipstick and retreat into a make-believe world of her own.

21

Bing: Homecoming
and Feet of Clay

IN MANY WAYS 1945 was the peak beyond the peak in Bing's career. He had two movies in release, *Road to Utopia*, probably the best of the *Road* movies and certainly the most meta, and *The Bells of St. Mary's*, a sequel to *Going My Way* in which he returned as Father O'Malley but this time had the beautiful and very charming Ingrid Bergman as his costar. On record he captured the mood of the whole country and the imminent return of soldiers with "It's Been a Long, Long Time," a number-one hit written by Jule Styne and Sammy Cahn on which he was accompanied only by Les Paul on guitar.

"Bing was a sucker for guitar and that particular song was a case of you don't have to play a lot of notes, you just have to play the right notes," Paul said. In many ways "It's Been a Long, Long Time" is a return for Bing to the ardency and intimacy of his Brunswick period of the early 1930s, and the sexiness, especially when he sings, "Haven't felt like this, my dear, since I can't remember when," capering through the last words so that we feel his impatience for renewal, and for making up for lost time. He was still America's troubadour, expressing the national mood with his graceful authority, the lightness of his touch, and finally the way he bends a note on "long," which might have pleased the hard-to-please Billie.

"Next time I bring Sinatra," Bob Hope tells Bing as they travel to Alaska in *Road to Utopia*, and Hope also sings that the girls in igloos might like Bing because they "don't wear bobby sox," a reference to Frank's young female bobby-soxer fans. These were reminders that Frank was gaining on him in popularity, but Bing was still king in 1945, so much so that he could allow Ingrid Bergman to dominate *The Bells of St. Mary's* with her blooming smile and a long comic sequence where her Sister Benedict teaches a young bullied boy how to box. Bing and Bergman had something in common in that they both wanted to work constantly because neither of them liked what they found when they went home.

Off camera, Bing was starting to chafe against the restrictions of a marriage that was now only for show. In a letter to a priest, he wrote that he loved his wife Dixie but "hated what she had become," and he felt she had been spoiled by too much money and free time. Bing fell in love at first sight with the beautiful blonde Joan Caulfield and started a clandestine relationship with her, and he even turned up slightly drunk to a recording session, allowing a photograph to be taken of him with a hole in his pants. Bing had become an institution, but he was human, and he couldn't play the part of Mr. Perfect American Success all the time.

Bing avoided gallstone surgery because of the memory of what had happened to his best friend Eddie Lang, who had died in 1933 following a tonsillectomy. A *Life* magazine writer noted that Bing was more giving with casual acquaintances than with anyone who could have been considered a friend, and Bing was very aware of his own faults. In a letter to his brother, he wrote, "I don't know whether we Crosbys expect too much or give too little."

Fred Astaire was not happy when he was assigned Joan Caulfield as a dance partner for a Technicolor teaming with Bing called *Blue Skies* (1946), but Astaire was told that Caulfield was Bing's girlfriend and he wanted her in the picture, and that was that. There definitely seems to be something going on between Bing and Caulfield on-screen in this movie, and Bing relates to her in an intent way that he'd never related to a leading lady before. He is surprisingly agile in his dance routines with the great Astaire, and he sings "White Christmas" again for the troops.

On the airwaves that year, Bing's recording of "Symphony" had a ghostly delicacy, but when he finally got around to Cole Porter's "Night and Day," which was recorded in 1944 but only released in 1946, it became clear he had waited too long. Porter was not a Bing songwriter, too intense and too sophisticated, and Bing's timbre was starting to get a little shaky at this point, with vibrato used for expedience rather than expressive purposes. And unlike Frank, for whom this sort of song was meat and potatoes, Bing couldn't do a big finish anymore. Some of the recordings he did at this time were subpar, and he knew it, for when this was pointed out he only said, "That's all right, let 'em see that I'm human."

Bing finished out the 1940s with another flurry of movies, just as he had done at the end of the 1930s. He plays opposite Caulfield again in the sleepy *Welcome Stranger* (1947), and at one point in the movie it is said that he's as "good as Frank Sinatra" after he sings, but he was getting ever more distant. As an older woman, Caulfield said that Bing "had a little bit of ice water for blood."

He played a character named Scat Sweeney in another *Road* movie with Hope, *Road to Rio* (1947), but any actual scat vocalizing was a thing of the past for him. He does sing the Jimmy Van Heusen–Johnny Burke ballad "But Beautiful" to Dorothy Lamour, but his voice was starting to get a hollow quality, as if only the surface of it were left. The humor here is all glib throwaway one-liners that are delivered so fast by Bing and Hope that they aren't allowed to land, and this is another form of retreat. Yet one of those jokes does come through: it is said that Bing has told a girl his name is Frank Sinatra.

The Emperor Waltz (1948) was an attempt by Billy Wilder and his cowriter Charles Brackett to do an Ernst Lubitsch–type musical comedy with Bing and Joan Fontaine, but as Otto Preminger found out in the mid-1940s, only Lubitsch could do Lubitsch, and they wound up with not whipped cream but sour cream. There's far too much dialogue in this picture, and it is all mistimed by the players, a fault that turned up again when Bing worked with Frank Capra on *Riding High* (1950), another attempt to return to the feeling of the 1930s, a film that is stuffed with character actors past their prime.

Manny Farber wrote a negative review of *Riding High* in which he unfairly criticized the handling of the character played by Clarence Muse, an African American actor who did more than just about anyone else to dignify, complicate, and humanize the small roles he was given in this period. Farber was trying to write about how insulting roles were for Black actors at this time, but he was mistaken in picking out Muse here; he was right in general but wrong about Muse and Muse in this movie. Capra was apoplectic about this Farber review in his memoirs, but it signaled that times were at last starting to change, and it would take a lot of all types of urging on all sides to change them.

Bing was still seeing Joan Caulfield and doing anything he could to secure a divorce from his wife Dixie. The clandestine couple had appeared on the cover of *Life* magazine together in 1946, Bing looking at her quizzically but with love, and Caulfield kept on hoping. Patricia Neal said in her 1988 memoir *As I Am* that she shared a boat crossing with Caulfield in 1948, and Neal was also having a tortured love affair with a married man, Bing's friend Gary Cooper, but she couldn't talk about that to Caulfield. "She confided to me that she desperately wanted to marry Bing Crosby," Neal wrote.

Bing recorded a few tunes with his oldest son Gary in 1950, and the results were uncomfortable. Gary's voice is rough and he has pitch problems, but Bing tries to finesse this when they sing in counterpoint, supporting his son's voice with his own sound underneath. Bing's way with a problem was to act like it didn't exist, and this worked fine for him in many areas of his career and life, but not all of them.

Mr. Music (1950) is only notable for guest appearances from Groucho Marx, who seems to make Bing uncomfortable, and Peggy Lee, with whom he comes alive rhythmically for "Life Is So Peculiar," a hint that the early Bing was still there if he could be stimulated out of his hiding place.

22

Billie: Lover Man

BILLIE ASKED DECCA for a background of strings for her 1945 recording of "Lover Man," and she got them because Milt Gabler had a hunch that the song would be a hit for her, and it was. The strings gave her that lush sense of grandeur that she was so drawn to, and she also got some very dramatic strings for "Don't Explain," another of her own songs, drawn from a moment in her own life, when she caught her man of the moment with lipstick on his collar. Billie is in full tragic chanteuse mode for "Don't Explain," and the strings cushion her like a soft bed.

Decca was where Bing and Ella were singing, and now Billie would sing for Decca as well, which looked good for her, but she lost $35,000 in 1946 after going out with a big band when all the big bands were starting to fold. She knew that her mother Sadie was ill before she went out on the road, but when Billie got a telegram that Sadie had died, she took it hard. There was some guilt that Sadie had died alone, and there might have been some relief, for Sadie could be a clinging pain in the neck, but now Billie was officially alone herself.

Greer Johnson got Billie a prestigious legit gig at Town Hall, for which Ella and Leonard Bernstein offered printed testimonials to her artistry. As they were going to Town Hall, Billie said she wanted a new dress for the second half of her recital, and Johnson got nervous that they wouldn't make it there on time, but they did. The first act of the performance was a triumph for her, and she was elated afterward, but Johnson was told when she came off for the intermission that Billie's apartment had been robbed. No rose for Billie without a thorn.

Johnson asked Billie's musicians not to tell her about the robbery until she had finished the whole show so as not to ruin it for her, and they agreed, but maybe Johnson didn't understand her and her talent as much as he thought he did. Billie used everything bad that happened to her like a method actor would, and she was singing so many sad songs now that any fresh sadness was put to use.

She was still capable of singing with a light touch, as proven by the somewhat distant and fast-paced way she delivers her lyrics at the start of "Good Morning Heartache," but her attraction to the deepest sadness wins out here in the end, especially when she sings, "You're the one who knew me when," a very sad line for her at this point. Billie was only thirty years old, but she sounded like she had lived several lifetimes of despair already. She was making an example of herself now as a woman of her race and her era. This was her artistic, personal, and political project, as if to say, "See how bad this is for me? Do something about it."

Billie had a brief affair with the white drummer Roy Harte, who enjoyed her raunchy company. He remembered her telling him, "I'm only gonna do four tunes on the second show tonight. Start your hard-on!" She could be lots of fun, and she could be serious too. When they made love, Harte remembered her crying out, "Use me, use me!" They discussed this afterward, and she developed a whole philosophy with Harte about this idea, he said, of being used and used well. "She'd read newspapers, down south," he said. "She'd point out racial things I wasn't aware of."

Her manager Joe Glaser signed her up for a movie called *New Orleans* (1947), in which she would sing with Louis Armstrong, but she would be playing a maid. Billie tried to be optimistic about it—"She's a really cute maid," she said to Leonard Feather—but eventually a rightful amount of resentment started to creep in. Billie's character was made to wait on the white ingenue (Dorothy Patrick), and her feelings were mollified a bit only when the director Arthur Lubin told her that she made Patrick look like "a hole in the screen."

New Orleans is something like Bing's *Birth of the Blues* in its attempt to dramatize the racial basis of jazz music, but on a much lower level, even if it had the highest musical talent in Billie and Louis. For his part, Louis was thrilled to be playing with her on-screen. "Billy and I are doing quite a bit of acting (ahem)," he wrote to a friend. "She's also my sweetheart in the picture . . . ump ump ump. Now isn't that something? The great Billie Holiday, my sweetheart?"

Billie and Louis were similar at this point in that neither of them dug the bebop movement in jazz that was being pioneered by Dizzy Gillespie and Charlie Parker. They were set in their ways and liked to stay within the range in which they were comfortable as musicians, and this rejection of bebop made sense for Louis but less so for Billie. Here they both were in 1947 in a movie called *New Orleans* in which they were supposed to explain how this jazz music came to be, and this had the effect of placing them both in the past rather than the present or future. But Billie cared above all about lyrics, and maybe the speed and abstraction of bebop went against her dramatic instincts.

Gillespie was uncomfortable with Louis's onstage antics and how they were meant to come across to white audiences, and Billie herself was aware of this. Dan Morgenstern overheard this subject being talked about with Billie present, and he remembered Billie saying, "God bless Louis Armstrong, he Toms from the heart."

Crude Joe Glaser had all-powerful control as manager over both Louis and Billie. He had signed Billie up for a movie she was ambivalent about, and now Glaser insisted that she go into the hospital for a three-week cold turkey cure for her heroin use, for she was getting very unreliable at her club dates, but the only thing this did was draw more attention from the narcotics bureau to Billie as a drug user, especially when photos of her were published smiling in her hospital bed as if she considered the whole thing a publicity joke; she had in fact gotten heroin from her nurse. Louis went to visit her during her hospital stay, which pleased her.

Her recordings for Decca were getting sparse, and her 1947 version of "Easy Living" makes for a sad contrast to her record of that song from ten years earlier. She sounds very tired, as if the living is easy because she just doesn't have the energy for anything else now. You could say that it is a different interpretation of the song, and it is, but her first recording of "Easy Living" is a multilevel paradise, and this new one is a steep comedown, partly because it somehow sounds insincere, as if she is remembering a time that no longer exists and is mocking it. Even her musical backing sounds insincere.

Billie almost overdosed when she played in Chicago, and things were coming to a head with Glaser, who had been talking to narcotics agents about her since at least 1945. Billie was playing on a bill with Louis in Philadelphia, and at the end of the engagement she could tell that something was up when she went to get her things at her hotel. As she attempted to make a getaway, police started shooting at Billie's car, which was headed back to New York.

Billie was arrested in New York after cops found heroin in her hotel room. She was driven back to Philadelphia to face trial in May of 1947, and she pleaded guilty. The judge sentenced her to a year and a day at a federal reformatory in West Virginia for possession of narcotics. In her book *With Billie*, Julia Blackburn questions just how addicted Billie was to heroin given that she did not have any of the classic withdrawal symptoms after she was taken to prison. Her admission document to jail read, "Has done singing and housework."

Billie bided her time during her yearlong prison sentence, which was fairly uneventful. She'd been in places like this as a girl. She kept her head down, knitted, and got along well with others, and so she earned an early release in March of 1948. But the moment she got out and was in the clear, she sought to make a connection for heroin. Billie told her pianist friend Bobby Tucker that like some of the others in jail, she had been counting the days until she could get some heroin again. Tucker said that Billie had "gotten to the place where she was melodramatically romantic about her mother," and that she resented how Sadie had been rejected by the Fagans.

As a convicted felon, Billie was unable to obtain a cabaret card, which would allow her to work in New York clubs, and so she had to get around that somehow. She played at Carnegie Hall the month she got out of jail, and the place was packed; there were even people sitting on the stage with her. "They came to see me fall on my ass," Billie had said beforehand. Bobby Tucker felt that Billie sang at her very best that night,

Billie at Carnegie Hall, 1948. *Photo by William P. Gottlieb, courtesy of the William P. Gottlieb Collection, Music Division, Library of Congress*

but it was not recorded. She sold out a second show there three weeks later and played on Broadway for a week in June.

Billie took up with a guy named John Levy, probably the worst of all her boyfriends, though there is competition for that title. Levy was a partner in a nightspot where she performed called Club Ebony, and the management looked the other way about Billie not having a cabaret card to work in New York.

Billie would goad Levy to beat her up, as she had done with pimps when she was a girl on the streets of the Point in Baltimore, and she would beat him up too. He rented her a nice apartment and bought her gowns and furs and a green Cadillac convertible with a driver, but this he looked on as an investment, for he took total control of her and her earnings.

In 1949 Billie recorded "Girls Were Made to Take Care of Boys," almost certainly the worst song she ever sang, and she also did "I Loves You, Porgy." When Greer Johnson asked Billie why she didn't do this song at clubs, Billie told him that she thought Gershwin's *Porgy and Bess* had not "done much for the race," though she often kept these thoughts close to the vest.

When she returned to "My Man" in 1949, it was very different from her more circumspect earlier version: stark, slow, tragic, and very intense, with just a piano backing. She puts all her hurt and perverse defiance into this performance, especially when she sings, "But I don't care" with childlike insistence.

Could it be said that Billie chose her men as muses, the way that Joni Mitchell later did? If so, the choices and the results were so extreme that it's hard not to recoil from them. John Levy told her musicians that he would beat Billie up "so she sings good."

On New Year's Eve in 1949, Billie got arrested again at Billy Berg's in Hollywood. Jimmy Rowles said he heard a violent argument between Billie and Levy in the kitchen and heard her throwing plates, and then a man staggered out of the kitchen with a twelve-inch butcher knife buried in his left shoulder, and there was blood everywhere, and it was chaos.

Piano player Bobby Tucker had a more complex view of what happened. He said that Billie was in the kitchen with several guys, including the gangster Johnny Stompanato, who was later stabbed himself by Lana Turner's daughter Cheryl Crane. Tucker said that one of the guys got flirty with Billie, and she wouldn't have minded that, but Levy was there, and so Billie made a fuss about it and Levy had to respond. Tucker also said that Levy was scared because there were three guys.

Levy grabbed a knife, and the man who got it in the shoulder was just a bystander in that kitchen. To make it even worse, Tucker said,

Striking, if misspelled, advertisement for a 1949 appearance by Billie at the Sacramento Auditorium. *Courtesy of Wikimedia Commons*

Billie started throwing bottles. She had created this scene, she had created this mayhem, and now she was taking control of it. Tucker didn't think Levy was tough enough to play his role for Billie. "He was all mouth," Tucker said.

Billie was arrested yet again in January of 1949 when her hotel room with Levy was raided and opium was found, which Billie had attempted to flush down the toilet. George H. White, the federal narcotics agency's superintendent, said that he went after Billie because some of the "little colored prostitutes on drug charges" complained to him that Billie was on drugs but the police didn't do anything about that. White also said that Billie lived an ostentatious lifestyle, via her own earnings via Levy, and that made her a target. He said that when she was arrested, she was completely calm.

The state did not have a strong case against her this time. Her lawyers checked Billie into a hospital, where once again she displayed no heroin withdrawal symptoms, and she got the staff to play bartender for her, drinking her share of crème de menthe and brandy.

Billie used her own image here to her advantage in court, going into a "my man" routine about Levy and how she just did what he told her to do. She was acquitted in May, and she went back to her lush, rough life, defiantly recording a Bessie Smith tune, "Ain't Nobody's Business If I Do," with a blaring horn background—a far cry from Teddy Wilson's tinkling piano and Lester Young's caressing tenor sax from the 1930s. Whatever else had been lost with Billie, a very sassy and mordant humor was still there.

A 1949 photo session with Carl Van Vechten was not going well until he showed Billie his photos of Bessie Smith, which made Billie cry. Inspired now, she shot photos with Van Vechten all night, some in full color. In one of these shots, Billie holds an African sculpture and her face stares directly into the camera with great pride and great outrage. Another of these photos catches Billie looking down but with her eyes visible, and the camera captures a deep, nearly unfathomable torment.

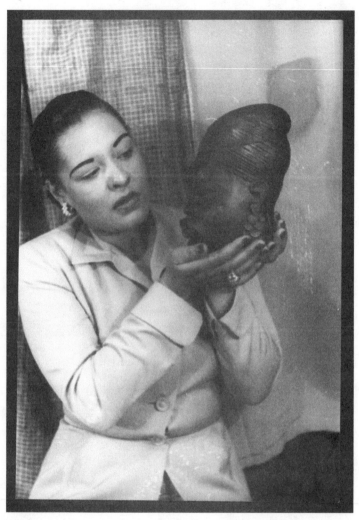

Another Carl Van Vechten photo of Billie holding the African sculpture.
Photo by Carl Van Vechten, courtesy of the Van Vechten Collection, Prints and Photographs Division, Library of Congress

23

Ella Bebop

Bobby Tucker played piano for several female singers, and he noted some similarities in their lives. He said that he once saw Ella play a gig at the Apollo in the 1940s with sunglasses on because she had a black eye from a boyfriend, and then he saw Billie playing the Apollo right after Ella's engagement and she was also wearing sunglasses to hide her own black eye. But this was a pattern for Billie, whereas with Ella it seems to have been an isolated incident.

Billie had not changed her opinion of Ella by the late 1940s, according to singer Billy Eckstine. She'd start complaining about Ella to him and would say she couldn't stand Ella's singing, and he'd say, "Bullshit, you know the girl can sing, don't give me that shit." But Billie wasn't having it: "William, goddamn it, that bitch can't sing at all, man." And Eckstine would tell her, "You're wrong, Lady, you know damn well that girl can sing." Billie would not back down, yet she would sound less certain. "Oh, bullshit," she'd say. "I don't understand how you can think that shit. That's horrible."

Eckstine said that Ella "used to love Lady's voice," and he noted that Ella was "a different person" in comparison to Billie, that Ella was "a calm person." It could be that Billie still saw Ella as that girl off the streets in 1935 who wasn't good enough, in her view, to sing with Chick Webb's band. But Billie was a singer for whom the words were everything, and sadness was the ultimate emotion for her to be explored. Ella was

Ella found a new freedom singing bebop. *Photo by William P. Gottlieb, courtesy of the William P. Gottlieb Collection, Music Division, Library of Congress*

interested above all in melody, and she almost always kept the words of a song at a respectful distance.

The jazz clarinetist Tony Scott told Bobby Tucker, "With a singer like Ella, when she sings 'my man has left me,' you think the guy's going down the street for a loaf of bread. But when Lady sings it, man, you see the bags are packed, the cat's going down the street and you *know* he ain't *never* coming back."

The emergence of Sarah Vaughan as a star vocalist in this period is also something that threw Billie. We can feel her ambivalence about

Vaughan in what she told her ghostwriter William Dufty for her memoir, in which her stories about Vaughan are all over the place. Billie claims she helped Vaughan learn how to dress, and she even claims she helped Vaughan out of a drug charge, but then she says that Vaughan snubbed her at a club after Billie got out of jail. Vaughan said later that if this happened, it was only because she hadn't seen Billie.

Lena Horne had approached Billie with deference and admiration, and so Billie had taken Horne under her wing. But Horne was Billie's sort of singer: she was also attentive to the words of a song, and Horne's distinctive style was to attack them. Ella and especially Sarah Vaughan were using a song in this bebop era as a vehicle for their voices, and Vaughan's blatantly show-offy use of vibrato, which she poured over her vocals like syrup over ice cream, must have annoyed Billie greatly since she was so anti-vibrato. At the same time, Billie was envious of Vaughan's instrument and aware that her own small voice was starting to lower and get even smaller and rougher.

There is a photo of Billie and Ella together from 1947 after a poll winners' midnight concert at Carnegie Hall. Ella is wearing a low-cut gown and beaming ecstatically for the camera, clearly thrilled to be sitting next to Billie, while Billie is holding herself away from Ella physically and her smile seems less than sincere. Being polite was never Billie's bag, but she's trying to be here.

Ella had started doing the scat vocal "Flying Home" in 1943 in her act, and through years of practice and experimentation she had perfected it, so that when she recorded it for Decca in 1945 it was a Joycean masterpiece where she picked and quoted snatches from the multitude of songs that existed in her head and her head alone. "How High the Moon" was another scat set piece she was working up, but when she first recorded it in 1947 her voice was in such ragged shape that she could barely sustain certain notes, a hint that she was overworking.

Her manager Moe Gale was still sending her out as a single to any town with a pickup band. Ella would show up with her old Chick Webb arrangements and the musicians could barely play them, and she'd get very mad about it and stay in her room with her cousin Georgiana in between sets. She didn't think about getting new management yet. Surely

Ella knew how Joe Glaser treated Louis and Billie, and at least Gale was better than Glaser.

Ella was recording with the Ink Spots, and she did duets with Louis Jordan and Louis Armstrong. She still did more than her share of novelty songs, which she enjoyed, like "Stone Cold Dead in the Market," and the hits Ella had with material like this could not have pleased Billie.

But Ella's voice was slowly opening up and strengthening. Her 1946 recording of "(I Love You) for Sentimental Reasons" is very close to her mature style, but there is still some youthful hesitation holding the sound in and keeping it from expanding to full volume, a pinched quality that marks most of her early work.

Ella was more focused at this time on being the queen of bebop. On "My Baby Likes to Bebop" from 1948, Ella sings of how the rhythm is now off the beaten track and that "the squares keep trying just to beat it back!" There's a famous photo of Dizzy Gillespie staring at Ella with a sighing sort of adoration on his face as she sings, and that's partly because Ella was the star emblem he needed for the kind of hard-edged, abstract, postwar music he was developing.

Ella is looked on adoringly by Dizzy Gillespie. *Photo by William P. Gottlieb, courtesy of the William P. Gottlieb Collection, Music Division, Library of Congress*

Ella toured with Gillespie, so she was right there with the vanguard of this new music. Ella, who was so often drawn to the most commercial songs, was magnetized now by this more difficult sort of jazz, which demanded to be listened to closely. "When the band would go out to jam, I liked to go out with Dizzy because I used to get thrilled listening to them when he did his bebop," Ella said.

Gillespie encouraged her to come out for these jam sessions and bop with her voice as one of the instruments in the band, and his band members, who had viewed Ella at first as a swing-era concession to get audiences in, soon gained respect for her improvisations. Her wide-ranging musical brain was perfectly equipped to take in the deconstructed rhythmic lines of bop and the abundance of chords that Gillespie used, which suited Ella's "more is more" musical joy.

This was a very happy time in Ella's life. "We would go into the towns and go to the clubs," she said. "There'd be a nightclub or somewhere to go, and the band would start playing and we would get up and that was it! We used to take the dance floor over. Do the Lindy Hop . . . we'd go with the old Savoy steps."

Ella grew close to bassist Ray Brown while touring with Gillespie, and back in New York they were seen together out and about where bop was being played. (Brown is sitting next to Ella in that photo with Billie.) Brown joined her on tour to play for her and be with her, and in late 1947 he asked her to marry him, and she very enthusiastically said yes.

Brown was good looking and young (twenty-one years old) and a bop musician, so he could travel with her and keep up with her, and Ella was thirty and just about to enter her musical prime. Everything was coming together for her, personally and professionally. When the Gillespie band was about to embark on a major tour of Europe, Brown chose to stay with his new wife and tour with her, which was a professional sacrifice for him. Ella traveled to England to sing with Brown, and they viewed this as a honeymoon trip.

Her manager Moe Gale was getting Ella good money now, and she was intent on pleasing her audience, so much so that she began singing "The Woody Woodpecker Song" in her act and kept it there for two years. By 1949 Norman Granz had Ella singing in his Jazz at the

Philharmonic performances, and he was eyeing her intently and thinking of winning her away from Gale. Billie had been his favorite singer, but now that he saw how audiences responded to Ella, Granz was switching his allegiance to her.

In April of 1949, Ella co-headlined with Artie Shaw at Bop City, a new jazz club in New York. Highfalutin Shaw brought in a forty-piece orchestra to play Debussy and Ravel, and the audience grew restive, so Ella brought out her most crowd-pleasing bop songs for them. Billie was in the audience that night, and so when Ella sang "Lady Be Good," she addressed her directly and sang, "Oh, Lady Day be good." Did Billie warm to Ella in a public moment like that, or did her ambivalence about Ella only deepen?

It was Ella's scat solos that were making her into a star of live music performance, but there came a point when she started to yearn to prove herself as a singer of ballads. Ella began to downplay her "riffing" in interviews and say that she liked to sing love songs best. "As far as the audience is concerned I could sing 'How High the Moon' all night," she said, chafing against what she was beginning to feel was a limitation.

Ella saw the kind of critical acclaim that Billie was getting for "Lover Man" and "Don't Explain" and slow torch songs like that. She wanted to prove herself in this area and make her own claim on the sort of material that was the forte of her idol, the woman she had asked for an autograph in 1935.

In September of 1950, Ella made a recording breakthrough, a long-playing collection of Gershwin tunes where she was accompanied only by the pianist Ellis Larkins, who plays the prettiest and juiciest chords for her. On *Ella Sings Gershwin*, her first major album, Ella's voice is naked, tender, full of feeling, so intimate and uncovered that it feels like you could reach out and touch it. Her voice is Bing-like in its authority here, gold being poured from a cup just like his at its best, and that voice is devoted to a single composer.

Lee Wiley had recorded albums devoted to Gershwin and Rodgers and Hart ten years before, but Wiley was a cult figure and an acquired taste as a woozy song stylist. Ella was the singer who got people thinking about popular American songwriters of the 1920s and '30s as artists with consistent points of view, and she owns certain Gershwin songs on this first album, especially a girlish, yearning "I've Got a Crush on You" and "How Long Has This Been Going On?"

There are only hints here of the small, forlorn sounds that had been holding her back before. Her singing voice has finally opened up fully and expanded on *Ella Sings Gershwin*, and she does direct, caressing things with it that had rarely been done before by a popular singer. Ella was singing now in a totally unprotected way technically, holding nothing back or in reserve, and this led her into unprotected areas of touchingly reserved emotion as well. This was a liberated Ella who was throwing her hat into the ring as a creative artist.

24

Judy and Frank at MGM

JUDY HAD STARTED shooting *The Clock* (1945) with cautious director Fred Zinnemann, and she was not happy about the way things were going. This was her first straight part in a nonmusical movie, and she knew how important it was to her career, so she went to L. B. Mayer and asked that Zinnemann be taken off the film. Judy wanted Vincente Minnelli as her director, for she had seen how beautifully he had showcased her in *Meet Me in St. Louis,* and she wanted that special kind of attention again. Zinnemann was sober and heavy spirited, whereas Minnelli was sensitive and wild, just like she was.

Judy and her director fell into a romance while they were making *The Clock,* an affair that they flaunted in front of the crew. This added closeness between them deepened further when they attempted to help her tortured leading man Robert Walker, who was in agony over divorce from his wife Jennifer Jones. Walker was far more troubled than Judy, and this had the effect of taking Judy's focus off her own troubles. She was always at her very best when moved to care about the well-being of someone else.

Judy was far from an ordinary person, but she somehow knew how to play one in *The Clock,* maybe the best or most perfectly controlled film she was ever in. Everything was shot on the MGM lot, but Minnelli knew his New York, and he managed to get the feeling of a bustling and impervious New York into the movie.

Joe (Walker) is a soldier on leave in Manhattan, and he meets Alice (Judy) by chance when she loses a heel on her shoe in crowded Penn

Station. Alice's defenses go down very slowly and realistically as she spends the day with Joe. She laughs at him a little and even sends him up, which is the way Judy shows love, and Judy lets us see the exact moment when Alice falls in love with Joe and his innocence.

Alice and Joe are separated in an overcrowded subway station, but they find each other eventually under the clock at Penn Station. Not wanting to lose each other again, they do everything they can to get married, but the rush of it makes Alice break down in tears afterward, and Judy goes up to and almost right over the edge of overplaying in this scene, but Minnelli helps her to shape this outburst of emotion just enough and ends the film with a lyrical crane shot of Alice getting lost in a crowd. *The Clock* was a notable change from her previous MGM movies directed by hacks, tyrants, or committees, and Judy knew it.

Minnelli loved to play Pygmalion for a woman, and he gave Judy the sense of glamour and sophistication that she had been longing for all through her adolescence. But this did not mean that she was focused only on Minnelli. She had a brief dalliance with Orson Welles, for she was unable to resist brainy men, and her makeup woman Dorothy Ponedel told a funny story about a night when both Minnelli and Welles were mistakenly invited to dinner at the same time. As Welles was coming up the drive, Ponedel had to run out and tell Minnelli he would have to eat in a restaurant with Judy because her stove was smoking.

Louis B. Mayer thought that Minnelli would help to keep Judy in line. Mayer wanted her to sign another contract with MGM when her old one was up, for she was a valuable box office property, and so Mayer encouraged their marriage, which took place on June 15, 1945, with studio spy Betty Asher as Judy's bridesmaid. The couple took off to New York for a honeymoon trip, and Judy threw her pills into the East River while Minnelli watched. His old boyfriend Lester Gaba met up with them, and Gaba was very unhappy about the whole thing.

"I'm going to have a baby, Mama," Judy told her mother Ethel over the phone. "Do you mind?" Before she started to show, Judy shot some numbers with Minnelli for a Jerome Kern biopic called *Till the Clouds Roll By* (1946), in which she plays musical star Marilyn Miller and sings "Look for the Silver Lining" with a smudge on her face and "Who?" in a yellow dress. There was much hilarity when pregnant Judy pointed out how funny it was in her condition to have her singing this song to a large group of men.

Frank very ill-advisedly sings "Ol' Man River" in would-be dialect in a white suit on top of a drum at the end of *Till the Clouds Roll By*, a much worse idea than any of Bing's versions of this song. But Frank's singing of "Ol' Man River" is what got him his MGM contract from Mayer in the first place, and so of course Mayer wanted him to put it on film.

In Frank's first movie for MGM, the Technicolor musical *Anchors Aweigh* (1945), he plays a lovelorn sidekick to Gene Kelly, and he is a hopeless dancer, staring at his feet Ruby Keeler–style and just barely getting through. He blinks constantly, and he's such a wimp in this picture that even milquetoast character actor Grady Sutton is threatening to him. Frank couldn't understand why movies took so long to shoot and was cranky and difficult about it, mouthing off to the press and winning no friends on the lot, though the inevitable Lana Turner won his full attention.

After finishing *Anchors Aweigh*, Frank went back to New York, where he was king of live entertainment. His pal "Toots" Shor, a colorful saloon-keeper, had arranged to meet with President Roosevelt through Robert Hannegan, the Democratic National Committee chairman, and he brought Sinatra along with him to the White House. Hannegan introduced them, and Roosevelt turned to his secretary Marvin McIntyre and said, "Mac, imagine this guy making them swoon. He would never have made them swoon in our day, right?"

Frank's smile grew fixed when he heard this remark from the president. Implicit in what Roosevelt said to him, Frank felt, was prejudice against him as an Italian American, but he brushed off the slight and continued to idolize Roosevelt anyway. Frank was only really impressed by world leaders, and if one of them wanted to insult him, he'd just have to take out the humiliation he felt on someone else in his ever-growing and changing entourage.

He got a frenzied reaction from his bobby-soxer fans at the Paramount Theatre in New York—so much so that his ballads could barely be heard above the clamor, which almost never died down. At one performance,

Frank was hit in the face with an egg by a disgruntled guy whose girl-friend was in love with him, and outside the theater a group of sailors threw tomatoes at Frank's image on the marquee. This showed just how much male resentment there was about Frank during the war.

His wife Nancy had moved out from Hoboken to the home in Hollywood, and they gave a big New Year's Eve party on December 31, 1944, that was attended by L. B. Mayer, Judy, and Gene Kelly. Frank showed his antiauthoritarian side by getting up and doing a piece of special material that poked fun at Mayer, and Judy sang some very enthusiastic backup for this parody piece with Kelly. Mayer managed to smile, but he was not amused, and it was clear that Judy took to Frank's underdog rebelliousness right away.

Frank was always getting bad publicity, and his publicist George Evans worked overtime to fix many of his problems in this area. Evans arranged a USO tour where comic Phil Silvers made fun of Frank, and this went over well with the soldiers. Back in Hollywood, Frank was rarely at home, for he was always in love with some girl or other, most seriously a blonde bombshell named Marilyn Maxwell. His new idol was Humphrey Bogart, and he worked hard to get invited into the social circle of Bogart and his foxy young wife Lauren Bacall.

Frank put his foot in his mouth about the USO tour to the press, complaining about it, and this canceled out any good it had done for his image. So when Frank spoke to Evans of his feelings about racial injustice, Evans saw that this might counteract some of the bad publicity Frank had again been getting. He sent Frank out on a tour of speaking engagements in 1945 at integrated high schools where there had been tensions. Frank's talk went over well at an integrated school in Harlem, but things were a lot tougher in Gary, Indiana, where he faced down a hostile audience of angry white steelworkers and their kids.

Frank's new image as a figurehead of racial tolerance was cemented by a short film called *The House I Live In* (1945), where he plays himself and talks to some kids about treating each other as equals no matter what your race or creed and sings the title song, which was penned by Abel Meeropol, who had written Billie's "Strange Fruit." This short earned him some pushback in the right-wing press, but it was nothing he couldn't handle. This was Frank's best self being put forward, yet he was also a man who idolized the gangster Bugsy Siegel and sought to emulate him.

He behaved in a totally unprofessional and very impatient way on the set of *It Happened in Brooklyn* (1947), yet he never looked more beautiful in movies than in the sort of glowing MGM black-and-white cinematography that turned all of its actors into gods and goddesses. Frank is sensitive and appealing here, listening closely to others and singing "Time After Time" with consideration and feeling. His appeal is most evident in the attractive contrast between his fawn-like looks and his tough Hoboken speaking voice.

Jimmy Durante tells Frank in *It Happened in Brooklyn* that it was "heart" that made Bing great, and that his own songs need to come from the heart, and this isn't entirely true. Bing was rarely direct about his feelings, as Frank was, and he also had a sense of rhythm that Frank lacked. When Frank tells Peter Lawford in this movie that a song doesn't have a beat, he taps on a piano with his hand but can't seem to find a beat himself.

Judy stayed at home for a while before giving birth, but she had filmed a highly sophisticated number for the movie *Ziegfeld Follies* in July of 1944, and that picture finally got released in 1946. Her song, "A Great Lady Has an Interview," was originally written by Kay Thompson and Roger Edens for Greer Garson, who turned down the opportunity to satirize her own image as a prestigious grande dame of MGM. The number was staged by Charles Walters but filmed by Minnelli, and Judy closely imitated the way that Thompson delivered this material with a group of clapping chorus boys.

Judy makes her entrance in a white gown from a bright orange passageway and flounces around for her all-male press claque before crying, "You have caught me pitifully unprepared." This is a reference to the way that Garson began her notoriously lengthy Oscar acceptance speech for *Mrs. Miniver* (1942) by saying "I am practically unprepared" before going on talking for five to six minutes. So this is very inside baseball show business stuff, and Judy is in her element with it.

She delivers this mainly patter routine with a kind of barely controlled camp frenzy that makes it one of the gayest things ever put on-screen, hip and decadent and devoted to pure colors, adoring and naughty men, and stiletto-like female irony. This Judy number in *Ziegfeld Follies* is a heady brew, slashed visually by the green of the scarf she deploys like a weapon and the morbid orange of that passageway she emerges from (orange was Frank's favorite color). The whole routine couldn't be less wholesome, or less like the Mickey and Judy movies that had made her name.

When Judy asked producer Arthur Freed how he liked the number after Freed watched a rehearsal, he replied, "I think Bing Crosby is going to win the Academy Award for *Going My Way* this year," as if only a reference to Bing's "hip" but conservative Father O'Malley could possibly counteract the gay hothouse posturing he had just witnessed.

Another movie Judy had shot before her pregnancy, the Technicolor musical western *The Harvey Girls*, was also released in 1946. Her former lover Johnny Mercer provided the lyrics for the songs, which included the showstopping "On the Atchison, Topeka and the Santa Fe," a very high-spirited and detailed production number that occurs near the beginning of the film. Judy's singing voice is still fairly high here, and she belts out the number with great power, using her voice as a kind of weapon and infusing her adventurous heroine with joy and a spirit of adventure. Angela Lansbury is a strong scene partner for her as a competitive saloon girl, but Judy has no chemistry with her leading man John Hodiak, and so the whole of the film, which begins to resemble a revue for other MGM contract players, doesn't live up to the classic opening.

Judy gave birth to her daughter Liza in March of 1946, and Frank later told his last wife Barbara that he was present for Liza's birth and ordered pizzas for everybody, though he might have been thinking of the later birth of her son Joey, when he definitely was there at the hospital. Judy suffered from postpartum depression. She signed a new five-year contract with MGM, and she knew almost immediately that she had made a mistake. Judy hated working there and couldn't stand it anymore, but Minnelli kept trying his best to reassure her, for he had his own career to think about.

While she stayed at home, a new musical vehicle was readied for her that Minnelli could direct, *The Pirate*, which was based on a play that had starred Alfred Lunt and Lynn Fontanne on Broadway. This was the project that Judy thought would really let her be seen as a sophisticated adult performer, a whole film with the knowing insider tone of her segment in *Ziegfeld Follies*, but it was troubled for many different reasons from the start.

A first script proved unsuitable, and a role for Lena Horne as a friend and confidante to Garland's character was regrettably dropped. Gene Kelly was chosen to play her leading man, and Cole Porter had been brought in to do a score. Kay Thompson's arrangement for Judy's frenzied big number "Mack the Black" was rejected by both Judy and Porter, and Minnelli kept seeking to expand Kelly's role and offer him chances for acrobatic dances that showcased his muscular body in tight and scanty costumes.

Judy started taking her pills again, excessively, and she missed 99 of the 135 rehearsal and shooting days. When she did appear on the set, Judy would often seem drugged from all the barbiturates she was taking, and the amphetamines she was taking to counteract them started to make her paranoid. Finally, while she was shooting a number where fire was involved, Judy had a breakdown on the set and started shouting, "I'm going to burn to death! They want me to burn to death!" and had to be led away, both laughing and crying hysterically. She told the columnist Hedda Hopper that her phone was tapped and that her mother Ethel was "doing everything in her power to destroy me."

What Judy wanted was to go back to live performing and hear applause again, and she blamed her husband for saddling her with another long-term MGM contract. She was torn apart by drugs and depression and the very real sense that she had no freedom, that she was monitored by all of MGM and Ethel and now Minnelli, for MGM actually was tapping her phone. The year 1947 was a turning point for Judy where the pressures of working for the studio, her failing marriage, and her addiction to prescription pills started to take their toll.

Suppressed and frustrated sexuality was one of her key problems now, and it found its way onto the screen in *The Pirate*, which does not exist in the form it might have. Minnelli shot a dance number between Judy and Kelly called "Voodoo" that was so sexually charged that an apoplectic Louis B. Mayer ordered the sequence cut and burned after he saw it. Mayer was also against the strong sexuality of Kelly's pirate ballet sequence, where Judy's character imagines him as a sexual dominant in very tight shorts, but that scene managed to stay in the picture.

Kelly dominates *The Pirate*, at least partly because Judy was so unwell when they made it and they couldn't shoot much with her. She forces a lot of her scenes here, seeming to imitate Katharine Hepburn's "I'm alarmed!" mannerisms and falling back on her own "I'm befuddled" tricks. What Judy appears to be trying to keep at bay is the realization that this movie is partly about her many problems with her husband.

She had married a very talented man who was likely gay by nature and bisexual by opportunity, which relates back to her beloved and lost gay father, who was the only person in her life who had given her unconditional love. Judy was drawn to men like Minnelli and her leading man Tom Drake for a reason, and this was bound to lead her to bad feelings all around and disappointment that could not be assuaged because it could not be named or seen clearly for what it was. This unspoken area of psychic trauma was partly what began to send her over the deep end.

There are so many bad vibes in *The Pirate*, and it does feel like scenes are missing. It cost a lot of money, almost $4 million, and it made less than $3 million, so it could not be counted as a financial success either. Judy was sent to a sanitarium after her crack-up, and she had many people around her who were very concerned about her, especially Carlton Alsop and Sylvia Sidney, who was a major star in Paramount melodramas of the 1930s. Sidney was "crazy about her," she said, and cooked for her. She wanted to "preserve that talent."

Judy returned to MGM to make *Easter Parade* (1948) with Fred Astaire after Gene Kelly had to drop out because he broke his foot. The score was by Irving Berlin, about as far away from the tense sophistication of Cole Porter as Judy could get, and she was tough enough to stand up to the revered Berlin when he tried to tell her how to do a song, poking him in the stomach with her finger and saying, "Listen, buster, you write 'em, I sing 'em," which Berlin loved.

Judy sometimes looks in *Easter Parade* like someone who has barely had any sleep in years and then suddenly has gotten too much of it. She seems frazzled and worn out at times, as if years of forced smiling for

Busby Berkeley movies had left their mark, but the movie itself has a lot going for it elsewhere. Astaire kills with his "Steppin' Out with My Baby" solo, and Ann Miller also kills with her own "Shakin' the Blues Away" tap solo, in which she pulls away the front of her yellow dress and all the material in back always looks like it's about to trip her up. Astaire and Judy click when they sing Berlin's "I Love a Piano" and "When That Midnight Choo-Choo Leaves for Alabam'," where he really responds to her and takes visible delight in her talent, and their tramp number became a classic.

Judy was needed for an appearance in the Rodgers and Hart biopic *Words and Music* (1948) with Mickey Rooney, but her health was breaking down again, and it took a while before they could lead her to the set to do "I Wish I Were in Love Again," a song that ideally suited her drama queen proclivities. She gets through this routine on sheer nerves, and there's a lovely moment here when Judy closes her eyes as she sings with Mickey and presses her face against his, a fleeting insight into how much she loved him that is brushed away finally by a sock-it-to-them ending that has an exciting edge of teeth-baring contempt to it. When preview audiences clamored for a second Judy number, she obliged with "Johnny One Note," which was filmed later when she was feeling better.

Judy had been making movies for the Arthur Freed unit, but she functioned better when they placed her with the smaller Joe Pasternak unit for *In the Good Old Summertime* (1949), a period musical version of Ernst Lubitsch's *The Shop Around the Corner* (1940) that is notable for her very physical rendition of the chestnut "I Don't Care," which is very her and very of an earlier time, ending on bended knee. Everyone involved in this picture made sure that Judy felt loved, but the result on-screen was mild and removed all of the emotional stakes of the original film.

Annie Get Your Gun had been a success on Broadway with Ethel Merman in 1946, and so Freed bought this property for Judy. She was uncertain if she was right for the role of Annie Oakley, and her fears mounted when Freed assigned her Busby Berkeley as director. Her leading man Howard Keel broke his leg when the tyrannical Berkeley ordered a horse he was on to gallop faster, and Berkeley offered no help to Judy.

She would come in ready to work, but then Berkeley would start yelling at her and she'd have to leave the set and go home. Her hair started to fall out because of her amphetamine use, and she went in for a series of six shock treatments to try to treat her anxiety. *Annie Get Your Gun* was a star vehicle, and if Judy was sick or not getting something right, they couldn't shoot around her.

The rushes started to come in, and Judy looked lost and demoralized, exhausted and uncomfortable with the role, and there was no one to help her. Why did Freed give this job to Berkeley when it was known that Judy hated him and was frightened of him? As a very commercially valuable star to the studio, why didn't Judy demand another director for herself, someone who could have worked with her on the part of Annie Oakley, which was not a natural fit for her? Freed hated the footage that had been shot, fired Berkeley, and brought in Charles Walters, who told Freed that the project couldn't be salvaged at this point. Finally, the worst happened: Judy herself was fired from the picture, and it was later reshot with Betty Hutton.

Frank was always drawn to people in trouble. He loved to help them in any way he could so that he could luxuriate in the feeling of his own generosity. At some point in 1949 he reached out to Judy, and she accepted his attentions gratefully. In a love letter from Judy to Frank that was recently sold at auction, she enthused about the "great amount of happiness" he had given her and how she would never forget the hours they had spent together.

Judy had become friendly with the good-natured Joan Blondell, who had been a key player at Warner Brothers in the 1930s, and one night she called Blondell and asked her to come over for dinner. Blondell said that she had already had dinner, but Judy insisted she come over anyway to talk. When Blondell got there, she saw that a fancy dinner had been laid out. They had some drinks, and Judy finally said, "I'll have to be honest with you." She admitted that she had been set to have dinner with Frank and he had stood her up.

Blondell was sympathetic, but then Judy went upstairs to "take some aspirin," and when she came back down, she spoke frenetically about being humiliated that Frank had stood her up. Blondell knew that Judy had taken more than an aspirin as she went on about being in love with Frank and how he was in love with her and that she hoped to marry him.

Frank's own film career was also on the downswing. He was loaned out to RKO to play a priest in *The Miracle of the Bells* (1948) and was so unconvincing in this sexless role that his performance has a small amount of camp value. Bing had his greatest commercial success as Father O'Malley, but Frank looks totally out of place in a clerical collar.

Back at MGM, Frank was put in tight, fancy clothes that look like they were deliberately designed to embarrass him in *The Kissing Bandit* (1948), where he plays a prim and hapless virgin whose eyes widen whenever he gets an idea. This MGM version of "Frankie" was not an appealing persona, and it could not go on much longer. His leading lady Kathryn Grayson said that she "couldn't stand kissing him" because he was "so scrawny."

Frank's relationship to the press worsened. He hit columnist Lee Mortimer from behind, and he was told by his publicists to lie and say that Mortimer had called him a dago, and so Frank told this falsehood, but then he was forced to admit that he had lied when the case came to court, and he eventually paid Mortimer off. Worse than this, Frank had spent four days in Havana, Cuba, in 1947 at a mobsters summit and was seen bringing a briefcase when he got off the plane, which caught the attention of the feds.

Years later Hank Sanicola, a key member of Frank's entourage, told Peter J. Levinson that he helped Frank pack a suitcase full of cash to bring to Lucky Luciano down in Cuba, a sum that was reportedly anywhere from $100,000 to $3.5 million. "It was one of the dumbest things I ever did," Frank himself told writer Pete Hamill. Worst of all, Frank's defense of himself in the press sounded weak, for he was always a very bad liar.

Frank's wife Nancy threatened to abort their third child if he didn't settle down, and she carried this out, the ultimate power move for her. His mother Dolly didn't like Nancy because Nancy had a strong will and couldn't be pushed around, or pushed out of the picture. Nancy got pregnant again and this time she had the baby, a daughter named Tina, in 1948.

Frank hired a tough governess named Georgie Hardwick to take care of his kids. Hardwick was a strict disciplinarian who had been in charge of Bing's four sons in the early 1940s, and they were not fond of her. But Nancy Jr. said in later years that Hardwick "transformed me into an unspoiled child," so either Nancy Jr. was being diplomatic or different methods work for different children.

Frank was getting drawn more and more to Ava Gardner, who knew just how to keep his attention by showing some interest and then dropping him, making out with him but then not going to bed with him. His mother Dolly loved Ava's adventurous spirit, and she encouraged Ava's romance with her son, but Ava was uncertain about her feelings for Frank. She was still hung up on her second husband, the inevitable Artie Shaw, and she did not like Frank's mobster pals.

On the radio, Frank bridled as his material worsened. Bing could sing just about any song and get away with it, absorbing it into his all-encompassing Bing-ness, but Frank had to like the songs he was singing or he couldn't put out for them. A particular low point was when he was forced to sing "The Woody Woodpecker Song," which Ella was singing with no qualms in her live act; he sounds like a miserable kid being kept after school.

Two more teamings with Gene Kelly at MGM, *Take Me Out to the Ball Game* and *On the Town* (both 1949), only emphasized Kelly's star mastery and Frank's own second-banana feeling of worthlessness, and this was something he had in common with Judy after her experience with Kelly on *The Pirate*. They both hated MGM, and they were both broken in very different ways, and so they took some solace in each other.

The press was hounding both of them. Is SINATRA FINISHED? asked a headline in *Modern Television & Radio*. A tabloid called *Hollywood Nite-Life* had outed Judy as a drug user in the summer of 1948, and this immediately changed the way people in Hollywood looked at her. Judy's problems had been known before to people at MGM, who viewed them with sympathy, especially when she was suffering through the making of *The Pirate*. But now that the whole town knew, and now that she had been fired from *Annie Get Your Gun*, she was starting to get looked on as a pariah. Judy's punishment for her drug addiction was disapproving looks. Billie's punishment for her own drug addiction was a prison sentence and police harassment.

Judy didn't need to find a street connection for her drugs as Billie did but got them from doctors, and she had innumerable doctors and pharmacies to get her the pills she wanted. People who gave parties knew now to lock up their medicine cabinets if she was attending, for Rosalind Russell found her whole medicine cabinet empty after Judy came to a party at her house. "I am an addict," Judy told a group of attendant doctors. "And when I want something, I can get it." Sylvia Sidney witnessed a young Liza running screaming from her mother when Liza smelled the by-product of a drug Judy was taking called paraldehyde.

Louis B. Mayer himself loaned Judy money for another hospital stay, so wicked old L.B. did want to do right by her. Frank sent Judy flowers in the hospital along with perfume and a phonograph with some records, which delighted her. While in this hospital in Boston, Judy befriended a group of disabled children, and it was a proud day for her when she helped a little girl who had stopped speaking to learn how to talk again. But Minnelli was horrified when she told him that she lied to her therapists. It was at that point, he wrote in his memoirs, that he knew Judy wasn't serious about getting well and that it was a game to her that she played to spite any authority figure she came in contact with.

Mayer told everyone to be cheerleaders for Judy when she came back to the studio to make *Summer Stock* (1950) with Gene Kelly, but she was overweight from her hospital stay and ordered to lose the weight, and this meant more pills, migraines, and insomnia. "I was in the trap again," Judy said, and she would barely work for director Charles Walters, who finally had to resort to making a show of his despair in front of her and saying that the studio was on his back, which briefly got her on his side. Anybody who was against MGM had her full sympathy.

"Everyone can't be a Bing," Judy sings in her first number in *Summer Stock*. "If you feel like singing, sing!" Her eyes look exhausted here and her pep is all surface, but she is in great voice, and she flings this first song out at us defiantly, as if she hates her own talent and how it led her to be caught in "the trap" of MGM to begin with. *Summer Stock* was a return to the Mickey and Judy "let's put on a show in the barn" pictures of her adolescence, and Judy was understandably fed up with this kind of thing. In her scenes, she plays "I'm fuming!" and "I'm frazzled!" far too much for comfort.

Judy was called back to do one more number after the movie was finally finished, and she had lost a lot of weight by this time. She had always wanted to sing the Harold Arlen and Ted Koehler song "Get Happy," and so Judy told the studio that she would only come back if she could do this tune. She showed up on the first day of shooting for "Get Happy" too drugged to do anything, and a fed-up Joe Pasternak wanted to let her try to shoot it, but assistant director Al Jennings convinced Judy that there was a technical problem and she'd have to come back to do the song the following morning.

Judy had told Minnelli that one really great musical number might make the whole of *Summer Stock* worthwhile, and she was right about that, for "Get Happy" became another of her classic routines. The angry Judy of the other scenes is suddenly replaced by a streamlined Judy in black coat and black hat, moving around like some snazzy fawn on legs that she shows off as a sexy male chorus claps for her Kay Thompson–style.

Everything comes together for Judy in this one number: the male-female costume, the cerise backdrop with white clouds, the adoring yet distant male dancers, and the words of the song itself, which promise that it's oh so peaceful on the other side. Judy's showmanship has a death wish in it, a longing to end the pain of living, yet there is no one more alive to pleasure and fun than she is.

Judy wasn't the only one in trouble at MGM. Frank was released from his own MGM contract in April of 1950 after he made a wisecrack in the studio commissary that too many people heard about. Louis B. Mayer had broken his leg in a horseback-riding accident, and when one of Frank's entourage asked, "Hey, did you hear about L.B.'s accident?" Frank replied, "Yeah, he fell off of Ginny Simms." Simms was Mayer's mistress, and L.B. did not take kindly to the joke when it was told to him. Frank was called into Mayer's office, and Frank did something he almost never in his life did: he apologized. But it was too late. Mayer wanted him gone.

Mayer offered Judy a full year off with salary and hospital bills paid if she agreed to be treated at a clinic, but Judy was aware at this point that her mother Ethel had looked into having her committed to an asylum, and she was very afraid of this. When June Allyson dropped out of *Royal Wedding*, Judy was asked if she could step in, even though she was trying to get her health back together, and she said yes. This was "one of the really classic mistakes," she said later.

Judy was trying her best on this movie, but Dore Schary, the economy-minded vice president of MGM, was taking on more and more responsibilities now. To Schary, Judy was an expensive liability to MGM and a symbol of the more indulgent days when movies could be allowed to run way over schedule. When she was an hour late for a rehearsal, director Stanley Donen told Schary he had had enough, and Judy was fired from the movie.

The public humiliation of this firing sent her into deep despair, and she attempted suicide by cutting her neck with a piece of glass in June of 1950. This suicide attempt got into the papers, forever changing the public perception of Judy. "I wanted to black out the future as well as the past," she said in 1957. "I wanted to hurt myself and everyone who had hurt me."

Her MGM contract was terminated in September of 1950, and at age twenty-eight she looked to be finished. Judy had appeared on Bing's radio program several times during the 1940s, and his people reached out to her to make an appearance. This radio performance was crucial for her if she wanted to continue any kind of performing career, and she was very nervous about it.

Hal Kanter, one of Bing's writers for his radio show, remembered the scene before Judy went out to face the audience. "She was standing in the wings trembling with fear," Kanter said. "She was almost hysterical. She said, 'I cannot go out there because they're all gonna be looking to see if there are scars, and it's gonna be terrible.' Bing said, 'What's going on?' and I told him what happened, and he walked out onstage and he said, 'We got a friend here, she's had a little trouble recently. You probably heard about it—everything is fine now. She needs our love. She needs our support. She's here—let's give it to her, OK? Here's Judy.' And she came out, and that place went crazy. And she just blossomed."

There is an edge of desperation in Judy's singing voice after Bing introduces her to sing "Get Happy" on his show, but the way she puts it over with determination at a faster tempo is a heartbreaker for anyone who knew about her troubles, which was pretty much everyone in 1950. It meant a lot at that crucial moment that King Bing was pulling for Judy and was in her corner.

25

Bing and Dixie

JOAN CAULFIELD FINALLY gave up on thinking that Bing would ever divorce Dixie and marry her, and she got married to the producer Frank Ross in 1950. Having set aside this relationship, which he had hoped to make permanent in the late 1940s, Bing was focused now on trying to help his wife, but this proved difficult.

"He would put out the money to have the head psychiatrist from the major hospitals in this town come to our house every day for two-hour sessions with my mother," said their son Gary in a 1987 interview. "And my mother would white-knuckle it. She'd sit there, she wouldn't drink. And then my dad would leave town and it wouldn't be a matter of a day; the doctor wasn't coming anymore and Mom was drunk. . . . It used to infuriate him. He couldn't figure it out. If you're doing something that hurts yourself, why you don't stop doing it."

Bing distracted himself from this ongoing problem, as always, with work. He made another movie with Frank Capra called *Here Comes the Groom* (1951), which is notable for an appearance by Louis where they sing together with Dorothy Lamour and a bouncy Hoagy Carmichael and Johnny Mercer tune called "In the Cool, Cool, Cool of the Evening."

Bing then made a picture that directly reflected on his vexed relationship to fatherhood, *Just for You* (1952), in which he plays a Broadway producer who doesn't have time for his children. His young son Jerry (Bob Arthur) writes songs, and Bing's character is very verbally rough on his kid's fledgling musical efforts. When his wounded son leaves the

Bing as a troubled father in *Just for You* (1952).

room afterward, Bing makes a slightly befuddled face that speaks to his own cold side.

Father and son fight some more, and there is an upsetting moment when Jerry tells him, "You don't have to love somebody just because he is your son." A young Natalie Wood plays Bing's daughter here, and her character is saddled with a drunken babysitter who is quickly fired. Bing offers to tell his daughter "why people drink" but soon swerves away from that. "What do you think fathers are for?" he asks her, and she replies, "To make money and be famous?"

Just for You keeps going right up to the edge of confronting Bing with the problems he had in his own life, but by the end it flinches from going all the way with that and settles for an unconvincing happy ending. Bing's character is depicted as an oblivious jerk in most of his scenes with his son Jerry in this movie, and Gary was the name of his own unhappy son, the unhappiest of his boys.

Bing got back on the *Road to Bali* (1952) with Hope, in color this time, and their delivery of dialogue had gotten so ultra-fast at this point that Hope sometimes gets laughs he shouldn't get and some of the better one-liners get buried. As always, Bing was professional and most encouraged by silliness, but there was a new crisis now in his personal life.

Dixie was diagnosed with ovarian cancer, and her doctors decided not to tell her she was dying. Bing was set to go to Europe to film a drama called *Little Boy Lost* (1953), and if he canceled the trip, he was told, Dixie would know that something was wrong. So Bing went to shoot that mild movie, and Dixie got sicker and sicker. Judy briefly stepped in to host Bing's radio show when Dixie was on her deathbed in late October of 1952, which is when Bing returned home, and Dixie died on November 1.

Dixie's funeral was "a circus," said Bing's son Gary, with photographers standing on gravestones to try to get shots, and Bing wept openly, as if no one else was there. There is a photo of him with his head in his hands that is deeply anguished, and the price of his fame was that he was not allowed any privacy in a moment like this.

Bing released a modest as-told-to memoir in 1953 called *Call Me Lucky*, and he started to think about retirement. Yet he returned in full force in 1954, releasing a retrospective five-record set called *Bing: A Musical Autobiography* in which he takes us through his whole singing career and sings some new versions of his 1930s hits. The green cover shows the hallmarks of Bing-ness: a hat with a feather, a pipe, a golf club, and loud clothing with colors that clash. No face is needed. Everyone in America in 1954 could look at this cover and know who it was supposed to be.

Bing's patter on this marathon retrospective recording is convincingly self-deprecating. He hopes that this set of albums won't be too dull but thinks that it might make for easy listening if "you're snowbound or there's a bus strike." He lets us know that some keys have been changed and lowered for him, but he has a nice bright tone on most of the old numbers, which are taken out and dusted off and then put back in the closet.

White Christmas (1954) was a color remake of *Holiday Inn*, and this time a minstrel show is done without blackface of any kind. It was the 1950s now, and the civil rights movement was consigning such things to the past, and so this number is an unpleasant and partly watered-down last gasp. Bing was not too happy with this movie, in which Danny Kaye was supposed to be a substitute for Fred Astaire, but it has had a continual life on television during the holidays. When Irving Berlin played a few new songs for Bing that he had written for the picture, the great songwriter found he couldn't continue due to nerves, and so Bing reassured him. "Do you like them, Irving?" he asked Berlin, who nodded. "Then they're good enough for me," Bing told him.

Most notable that year was Bing's attempt at dramatic acting in *The Country Girl* (1954), an adaptation of a Clifford Odets play for which he was nominated for an Academy Award. He plays Frank Elgin, an insecure alcoholic has-been and people pleaser who is trying to make a comeback onstage with the help of his embittered wife Georgie (Grace Kelly) and a wily theater director named Bernie Dodd (William Holden).

Frank Elgin is written as weak, insecure, manipulative, and a liar, and so he is totally unlike the awesomely assured and cool Bing. This part was meant as an acting challenge for the Old Groaner, and Bing rehearsed for it diligently, but like a kid being kept after school. *The Country Girl* would seem to relate to aspects of Bing's own personal life in its themes of a couple whose relationship has been destroyed by alcohol and Frank's failure as a father, but it does not touch Bing himself, and this is entirely due to the ham-fisted direction of George Seaton, who pushes Kelly and Holden to shout at each other in their confrontation scenes and grandstand too loudly too often.

In the crucial scene where Frank's son runs away from him and gets hit by a car, Bing makes an anguished face in close-up, but it is all surface, as if he is imitating other actors he has seen in dramatic roles. Like Kelly, who won an Oscar for her strenuous performance, Bing is miscast here. He doesn't have the right kind of self-loathing for this part, for he likes himself just fine and rated himself very smartly. Frank Elgin is the sort of man who makes a suicide attempt just to get attention, and this does not suit Bing or his persona one bit.

A widower now, Bing dated Kelly a bit, which was one positive thing to come out of shooting *The Country Girl*. When interviewed by Edward R. Murrow for Murrow's TV show *Person to Person*, Bing seemed totally assured, insisting that as a youth he was a "studious" lad who spent most of his time in "reading rooms." But his house looks forbidding and deserted somehow, and it is clearly an unhappy place. There is an image of Jesus on the wall, and Bing shows some of the late Dixie's china for the camera.

Bing is in complete control on this program, and part of his allure is that there is a rather large part of him that does not care about anything, which is very different from Billie's "don't care-ish" armor. Billie actually cared too much. Bing, who had been caught crying at his wife's funeral, knew that you shouldn't give too much of yourself away, to the public or to people in your life. If you do, there might not be anything left after a time.

Bing was all about conserving his resources now, and he felt his resources vocally and emotionally were limited. He had entered an era where putting your heart on your sleeve was the fashion, and so he rose above that but began to recede into an emeritus role as star and singer, gracefully, with a little smile that said, "I'm still here if you want me, but don't ask too much of me."

26

Billie's Clef Blues

BILLIE'S REGULAR ACCOMPANIST Bobby Tucker had left her to work for Billy Eckstine because he couldn't stand seeing John Levy punch her in the face or the stomach and knock her down when she would ask for a little of her own money. When they fought, Billie would sometimes break a bottle over Levy's head or cut him with a knife or a piece of glass, and one time she broke a television set over his head. She kept a razor blade at the top of her stocking, but this was just for show; she rarely if ever used it.

What Billie wanted Billie got, and she wanted pianist Carl Drinkard. Billie had heard Drinkard play and requested him, but he was intimidated by her and tried to beg off. When he was on a break one night, Drinkard spotted Billie. "Now when you first saw her, even if you didn't know who she was, you would say to yourself, 'Truly I don't know who this woman is, but she must be *some*body,'" Drinkard said. "She wore a white sequined gown, sequined from top to toe like the suits the warriors wore to the Crusades . . . so she walks over to the piano . . . she points at me and she says, 'You—you're coming with me!'"

Billie took Drinkard for a drink and had her own favorite, a lethal combination of brandy and white crème de menthe, and then she brought him out to play for her at her own show. Drinkard was frightened, but he got through it, and afterward Billie told him, "From now on, you belong to me! You're going to be my piano player!" And that was that.

John Levy set up a disastrous tour that was not promoted properly, and her band wound up stranded with no money in South Carolina, and so Levy's days were numbered. Drinkard had not gone on that tour, but he played for Billie again when she got back. He remembered that she would often tell him, "Carl, if I had to live my life without drugs, life wouldn't be worth living."

"Lady was an ironical person," said Drinkard. "Lady was the first to say that no one *else* should use stuff. She was very emphatic about this; she could not endorse the use of heroin, *except* for herself." She'd tell Drinkard that only she was strong enough to handle it, but Billie also told him, "Don't you end up like me." Along with her drugs, she was also putting away a quart or so of gin a day, and so for Billie it was anywhere but here and anything but sober.

She had a success at a date with Miles Davis in Chicago at the end of 1950, but Decca didn't sign her up again, and she cut just four sides for Aladdin Records in 1951. A live concert was recorded at the Storyville club in Boston, and it revealed that her voice had started to sound like it had been beaten up regularly for many years. Speaking to Nat Hentoff for *DownBeat*, Billie claimed she was married to her new man, Louis McKay, a guy she had known in Harlem in the old days, but McKay was still married to another woman then and had kids with her.

In this same interview, Billie talked about how much she loved Jo Stafford's singing. "I've been listening to her for six or seven years," Billie said and added, "She sounds like an instrument," which was her highest compliment. Stafford's tone at this time was the clearest and purest in the business, and she could hit notes that somehow seemed to shimmer without using almost any vibrato, and so of course this got Billie's attention.

In 1952 Billie began recording for Norman Granz's Clef Records, and she stayed within an increasingly narrow range for repertoire. "I don't dig all this modern stuff," she told *Melody Maker*. "Jazz is not what it used to be. For me, Benny Goodman is still the greatest." Billie was presenting herself as a back number now, or appealing to nostalgia. The covers of her Clef albums featured drawings and then even light-skinned models instead of Billie.

Granz sounded dutiful about her. "Billie was a great artist and she needed recordings, so you did them," he said, but he was far more enthused now about how Ella was spreading her wings while Billie was shutting down. Oscar Peterson played piano for Billie on these first Clef dates, and his propulsive, note-filled style was very different from the tinkling background she'd gotten from Teddy Wilson in the 1930s, but Peterson does give her a raindrop-like, Wilson-ish intro for her melancholy return to "These Foolish Things."

At age thirty-seven on her first Clef recordings, Billie sounds like she's had about two hundred years of strife, and she offers the definitive version of Cole Porter's "Love for Sale," partly because she's the only singer of that time who actually knew what that song was about; she reflects on the lyrics, considering them and letting her own memories saturate them. Billie may not have been into bebop, but her way of letting it all hang out emotionally was just starting to come into fashion in the performing arts in the 1950s.

Annie Ross stepped in for Billie at a gig at the Apollo with Duke Ellington, and Ross told Ellington that she was afraid to meet Billie because Billie was known for telling you if she didn't like you, but Ellington reassured Ross: "No, she's not like that at all," he told her. "She's really a lovely lady." Billie was very encouraging with Ross, and they became friends.

Billie appeared on the third episode of an exploitative TV show called *The Comeback Story* in 1952, which made clear that the notoriety of her drug arrests had overshadowed her image as a singer. Only audio of that show has survived, and what it reveals is that Billie so wholeheartedly participated in the anti-drug "up from the ashes" message of this program that she also seems to be sending it up.

Her pianist Carl Drinkard observed the games she played with her new man Louis McKay, how she would goad him into hitting her and then look refreshed afterward. She told Drinkard that McKay was the best in bed that she had ever had, and so at least he had that in his favor, even if he was another pimp type like John Levy. McKay also got her the heroin she needed and bought it in large quantities, and that was the most important thing to her. In the 1920s blues tradition of Bessie Smith and Gertrude "Ma" Rainey that Billie grew up on, the male was often seen as an instrument of sexual pleasure, and he often had to be bought or paid for to keep him around for an extended period, an inversion of both white and Black middle-class morality of this time.

In some ways Billie was still the unsupervised little girl from the Point in Baltimore. She liked to keep her hand in as a thief at stores, heisting a few items, and McKay would pay for them and be careful not to let her see him doing so, which would have spoiled her fun. Annie Ross remembered Billie getting away with some pretty high-priced jewelry at a shop in Paris. Her constant companions were two Chihuahuas, one named Chiquita and one named Pepe. Drinkard said that Pepe had been given to Billie as a present by Ava Gardner.

Billie was very possessive about the people in her life, and Drinkard felt that pull. "Anybody that belonged to her, belonged strictly to her," he said. "She didn't want them to make a move—to breathe—without her permission." It was getting heavier and heavier to be around her, psychologically and physically, and Billie even got Drinkard to hit her once after she unexpectedly belted him hard in the face and broke his glasses while she was very drunk. He said she had a "faggot heart," her own phrase for people who showed too much of their feelings.

When Billie would get certain female fans at her shows, she'd sometimes send them to Drinkard and say, "You want these bitches, Carl?" She could play the masochist with some men, but with women it was different. "Sure I've been to bed with women, Carl," she told Drinkard. "But I was always *the man*."

Drinkard said that if you acted like you didn't care about Billie she would do her utmost to get you to love her, but if you showed you cared for her she would cut your heart out. A chauffeur who was arrested with drugs in her car took the rap for her and didn't even mind when Billie wouldn't talk to him after he got out of jail; he loved her that much.

Billie needed a passport for a tour of Europe in 1954, and so she had to go back to the Good Shepherd home in Baltimore to get her birth certificate; she sang a song for the inmates, which did not make the staff happy. The tour was successful, and there is a definitive live recording of Billie singing "I Cover the Waterfront" in West Germany with Drinkard's very expressive accompaniment. This is Billie at her latter-day best, her voice piercingly clear again, and so deeply into the lyrics of the song that every one of the images can be felt. She socks over the words "hurts" and "knocks" and "desolate," and she really makes us feel that her heart has an ache that's as "heavy as stone." Billie was as in touch with "the great unknown" at this point as any artist alive, so much so that she could immerse herself in the terror of encroaching nothingness with an authoritative sort of calm.

Billie had a very good time playing in London and got a loving response from her audiences, but back in America, her drug habit put her in a very embarrassing situation. Norman Granz had programmed Billie as a guest star for one of his Jazz at the Philharmonic concerts. Ella was on the bill with her, and she was very enthusiastic about Billie's partic-ipation. To Ella, Billie was still an idol and someone who inspired her.

Billie did very well in the first half of the concert, according to Oscar Peterson. "She laid waste to the audience—killed them," he said. But after the intermission, when Peterson went to look in on her, he found Billie in an altered state. "I took one look at her, and she was like the sphinx, like a graven image," Peterson said. When Billie got back out onstage, she kept missing the intro to her song, and when she did start singing, Billie couldn't seem to find the beat.

This was at Carnegie Hall and with a large audience, and with Ella there watching as Billie faltered very obviously and embarrassingly. Granz had to finally get up and lead Billie off the stage, and she blamed Peterson for this fiasco. Peterson never recorded with her again, for he said that Granz knew that "I didn't dig being put in that position." The drug that Billie felt she had mastered was finally starting to master her.

27

Frank's Fall and Rise

FRANK'S SINGING VOICE was always fragile, and that was part of its appeal. By the early 1950s his voice was beginning to get the darkened sound of someone who is getting over a cold, or someone who has been out all night drinking, and that sound could be very expressive and striking, but it could give out at any moment.

He was madly in love now with Ava Gardner, and he needed a divorce from his wife Nancy, and this caused all kinds of trouble. "Frank was a guy—call it ego or what you want—he liked to suffer out loud, to be dramatic," said Mitch Miller, his A&R man at Columbia Records. "There were plenty of people, big entertainers, who had a wild life or had big problems, but they kept it quiet. Frank had to do his suffering in public, so everyone could see it." Miller also called Frank "the sorest winner I ever met."

Frank threatened suicide, calling Ava up and letting her hear a loud gunshot. When she ran to his room, Ava discovered that he had fired a shot into his pillow, and this hit the papers in differing versions, for Sinatra was always good for headlines. His passion for Ava made Frank more human, and a far greater singer than he had been; she was the essential added ingredient, and he knew it. Ava was masculine and wayward, and she was his match, yet she always outmatched him. She spoke to Artie Shaw about Frank, and Shaw said that Ava told him Frank was too gentle for her.

At an engagement at the Copacabana nightclub in Manhattan, Frank's voice finally cracked, and he couldn't get any sound out at all. This is when Lee Mortimer and other columnists who hated him pounced and called him washed up. Right-wing journalist Westbrook Pegler actually compared Frank to Hitler in print, and now the war was supposedly over.

At his lowest, Frank traveled to Spain where Ava was shooting *Pandora and the Flying Dutchman* (1951). When he was hounded by reporters who asked him if he had anything to say, Frank said, "Yes, Bing Crosby is the best singer in the world." Bing was still very much on his mind. He played Bing in a sketch with Bob Hope on TV, and in London he sang "Ol' Man Crosby" instead of "Ol' Man River."

Frank got himself his own television show, but he was jumpy and uncomfortable and it went badly. Eddie Fisher was the new teen idol at this point, and Frank felt discarded. Manie Sacks, one of his entourage, found Frank sobbing on the floor of Sacks's kitchen with the oven door open and the gas on. Suicide was on his mind, yet he couldn't bring himself to go through with it.

His trip to Havana for Lucky Luciano got him called in to testify before a government committee against organized crime headed by the senator Estes Kefauver, who at first wanted Frank to appear at the hearings on television and answer questions. This likely would have killed his career for good, and his attorney Sol Gelb got him a private meeting with the senator instead in March of 1951 at 4 AM in an empty office in Rockefeller Center.

Frank was scared to death, and he didn't know what Kefauver and the lawyer Joseph Nellis had on him. He tried to remain calm, but calm was not his thing. When asked about the suitcase he brought down to Havana, Frank claimed that it contained sketching materials, crayons, and shaving equipment.

According to Frank, all of his meetings with gangsters like Luciano and others like the Fischetti brothers had been coincidental, but Nellis wasn't having it. Frank started to wring his hands. "You're not going to put me on television and ruin me just because I know a lot of people, are you?" he asked. They were considering it, but Frank just narrowly avoided being called for the TV hearings.

He was offered $25,000 by Universal to appear in *Meet Danny Wilson* (1952), where he played a singer involved with mobsters. This movie was written by Don McGuire, a member of Frank's entourage who had keen insight into him, and so even though it was looked on as a comedown from MGM, *Meet Danny Wilson* was actually a step forward for Frank as an actor and a singer. His character is a hothead like Frank, and in the first scene he gets into a fight with a guy who calls him a runt. Frank's Danny winds up in jail for hitting a cop, and he sings a blues song in his cell. This is all a far cry from his virginal Frankie persona of the 1940s.

Frank sings a lot of songs in *Meet Danny Wilson*, and he has a new power and authority to go along with the delicacy that made his name. When he does "She's Funny That Way" at a club audition, cleaning people are seen stopping their work to watch him and marvel at his soulful sound. Singing at the club for an audience with no microphone, he does "That Old Black Magic" and "When You're Smiling" with very expressive hand gestures, including a very charming "grand" Egyptian sort of hand gesture to punctuate a pause for "When You're Smiling." Gangster Raymond Burr, however, is unimpressed. "Personally, I'm a Crosby fan," he says.

Frank and his leading lady Shelley Winters hated each other, and she recounted their nasty fights at length in her memoirs, but they have a spark together on-screen. At one point Frank's Danny yells at both Winters and his accompanist, and then he apologizes. Screenwriter/crony McGuire knew that Frank never apologized for anything himself, maybe because if he had started, he never would have been able to stop.

Frank made a breakthrough on record with "I'm a Fool to Want You," a very heavy torch song that he has a writing credit on because he altered some of the lyrics for himself. This was the first time he really put his heart on his sleeve about his somewhat unrequited passion for Ava, and the surge in volume he gets here on the words "time and time again" is hair raising in its wounded intensity. But this key Frank song was put on the same platter as the worst piece of material he ever recorded, a novelty tune called "Mama Will Bark."

Frank made another suicide attempt, this time with pills, but it was just another ploy to get Ava's attention, and she knew it and resented it. They were the ultimate in "I can't live with you, I can't live without you," and all with the press on their heels. Frank finally married Ava in November of 1951 after securing a divorce from a very reluctant Nancy Sinatra, but they did nothing but get jealous and fight and make up and fight again. Yet the making up seemed to make it all worthwhile.

Ava was now a major movie star at MGM while Frank's career sank lower and lower. He tried to court the press he had scorned, and he had serious vocal trouble on his TV show, especially on an episode that had Jackie Gleason as a guest. But he had a goal in sight: Frank read James Jones's bestseller *From Here to Eternity* and he knew that he was perfect for the role of Maggio, a volatile runt and loser who pays the price for standing up for himself. He read the novel over and over again and sent continual telegrams to Columbia studio head Harry Cohn, who had purchased the film rights to the book.

Frank was booed at a concert in his native Hoboken after he "hit some clinkers," said his boyhood friend Tony Macagnano, and people threw fruit at him. "Oh, did he get mad," Macagnano said. Frank vowed never to return to Hoboken again. He became more and more desperate to get the part of Maggio in *From Here to Eternity*, telling Harry Cohn that he would even forgo a salary and just play it for expenses.

This piqued Cohn's interest, and he was further intrigued when Ava begged Cohn's wife Joan to get Frank a screen test. Ava even met with Cohn and told him that she'd do a picture for him for free if he'd just let Frank do a test. She knew that their volatile relationship couldn't suffer his career being on the skids for much longer.

Their fights grew more and more elaborate and boisterous, and they used other people as bait for their jealousy. In her memoirs, Ava remembers a brawl where Frank finally offered her a "a truly memorable exit line": "Okay! Okay! If that's the way you want it. I'm leaving. And if you want to know where I am, I'm in Palm Springs fucking Lana Turner." He then took off in her car.

Undaunted, Ava set about beating him at his own game. She had her sister drive her to Palm Springs, and she climbed over the fence of the house where Turner was staying with her business manager Ben Cole. When Turner opened the door, Frank wasn't there, and they all decided to get drunk and tell some stories, and when Frank arrived and found Ava there with Turner, he was furious. Ava was mocking, Frank insulted Turner, the cops were called, and the fight that ensued has given rise to some colorful rumors, but the bare facts prove that Ava always managed to win their arguments.

At a Hollywood rally for Adlai Stevenson, Ava first uttered her most famous line about Frank. As she listened to him sing onstage, some reporters kept asking her questions, and one stringer from Chicago said, "Hey, Ava—come on! What do you see in this guy? He's just a 119-pound has-been!" Ava stared straight at him and said, "Well, I'll tell you—19 pounds is cock." There was an explosion of laughter from the press corps as the stringer stood frozen at her audacity and Ava went back to staring lovingly at her husband singing onstage.

Not one to waste a great one-liner, Ava used it again on the location shoot of *Mogambo* (1953) in Africa, but this time she amplified it and made it even funnier. After her irascible director John Ford introduced her to the English governor of Kenya and his wife, he provokingly said, "Ava, why don't you tell the governor what you see in this 120-pound runt you're married to?" Ava replied, "Well, there's only 10 pounds of Frank but there's 110 pounds of cock!"

There had to be some explanation at hand, for Frank had accompanied her on location and was sulking all over the place until he got a telegram saying that he was to return to Hollywood to screen-test for Maggio. After he left, Ava found that she was pregnant with his child, and she arranged to be flown into London to get an abortion. She had already miscarried a baby of his after one of their most physical fights, and she knew she didn't want to have a child with him. While shooting *Mogambo*, she got pregnant a second time, not by Frank, and had to get a second abortion, and all of this had to be kept from Frank.

Alan Livingston at Capitol Records took a chance and signed Frank to the label because he believed the talent was still there, but when Livingston mentioned Frank's name to his distributors a loud groan of derision went up in the room. Practically everyone felt now that Frank was a has-been, that he was finished.

Director Fred Zinnemann wanted Frank for *From Here to Eternity*, partly because the most favored candidate, Eli Wallach, had come across as too physically strong in his own screen test. And so Frank finally won the role of Maggio, and no horse's head had to be put in anybody's bed to secure it, but that has never stopped the Mafia rumors.

This was a cinch of a part for Frank, with several drunk scenes and a pitiful death scene for good measure, and the film itself was a nearly preordained hit, dominated by the method intensity of Montgomery Clift, who helped Frank with the role of Maggio, and a scene on a beach where Burt Lancaster and Deborah Kerr kiss in the surf.

From Here to Eternity is one of those famous movies of this time that looks pretty sterile now. It was clearly made at a point when censorship was strangling the life out of many pictures, but it put Frank right where he needed to be. All he required to make a comeback complete was an Academy Award, for Maggio was an Academy Award sort of role, but those contests are also popularity contests, and Frank had alienated a lot of people. His future still hung in the balance.

Frank started recording his first long-playing record for Capitol, *Songs for Young Lovers*, and it revealed a mature Frank with a darker sound who had taken the lessons he had learned from Billie to heart; he uses barely any vibrato now, and he bends some of the notes, as Billie had suggested to him. Frank is clearly giving thought as well as feeling to his phrasing, and he gets a lot of dramatic value out of a device that was entirely his: closing the vowel sound of a note as he holds it for an extended period. This technical choice has the effect of protecting the note and also making it sound angry, and this is the exact opposite of the open, unguarded, tender voice that Ella used on *Ella Sings Gershwin* in 1950.

Frank sometimes indulges in one of his worst habits here: adding extra words to a lyric to linger over certain emotions (he sings the word "shining" five excessive times on "A Foggy Day"), but otherwise he is a new man on this album, alert and dangerous and fully involved in the dramatic tension of Cole Porter's "I Get a Kick Out of You," with its drum kick. This album was arranged by George Siravo, but it was conducted by a key new collaborator, Nelson Riddle. The cover shows the now-classic Frank image, the noir outsider staring at a young couple as if he might like to offer them advice.

Frank's personal life was a shambles, for he knew he was losing Ava, the love of his life. He made his most serious suicide attempt in November of 1953, when Jimmy Van Heusen found him semiconscious on the floor of his room with his left wrist deeply cut. Van Heusen saved him, and this was a good deed that would not go unpunished.

A lovelorn Frank followed Ava to Rome, where she was shooting *The Barefoot Contessa* (1954), but she had already moved on to a famous bullfighter named Luis Miguel Dominguín, and so the press for Frank in this situation was deeply humiliating, but it also earned him some much-needed sympathy. While he played at the Beachcomber club back in Miami, headlines blared that Ava was now seeing the good-looking Italian comedian Walter Chiari, and so Frank brooded and drank and got deeper and deeper into his torch songs. But he had made a recording of "Young at Heart," a song of renewal, that was fast becoming a hit, and *Songs for Young Lovers* was selling well.

Frank did a live TV broadcast of *Anything Goes* with Ethel Merman in February of 1954, and he tried very hard to reach and warm up his tanklike leading lady, to no avail. When Frank kisses Merman, she refuses his kiss and keeps her eyes open and doesn't kiss him back. The Merm was set in her ways and didn't like competition of any kind, and she functioned far better with Bing in the 1936 movie of this show, for Bing allows her to do her thing and doesn't scare her with such direct contact. As a reminder of Der Bingle, Frank sings "you're Crosby's salary" here when he does Cole Porter's "You're the Top." At this time Frank also sang a medley with Bing on the radio where their voices balanced each other touchingly on the song "Among My Souvenirs," as if Bing's mellowness could calm Frank's anxiety.

Frank's competition for the Oscar in March was not strong: two actors from *Shane*, the villain (Jack Palance) and the little boy (Brandon De Wilde); Eddie Albert in *Roman Holiday*; and Robert Strauss in *Stalag 17*. Hopeful but nervous, he brought his children Nancy Jr. and Frank Jr. to the ceremony. Donna Reed won best supporting actress for *From Here to Eternity*, but William Holden in *Stalag 17* beat Montgomery

Clift for best actor. Adoring Nancy Jr. whispered to her father, "Don't be too disappointed if you don't win, Daddy." He whispered to her, "Don't you be, either."

Mercedes McCambridge presented the award for best supporting actor, and when she read out the nominees Frank's name got some applause. After McCambridge read out, "The winner is Frank Sinatra in *From Here to Eternity*!" she did a little jump of joy, and Frank bounded up to the podium and was a bit inarticulate at first, as if he were too stunned to speak. He mentioned that this was a new kind of thing for him and that he had done "song-and-dance-man-type stuff," and then Frank said that "they're doing a lot of songs here tonight, but nobody asked me." He ends by saying that he is "absolutely thrilled" and blows the audience a big kiss.

Lots of people in the industry didn't like Frank, but still they were glad that he got it and glad about his comeback. Louella Parsons wrote later, "I ran into person after person who said, 'He's a so-and-so but I hope he gets it. He was great!'" There was a get-together in his honor at his apartment that had been put together by Jule Styne, and Gene Kelly and Sammy Cahn were there, and various starlets, but Frank ducked his party and went out on a walk in Beverly Hills instead with his award. Even when he got stopped by a cop, the thrill of his win did not lessen, and neither did the need for solitude that went with it.

28

Judy on the Comeback Trail

JUDY WAS IN thrall now to a new man: Sid Luft, a big tough enforcer sort of guy, a gambler, a spender, and a brawler, and about as far away from Vincente Minnelli as you can get. She accepted a gig at the London Palladium, and Minnelli suggested that she sing "Rock-a-Bye Your Baby with a Dixie Melody," an old Al Jolson tune. Judy had Kay Thompson and Roger Edens to help put together her act, where each hand gesture and each aside to the audience were all carefully planned. Fanny Brice gave Judy a tough-love pep talk beforehand, which was key.

Judy killed them at the Palladium, and Luft next got her the Palace in New York to play in, a theater that had once been the height that any vaudevillian hoped to reach. She spent the night with Johnny Mercer before opening at the Palace, rekindling their connection, and she triumphed again, doing Brice's signature song "My Man" and "Shine On, Harvest Moon."

What Judy was doing at this point was very similar to the image that had been built for her at MGM as the spirit of old show business and a link to the past, but she was performing now on her own terms, in her own way, with control over what she did and how she did it—and control over her audience, which regularly went crazy for her. Judy was awarded a special Tony Award for her Palace show, an acknowledgment from the theater community of what she was bringing back to live entertainment.

Judy married Luft in June of 1952, and he took control of her finances, buying a lot for himself and underpaying or outright stiffing her staff. There was a drunk-driving incident that devolved into a brawl, with Judy smacking one of the other drivers and Luft punching another one in the nose, and this made the papers. But Luft was good for Judy in some ways. He protected her, and he let her eat what she wanted. Luft knew enough not to ever give her orders of any kind because she always needed to rebel against orders and do what she wanted after so many years of being told what to do.

A plush contract with Warner Brothers augured a comeback in movies for Judy, and she had a new baby in 1952 whom she named Lorna. So many things were good for her and had improved, yet there was the same disorder underneath that led her to keep cutting herself to get attention, and her tumultuous relationship with her mother Ethel had reached a crisis point.

There is home movie footage of Judy and Ethel that was included in the 2019 documentary *Sid & Judy*, and it is extremely revealing. Judy and Ethel are outside on a terrace, and Judy looks at her mother closely and then impulsively hugs her tight. Ethel is clearly delighted by this hug, beaming to the camera afterward with a corny smile, but Judy retreats from her mother physically right afterward, holding herself back, as if she thinks she has made a mistake.

When Ethel started acting the part of stage grandmother with Liza, Judy was pushed over the edge, and they got into a very bad fight. Judy broke with Ethel, telling her she never wanted to see her again and that Ethel was never to see Liza again, and Ethel attempted suicide with pills afterward. Recovered from this, Ethel started giving interviews to the press about her daughter, telling columnist Sheilah Graham, "Judy has been selfish all her life. That's my fault. I made it too easy for her."

Cut off from Judy's money, Ethel got a job as a riveter, and she was going to that job when she had a heart attack and died in January of 1953. At a party shortly after this happened, a drunken Johnny Mercer attacked Judy in front of everyone and said, "Why did you let your mother die in a parking lot?" Judy burst into tears and ran to the bathroom, where she cut her wrists. The party broke up and everyone went home.

When told that Judy and Luft were going to produce her comeback movie *A Star Is Born* (1954), Arthur Freed said, "Those two alley cats can't make a picture." All of Hollywood was skeptical, but Judy and Luft were given carte blanche by Jack Warner, and they set about choosing a leading man to play the drunken matinee idol Norman Maine. Frank was approached, along with Humphrey Bogart and Errol Flynn, but they finally settled on James Mason, the best possible choice. George Cukor was chosen as director, Moss Hart would do the script, and Harold Arlen and Ira Gershwin would do the songs, so *A Star Is Born* was to be top of the line in every department.

The production was shut down after ten days of shooting so that they could start over in CinemaScope, at a loss of $300,000. Judy's insomnia, pill taking, and absences started again, and Cukor wrote his close friend and colleague Katharine Hepburn that he lost all sympathy for Judy's problems when she would report sick and then be seen at the racetrack during the day or the Mocambo in the evening. He decried her "ruthless selfishness," but she was the star and the producer and could do as she liked. When they were finished, it was felt that another musical number from Judy was needed, and it was Luft's idea to do the lavish "Born in a Trunk" sequence, which featured many different songs for her to sing.

A Star Is Born begins with an ingeniously conceived and vividly shot sequence in which Judy's struggling singer Esther Blodgett covers for Mason's Norman Maine at a benefit when he drunkenly comes out onstage with her. Cukor gets a real sense of danger and tension into this opening, and it is clear that we are as far away from the stultifying wholesomeness of an MGM "meet-cute" as we can get. Mason is the strongest scene partner that Judy ever had, and the storyline itself, about a star on the rise in love with a star in decline, allows her to survey her own troubles from a creative distance that suits her beautifully at first.

Maine goes looking for Esther afterward, and he finds her at a jam session where she is singing a new song with the boys in the band, "The Man That Got Away." Judy's Esther is trying the tune out for the pleasure of it, with no obligation, no need for a professional presentation, and no need to be MGM beautiful. Warner Brothers had been the studio of Bette Davis and James Cagney, and things didn't need to be perfect there, as they did at MGM; they could be real, they could be disorderly, they could be tough, and Judy thrives in this atmosphere, messing her hair while she sings for the first time on-screen and letting loose with a voice that has the power now of a waterfall, a rippling wall of sound that is unlike the sound of any other singer.

Judy took a technical risk with this song. Hugh Martin had been brought in to do vocal arrangements, and he played his version of the tune for her, which made her angry at him. Judy told Martin that she wanted to do "The Man That Got Away" in a much higher key. Martin warned Judy that this would be too high for her, especially when she got to the section that started "fools will be fools," and that she would wind up shouting, but she was adamant.

"There has to be a flash of something extraordinary at this moment," Judy told Martin. "If I croon the damn song, why would Norman Maine see the possibility that I might be a star?" Arlen, Gershwin, and Cukor were all on Martin's side in this argument, but Judy would not budge. Martin was very leery when he attended the recording session for the song. "She warmed up on takes one and two," he said. "Then, on take three she let us have it—all stops pulled out."

Like Frank's voice, Judy's was a voice that had seen trouble and had come through, but Judy had a quality that Frank never had: mordant humor. And it is this scary humor of hers that jolts her performance alive in *A Star Is Born*, for there is a scream in that famous vibrato she has, and it comes from down in the depths of some insomnia hell.

Esther has had a rough time coming up in show business, and she has a rough time even after Maine starts doing anything he can to help her career, and so the "Born in a Trunk" number relates directly to Esther's struggle to achieve stardom. Judy takes some expressive panicked breaths when Esther sings "It's a New World" to Maine after they are married, for she always prized emotion over technique and smooth phrasing.

A Star Is Born features one dazzling set piece for Judy after another, and maybe the most dazzling is the extended scene where Esther mocks a production number she is doing at the studio with Maine as her adoring and lustful audience of one. This is Judy at her campy, mocking, hilarious best, using humor as a weapon against the deepest despair. When you go down to the lowest lows, you get the highest highs too.

Judy is given a Big Scene where she speaks to the head of the studio (Charles Bickford) about Maine's drinking, wondering plaintively why he has to destroy himself. It is a scene full of little jags and hesitations, and it is truthful and moving, but it is also ever-so-slightly hammy. There comes a point in *A Star Is Born*, which is certainly one of the most lavish vehicles any star ever had to show off in, when everything starts to feel like too much of a good thing. In her last Big Scene, after Maine's suicide, Judy's Esther shouts at a friend in a very high voice, and the high emotional pitch of this nearly three-hour picture has begun to feel exhausting.

A Star Is Born received ecstatic reviews, but after its release it was badly cut by Harry Warner, who seemed to want to destroy it, and so the full experience of her comeback movie got lost. Judy was nominated for a best actress Oscar, and it was expected by some, not least herself, that she would win. She was in the hospital that night after having given birth to her son Joey, and they had her wired for sound so that she could give an acceptance speech right from her hospital bed after Lauren Bacall accepted for her at the theater.

But Grace Kelly won for *The Country Girl*, the movie where Bing had tried to be a drunken has-been, and Judy later made this loss into a funny story, as was her wont, describing how the press guys tore out her microphone and tore down a tower outside her window and didn't even say good night to her.

Why did Frank win his comeback Oscar for *From Here to Eternity* while Judy got snubbed for hers? He had behaved badly on sets for years, and he didn't have a drug problem as an explanation for his bad or unprofessional behavior, but he had humbled himself to come back, taking a victim part in an ensemble picture, and everyone knew that Ava had thrown him over.

Frank was always getting himself humiliated, and he had a taste for the abject. Judy only playacted at being abject, and the cost overruns on her epic, colorful star vehicle were well known around town. Her urge to go to the racetrack rather than do her job did not endear her to anyone. There was a feeling, perhaps, of "Who does she think she is?" in spite of her great talent, which no one argued about.

Kelly was a classy ingenue made good who had deglammed to play an older, embittered woman, and she was on-screen that year as a luscious and spirited beauty in Alfred Hitchcock's great thriller *Rear Window* (1954), which added to the good feeling about her. She was miscast in *The Country Girl* but struggled mightily to overcome that, and such effort is often rewarded. Judy's greatness and her excessiveness needed to be rebuked, and this rebuke was made to feel final.

29

Frank and Ella
Make Album History

THE LESSONS THAT Frank had learned from Billie are particularly apparent on his album *Swing Easy!*, which was released in August of 1954 and was his first musical project with arrangements by Nelson Riddle. Frank bends notes here the way Billie had advised him to and even revives some of her "dying fall" sounds from the 1930s, in his own way. This sense of lineage comes through particularly on "All of Me," a song that Billie had made her own, which is done in Frank's own virile style, with his surging attacks of volume and his added words for extra intensity.

Frank also did a Bing song for this album, "Wrap Your Troubles in Dreams," but the effect is totally different, for Frank is never a reassuring singer—he's excitingly unpredictable, and he knows that dreams aren't going to last for long. Frank even took on Judy's "Get Happy" and makes it his own with the aid of Riddle's very edgy and driving arrangement backing his multileveled reading of the lyrics, which depends on playing around with phrasing to create a profound sense of unease. With these tracks on *Swing Easy!*, it was as if Frank was throwing down and announcing that he was going to take on all comers from Billie to Bing to Judy as greatest singer in the land.

But one singer he did not take on was Ella, and the reason for that is apparent in the recordings he did with Ella and Louis in 1954 for an animated version of the musical *Finian's Rainbow* that never got made.

Attempting to duet with Louis on "Ad Lib Blues," Frank can't scat at all; he is off pitch, off rhythm, off everything. And so he was not likely to offer his own scat versions of "How High the Moon" and "Lady Be Good." Frank had not been a swing singer, and he would never be a jazz singer like Ella or Billie or Bing, who could have handled an ad-lib duet with Pops with aplomb.

For his own ambition Frank wanted to prove himself now as a movie star and actor, and he did so in *Suddenly* (1954), a small independent picture where he served up some very frightening ice-cold evil in close-ups as a would-be presidential assassin. It is clear in *Suddenly* just how influenced Frank was by James Cagney (he enthusiastically hosted the American Film Institute Life Achievement Award for Cagney in 1974) and also by his friend and idol Humphrey Bogart. Frank's character here is a sadist, and he gets this across in a startling scene where he smiles as he straightens Sterling Hayden's broken arm, taking pleasure in inflicting pain. The movie itself does not live up to Frank's performance, but he showed here that he was willing to push himself and explore the darkest areas of his extremely dark psyche.

For his entrance in *Young at Heart* (1954), a color remake of *Four Daughters* (1938) where he plays the outsider John Garfield part, Frank gets a star close-up turning around in a door, and this movie cleverly places him for viewers in an earlier Warner Brothers context. This successful picture almost made up for the fact that Frank had nearly won and then lost the lead role in *On the Waterfront* (1954), which went to Marlon Brando.

In 1955 Frank had four feature films in release and he also put out what he called "the Ava album": *In the Wee Small Hours*, a long-player featuring Riddle arrangements on songs of lost love and a cover where a lonesome Frank stands smoking a cigarette against a sickly blue-green street background. This collaboration with Riddle would popularize the idea of the concept album, a suite of songs chosen to dramatize a theme or idea or even a narrative. Gone were the days at Columbia when Frank's anguished performance of "I'm a Fool to Want You" would be placed on the same platter as "Mama Will Bark." Frank had control now, and for all his ambition to be taken seriously as an actor, he knew that his singing ability was his ace in the hole.

Frank accesses his dark side in *Suddenly* (1954).

Frank in the 1940s was a good singer but he was a show-off singer, with "vulnerable" gimmicks, and he was willing to be very commercial; his musical accompaniment, usually by Axel Stordahl with his ever-present harps, hadn't mattered much. Frank listened to classical music regularly, and he wanted to be taken seriously as a musician as well. His lowered voice now was a nighttime sound, and it was a voice that might break, and so the Riddle accompaniments were there partly to cradle it.

Frank broke down crying after he finished singing "When Your Lover Has Gone," a track that Lester Young loved in particular. Billie's version of that song is snarly and hard edged, for she didn't take love as a concept as earnestly as Frank did; to her it was a kind of sick joke. Frank felt he had found his perfect woman in Ava, and she seemed lost to him in 1955.

He doesn't wallow in his despair on *In the Wee Small Hours* but gives it structure. Frank knows when to end a note abruptly and not hold on to it, and he uses crisp final consonants to aid this effect of moving on. Riddle uses a lot of ominous descending figures in his broken, modernist arrangements, which feel like fragments of sound, a little of this, a little of that. These Riddle charts get across a feeling of quiet desperation, searching, and mental disorder, as if a despairing mind is looking anywhere for comfort of any kind.

Frank uses his highest notes expressively now rather than just for their own sake, everything in its place as he moves from one Riddle sound island to the next, and he even touches down on some fragile bass notes, which might have been a way of competing with Dick Haymes, a singer that Frank still thought of as a rival who was capable of hitting very low notes.

Frank sometimes sounds so anguished on *In the Wee Small Hours* that he can barely keep going forward to look for solace. He is often using a very naked voice here, so that you could reach out and touch its rocky texture, but at the same time he has enough control to use little to no vibrato, another nod to Billie.

A live TV musical production of *Our Town* where he was very miscast as the narrator would have best been avoided, and Frank seemed to know it, behaving as if he were due for another engagement somewhere. Frank was signed to play the lead in the movie version of the Rodgers and Hammerstein musical *Carousel*, but he walked when told that every scene would have to be shot twice for technical reasons, and this might have been just a convenient excuse because he was uncertain if he could sing such a demanding score. But Frank agreed to play Nathan Detroit in Samuel Goldwyn's expensive adaptation of the Frank Loesser musical hit *Guys and Dolls*, even though it meant being second banana to Marlon Brando. He is overqualified for his part, but the movie is lucky to have him.

Frank was a swinging bachelor in *The Tender Trap* back at MGM, where he has to choose between lots of sexy girls, a sensible and attractive lady (Celeste Holm), and a very calculating virgin (Debbie Reynolds). This being an American movie from 1955, the calculating virgin wins, and Reynolds verbally espouses Frank's appeal when she says that he is attractive "in an offbeat, beat-up sort of way."

But his most important picture in 1955 was *The Man with the Golden Arm*, an adaptation of Nelson Algren's acclaimed novel about a drug addict. This was his most determined Oscar bid, and Frank put himself into the hands of director Otto Preminger and approached the project with the utmost seriousness.

The Man with the Golden Arm starts promisingly with graphic Saul Bass credits and a jazzy, blaring Elmer Bernstein score. The first long

Frank in Otto Preminger's *The Man with the Golden Arm* (1955).

take, a Preminger trademark, ends with Frank's Frankie Machine look-ing through a bar window with longing. Like *Guys and Dolls*, a stylized musical, this is a movie that takes place on obvious studio sets, and this does not aid any attempt at realism.

Frank's Frankie Machine has just gotten out of jail, and he is wised up and solitary. When he sees a one-armed man forced to do a dance for a drink, Frankie looks down as if he is shamed, but then he smiles, and this unusual reaction shows that Frank is willing to delve deep into the complexity of this part, like Billie used to do in the 1930s for songs like "Some Other Spring."

The fatal flaw in *The Man with the Golden Arm* is the very overdone performance of Eleanor Parker as Zosh, Frankie's wheelchair-bound, guilt-tripping wife. Zosh is a bum part, but Parker makes it far worse than it might be, though we do also have Kim Novak doing her best here to cancel Parker out with her own soulful performance as a girl who loves and believes in Frankie. Novak would be one of Frank's more serious affairs at this time. To impress her, he would even get together a group of professional musicians in a Capitol studio late at night and serenade Novak with a private concert of love songs.

Frank reportedly observed an addict going through withdrawal so that he would know how to play his withdrawal scene in *The Man with the Golden Arm,* and this research paid off, for it is his most memorable scene in the film, with Preminger's camera following him as he opens himself up to the idea of physical pain and looks like a wounded bird writhing around on the floor. In spite of this commitment, Frank lost the leading actor Oscar to Ernest Borgnine for *Marty.*

Frank's career on records and in movies was reaching a new peak, and Ella's career was slowly coming to its own peak after years of recording and playing one-nighters. Ella and her husband Ray Brown had adopted the son of her half sister Frances and called him Ray Jr., and they had an apartment in Queens where Ray Jr. was taken care of by Ella's aunt Virginia, who had taken Ella in after her own mother had died.

There were tensions in her relationship with Brown because he insisted now on traveling with the Oscar Peterson band, which he knew was better for his own career, and Ella wanted him to play with her. When Brown got back from playing with Peterson, he joined Ella on another Jazz at the Philharmonic tour for Norman Granz.

Ella was still recording for Decca, and Granz bided his time to sign her up for his own label. In 1951 Ella recorded an evocative Nat King Cole song called "Because of Rain," which deserves to be better known, but she insisted on doing her own version of the novelty hit "Come On-a My House." Her touring schedule was one of the busiest in show business, and the strain started to show in her marriage. She was seeing less and less of Brown when he chose to tour with Oscar Peterson instead of her, and finally her marriage with him ended in divorce in August of 1953.

"When my husband and I broke up, I got a little bit despondent," Ella said. "I cried and cried, and my cousin said, 'Oh, take her to a bar. I can't stand her crying.' So I went into this bar, and there was this pleasant bartender. 'What'll you have?' he asked. I jumped and said, 'I'll have a Manischewitz!' The whole bar said, 'Manischewitz?' The bartender said, 'If she wants it, she'll get it.' That's how much of a drinker I was," she laughed. There was no lasting bad feeling between Ella and Brown, for he joined her on a tour in October of 1953.

Granz was patiently waiting to manage Ella when her contract with Moe Gale was up in December. He said that Ella was very cautious when it came to making changes in her life, but Granz finally won her loyalty after he paid off a tax bill that she owed because Gale had neglected to pay it on her behalf. Ella was horrified when she learned of Gale's failure to pay taxes on her earnings, and so she was grateful to Granz for helping her out of this trouble. She signed with Granz as her manager, and he set about making her a top attraction live and on record.

In early 1954, just after signing with Granz, Ella was rushed to the hospital because she had a node on her vocal cords. "It was serious," said producer and club owner George Wein. "At the time it was thought that she'd never work again. Trouble with her throat. It was kind of hushed up, but it was serious." After an operation, Ella took no chances and stayed completely silent for six weeks.

Fully recovered by March, Ella went into the studio to record another album with just Ellis Larkins as her accompanist on piano, *Songs in a Mellow Mood*, where she stuck mainly in her alto range for a thicker sound and stayed away from higher notes for the time being. She does a fabulously ornamented "My Heart Belongs to Daddy" here and takes a risky pause on "You Leave Me Breathless."

In June of 1954, Ella was booked into Basin Street in Manhattan and given a party to celebrate her nineteenth year in show business, with Pearl Bailey, Harry Belafonte, Eartha Kitt, and Dizzy Gillespie all paying tribute to her. Ella finally got up and said, "I guess what everyone wants more than anything else is to be loved. And to know that you love me for my singing is too much for me. Forgive me if I don't have all the words. Maybe I can sing it and you'll understand." They played some of her records, including "A-Tisket, A-Tasket," and she joined in and cried a little with happiness, with all her colleagues around her.

In July, Ella and her accompanist John Lewis and her assistant Georgiana Henry were bumped off a first-class Pan Am flight to Australia to make room for some white passengers when they made a stopover in Honolulu. Because they were forced to stay in Honolulu for three days without a flight, Granz had to cancel Ella's Australian concert, and the airline hadn't even let Ella and her group collect their clothes and personal belongings from the plane before it took off without them. Granz brought suit against Pan Am for discrimination, and the case was settled for an undisclosed sum.

Granz got Ella a part in *Pete Kelly's Blues* (1955), in which she plays a nightclub singer and sings "Hard-Hearted Hannah" in a calm, stately sort of way. While she shot this movie in Hollywood, Ella was booked into the Mocambo after Marilyn Monroe put pressure on the owner to let her play there. Monroe, who was one of the biggest stars in Hollywood then, even said that she would come to Ella's engagement every night for a week to get her some publicity, and this idea worked. On opening night of Ella's engagement at the Mocambo, Frank and Judy were both there to hear her perform. The feeling was beginning to dawn that this woman who had been singing for twenty years was special, an encyclopedia of song who wanted to sweep up and save and treasure every tune she could.

But in October of 1955, Ella was confronted again by racism. She was playing in Houston, Texas, to an integrated audience, and the vice squad of that city was looking for trouble. When they busted into her dressing room, the Houston cops found Ella and Georgiana and Granz watching Dizzy Gillespie and saxophonist Illinois Jacquet playing a dice game. Granz perceived right away that a crooked cop wanted to plant drugs in her restroom, and so Granz brushed past the other officers and stared at this cop, who could then do nothing. "I ought to kill you," the cop said, pushing his gun into Granz's stomach.

Ella and her friends were brought to the police station and charged with being party to an illegal dice game, and the press was all over the place because they had been alerted that there was going to be a drug bust. Though this false charge had been averted, photos of the arrest were taken anyway, and Ella looks like she is in an agony of embarrassment, stiff with affronted pride and "this can't be happening" fear. "They took us down, and then when we got there, they had the nerve to ask for an autograph," Ella said later.

To finish up her Decca contract, Milt Gabler was forced to issue some performances Ella had done on Bing's radio show with John Scott Trotter backing because she was too busy to come in and record. "We would never use John Trotter to accompany Ella," Gabler said, "but she had done some standards on the show and we just took it from the transcriptions."

Granz loved to record his star vocalist, and so there are recordings of live performances from 1956 at the Shrine and at Zardi's that display Ella at her peak vocally. Her "Cry Me a River" at the Shrine is very cool, and she folds "I Cried for You" into it because she loves to set songs side by side; she is greedy for melody, and up for any rhythmic dare. "Am I still / Still in key?" she wonders on an incendiary "Air Mail Special" at the Shrine, for as Will Friedwald has pointed out, she had to improvise all of her scat numbers in key.

Ella's repeated "all right" to her audiences on her live records can mean many things: assent, annoyance, good humor, bad humor. It is all purpose, but don't trifle with it. When her audience asks for a blues number at Zardi's, she offers a speedy "Joe Williams Blues," and when they seem to challenge her she says, "Oh, you want a *slow* blues," but just moves on, for a slow blues does not interest her.

Ella doesn't really know the words to "Gone with the Wind" at Zardi's, but she tries it anyway, for even if Ella doesn't know the lyrics to a song, she can just make some up—if she wants that melody, she will have that melody. "You want it fast or slow?" Ella asks her audience. "Slow?" she inquires, and then when Ella hears something from the audience she cries, "Sexy?!" as if "sexy" is a concept she likes very much.

Ella makes a joke about Eddie Fisher and his Coca-Cola sponsorship and then advises her audience, "Go ahead and get high, you still have to pay for it!" She sighs a crestfallen "all right" when the audience requests "The Tender Trap," for she would give the people what they wanted, even a bad popular song. "That's a number we recorded in case you get tired of Frank Sinatra's," she says.

Granz renamed his company Verve and planned to build it around Ella. Oscar Peterson had recorded a series of albums for Granz dedicated to popular songwriters of the recent past, and these had been so successful that Granz decided to set Ella up with a similar project that would make her into the First Lady of Song. This composer survey would start, Granz announced, with Cole Porter. Ella had always shown an affinity for the naughtiness of Porter's "My Heart Belongs to Daddy," but how she would fare with his other numbers was an open question.

Granz paired hip jazz song stylist Anita O'Day with arranger Buddy Bregman for her own first Verve album called *Anita* (1956), and this worked out so well that Granz put the young Bregman with Ella for her Cole Porter album, which was conceived as one LP but gradually grew into a two-LP set because Porter had written so many songs that they wanted to cover.

There is always thought behind Bregman's arrangements of the Porter songs on this all-important album for Ella, and surprises and variety. The somber beginning of "Anything Goes" is unexpected, and having Ella do "Miss Otis Regrets" mournfully without any humor or anger and just piano accompaniment is another inspired idea. Bregman gets out some swinging brass for "Too Darn Hot," and Ella swings it pretty hard, just as she swings a fast backing of "It's All Right with Me" and lets the blaring horns push her to sound convincingly tough.

Of all the thirty-two songs Ella does on this Cole Porter set, only "Just One of Those Things" and "I've Got You Under My Skin" don't really suit her; she didn't like the name-dropping verse in that first song. But every other Porter song here stimulates her to heights she had never reached before on record, both technically and otherwise. By concentrating on the melodies that Porter wrote, Ella brings out the pent-up emotion within them, especially on "Begin the Beguine." She understands that the simmering way a song like "Begin the Beguine" is written is meant to be sexual, with a delay, another delay, and then a release.

Ella is most encouraged and tickled by the naughty Porter songs. She gives "Love for Sale" a kind of camp wink at first, but some musical plunges in her delivery start to make it sound sexy, and then a slight melancholy starts to creep in, but none of the grinding despair that Billie brought to this song. Ella had been a lookout at a brothel, not one of the girls who climb the stairs with customers, and so her point of view on this world is one of curiosity, vicarious imagination, and finally objective sympathy. This is a great and complicated reading of "Love for Sale," filled with contrasting feelings.

Bregman's excitingly spare introduction for "Night and Day" with drums and horns allows Ella to start on the beat and build slightly in volume before she pulls back on the phrase "so a voice within me" in a way that is extremely sexy because it is withdrawing for a moment from the forward motion established at the start. Ella was a singer who explored the melody in order to get to the truth of a song. What she is offering on her Cole Porter set is the platonic essence of his songs, unadorned, nearly without interpretation most of the time.

Ella was not a belter like Judy and Frank. She husbanded her sound, traveling up and down rather than up and out to an audience, and she had perfected a smoothness of tone that is something like Bing's gold being poured from a cup, but with far more vocal range, which is part of why Bing was so enthused and admiring about her singing. There is barely a hint of vibrato when Ella holds notes on this Porter album, just the suggestion of a breeze here and there.

Ella was an artist for art's sake at heart, and if you listen to her closely on this Porter album, there is an urgency in her caressing of these songs, and a tender care, especially on "Easy to Love," where she sticks fairly close to the melody but puts it over in such a hushed, attentive way that her high notes on "seem a shame" get across everything that might have been intended by the songwriter.

For Ella doing a composer songbook album for Verve was like running a marathon, and she had the stamina for it. "There were hardly any second takes," said pianist Paul Smith. "The Cole Porter and some of the other ones were just kind of *ground* out—that's the only way I can describe them. We'd run down the verse, just to make sure she knew it, and bang, we'd record it!"

When Granz played the album for Porter himself in his suite at the Waldorf Towers, his only comment was, "What diction she has!" *Ella Fitzgerald Sings the Cole Porter Song Book* was released in the spring of 1956, and it was seen as a kind of event in the world of recording and sold very well. It remains a classic, endlessly replayable and renewable, just as Frank's *In the Wee Small Hours* is.

Ella played at Storyville in Boston, and she had a short affair with drummer Gus Johnson, who said that she still had some of the insecurities of her youth. "She's self-conscious," he said. "She's very sensitive, and if she saw you talking, she might think you were saying bad things about her. . . . She wanted people to love her. She's beautiful to me, but she was always trying to improve herself in everything she did."

Ella next did her first album-length recording with Louis, *Ella and Louis* (1956). "When she made the album with Louis, she insisted that he select the tunes, and she sang them all in his keys even if they were the wrong keys for her," said Granz. Louis came in tired from his constant touring and one-nighters, yet there is no sense of strain from either of them on *Ella and Louis*. In fact, Louis seems to up his singing game here in response to Ella, exploring the words of "Can't We Be Friends?" reflectively and letting her cool, smooth voice pour balm over his rough, gentle one. His treasurable gravel vibrato at the end of words is so pronounced that it nearly detaches from the notes themselves, especially when he lingers over them.

Ella and Louis is so delightful because Louis and Ella sound so different and yet their viewpoints are so similar when it comes to giving joy to their audience, and their interplay is full of fun and encouragement. On "They Can't Take That Away from Me," Ella repeats the word "never" for emphasis, Frank-style, and Louis croaks, "Swing it, Ella!" and he wants to keep this song going: "Will you repeat that again, dearie, please?" he asks. The tunes here stretch out and often last for five to six minutes, and Oscar Peterson is on piano and Ella's former husband Ray Brown is on bass, and so this is a case of musical heaven. The photo of Ella and Louis on the cover of this album is likably modest and casual, but it is deceptive. If America ever had royalty of any kind, these two people, Ella and Louis, were American royalty.

Ella closed out 1956 with another marathon songbook project with Buddy Bregman, this time devoted to Rodgers and Hart, and this set posed her a special problem. The Richard Rodgers melodies are sweet while the Lorenz Hart lyrics are tart and often despairing, and so Ella was unable to bring out the core of the songs by concentrating on their melodies. Whereas Frank could dig into the Hart lyrics for "It Never Entered My Mind" or "Where or When," Ella found herself lost with the sugary melodies of "There's a Small Hotel" and "Mountain Greenery." She tries her best with "Ten Cents a Dance," even seeming to assume a character by the end, with a heavier vibrato, but this just isn't her thing.

The Rodgers melodies bring out her most girlish side, with cutesy pinched vowels that finally begin to grate.

Buddy Bregman was clearly overextended in 1956 with these two massive Ella projects, and this became apparent when he worked with Bing that year on an album called *Bing Sings Whilst Bregman Swings*. Bregman, who was the nephew of songwriter Jule Styne, had been working as an orchestra leader on a radio show hosted by Bing's troubled son Gary, and so this gave him an in with Bing, who insisted on recording at 9:00 AM, when he felt he sounded his best. This was in marked contrast to Frank, who only wanted to record late at night.

Bregman's accompaniment to "Heat Wave" for Bing on this album is full of what Frank would call "clams," or wrong notes, but Bing just sails along anyway, unperturbed. He recorded several long-playing albums in this period, including one called *Songs I Wish I Had Sung the First Time Around*, where he gives an urgent reading of "Prisoner of Love," the signature tune of his one-time rival Russ Columbo. "Is that note at the end of the first chorus a little gangrenous?" he wonders after crooning a very old-fashioned tune called "Lady of Spain."

On record Bing may have been pleasantly coasting in comparison to Frank and Ella, yet he was fully in charge when he costarred with Frank in *High Society* (1956), a musical version of *The Philadelphia Story* (1940) with Cole Porter songs in which Louis plays a kind of Greek chorus role that allows him far more latitude than anything he had done on-screen before.

Bing's character C. K. Dexter Haven is producing the Newport Jazz Festival, which is why he has engaged Louis, and he looks great at age fifty-three, still Mr. Cool with his pipe and brown shoes and his ultra-low speaking voice, which seems to put people into a trance and keep them at arm's length. Bing's Dexter is heir to a fortune and totally secure, whereas Frank's character Mike is a resentful interloper, a reporter with a chip on his shoulder. They are perfectly cast.

Frank had begun to lose his hair at age forty, and so he is outfitted with a very attractive hairpiece in front in *High Society* that looks like a dark wave coming in, and he is beautifully dressed too, in a black hat with a white ribbon and a light-pink shirt with a black tie. Frank knows he has to be at his very best to compete with Bing, and so he gets out his heaviest artillery in a scene where he attempts to seduce Dexter's ex-wife Tracy Lord (Grace Kelly), turning a look on her that is so direct and intense that it might be said to be irresistible, but in the way that you cannot resist a hurricane or an earthquake.

It helped that Frank was in awe of the classy Kelly and was dying to make a play for her, according to his valet George Jacobs, but he felt stymied because Kelly had seen him as a rejected has-been on the location shoot of *Mogambo*. Of far more concern to Frank was that his idol Bing had actually dated Kelly himself, and Bing was there shooting with them, so if he failed with Kelly he would be failing in front of Bing.

Jazz is everywhere in *High Society*, and this gives Bing an advantage over Frank that he takes up serenely, like a monarch, while Frank does everything he can to look and sound his best. Neither man was ever more winning on-screen, or likely anywhere else, and this comes to a head when they do a duet, "Well, Did You Evah!" When Bing sings, "Ba ba ba ba boom," Frank crankily sings back, "Don't dig that kind of crooning, chum," to which Bing rejoins, "You must be one of the newer fellows." The crew of this movie nicknamed Bing "Nembutal" and Frank "Dexedrine," meaning that they worked well together.

Frank and Bing face off in *High Society* (1956).

When Frank sings a slow love song to Kelly toward the end of *High Society*, he does everything in his power to entice her, caressing her with his hands and with his voice and then kissing her passionately. Kelly clearly has no interest, reserving her most enraptured smiles for Bing when he casually sings "True Love" to her on a boat, but everybody comes out well in this movie. Frank was always at his best as a loser while Bing glided through life as a winner, and this is what *High Society* is about.

In his own interview with Edward R. Murrow in 1956, Frank seems very insecure, boastful, and faintly menacing, like a low-level gangster trying to feel big, even though Frank was very big in show business at this point, close to the biggest. His new album from that year *Songs for Swingin' Lovers!* was felt as a rebirth, a sign that you could have a second act in American life and come back even better than before, with a greater authority.

Frank does lots of old songs on this long-player and revitalizes them, bringing a nearly Bing-like ease to "It Happened in Monterey," but earthier, with unbanked passion. Nelson Riddle's intensely sexual arrangement of Cole Porter's "I've Got You Under My Skin" for Frank on this album is a high-water mark in their musical collaboration, especially during its momentously building instrumental section before Frank comes back in.

Frank makes "Pennies from Heaven" his own just as Bing and Billie had in the 1930s, as if to say, "If you want the things you love, you must have showers, and I'm living proof, folks." Billie's influence still shows in the way he'll do a dying fall in pitch or stay behind the beat, but the loud burst of a sustained high note at the end of "Too Marvelous for Words" is entirely Frank.

Don McGuire, the Frank pal who had written the perceptive *Meet Danny Wilson*, was the writer and director of *Johnny Concho* (1956), a western where Frank plays a self-loathing bully who has a powerful brother and is despised by the people in the town he lives in. The film was produced by Frank and Hank Sanicola, so this was the tale of an antihero created for him by his inner circle, and the result was remarkably and bravely unflattering.

"A man gets scared when he knows he's wrong," Frank says in *Johnny Concho*, a line that relates directly to his own character and what his friends knew about it. There is even a point in this picture where Frank's Johnny denounces the "scum" he was once a part of, and this feels like McGuire getting Frank to disassociate himself on-screen from the Mafia, though in life his mob connections continued unabated.

Frank was hanging out with Humphrey Bogart and Lauren Bacall and their orbit of friends, which Bacall herself dubbed the Rat Pack, and Judy, who lived close to Bogart and Bacall, was often an enthusiastic member of the Pack, along with Sammy Davis Jr. and Dean Martin. They even named Judy "first vice president" of their club, which was dedicated to drinking, staying up late, and not giving a damn. George Jacobs observed that Judy was the only one who got seriously drunk at these get-togethers.

Frank was protective of Judy to an intense degree. Once when they were in the nightclub Ciro's, a man asked Frank, "Who's the broad?" and Frank sprang into action, pushing the guy into a phone booth, punching him, shutting the door, and then opening the door to say, "The lady's name is Garland . . . spelled G-A-R-L-A-N-D," and of course Judy thrilled to such theatrics on her behalf.

Whenever she needed an ego boost, Judy could always count on Frank and his sexual generosity, but he could put her in awkward situations. She was there for a brawl he had with a reporter after they had gone to see Mel Tormé sing, and when he brought the Pack to see her sing in Long Beach, Judy asked Frank to do a song with her onstage and he declined, but Humphrey Bogart gamely and drunkenly offered a bar or two of "My Melancholy Baby" for the crowd. "If you want to hear any more, you know we can stay here all night!" Judy cries breathlessly in a recording that Frank had made of this Long Beach concert, and at one point she even says the Rat Pack catchphrase "ring-a-ding-ding."

CBS offered Judy $100,000 to do a ninety-minute live special in September of 1955, and she accepted it because she needed the money for her high-spending husband and her children. But Judy took too many sleeping pills the night before the show was set to air, and she could barely move or talk right up to showtime. Everyone panicked, and it was very touch and go, but somehow she woke up enough to get through it, and the result was that the forty million people who tuned in saw her fairly groggy and at less than her best.

Judy had signed for a second live CBS special in 1956 for a program that would run for just a half hour, and this time she was not groggy but behaves in a very manic way, getting so aggressively tactile with her accompanist Joe Bushkin that he nearly gets thrown by the mauling she gives him. Judy can't seem to stay still for a moment on this special, and there is clearly something wrong when she speaks to the camera and does a long, intense, rambling monologue about her love for her son Joe; it's the sort of corny bit she used to do in the late 1930s at MGM, but now it is cracked, distorted. Whatever pills she was taking were part of what was wrong, of course, but Judy seems here like someone who is having a nervous breakdown on camera.

CBS canceled her third special, and Judy and Sid sued CBS for libel after this was reported, which resulted in a journalist named Marie Torre spending ten days in jail for not revealing the CBS source for her story. Columnist Dorothy Kilgallen commented, "I must say I never thought I'd see the day when anyone would be tossed into the jug for saying Judy Garland had problems."

Judy recorded some albums at this time, but the material she was offering and the all-out way she was performing it for platters like *Miss Show Business* (1955) and *Judy* (1956) were more suited to a live performance in a large theater than to record. Unlike Frank, Judy was singing old songs but too much in the old Al Jolson way, and she often let her famous vibrato run rampant.

Her album *Judy* leads off with the bongo drum arrangement of "Come Rain or Come Shine" that Nelson Riddle did for her after first giving it to his lover Rosemary Clooney as an uncredited ghost assignment. Judy was very angry when she heard Clooney singing this song with bongo drums, and she confronted her after a performance: "You stole my arrangement!" Judy cried, and Clooney had to explain the situation to her. Judy kept it, of course.

Judy was there for Frank's performance at the Copacabana on New Year's Eve of 1956, and this was the start of a very heady, busy, and creatively productive year for him. Humphrey Bogart died in January of 1957, and so Frank did everything he could to cheer the widowed Lauren Bacall, but he was seeing lots of other women as well, as many as he could fit in.

Frank's new album *Close to You* (1957) was very much an experiment in which he did songs with only the backing of a string quartet that included Felix and Eleanor Slatkin, married musicians he very much admired who were two of his closest friends. It had taken eight months to record this album to everyone's satisfaction, and Frank was proud of the result, even if he hit some shaky or damaged notes that a fuller sound behind him might have cloaked or finessed.

Close to You is an album where Frank really sounds like he's been out too many nights. When he sings his old hit "I Couldn't Sleep a Wink Last Night," he sounds now like he hasn't slept in days. As a joke, Frank recorded a tune called "There's a Flaw in My Flue" and did it in all seriousness, as if he wanted to prove he could make anything sound sad and sexy, and maybe that the words he sang didn't matter so much, an Ella point of view.

Nelson Riddle's arrangements for Frank are at their very best on *A Swingin' Affair!* (1957), and Frank is in great voice, floating above Riddle's version of "I Got Plenty o' Nuttin'," which he puts over with some snazzy phrasing, and a brassy "Night and Day" with horns and strings and even a tuba interlude. He skips the word "yearning" in the lyrics of "Night and Day" and makes us feel its loss, and his tone throughout is clean and sharp yet bendable. Riddle loves descending figures, which he uses to give edge and tension to the songs that Frank sings, and there is the sense on this album that the party might be over at any moment and we'd all better have our fun fast. Riddle's piano and maraca intro to "Lonesome Road" is particularly ominous, a real Frank sound.

Riddle also arranged the hit single "Witchcraft" for Frank, a classic lightly swinging Riddle-Frank sex song that was only revealed as more than a little silly when Bing recorded it, and Frank found time to conduct an album with Riddle arrangements for one of his regular lovers, Peggy Lee, called *The Man I Love*, her voice at its most naked and yearning for him.

For *Where Are You?* (1957) Frank chose Gordon Jenkins as his arranger, for he had liked the string arrangements that Jenkins had done for Judy in the late 1940s for some of her Decca singles. "With Gordon Jenkins, it's all so beautifully simple that, to me, it's like being back in the womb," Frank said. *Where Are You?* is an all-ballad album, and the far more straightforward Jenkins gives it a linear, supportive sound far removed from Riddle's fragmented modernism. Frank retreats to an earlier comfort zone here, with his new power and volume and also some vocal damage that he uses for expressive purposes.

He wallows in and owns David Raksin and Johnny Mercer's "Laura," making it sound like it is coming from a ruined man who is remembering a girl he loved in his happier youth. Jenkins provides forty-five seconds of a heavy strings intro before Frank starts an unsettling "Autumn Leaves," and Frank brings the same sort of French feeling of virile despair to a second recording of "I'm a Fool to Want You," which he puts over with the self-pitying bravado that had finally won him his male fans.

So 1957 saw three very different and major albums from Frank, and he also had three movies in release. *The Pride and the Passion* he took just to chase after Ava in Spain, and that didn't work out well on any level, but *The Joker Is Wild* gave him one of his best parts as singer Joe E. Lewis, who became a comic after the mob cut his vocal cords. Frank adjusts his singing style in the early scenes set in Chicago in the 1920s, milking and selling a song the way that Al Jolson and Eddie Cantor used to. Because Frank is a great singer and his greatness is established in the first twenty minutes of the movie, the loss of his singing voice feels particularly cruel, and the scene where he crawls out of his hotel room covered in blood is surprisingly grisly.

Frank's Joe E. Lewis becomes a burlesque comic in New York, and the humiliation he experiences suits humiliation-prone Frank very well. He hears Bing sing his 1930s hit "June in January," and we see Bing in silhouette as the vocal plays. This is the crooner who haunted every male singer of that time, though his influence was fading by 1957.

Frank's Joe has some success as a stand-up comic, and Frank delivers the one-liners professionally but without joy, and that was likely true of Lewis himself, who was a friend of Frank's in real life. Frank excels in a long drunk scene here, and overall *The Joker Is Wild* contains one of his most committed performances and is also one of his best movies. The big dramatic incident happens fairly early, and afterward this picture catches the formlessness of life, or of a life, much more than biopics usually do.

Frank ended the year with one of his very best vehicles, a movie of the Rodgers and Hart show *Pal Joey*, in which he plays a heel caught between two beautiful women: rich and imperious former stripteaser Rita Hayworth and vulnerable chorine Kim Novak. Frank gets to do one great song after another here, most notably his best-ever "The Lady Is a Tramp," sung directly to Hayworth.

Director George Sidney frames Frank with a blue light above him for this number, and what's really thrilling is the combination of his driving voice and the light, effortless movements of his body as he sings, the way he uses his shoulders, arms, and hands. "The Lady Is a Tramp" is a key Sinatra song because he both loves and hates this free-spirited woman he sings about, and he also identifies with her: he wants her, he scorns her, and he is her. That's what art on a high level can be.

Bing always proceeded more cautiously than Frank. In 1957 he married his second wife Kathryn after dating her off and on for several years. She fell in love with Bing when he saw her on the set of a movie in the mid-1950s and said, "Hey, Tex," in his lowest, smoothest tones (she was from Texas). It was the sound of his voice that got her, but Bing was hesitant to marry again, mainly because Kathryn was thirty years younger than him, and he was concerned about how it would look. He was that conscious of his image, but he finally felt that such things were not so important.

Bing was a pleasant throwback on records like *New Tricks* (1957), which gathered together some songs he recorded for the radio, and these tracks furnished proof he was still a rhythm singer. But on-screen he took a real risk in *Man on Fire* (1957), a movie in which he played Earl Carleton, a bitter and spiteful man fighting his ex-wife (Mary Fickett) for custody of their son.

"Winners like to be civilized," Earl says to his ex-wife's new husband, "losers go for the groin." Bing is believably nasty in *Man on Fire*, and he is nasty in several different sorts of ways; he had it in him. "Come on, get your little bucket butt over here," he tells his on-screen son here, using Gary terminology, and his character is a Catholic who doesn't believe in divorce, yet this characterization is not really a self-portrait.

There is a scene in *Man on Fire* where Bing's Earl cruelly mimics a female employee as they sit together at a bar, and this pure meanness is shocking coming from Bing. It's surprising that he took this part, and it's also surprising that he doesn't "act" it as he did his role in *The Country Girl*, which would let us know that he is actually nice easygoing Bing underneath; instead he fully inhabits this very unlikable man he is playing.

When a female judge awards custody to the mother (there is a male secretary in court to get across how gender roles are starting to change), the cold-as-ice reaction of Bing's Earl is truly horrible. There is a scene beyond this one where Bing's character looks into a mirror and confesses his self-loathing, and it feels very real. Bing wasn't self-loathing himself, yet for this part he dug very deep and found the emotion he needed, and this showed that even the blithest winners like Bing have something like this way deep down inside them somewhere. There is another very upsetting scene toward the end of the film where Earl gets into a physical scuffle as he tries to kidnap his son, and then there is an ending where Earl is not redeemed but simply outmaneuvered by his ex-wife and her new husband.

Within the full context of Bing's life and career, *Man on Fire* is revelatory, and it is certainly the best dramatic performance he ever gave. It is so uncompromising and so filled with impotent male anger that it raises questions about what Bing might have been keeping down inside of himself. He didn't get any award nominations for this performance because it is not flashy, and also because it is so deeply unflattering and disturbing; there is nothing enjoyable or easy about it, and he had made his career on ease and pleasure. Bing had been overtaken by Frank in movies and especially on record by 1957, even if he managed to dominate *High Society*, and so maybe this performance in *Man on Fire* was his way of staying competitive, not in the short run but in the long run of posterity.

Louis did an encore record with Ella in 1957 called *Ella and Louis Again*, a double album where they each soloed on some tracks. Louis makes a joke at one point about all the material they're doing: "Norman Granz says one more!" he cries, and Ella sounds very amused by that, an indication that Granz was very demanding of his star vocalist. Ella does a little shout-out to Bing on "These Foolish Things" and imitates him when she mentions "the songs that Crosby sings . . . boo boo boo boo boo." But this was Billie's song, and Ella's "Comes Love" here is far too cute.

Yet when Ella appeared on the same bill with Billie at the Newport Jazz Festival in July of 1957, Ella triumphed in spite of a microphone that kept giving her feedback, especially on her scat specialty "Air Mail Special." Johnny Mercer introduced Billie, who came out and did her expected songs, like "My Man" and "What a Little Moonlight Can Do," with a much-diminished voice that paled particularly next to Ella's flexibility and control of her world-class instrument.

Ella had been performing regularly for a long time, but her musicians noticed how nervous she would be before a show. She would often wonder out loud if the audience would like her, which was all-important to Ella. In her life offstage, Ella admitted that she was sometimes lonely. "I want to get married again," she told the *New-York Mirror*. "I'm still looking. Everybody needs companionship."

It was reported in the summer of 1957 that she had married a Norwegian man named Thor Einar Larsen, but Ella told the press that they were not married yet; she very much seemed to enjoy the attention. Ella even went to the trouble of furnishing a flat for them in Oslo, Norway, but this all collapsed in August when Larsen was convicted of stealing money from a woman to whom he had been engaged. Disappointed once again, Ella concentrated on her work.

Unlike Bing, who could do practically any song handed to him, Ella was not suited to all types of material, but Granz always ignored that, and this was most apparent when he got Louis and Ella back together in 1957 to record songs from *Porgy and Bess*, an album that was released in 1958. The initial track, where they duet on "Summertime," is magisterial, but Ella is unable to play Bess convincingly. She had no sense of drama, and the moments where she is acting the role with dialogue only show that she is game and willing to try.

Another very ambitious project for Ella in 1957 nearly ended in disaster. Granz wanted her to record a three-album set with Duke Ellington, and when Ellington showed up with his band it was clear that very little had been prepared and that they would all have to take a chance that things would work out, and they mostly did, because Ella and Duke together were a magic combination.

"It was a panic scene," Ella remembered, "with Duke almost making up the arrangements as we went along. Duke is a genius—I admire him as much as anyone in the world—but doing it that way, even though it was fun at times, got to be kind of nerve-wracking."

"We planned far in advance, but in the end Duke failed to do a single arrangement," said Norman Granz. "Ella had to use the band's regular arrangements. She'd do a vocal where an instrumental chorus would normally go. . . . Really, at one point she became so nervous, almost hysterical, that she began to cry. Duke went over to her and said, 'Now, baby,' in his most gentle tones. 'Don't worry, it'll turn out fine.'"

But Ella seriously considered walking out on the project and had to be persuaded by Granz and Ellington's right-hand man Billy Strayhorn. "Ella really was very upset, and she didn't want to do it," Granz said. "She wanted to walk out. . . . Strays [Strayhorn] spent a lot of time holding Ella's hand and saying, 'There, there, it's going to be okay. Don't worry.'"

The first track, "Rockin' in Rhythm," is a marvel of controlled chaos, with tense and risky playing from the musicians and Ella proving that she can fit herself smoothly and delightedly into anything they throw at her. Ella's Duke Ellington songbook is a melody splurge, and she takes all of his melodies in with that nearly imperturbable stamina of hers. Some of the horn playing here is next level, and Ella interacts with it as both guide and instrument herself.

The band's lack of preparation shows sometimes, yet it doesn't finally matter, and there is variety on the first record, so that Ella can offer her most naked voice for a "Solitude" done with just guitar. But her voice sounds far too innocent on Strayhorn's great and very difficult "Lush Life," which Frank attempted once in the recording studio and then gave up on.

During a birthday celebration for Louis at the Newport Jazz Festival, where Ella was in attendance, Louis was very uncharacteristically angry. When a cake was wheeled out for him, Louis played "The Star-Spangled Banner" and then stormed off the stage. Producer George Wein had asked him to vary his program and include some songs from his Hot Five days of the 1920s, but this was not the only thing that Louis was mad about.

Times were changing, and it had taken Louis a while to adjust. There had come a point when Gordon Jenkins had to timidly ask Louis to stop singing the word "darkies" in the song "When It's Sleepy Time Down South" and sing the word "people" instead, and Louis was defensive about this at first. He had been singing it that way all his life, and now it wasn't right anymore? But this defensive reaction gave way to a blistering interview to a student reporter named Larry Lubenow in September of 1957 about the situation down in Little Rock, Arkansas, where nine African American students had been barred from integrating a school.

Louis had accrued lots of goodwill from his white audience through the years, and this was looked on with skepticism and outright contempt by some of his Black colleagues, especially the younger musicians coming up like Dizzy Gillespie and Miles Davis but also Duke Ellington, who was of Louis's generation and very intent on presenting a smooth and glamorous image. But now Louis used that goodwill and cashed in his chips on it at a crucial moment in American history.

Louis had been set to go on a goodwill tour of the Soviet Union for the American government, but now he said he could not represent this country if it continued to brutalize his people and treat them like second-class citizens. Louis blasted President Eisenhower and Arkansas governor Orval Faubus in very profane terms that had to be cleaned up for print, and he then sang his angry version of "The Star-Spangled Banner" for Lubenow with curse words added.

The story went out, and it caused controversy immediately. Sammy Davis Jr. blasted Louis for playing to segregated audiences, but Louis's words had been heard. President Eisenhower eventually ordered troops to help integrate the schools in Little Rock, and Louis's interview was likely one of the reasons why this happened. When Ike sent in the National Guard, Louis sent a telegram to congratulate him.

Strangely enough, no one was eventually happier about this confrontation than Louis's manager Joe Glaser. "Now the people who've been calling him an Uncle Tom can see that he's a real, real man," Glaser said in an interview. Less than a month after Louis's interview, Ford Motor Company wanted to fire Louis from an upcoming TV special with Bing and Frank, but CBS wouldn't budge, and surely Bing would not have countenanced such a thing. Louis's career sailed forward.

Bing was unhappy that Frank would not come to rehearse a complicated medley that they would be doing with Rosemary Clooney on this TV show. "Frank's gonna blow it," Bing told Clooney. "He's gonna blow it, and you and I are gonna have to bail him out." There was a tricky key change for Frank in the medley, and Bing and Clooney both knew he wouldn't get it if he didn't rehearse it.

Sure enough, when they were performing the medley live on TV Frank started "Blues in the Night" and sang "My mama done told me" and then cried, "What?!" when he didn't recognize the key. Bing and Clooney both broke up laughing, and Bing commented, "That key, she didn't tell ya." But Frank got away with it, partly because Bing was such a gracious host.

Frank soon had his own TV show again, but it wouldn't work too well because he was jumpy and edgy and decidedly not a gracious host—this was never his medium. That October of 1957, when his new television show premiered, Frank issued an overdone broadside against rock 'n' roll music: "It fosters almost totally negative and destructive reactions in young people," he claimed, and went on to condemn it as "dirty" and a "rancid-smelling aphrodisiac" with songs written and played "for the most part by cretinous goons."

Frank kept listening to rock music hits in 1957 and trying to figure out why young people liked them, and he came up empty, and it drove him crazy. Bing was also perplexed and unhappy by what he heard of rock 'n' roll at this time, and thought that it was a simplistic musical regression, but Bing would be far more circumspect about this publicly than Frank would.

In spite of the threat of rock music, Frank, Ella, Louis, and Bing were all still thriving, but Judy's career was in the doldrums, even if her albums began to slightly improve. Gordon Jenkins got Judy under a measure of control for *Alone* (1957). Her rather jazzy ending to "Mean to Me" on that album is enough to make us wonder how she might have functioned with a small jazz combo, but Judy's need to plunge herself into emotional puddles generally takes her away from rhythm as a means of musical expression. "With Judy, I'd just lock the door of the studio, and make her do it again," Jenkins said. "But if Frank wants to go home, he generally goes home."

Judy in Love (1958) is her best studio album because Nelson Riddle was the arranger for all the songs, which include an up-tempo and beautifully streamlined version of her old standby "Zing! Went the Strings of My Heart" and an ultra-slow setting of "I Can't Give You Anything but Love, Baby" with those Riddle sound islands rising up around her voice as she quivers over each word. *Judy in Love* is a concept album such as Riddle was doing with Frank at this time, and Riddle made a substantial contribution to Judy's repertoire. But Judy didn't show up for some of the sessions, and so parts of the album had to be overdubbed.

Judy's live performances of this time, which were sometimes conducted by Gordon Jenkins, often ended in disaster or great trouble. There was a serious suicide attempt during a brief American tour and Judy had to get stitches in her wrists, yet she insisted on going on singing afterward as if nothing had happened. Judy walked out on a noisy Las Vegas engagement on New Year's Eve of 1957, and she was fired from a stint at a Brooklyn nightclub, and debts piled up. There were so many expenses that she often lost money on her tours.

Judy was not singing live as much by 1958, partly because she had gained a great deal of weight and was feeling bad about herself. When she performed in London, the press was very cruel about her weight gain, and afterward she sought refuge in drink. According to Frank's valet George Jacobs, who saw all the traffic at Frank's house, a drunken Judy often "made major sexual demands on Mr. S, showing up on Bowmont Drive at all hours of the night for a shoulder to cry on . . . she wanted Mr. S to hold her, to love her, to make her feel beautiful again, and he did. Sinatra had the highest regard for Judy and her talent." Jacobs said that Frank loved Judy the way he loved his first wife Nancy, but Judy insisted on a sexual component to their relationship even when Frank wasn't feeling it or wasn't in the mood.

Judy complained about the limits of her ongoing affair with Frank to her friend Harry Rubin. She had fallen into a pattern of fighting and making up with her husband Sid Luft, and she was addicted to the drama of this Frank and Ava situation while Luft spent her money as soon as it came in. Judy's act at the Cocoanut Grove was recorded live in August of 1958 with a Guy Lombardo-ish accompaniment, and she was not in good voice, but she got some good notices.

In October Judy played at the Sands in Las Vegas, and Frank and entourage came in to support her. At one of her shows, Frank and Dean Martin got up and did a heckling routine that Judy played along with, and the audience ate it up. But a diminished voice was noted by *Variety* when Judy played in Miami in early 1959, and her engagement was looked on as a flop, whereas Frank's own engagement there right afterward was a sellout success.

Judy did a cockamamie Gordon Jenkins concept album called *The Letter* (1959), which was an attempt at a sort of mini-movie narrative about a doomed affair where sexy John Ireland acted the role of her lover. Judy is in better voice here, but she rightly sounds a little skeptical about the whole thing. In November of 1959, Judy contracted acute hepatitis and nearly died from it, and a doctor told her that she would likely survive only five more years and would be an invalid. Her career seemed to be over.

Frank's career could not have been in better health. He reached his creative height as a singer in 1958 with two of his very best albums, *Come Fly with Me* and *Frank Sinatra Sings for Only the Lonely*, which make for quite a contrast. The Rabelaisian Billy May was the arranger for *Come Fly with Me*, a concept album where each song is meant to take you to another jet-setting location around the world. May is very flexible and inventive here, and humorous; he's bold where Riddle is indirect.

The Sammy Cahn and Jimmy Van Heusen title number couldn't be more enticing or swaggering, especially when Frank sings, "Once I get you up there" with a clear sexual overtone. *Come Fly with Me* offers a kind of modern Frank-ian paradise where possibilities are limitless. The abrupt ending he does to "On the Road to Mandalay" is unexpected and gets across his utopian restlessness, and on "April in Paris" he cleverly starts with lyrics from the middle of the song, which creates the feeling Frank wants of shaking things up, of not settling down or settling for anything. He hasn't found what he's looking for yet, and he's no quitter!

Let Bing sink into the suburbs with his pipe and slippers: Frank is out to get the brass ring. He even bestirs himself to do some hard swinging with May's musicians on "Brazil," which really is a melodic heaven, and he does "Blue Hawaii" without any expected Hawaiian sounds, leaving that to Bing. It all ends with another Cahn and Van Heusen song called "It's Nice to Go Trav'ling," which lets us know that only sheer exhaustion will stop Frank from looking for a good time.

Frank was seriously seeing Lauren Bacall now, and there came a point where he offered to marry her, but this was all a very delicate business. Bacall was certain she wanted to be with Frank, but Frank was far less certain that he wanted to marry again. He had finally gotten a divorce from Ava in 1957, but he was still hung up on her and went off to visit her when she fell off a horse in a bullring in Spain and damaged her face. Bacall was not happy about this visit, and she does not mention it in her memoir.

Frank and Bacall told super-agent Swifty Lazar of their marriage plans, and Lazar told columnist Louella Parsons, who wrote it up for the *Examiner*. Frank was not pleased with the headlines, and his reaction was to brutally cut Bacall off and out of his life. When she saw him at a social event soon after this, he pretended that she wasn't there and refused to speak to her. According to George Jacobs, Frank spoke of Bacall in very disparaging terms to his friends, and this was clearly the behavior of a tramp, not a gentleman.

The cover of *Only the Lonely*, which was Frank's own favorite album, shows him in clown makeup, making him a Pagliacci for America in the late 1950s. Nelson Riddle was back for this ultimate torch song collection, giving Frank grandiose backing for the Cahn and Van Heusen title tune. Several of the tracks are long; three are more than five minutes. This is a post-Ava album that acknowledges he is probably never going to get her back.

Riddle's strings on "It's a Lonesome Old Town" have the sound of pure anxiety, and sometimes Riddle has his instruments talking sardonically to each other as Frank pours his heart out. Frank is not in what could be called good voice on this record, but he uses the roughness of his tone and the fragility of his sound and even unsupported low notes for expressive purposes, another link to Billie, who was trying her best to do the same in the 1950s.

"Ebb Tide" is maybe the greatest track on this major Frank album. It begins with the grand sound of harps that seem ready to sweep us out to sea, and then there is a slowly building vocal from Frank, who sounds very weak at first, until he builds to higher notes on "I can tell . . . I can feel" and cuts off the word "feel" very dramatically before reaching up to very high notes on "really mine." From this vertiginous vocal height, Frank slowly descends back into a quiet, dreamy tone, his "rage against the dying of the light" voice fading away back to where it came from. For sheer drama, there is nothing like Frank's performance of "Ebb Tide" in the catalog of any other popular singer.

For the ultimate saloon song, "One for My Baby," which Frank truly owned, he makes each repeat of the word "baby" very specific, as if he is remembering everything about the love of his life, and this is method singing, Frank using everything he had experienced with Ava and putting it directly on record. His voice is ghostly, finally, as if he can barely get out the words, and this is because he is not singing this song: he is living it.

On-screen Frank worked with Judy's ex-husband Vincente Minnelli on *Some Came Running* (1958), an adaptation of a James Jones novel in which Frank plays a writer and soldier named Dave Hirsh who comes back to his Indiana hometown with a hanger-on good-time girl named Ginny (Shirley MacLaine). The way to Frank's heart in life and on-screen was to reject him and be unattainable, so MacLaine's clinging and adoring Ginny doesn't have a chance. Dave Hirsh is a perfect part for Frank, a resentful, superior loser with a portable Faulkner in his bag, a man who wrote a novel that is called "a powerful study of rejection" by a school-teacher (Martha Hyer). In his own way, Frank is extending Bing's image from the 1930s of a wandering man who is not going to settle down or settle for anything.

Frank's movie with Frank Capra, *A Hole in the Head* (1959), is far better than the two that Bing made with Capra in the early 1950s. Capra realized that Frank needed stimulation to make his first takes come alive, and so he devised some ways with the other actors to keep them fresh and keep Frank's interest high. Like Leo McCarey, Capra at his best was very good at capturing human behavior in long takes, and he gets the most out of Frank, Edward G. Robinson, Thelma Ritter, and Eleanor Parker, who is elegant and restrained here. Frank plays a widower who owns a Miami hotel and has a young son under his care with whom he sings "High Hopes," a paean to 1950s optimism.

Come Dance with Me! was a top-selling album for Frank in 1959, but with its brassy horns and short tracks it has a feeling of impatience and relentlessness that doesn't offer enough variation or focus. *No One Cares*, which Frank referred to as a "suicide album," finished out the decade for him on a note of unrestrained self-pity, with ever-sympathetic strings from Gordon Jenkins, who sometimes feels more like a fan than a collaborator like Nelson Riddle or Billy May.

Frank had established himself as the king of all popular singers in the 1950s, but there was one singer who intimidated him. "Ella Fitzgerald is the only performer with whom I've ever worked who made me nervous," he said in 1959. "Because I try to work up to what she does. You know, try to pull myself up to that height, because I believe that she is the greatest popular singer in the world. Barring none—male or female."

Frank was one of the most competitive people on earth, and he was not suited to the role of fan, but there was no way he could listen to Ella's albums in the late 1950s without knowing he could never touch what she was doing technically. He brought his A game vocally when Ella appeared on his TV show in 1959, sending out strong, clear notes when they duetted on the atmospheric "Moonlight in Vermont" and attempting to joke with her on "Can't We Be Friends?" In this television appearance Ella is very shy with Frank, closing her eyes and retreating into herself when she sings as she often did in concert, and the discomfort is mutual, for Frank is just as shy of Ella in his own very different way.

Jo Stafford's husband Paul Weston arranged Ella's next songbook album, a two-record set dedicated to the music of Irving Berlin. Ella never looked more confident than on the cover of this Irving Berlin record, sitting in a café in a beautifully cut black dress with a red hat perched on her head, and she had reason to be, for this is one of her best songbooks. Weston knew just how to showcase her kind of voice, and everything about this Berlin material stimulated her. Ella does the famous

Berlin songs in ways that could not be bettered, but she also revitalizes several of Berlin's more obscure gems as well. Many of these were tunes first introduced by Fred Astaire, and they suit Ella's cool side, but at the same time they bring out her warmth.

Even the words of Berlin songs often suit her, especially on "You're Laughing at Me" and "Let Yourself Go," and she gives her all to his melodies, finding particular beauty in "Russian Lullaby," "Remember," and "Reaching for the Moon," which has a perfect lyric for Ella: "I'm just the words waiting for the tune." But the best track on this Berlin album and one of the very best tracks Ella ever recorded is her ode to joy "Blue Skies," which begins with a serene scat solo to lift us up to musical heaven, goes into the lyrics, and then returns to scat variations on the melody, folding in some of Gershwin's "Rhapsody in Blue" just for sheer beauty. The only misstep on this Berlin set is "Supper Time," which is Ethel Waters's song, and too dramatic and despairing for Ella.

Ella played at Mister Kelly's in Chicago in the summer of 1958, and this resulted in one of her best live albums, partly because she was playing to a fairly intimate crowd, and she got surprisingly earthy with them at times. Frank is mentioned quite a bit: "We'd like to do a song made popular by Frank Sinatra," she says, and then wonders, "What song didn't get popular through Frank Sinatra?" Ella had her eye on her chief competition as well, for she does her own version of Frank's "Witchcraft," one of his key singles with Nelson Riddle, and makes it her own, swinging it both light and hard at once.

Ella knows she is doing a really inspired show this night at Mister Kelly's. She speaks of how she loves the "quiet and appreciative" audience she has had at Mister Kelly's and sounds very lovably sweet at many moments here. By the end, she says, "I'm hoarse, but I love it!" and goes on to say, "Although I sound like Louis Armstrong now, I'll try to do Ella for you." When she doesn't know the words to the verse for "Stardust," she smoothly makes some up in order to claim the pretty melody. Even though the melody was always the important thing to Ella, her skill at making up lyrics on the spot would soon become another notable aspect of her genius.

Things did not always go so smoothly. When she reached London with her musicians, British customs held her up to look for drugs. They strip-searched her ex-husband Ray Brown, took away some of her vitamin pills for analysis, and split a tube of toothpaste belonging to Norman Granz. Ella and company were detained for so long that a TV interview Ella was going to do had to be canceled. "I have never been so socially insulted in my life, and I have done some traveling," Ella said.

In 1959 Ella embarked on her most ambitious songbook of all, a five-album set of fifty-nine songs devoted to the music of George Gershwin with Nelson Riddle as her arranger. Riddle's daughter Rosemary remembered how different a Riddle session with Frank was from a Riddle session with Ella. "Boy, would I see the entourage for Frank," she said. "And it wasn't like you were going to walk up to him. As generous as he was in many ways, this was serious business. Whereas if Ella saw me, it would be this warm, cozy feeling."

So many songs were thrown at Ella for this Gershwin set that she could not possibly engage with all of them, and she was also forced to hold her voice in reserve a lot of the time just to get through all this material. But there are gems throughout, particularly a grand version of "The Man I Love" where Riddle's descending figures give the song a poignantly unresolved feeling, a "Love Is Here to Stay" that sounds cautious and teasing, and a very sexy "Embraceable You." This epic Gershwin project captures the sound of a person who is hopeful but who is ready to be resigned or detached if she needs to be, without fuss or self-pity.

30

Lady in Satin and Billie at the Met

BILLIE WAS BOOKED to play in Alaska by Louis McKay in 1954, and she didn't have proper clothing for the cold climate; she didn't even have a coat. When she performed, Billie would get up and sing a song like "Willow Weep for Me" with very long pauses. Her teeth would be chattering backstage in her dressing room, and she was badly malnourished.

Billie was haunted by the memory of Sadie. Her accompanist Memry Midgett remembered, "She seemed to worry a great deal about her treatment of her mother and she became depressed. . . . She felt that she had not done as much for her mother as she should have. . . . I never got the impression that she loved her mother, only that she felt guilty."

Billie couldn't relate to people unless she was manipulating them in some way, because she knew what people were. With Midgett, who was a young woman in her early twenties, Billie wanted proof that she cared, and then more proof, and then it would be, "Why do you care about me? Must make you as bad as me." She told Midgett that she had been a female pimp herself at age thirteen, likely one of her fantasies of power.

Midgett encouraged Billie to get rid of both McKay and her manager Joe Glaser, and Billie would think about it, but she just couldn't bring herself to improve her situation. One time Billie was all ready to part ways with Glaser, but then found that she couldn't walk down the escalator stairs to go in to see him. She just stood there and told Midgett that she couldn't, that she was too weak. But Midgett also saw that Billie knew her worth as an artist. Billie would wait for the audience to be totally quiet; she did not care about pleasing them, as Ella did. She was there to express herself, and that audience could take it or leave it.

Pianist Jimmy Rowles was annoyed that Norman Granz wouldn't allow more rehearsal time for Billie's recording dates, and he also didn't like that Ella would get sixteen instruments but Billie would record with just a combo, something that surely Billie herself took note of. But she had mellowed about Ella in conversation at this time, acknowledging what a fine singer she had become to her friend Alice Vrbsky, praising the way Ella used her "instrument" now. That girl who had asked for her autograph in 1935 had come a long way, and Billie knew it.

In an unaired radio interview from 1956, Billie says she is "crazy about Ella and Louis Armstrong, they're my favorites." Billie was very modest about her own achievements when interviewed by Mike Wallace, saying that she was expert "in my little way" but not as impressive as some performers she had known like Ethel Barrymore and her friend Tallulah Bankhead.

When Billie played in Vegas, she was not happy to perform for a segregated white audience. She was in very ill health now and often appeared dazed, and McKay made fun of her behind her back, according to her accompanist Corky Hale. When they were arrested on a drug charge in early 1956, Billie married McKay so that she wouldn't be able to testify against him in court.

To make some money, Billie had been working on an autobiography with journalist William Dufty, and it was published as *Lady Sings the Blues* in 1956. She was godmother to Dufty's son Bevan and loved being with him, and Billie sometimes talked about wanting children, but it was not in the cards. One time Billie asked Rosemary Clooney if she could be godmother to one of Clooney's children and charmingly explained, "It takes a very bad woman to be a good godmother."

There is a delightful and lengthy rehearsal tape of Billie from May of 1956 where she talks a lot of her trash, like a Richard Pryor character, and her hoarse laugh is very winning. When they rehearse "Everything Happens to Me," an early Frank song, Billie says that everybody does it "pretty," which is an Ella word, but she wants to try it "funky." Billie is in a very good mood on this tape, fun and vital and alive with ideas, musical and otherwise.

"Me and my old voice . . . it's not legit!" she says merrily, and she cries at one point, "I'm gonna walk by your house and throw a stink bomb!" When Jimmy Rowles mentions "What a Little Moonlight Can Do" and says that's a good one, Billie isn't having it: "I hate that song!" she insists, even though she had been singing it for twenty years. Billie is heard playing with her godchild Bevan, and she sings "Some of These Days" for him. And then she very unexpectedly sings another Sophie Tucker hit for her godson, "My Yiddishe Momme," doing it full out and in a high register.

This rehearsal tape is a revelatory insight into Billie, and it goes against her tragic image. The woman on this tape has a ready laugh, and she knows how to have a good time and how to entertain herself and others. Listening to this recording is like spending an afternoon with a very upbeat and funny Billie, and it provides a needed balance for all the sad stories told about her.

The happy side revealed on this tape is all the more heroic given what Billie always had to put up with. There was talk about a movie of her memoirs, but in the press they started mentioning Ava Gardner or even Lana Turner playing her on-screen, and Billie hit the roof when she heard this, going into a tirade over it with her friend Annie Ross. "Even if they get a white actress, the character she plays will still be colored," said an exasperated Billie in July of 1957. "If they change that, there's no story."

At the end of 1957, Billie appeared on television with Lester Young to sing "Fine and Mellow," and she takes in Young's solo on a fathoms-deep level that radiates out of her radically open and unprotected face. She is the reigning monarch of cool here, the stoned Queen of Jazz, living on sheer sensation.

Billie left Granz's Verve to sign with Columbia, where she had made her greatest recordings in the 1930s. She was listening to the albums that Frank was putting out, and they were inspiring both her and her soulmate Lester Young creatively. Frank himself praised Billie in the highest terms to *Ebony* magazine in 1958: "With few exceptions, every major pop singer in the US during her generation has been touched in some way by her genius," he said. "It is Billie Holiday who was, and still remains, the greatest single musical influence on me. Lady Day is unquestionably the most important influence on American popular singing in the last twenty years."

Billie's voice had declined into a wobbly rasp at this point, and so she had a musical idea. Why not record with a more-than-slightly corny orchestral backing as a contrast to this rough voice? Billie had heard what she wanted on an album called *Ellis in Wonderland*, and so she contacted arranger Ray Ellis to work with her on an album that would be named *Lady in Satin*.

Columbia record executive Irving Townsend was surprised by her request. "It would be like Ella Fitzgerald saying she wanted to record with Ray Conniff," he said. Conniff was an arranger who was working with Johnny Mathis, and Ellis was also working with Mathis and with Sarah Vaughan, singers who made elaborately pretty sounds.

Ellis was excited to work with Billie, but when he met her he was taken aback by how run-down she looked. Billie was getting reactions now like Ella got in 1935 when she had been out on the streets for a bit. Though Billie always had a place to stay, hard living had taken its toll. She wore her hair in a ponytail now, and she was painfully thin.

Lady in Satin became an improbable triumph for Billie partly because she picked some new songs for it, busting out of her "my man willow weep for me" rut, and she chose her tunes because of their lyrics, not their melodies. Her rendition of "I'm a Fool to Want You" rivals Frank's because he was singing about one specific person while Billie is singing more about an abstract concept, and she uses the ruins of her voice expressively here, with low rasps that sound like a death rattle, an actual dying fall, all tone gone. Ellis's Disney cartoon flourishes behind her make for such a total contrast that they somehow protect her and give Billie that lush feeling that she had always craved.

Billie knew that her voice was a wreck, and Townsend said she drank heavily to combat this knowledge during the sessions for *Lady in Satin*, but the drinking only made it worse, and she was imbibing straight gin, which made it particularly deadly. Billie recorded these songs even later at night than Frank liked to, at midnight and later. Ellis said that she often didn't know the songs. Billie had been used to doing variations on her somewhat small repertoire for years, and so exploring new tunes was difficult for her, but it wound up being rewarding.

Her version of "You've Changed" is a heartbreaker, and she wept while she sang it, whereas Frank sometimes broke down and cried after he was done with a torch song. Ellis had taken Billie to the Colony record store to look for one more song for the album, and this is when she had picked "You've Changed." The process was difficult. She was cursing out everybody in the joint, Ellis said, and cursing her dead mother Sadie, who hadn't been there for her and then was there too much and in the wrong way and now was gone for good yet ever present—the great unresolved love-hate of Billie's life.

A tour of Europe was a disaster. She got booed off the stage in Milan, and she was finally reduced to taking part of the door fee at a small club in Paris called the Mars. In early 1959, Billie was harassed over an obscure law that required convicted drug addicts to notify customs when they left the country. Frightened that she might be sent to jail again, Billie submitted to a grilling by three district attorneys in Brooklyn and came through it by acting meek with them.

Billie sang "Strange Fruit" on TV in England, taking on the full pain of it as she had so many times before, carrying the crushing weight of it even though she was obviously ill. She recorded a second album with Ellis that was botched when the producers adjusted the speed a quarter-pitch faster on some tracks, which makes her sound like a child star imitating a wrecked Billie Holiday.

On this album she references Frank by name and does two of his tunes, "All the Way" and "I'll Never Smile Again," but she really seems to enjoy an old Bing hit, "Just One More Chance." Billie has some good ideas here, and it's not her fault that the album doesn't work. One of the last lines on the last song on this misbegotten record is "Mama needs Daddy."

Lester Young died in March of 1959, and Billie was wounded when his family wouldn't let her sing at his funeral. She said to Leonard Feather that she would be next, and she likened herself to a ghost. Billie was very lonely now. "There were so many people flocking around her when she was at her height," said Annie Ross. "But when she became ill they didn't flock around no more." When Billie needed to rent an apartment, she did so as Eleanora Fagan because Billie Holiday was too notorious.

Ross would come around, her friend and assistant Alice Vrbsky was loyal, and her ghostwriter William Dufty tried to help her. Her legs and stomach were swollen, and she barely ever ate. She had cirrhosis of the liver, and this affected other parts of her body. Finally Billie had to be taken to the hospital, and she wound up at the Metropolitan Hospital in Harlem. Her lawyer Earle Zaidins brought the second Ellis album to play for her, and they joked that she could do a live album from the hospital and call it *Lady at the Met*.

Billie still liked to laugh. She phoned Zaidins in the middle of the night to tell him that a dripping tap was driving her crazy. "I wouldn't mind, but it don't *swing*," she joked. Billie even signed a contract to appear in a movie called *The Flaming Nude*, in which she was to sing a song called "Tired and Disgusted."

On June 12 she was arrested in her hospital bed after a nurse said she found drugs in Billie's room, or evidence of drug use. They took away her radio, her record player, the flowers people had sent her, and her telephone, and guards were posted at her door, as if this dying woman were a threat to the public.

It was at this point that Frank made a visit to his friend and mentor. He and his valet George Jacobs saw a line of picketers outside the hospital with signs reading, LET LADY LIVE, and when he got inside to see her, Frank praised *Lady in Satin* and tried to talk to Billie about all the things she could still do. Frank spoke of how she had taught him how to phrase lyrics, and Billie modestly said, "I may have showed you how to bend a note, Frankie, that's all." But surely Billie was proud of the effect that she had had on Frank's singing.

Billie then leaned in and whispered to Frank, "Will you cut the shit, baby, and get me some dope?" Frank hated drugs and hated anything to do with them, but he adored and respected Billie, and so he tried his best for her. Frank offered money to the doctors at the hospital to get Billie what she needed, but they were afraid of Mayor Robert Wagner, who was on a campaign against drugs and was capable of cutting off their funding if they were caught helping Billie. Frank tried to contact Wagner himself, but he couldn't get through. Finally Frank resorted to buying the heroin for Billie himself through a New York drug dealer, but he couldn't get it past the cops. Frank could have gotten into serious trouble himself, but he loved Billie that much.

Dufty and a press agent named Dorothy Ross made frantic calls to everyone they could think of to help her legally. When they got to Frank, he told them that Wagner hated him. They contacted Count Basie, Duke Ellington, and Sidney Poitier, and none of them responded. They also contacted Ella, and she also did not respond. Ella had been harassed herself by the police for no reason at all. She never took drugs and barely drank, and the police had done their best to humiliate her. And so she did not want to get involved in this situation with Billie.

It's worth wondering if Ella ever heard the negative things that Billie would say about her singing in the 1930s and '40s. Those kinds of things often have a way of getting back to the person being talked about. If Ella heard these things, did she also know that Billie had changed her mind, as she so often did, and that she was praising Ella's singing now? Praise doesn't travel as fast as negativity.

Ella idolized Billie, but she had seen her idol decline and make a fool of herself in public when they shared the same bill. Ella knew that people were constantly comparing her to Billie, as if listeners had to choose between them, and she was healthily competitive; she was now at the top of her field, whereas Billie was fading away. Ella was not as complicated a person as Billie was, but her feelings about Billie must have been mixed, troubled, and difficult for her to sort out. When she got that call from Dufty, it likely pained Ella greatly to decide to stay out of it.

McKay visited Billie and wanted to try to get the film rights to her memoir. He read the twenty-third psalm to her, and after he left Billie commented to Dufty, "I've always been a religious bitch, but if that evil motherfucker believes in God, I'm thinking it over." They were giving her methadone, and her health started to improve, but then she declined again when the methadone was stopped after ten days because the doctors couldn't legally continue to give it to her.

Billie got her record player back and kept listening to herself singing that old Bing song "Just One More Chance." Eventually she started to slip in and out of consciousness, and Dufty saw that her will to live was very strong but her body was giving up on her. On July 17, 1959, Billie died. She was forty-four years old. After her funeral, Billie was buried in the Bronx, and it was reported that McKay had Sadie's grave opened so that Billie could be buried on top of her, but the cemetery later said that Sadie's remains were moved to Billie's grave in 1961.

When Frank was told that Billie had died, he locked himself in his Manhattan penthouse and cried for two days, playing her records, drinking, crying some more, listening to Billie's voice some more. "I had never seen him hurt so much, even for Ava," said George Jacobs. Frank told Jacobs something that Billie had once told him: that you don't know what enough is until you've had more than enough. Billie had had more than enough.

Did Billie and Frank ever have an affair of any kind? Frank told Jacobs that they did, but he talked about this subject very differently to Quincy Jones. "One late night in Palm Springs, he told me about a crush he'd had on Billie Holiday when he was young, but you couldn't follow it through because of the times," Jones said. Frank told Jones, "Q, you couldn't get away with that back in those days, no matter who you were."

31

Judy and Barbra

THOUGH JUDY HAD been told that she would never sing again and wouldn't even live long after her serious bout with hepatitis in 1959, she was performing in London by 1960, and her voice had a new power and control; she also won over a difficult-to-please Paris after her first socko performance there.

Her husband Sid Luft passed off the management duties of her career to Freddie Fields and David Begelman, who planned a major comeback for Judy on records, on TV, and in movies. Luft tried to retain the money she was bringing in, and Fields eventually cut most of that off, but Begelman had his eye on her money himself, and Judy was soon embroiled in an affair with Begelman.

Fields set up a tour in America, and Judy was sent out on the road with a young woman named Stevie Phillips, who was immediately plunged into the chaos of Judy's life. In Phillips's horrifying 2015 memoir, which has a blunt and ungenerous tone, she describes the regularity and bloodiness of Judy's suicide attempts, Begelman's callous remarks about his star performer, and a knock-down drag-out physical fight that Judy had with Begelman's wife in a hotel room that spilled out into the hallways and went on and on.

The Judy in Phillips's memoir is a very sick person, foul mouthed, easily bored, and compelled to cut herself at the most unexpected times and in the most unexpected ways. Phillips writes that she once turned to Judy when they were on a plane and found that Judy had smashed her compact and made small cuts all over her face. But money was to be made from Judy, and Judy herself wanted to make a comeback, so Phillips and others would just clean her up as best they could and send her out onstage, and at this point no one was singing better than Judy was.

It was the addition of Mort Lindsey as her conductor that was the final magic ingredient for Judy's live concerts, for he whipped her arrangements into shape, streamlining and tightening them, and he came up with a very dramatic and exciting overture. On April 23, 1961, Judy played Carnegie Hall with Lindsey, and the performance was set to be recorded. Many famous names were there, and Judy knew how important it was that she ace this. A Capitol producer named Andy Wiswell went backstage to ask Judy if her drummer could play quieter for the recording, and Lindsey remembered Judy looking at him and saying, "Listen, you motherfucker, this is my night, and I don't care if you get a recording. I'm going to get it the way I want it. If I want the drums loud, they're going to be loud."

Judy was supposed to go on at 8:30 PM, but she made them wait until 8:45. Of course she wanted that sense of drama. *Will Judy show? Is she all right?* She insisted on talking to her friend Roddy McDowall beforehand, and he was sent for; he found her calm and ready. Benny Goodman was down front, and Ethel Merman was there. Harold Arlen was worried, but once Judy came out onstage, he told Alan King, "I think we're in good shape tonight."

Mike Nichols and Elaine May were in attendance, and Nichols had no expectations, but he was soon overcome. "Everybody loved Judy Garland, and I liked her, but I wasn't obsessed with her," Nichols remembered. "Then she comes out and she's like on fire from the first moment. You just thought, 'Holy shit! What is this?' We kept clutching each other and gasping and cheering and yelling and carrying on."

It was all just Judy now—no dancing boys, no supplementary acts as in vaudeville—and we can feel the full electricity of the moment on this Carnegie Hall album, her winning all these people back after they had given up on her: severe Henry Fonda overcome, Myrna Loy getting up to cheer, Hedda Hopper in tears. Judy is using all aspects of her voice here in a way that she never had before, particularly her vibrato, which she deploys as a weapon and also as an emblem of her vulnerability when she ends her quieter songs with it. "I do like to sing jazz, but they won't let me," she says at one point. "I don't know who *they* are," she admits. Was jazz to her just Benny Goodman still?

Though her image was one of excess and abandon, everything in this famous Carnegie Hall performance was carefully planned. If you listen to her concerts just before this one, particularly a poky version of this program she did in Amsterdam in 1960 with a different conductor, you can see that she always deliberately forgets the lyrics to "You Go to My Head" to get the audience on her side, and she does a similar thing with the "impromptu" version of "Who Cares?"

At Carnegie Hall, Judy whipped the audience into near pandemonium, and this was sustained by her gay fans on the second floor, who eventually rushed the stage just like the bobby-soxers who used to rush for Frank in the 1940s. Freddie Fields's wife Polly Bergen, who didn't like Judy, said that Fields actually paid these guys to do this, but surely they didn't really require remuneration. Gay people were forced to hide their lives then, and here was this tiny woman with this huge voice kicking over the traces and making a spectacle of herself, and it was such a relief. She was in pain but she was able to laugh about it, and that's a very gay quality.

Her frenzied ending to "Come Rain or Come Shine" gets a big rock-concert-like yelp from a male audience member, and she does a fabulously shameless dying baby bird vibrato at the end of "Stormy Weather." Judy does song after song at Carnegie Hall with increasing power and stamina, more and more, and then she finally says, "I know . . . I'll sing 'em all and we'll stay all night!" This was a line she had used before in her concerts, but it really lands here.

"I don't ever want to go home, I never," she dithers, very lovably. She knows how to milk that audience. "Do you really want more, aren't you *tired* of me?" she asks, and she knows she'll get a surge of love in return. Judy could never get enough reassurance that people loved her, but this level of mass adoration did thrill her. She hits a serious clam at the beginning of her signature song "Over the Rainbow" at Carnegie Hall, but it doesn't matter. After several years of aimless and sloppy work, Judy had finally reached her full potential as a great singer.

Her management set up movies for her again, and she made an appearance in Stanley Kramer's all-star *Judgment at Nuremberg* (1961) that got her a second Oscar nomination, this time for supporting actress. Judy does a light German accent as a woman called on to recount an experience in Nazi Germany, and Kramer exploits her as a wreck playing a wreck just as he exploits Montgomery Clift in the same film. She is very hammy here in her Big Scene in court, weeping, hesitating, milking the moment in a way that feels far less palatable without a song.

Judy added "What a Little Moonlight Can Do" to some of her 1961 concert dates, and she received a slam for doing so by columnist Ralph Gleason. "Jazz and Judy Garland are mutually exclusive," Gleason wrote, knocking her for trying Billie's song and also for the section of her Carnegie Hall concert where she claimed that she liked to sing jazz but seemed to have an outdated sense of what that meant.

"I sometimes feel that the audience has been looking at my Judy Garland face a long time and is ready for a change," Judy said in an interview at the end of this tour. "Change of pace in make-up and costume, within the bounds of characterization, of course, adds novelty and renewed interest. [Eddie] Cantor put on blackface. Jolson did, too. I don't use blackface, but I think it's the same principle when I make up for my tramp number or when I do a clown routine. It's one of the advantages of musical numbers. A performer can apply different kinds of techniques of make-up to give an audience a new look at his or her personality." So in the early 1960s, even though she made sure to mention that she did not or would not use such makeup herself anymore, Judy still basically saw blackface as just a novelty for a white performer's stage persona.

Judy did a TV special with Frank and Dean Martin in February of 1962, and after Frank is introduced he pulls a real power move with her, physically relating to her as if they are alone and making it clear that they have been very intimate with each other, which has the effect at first of his taking control of what should be her program. Frank looks over her slimmed-down body admiringly and even curtsies for Judy, putting his hands on her arms, and they might as well be in his bedroom rather than on national television.

But Frank is so wrapped up in his Judy seduction that he screws up the lyrics to "Too Marvelous for Words," and Judy's voice overpowers Frank and Dean when they all sing together, so there is a lot going on here, but Judy comes out of it the winner, for she is clearly into both of them and having a great time. When Judy messes her hair as she sings, it is a sign of abandon, sexual and otherwise. She is not going to be smooth and professional but is going to blow everything apart, destroy it all and take us somewhere better, which was always Billie's best impulse, but peak Billie did it on reefers whereas Judy used speed to take us there.

During this hectic period, Judy played a role in an animated movie called *Gay Purr-ee* (1962), pitching her speaking voice higher to be girlish as a social-climbing kitty named Mewsette who winds up getting sold into sex slavery and starts doing torch songs, including one in which she contemplates suicide. "River, river, won't you be my lover? Don't turn me down!" sings Judy's Mewsette, who in song sounds like a blowsy lady with a wide vibrato. This was rather dark fare for a film meant for children.

For *A Child Is Waiting* (1963), a straight drama in which she acted with disabled children, Judy plays Jean Hansen, a failed pianist who is looking for something that might give her life meaning. It is apparent Jean has been kicked around, and a female colleague suggests that she has been restlessly sexually promiscuous. Though Judy hated her brash young director John Cassavetes and showed up late and unprepared to the set, she is at her best in this movie: open, sensitive to the children, and subtle, choosing to underplay for a change.

Her antagonist in *A Child Is Waiting* is a hospital head played by Burt Lancaster, who tells her character, "Discipline is a part of life." This is the wrong thing to say to Judy, of course, who had pledged herself to living by heart and instinct, but there is a scene where Judy's Jean finally does have to discipline her favorite student Reuben (Bruce Ritchey), and Judy herself seems extremely upset by the implications of it.

Judy flew to London to appear in *I Could Go On Singing* (1963), an outright musical vehicle in which she plays a famous singer much like herself named Jenny Bowman. She was unhappy with the script and so she worked on improving it with her leading man Dirk Bogarde, who wrote many of her best lines of dialogue for her. Jenny is morbid and funny just as Judy could be, saying that she thinks being cremated would be "very sanitary and sort of chic!"

Judy was at her very worst during the making of this movie in England, physically harming herself numerous times. "How are things going today?" one of the producers was asked, and he replied, "Pretty good. She hasn't tried to kill herself today."

At one point during production Judy got Frank on the phone in Australia and told him, "I can't take it anymore, I'm saying goodbye." As screenwriter Mayo Simon remembered, "Sinatra called Hollywood, Hollywood called New York, New York called London, the producers called the guard outside Judy's hotel suite, who breaks in to find her semi-conscious, pill bottles everywhere. Judy is taken to a hospital and pumped out. She'll live; production is suspended."

It is here and here alone in *I Could Go On Singing* that she reveals Nightmare Judy on-screen, a black hole who can never get enough love or approval, and there is real dramatic tension in her scenes with Bogarde, who plays an ex-husband unsympathetic to Jenny's games and unwilling to allow her to swoop in and pick up her neglected son Matt (Gregory Phillips).

In the concert scenes, Judy has wild hair and wears heavy makeup and spangly jackets meant to cover that she's gained a bit of weight here. (Judy was really cursed in this regard because she was only four feet, eleven inches, and any small weight gain would show immediately on camera.) Her physical behavior in *I Could Go On Singing* is thuggish and off-putting, yet hard to resist. Director Ronald Neame films her singing the saddest song in the world, Kurt Weill's "It Never Was You," in a long single take that ends with a hard cut to Jenny in bed, as if both Jenny and Judy are so totally alone that performance and isolation afterward are the same thing. Audience applause can no longer reach her.

There is an extraordinary fight scene filmed in a single six-minute take between Jenny and Bogarde's David in *I Could Go On Singing* where Judy has morphed into a John Cassavetes sort of actor, dangerous and exploratory and intense, and when she shouts at Bogarde the effect is very intimidating. Judy had become a monster, but she could be an amiable monster. Fully aware of how trying she had been on this shoot, she told Neame on her last day, "You'll miss me when I'm gone."

Judy made an appearance on Jack Paar's talk show to promote *Gay Purr-ee*, and here she is slimmed down and ready to be the most entertaining of raconteurs, "one of the great talkers in show business," as Paar calls her. When she speaks of MGM and some of her fellow inmates there, Judy is mordant and catty in a way that makes the audience slightly nervous, and this made for riveting television. She says that her old rival Deanna Durbin had "one eyebrow—it never stopped in the middle—it went right across!" Judy is impish on Paar's program and none too accurate, but very funny, and her sculpted hair and black eyeliner give her a look that is sophisticated and a little depraved.

This talk show appearance got such a positive reaction that her managers pitched CBS a weekly television variety show for Judy. They got her a rich deal that meant that if she played her cards right and the show was a success, Judy would never have to work again if she didn't want to after the series ended its run. Judy was not someone who paid much attention to her finances, but she saw what this could mean for her and the freedom it might give her, and so she was determined to be at her best and make a success of *The Judy Garland Show*, which was set to begin taping in June of 1963. Miles away in New York, there was a young woman who was still missing her father with all her heart.

After the death of her husband Emanuel in 1943, Diana Streisand was grief stricken for years afterward, but she slowly began going out again, and she worked as a school secretary to help support her two children Sheldon and Barbara. To save money, Diana and her kids lived with her parents, and everybody was on top of each other. It was not a loving household.

Diana got pregnant by a man named Louis Kind, and her parents were adamant that Diana needed to marry him, and so she did in 1949, the year she had another girl, named Roslyn. Kind doted on Roslyn but disliked Diana's daughter Barbara, who had made a poor first impression on him when she demanded to be taken home from summer camp by her mother because she disliked it so much.

"I must have been pretty obnoxious," she admitted later, but Kind could be very cruel to his stepdaughter. There was one point when he was going to get ice cream for the kids, and Kind told Barbara that she was not pretty enough to have ice cream. Barbara tried hard to make Kind love her or notice her, getting him his slippers, practically groveling at his feet, but he was immovable.

In 1955, when Barbara was thirteen years old, Diana took her to a Fifty-Seventh Street studio in Manhattan and paid four bucks to get a record made of them singing. Diana did the operetta standard "One Kiss" and young Barbara sang "You'll Never Know" and Judy's "Zing! Went the Strings of My Heart" and bossed the pianist a bit, telling him what she wanted. She does a little mordent at the end of "You'll Never Know," and she already has her sense of attack, and her passion.

When the other kids were listening to Elvis Presley, Barbara was listening to her favorite male singer Johnny Mathis, with his smooth and technically splendid and otherworldly voice. When she was eleven years old Diana slapped her and Barbara pretended to be deaf for four hours, and Diana believed her, and this let Barbara know that she could act. She began suffering from tinnitus, a constant ringing in her ears where she heard the most high-range, high-pitch noises, and this set her further apart.

At fifteen the ambitious Barbara was playing in summer-stock productions in Albany, and at sixteen she graduated from Erasmus Hall High School and immediately tried to get any job she could in the New York theater. Barbara wanted to be a serious actress, and she took method acting classes. When she didn't have a place to stay, she would bring her army cot and sleep at the apartments of friends. Back in Brooklyn, Diana fretted about her daughter, and she always tried to make sure Barbara was getting enough to eat.

"I didn't like the reality of my life," she said later. "I felt like I knew certain truths. I wanted to be able to express my feelings and have people see themselves and feel that they could identify with me . . . I remember feeling as if I were chosen. I can't be specific, but I could feel people's minds, like I knew the truth, I could see the truth."

Barbara met a young actor named Barry Dennen when they were doing an experimental play together, and they grew very close. Gradually Barbara got herself a small entourage, like Frank had, but her entourage was gay guys, not wise guys: Dennen, who played her records of female vocalists like Billie and Ruth Etting and Edith Piaf after he heard her sing; Robert Schulenberg, who spent hours with her working on her makeup; and Terry Leong, who helped design her wardrobe out of thrift shop finds.

"Bob was the artist and he would always draw my face," she acknowledged as an older woman. "He was the only one, in a sense, who thought I was so beautiful when other people were calling me kooky and strange-looking or odd-looking. The way he drew and shadowed my face is what taught me how to put on make-up."

Dennen was enthralled by Barbara, who soon shortened her name to Barbra to make it more distinctive, and they had a love affair of some kind that was cut short when she caught him with another man. Dennen genuinely loved Barbra, and so he had tried to be straight for her, but of course that didn't work out. Unlike Judy, Barbra never made this mistake again.

Barbra was singing in clubs like the Lion and then the Bon Soir, and when Diana went to see Barbra there she was "just the trifle bit jealous" according to an unidentified friend of Diana's who is quoted in William J. Mann's book about Barbra's early years. Though Diana told Barbra that she was good after the Bon Soir show, she criticized Barbra's wacky clothes and said, "Sometimes the voice was a little thin. Maybe you should see a vocal coach."

Barbra became known nearly at once for the size and volume of her singing voice, and so Diana's comments might seem odd in retrospect, but Diana had been a soprano who took voice seriously, and what she was hearing was so unusual that it likely perplexed her. For Barbra had a kind of trick voice that stunned a lot of people because it suggested vastness in its highest register without actually being expansive and supported in the accepted ways. When a young Stephen Sondheim was taken to hear Barbra sing, he told his colleague Arthur Laurents that he felt her voice was "too pinched and nasal," and it was sometimes. But what Barbra had in her favor was a unique crystalline purity of tone on certain notes the likes of which had never been heard from any singer before, and a hummingbird vibrato so fast that it was barely a vibrato at all.

Barbra began receiving some good press, and she got herself on TV shows where she played up her image as a kook from Brooklyn who dressed outlandishly. She was on Jack Paar's television program when Parr himself was away, and Barbra sang "A Sleepin' Bee" with more conventional Diana-like soprano high notes. When Paar came back to his show, Diana was mortified after he made a crack about "that Barbra Streisand" that implied that Barbra was ugly, and Diana wrote Paar an angry letter and hoped that Barbra had not seen this particular episode. Part of Diana's tendency to be discouraging of Barbra's career in the beginning was her worry that her daughter would have to hear cruel remarks like this.

Barbra herself worried about her looks to an obsessive degree, which is why she loved spending hours with Robert Schulenberg being transformed into a beauty with winged eyeliner. Dennen knew how insecure Barbra was about her appearance, and so he had taken her to the Brooklyn Museum to see a bust of Queen Nefertiti, to show her a different beauty standard. He told Barbra that she would never be pretty, but that she could be beautiful in her own unconventional way.

When Barbra played at the Blue Angel, columnist Robert Ruark took the long view when he wrote, "She will be around 50 years from now if good songs are still written to be sung by good singers," but a *Variety* reviewer suggested that "a little corrective schnoz bob" might be considered, and so she was always made hyper-aware of her looks, and especially her nose. On a show called *PM East*, Barbra worried about her nose to Judy's old costar Mickey Rooney, who nicely asked, "What's wrong with your nose?" Barbra replied, "It's different."

The Mick said it was "a lovely nose" and even "adorable," but then Barbra pointed at his own nose, which was looking like a drinking man's nose at this point, and said, "How did you ever work?" Rooney started to splutter a bit, and then she said, "It fits W. C. Fields." Barbra was so on the defensive that she could be very tactless, and she was also still a teenager at this time. On another program, she told off producer David Susskind for not giving her a chance. "I scare you," she told him. "I'm so far out, I'm in."

Barbra got her big break when she was cast as secretary Yetta Marmelstein in *I Can Get It for You Wholesale* on Broadway. Myths have sprung up through the years that she was belligerent and difficult even at this early point, but she was mainly scared and determined not to show it. There have been many different versions of how she decided to use a chair on wheels for her showstopping number "Miss Marmelstein," and the most likely is that it was the idea of assistant director Herbert Ross, a key Barbra collaborator, but Ross let her think that it was her idea. Barry Dennen also took credit for it in his touching but sometimes unreliable 1997 memoir about their time together.

In April of 1962, Barbra was taken to see Judy record an album to be called *Judy Takes Broadway* with Mort Lindsey at the Manhattan Center. Barbra was not familiar with Judy, and this makes sense because Judy was largely inactive when Barbra was growing up, aside from *A Star Is Born* and live performances. Judy started at midnight, and she was hoarse and finally had to stop, and so Barbra was not impressed, but she did take notice of Lindsey and how supportive he was of Judy.

"Am I out of the spotlight?" Barbra asks in a live recording of her act when she was back at the Bon Soir. "I'll never be out of the spotlight," she says cutely, and she sure means it. Barbra uses her real pain over her breakup with Barry Dennen for "Cry Me a River," where she is the underdog out for vengeance, very "I'll show you" and "Listen to *this*."

This Bon Soir recording really captures the electricity of Barbra's live performing at this time, and there are audience cries of encouragement as she sings, as if they know they are seeing something very special. She is most comfortable high up in her own particular stratosphere of ultra-pure high notes and less secure on the shaky lower notes, but she is able to seize up this voice of hers to growl certain words for intimidating effect.

It took a lot of wheeling and dealing from her management to finally get Barbra in to do a studio album in 1963, for Columbia head Goddard Lieberson felt that she was a cult singer who would likely appeal only to a small group of gay cognoscenti and not the general public. Thirteen seconds of near silence go by before she starts to sing the first track "Cry Me a River" almost a cappella, and forty-four seconds go by before any strings begin to accompany her, and this underlines her sense of drama. She has said that she wanted her breaths to be heard on the album, and this could not have pleased breath-fetishist Frank.

Barbra sings the old Depression anthem "Happy Days Are Here Again," which she had performed in a dramatic skit on *The Garry Moore Show*, and does a deliberately strained super-high note at the end that she later regretted. She does old songs, retro songs, camp songs, and she does them lovingly, for this was the sensibility of her gay coterie. Barbra doesn't care about sounding pretty on this first album. Her vibe is "Take it and like it, buster," with aggressively crisp final consonants on words, and her urge is to be grand, theatrical, epic. She is an acquired taste.

Barbra made more TV appearances and had to skip a prospective show with Bing because she was so overbooked. She did four Harold Arlen songs for her second album, and her "Any Place I Hang My Hat Is Home" could not be more different from Bing's. Barbra's version is volatile, dangerous, and show-offy, and she does a riff like you wouldn't believe on the word "is" when she reprises this song at the end of the album. She also does a big daring high note beyond a high note at the end of the torch song "When the Sun Comes Out," which Judy had also been performing but never in this gobsmacking way. As singing maven Seth Rudetsky has pointed out, Barbra's authority is so total that on "Like a Straw in the Wind" she even switches a final consonant on the word "apart" and makes it "apard" just because she likes that sound better at that moment.

Barbra's whole thing is, I'm not trained, I've never had a singing lesson, so maybe you, too, misfit/outcast, might open your mouth and this huge crazy sound could come out and you'll show *them*; you'll conquer the world. Barbra did actually go to a vocal coach named Judy Davis at this time when she was having a bit of vocal trouble at a San Francisco gig, but only briefly.

She played at the Cocoanut Grove in Hollywood, where Bing had made his name thirty years before, and her new management Freddie Fields and David Begelman sent four limos to meet her at the airport. Begelman took Judy to see Barbra perform, most likely not at the Cocoanut Grove but at Harrah's in Lake Tahoe, and Judy was stunned by Barbra's voice, as so many people were. Since they shared the same management, it was thought that Barbra should appear at some point on Judy's new TV show.

Though Judy very much wanted this show to work, she was averse to rehearsing, and that lack of rehearsal shows on the first taped episode where Mickey Rooney guest-stars and they lightly send up their old MGM pictures, with Rooney parodying the way his characters would ignore and exploit her; this is a kind of exorcism for them. Judy looked at her very best in this period with snazzy clothes by Ray Aghayan, a mouth made big by lipstick and heavy eye shadow by makeup artist Gene Hibbs, and sculptured hair creations by Orval that she usually made a dramatic mess of as she sang.

The Judy Garland Show was a Kennedy-Camelot TV series, full of hope and a sophisticated insider tone, but with Jerry Van Dyke trying and miserably failing to be funny as Judy's sidekick, so we can't have everything. To her credit, Judy always looked very encouraging with Van Dyke, even as he ruined her program time and again.

Judy's strength was her singing, and so the episodes of her TV show would always end with a mini-concert that found her standing next to the trunk she was supposed to have been born in; she would tell a story and then offer a number or two. On the first episode Judy does the ballad "Too Late Now" and then goes right into "Who Cares?" and does a memorably wide-eyed face of skepticism after singing the line "Life is one long jubilee," as if to say, "Oh, really?" She is so open to her lyrics now that sometimes they take her by surprise.

Judy sings "Ol' Man River" at the end of this first episode, and the suits at CBS hated this choice; they wanted her to sing "Over the Rainbow," but Judy was insistent. She lived and breathed show business, but she was aware of what was happening in America with the civil rights movement. On September 16, 1963, Judy called a press conference to draw attention to the murder of four young Black girls in a KKK bombing of a church in Birmingham, Alabama, and at this conference a fund was started for money to pay hospital bills and funeral expenses for the victims.

She takes a moment to prepare before starting "Ol' Man River," and then she leads us through each image of it, keeping her face totally open so that each one can hit her and hit us. When the camera switches to a lower angle, the lighting is harsher, and Judy looks much older and worn down as she sings, "I get weary, and sick of trying . . . I'm tired of living

Judy sings "Ol' Man River" on her TV show.

and scared of dying." This is Judy herself singing, "I'm tired of living and scared of dying," and no one ever meant that more than she did.

By the end of this "Ol' Man River," Judy is hurling out the notes and letting her vibrato buffet her as if she is standing at the bow of a ship in a storm, and the power of her voice has the impact of a scream of anguish. Judy has taken in the pain of others and related it to the pain she herself feels, not in a self-centered way, but in a way that sees the pain from some great height of objectivity—that's what great art can do. She is just untouchable here.

Judy throws her mic cord over her shoulder in the second episode where she sings with Count Basie's band and swings very acceptably, and she even does a dance with her dancers, for this show was real variety or vaudeville, and top of the line in most ways. When Judy spoke on her TV program, her hushed dithering sounded gentle and detached, but watch out, darling, there might be a knife in it.

At the end of this episode, Judy stops everything cold with "A Cottage for Sale," immersing herself in every moment of this very sad song yet delivering it with a strange sort of lightness that is entirely hers and entirely new. Her performance here is stark and pure—dry, hushed, with no self-pity—and she does a sharp intake of breath at the end as she sings her last "A cottage . . ." and then "for sale."

After killing us dead with that ballad, Judy goes right into the upbeat and tongue-twisting "Hey, Look Me Over," which she sells even though she isn't too certain of the tightly packed lyrics. The show closes with a tune her father and mother used to sing in vaudeville, "I Will Come Back," which Judy always ended with a different name; on this second episode she goes the high camp route and claims, "Mary Miles Minter was a cousin of mine!" Minter was a silent-movie star involved in the scandal surrounding the unsolved murder of director William Desmond Taylor in 1922, and so this was a fairly obscure reference thrown out to her loyal gay audience, whose culture she had always been steeped in.

Judy's daughter Liza guest-stars on the third taped episode, and Judy kills again with her rendition of "As Long as He Needs Me" at the end of the show, judging every moment so sensitively and carefully and embracing herself at the end. All these personal-best performances of songs on The Judy Garland Show form the foundation of Judy's legend as a great singer.

Lena Horne was not happy that Judy didn't want to rehearse when Horne guest-starred on the fourth episode, but they worked up a rapport anyway. Judy is especially winning after Horne does "Meet Me in St. Louis" in her own particular way and Judy cries, "I didn't know it was a sexy song!" Judy was dating the ultra-studly Glenn Ford when she did her series, and he would sometimes come to watch her perform, and surely this was part of the reason why she was so moved to be in the zone for this show.

Judy took in all of her guests on her series and encouraged them to be as eccentric, zany, and intense as they wanted to be. It feels as if she wants to reach all of them on the most intimate level, and there is something very orgiastic about this. She was the opposite of show business phony, and that's actually what bothered CBS executives, who told her to stop physically touching her guests so much.

Episode 6 turned out disastrously, partly because there was too much drinking in the dressing room with guest star June Allyson, who is very clearly wasted when conversing with her hostess. Judy tells a story about L. B. Mayer and how he used to sing "Ah! Sweet Mystery of Life" for her and cry "steel tears," but she'd tell him it was marvelous every time: "No character at all," Judy says of herself. When she does the special-material opening to "San Francisco" that references Jeanette MacDonald, the word "Jeanette" comes out as a tuneless croak, and even the camera seems drunk, lurching at one point to find her. Judy finally winds up in the fetal position on the floor of the stage, pounding it with her fist.

This sixth program showed that Judy was an artist who couldn't do filler episodes, and she couldn't be great all the time; instead of finding a way to professionally coast through, she fragmented. In a way, *The Judy Garland Show* replays her ordeal at MGM in miniature with too much expected of her again, the medium of television using up her genius and then tossing her aside afterward. Bing had conquered all media in his heyday, but by the 1960s when radio was finished and he couldn't get many parts in films, he looked on television with apprehension. He felt that this particular medium gave the audience too much of a performer and eventually ruined them with overexposure.

Episodes 7 and 8 of *The Judy Garland Show* were similarly troubled, but on episode 9 a young Barbra guest-starred, and this would turn out to be an epochal meeting between one great singer on the way up and another on the way down. Judy's friend Tucker Fleming said that Judy was "nervous and anxious and jealous" waiting for Barbra to arrive on the set, partly because she was "very aware of how she looked" next to the younger singer.

"Can I replace you?" Barbra almost immediately asks Judy on this episode, and this is one of many sorry attempts by the writers to knock Judy down a peg, which was supposed to appeal to television audiences and make their star seem more human or down to earth. Barbra herself seems very nervous here, and Jerry Van Dyke's "comedy" is particularly painful, but once Judy and Barbra start to sing, this program becomes historic.

Barbra does "Bewitched, Bothered, and Bewildered" with lingering pure high notes, and then she does an angry, arrogant, and commanding "Down with Love," which Judy had tried on record. Barbra is nothing at all like Judy except in the bigness of her sound. For all her skittish laughter here, she is clearly a tough character at age twenty-one, whereas the middle-aged Judy is a leaf in the wind.

It was Judy's idea to do a duet with Barbra and sing her own signature "Get Happy" while Barbra did "Happy Days Are Here Again." When they sit down to do this duet, Judy smiles hard and really takes in a note that Barbra snarls, and their voices are thrilling together, but Judy can barely keep up; she is being overtaken, and she knows it. Judy is so open and unprotected on this TV show that her nerve endings are practically visible, whereas Barbra is so guarded that she might as well be carrying out a military operation when she sings.

"Don't you enjoy singing, doesn't it get all the rage out of you?" Judy asks Barbra during a teatime interlude, and this highlights another crucial difference between them. Barbra actually didn't enjoy singing; she still wanted to be a straight serious actress. Barbra had this extravagant singing voice, and she wanted to be noticed and she wanted to be a star, so she sang. Certainly Barbra puts a lot of rage into "Cry Me a River," and there is always anger somewhere beneath the surface with her, but it is not something she flings out at us like Judy does. She keeps it in check, or in reserve.

Barbra gets very stiff and flummoxed when Ethel Merman walks on for a brief guest shot with them and Judy allows Merman to take over. Barbra timidly speaks of getting the role of Fanny Brice in the Broadway musical of *Funny Girl*, a star-making part that she had steadily worked to secure for a very long and frustrating time, and Judy says to the Merm, "Watch your dressing room, and so forth."

Judy and Barbra sit on stools to do a medley together toward the end of the episode, and this is where they really interact in a profound way. When Judy starts "After You've Gone," Barbra is moved to say, "Pretty, pretty," as if she is genuinely impressed, for there is nothing showbiz phony about Barbra either. Barbra may sometimes be scared or overwhelmed on this show, but she also has a killer instinct that Judy never remotely had. Compared to Barbra, Judy really is the waif exploited by others that she liked to paint herself as.

When Barbra starts "How About You?" in their medley, Judy sees that Barbra's hair keeps covering her face, and so she very gently brushes it aside, a maternal gesture that is very touching. After Judy joins in and sings, "I like a Gershwin or Arlen tune," Barbra really laughs in response, disarmed a bit, maybe, because she feels that Judy has helped her out and isn't an enemy. This episode of her TV show doesn't feature Judy at her best as a performer, necessarily, but it does feature Judy at her best as a person.

Judy is a great audience member as she watches Barbra sing, doing everything possible to set her up and set her off well. As Barbra sings her up-tempo "Lover, Come Back to Me," Judy watches her very closely and lovingly and even starts to mouth the words a little because she is so deeply immersed in Barbra's performance and in love with her talent; there is nothing competitive about it.

Barbra does a silly laugh that she then youthfully reneges on, and this makes Judy laugh very hard, and then Barbra is thrilled when Judy unleashes her full voice for "You and the Night and the Music," crying out "Hey!" and "Yeah!" and mouthing "Wow" as Judy sings, and Barbra even lets out a little cry of pleasure when Judy finishes her last held note. This is all particularly wonderful because Barbra is clearly someone who does not thrill easily.

Duetting on "It All Depends on You," Barbra sings, "You're to blame, Judy, for what I do," and mimes shooting herself in the head, and this is Barbra, who never seriously considered suicide, doing this next to Judy, who tried to kill herself over and over again. Barbra explicitly rejected the sentiment of "It All Depends on You" verbally in a concert in 1994, mocking it, which means that she had moved far past the way Billie and Judy looked at life. But Judy gets to Barbra and really connects with her on *The Judy Garland Show*. At the end of their medley, Barbra even leans her head on Judy's shoulder, and again, she is not a touchy-feely person like Judy is.

As Judy continued doing episodes of her show, she started to seem heroic, and she also seemed alive in a way that few people ever are, hyperalert to stimuli. She had such stamina at this point; she was able to do a swelling song like "Through the Years" like nobody's business, all buildup to a big finish and then more buildup to an even bigger finish. TV Judy is a party animal who is pro-adventure and anti-boredom, and

Judy and Barbra connect on *The Judy Garland Show*.

she was inspired by Barbra's version of "Down with Love" to do her own competitive version on episode 12, singing it in a way that is both mordant and hopeful, without anger.

Judy did a Christmas episode with her children and sang "Over the Rainbow" at the end of it, but this was hardly a relatable family to please the CBS execs. After the Kennedy assassination, a tearful Judy insisted on singing a very raw "Battle Hymn of the Republic," and the network higher-ups were growing more impatient with her. When Martha Raye guest-stars on episode 18 and clowns it up, Judy looks very unhappy, as if she knows her days are numbered. She was giving her all every time she sang on her TV show and when she interacted with nearly all of her guests, offering the greatness of her perfected art, but all CBS wanted was a semi-classy cookie-cutter variety program to sell Contac cold tablets.

When she knew for certain that her show had been canceled, Judy started doing straight concerts in order to save money. She does her best-ever bongo-frenzy "Come Rain or Come Shine" on episode 21, getting a wave of applause even at the beginning and giving a little laugh at her own audacity after she does a barely controlled Dionysian finish that must have wreaked some havoc on her vocal cords, which often stand out thickly in her neck as she sends out her vibrating walls of sound. There is a sense on *The Judy Garland Show* sometimes that Judy is singing from the throat in a very heedless way rather than from the diaphragm, as if she can't be bothered with protecting her instrument and wants to gamble with it to see how many times she can win big.

On episode 22, which is maybe the best single episode of her TV series, Judy does her finest ever "Almost Like Being in Love," and after she sings the words "Glad I'm alive," she touchingly closes her eyes quickly as if to say, "Sure, why not?" Her conductor Mort Lindsey follows her lead with real stamina of his own, playing various instruments for each of her songs and always going the extra mile with the detailed arrangements. Judy does some of the tunes from her old Palace act, and she has far more control over them than she did in the 1950s.

By episode 23, Judy has started getting a little manic again, as if she knows she's really running out of time, and how many songs does she have for us that she can do or do again? The only performer whose repertoire was so vast that she could have gotten away with doing an hour-long concert every week on television was Ella, and Ella couldn't even get herself a TV special.

On episode 25, Judy enters jazz territory to do a song Sarah Vaughan had made her own, "Poor Butterfly," with a jazz pianist named Robert Cole, and she dramatically sings this tune near his accompaniment but not with it. She doesn't respond musically to his backing but keeps her performance separate from it, and this is a key moment that illustrates the difference between Judy and Ella as singers.

Judy does an Ella favorite, "The Nearness of You," on the last episode of *The Judy Garland Show*, employing dynamics very effectively, and then she sweeps up two very pretty new tunes for herself, "Time After Time" and "That Old Feeling," as if she has an Ella-like impulse to collect them before it's too late. Judy really blows out her voice again by singing from the throat on "Carolina in the Morning," and when she does "Almost Like Being in Love" again and gets to that line, "Glad I'm alive," this time she sadly lowers her eyes as if to signal, "Not really."

Judy looks into the camera at us on her TV show.

Judy tried to do the highly dramatic June Christy signature number "Something Cool" for her show but had to abandon it, and a lengthy clown pantomime number she had worked on also had to be abandoned. In the outtakes for Judy's series she is nice, funny, and apologetic with her crew if she screws something up, but when she sings "Here's to Us" in her clown outfit as a last song for the final episode, Judy is very bitter yet defiant.

Judy had given her best to this TV series; she had given her genius even. And it was not appreciated. It was not enough. Nothing was ever enough for the suits at MGM or CBS or for the public, most of whom saw her now as a fallen star who was always getting bad press. Yet in retrospect *The Judy Garland Show* is Judy's greatest triumph because the best songs from it can be endlessly shared online, and no one has to bother looking at any of the painful Jerry Van Dyke comic sidekick stuff.

On the evening that Judy taped the last episode of her show, her managers Freddie Fields and David Begelman were at the opening night of *Funny Girl* to see their new client Barbra, who had released a very beautiful all-ballad third album in 1963. A post-Billie Ray Ellis did some work on the arrangements along with her regular arranger Peter Matz, and there is a very pretty harpsichord backing for "Just in Time" that quotes some Bach for its intro. Barbra has found a new focus and control here, with far more supported low notes to go with the eerily pure high notes.

The verse for "It Had to Be You" on this third album sounds particularly like *buttah*, and her version of Frank Loesser's "Never Will I Marry" has all her declarative force and defiance. But Barbra herself had married Elliott Gould, the honey-bear-like star of *I Can Get It for You Wholesale*, and his career stalled while hers was steadily rising, yet he tried to handle this gracefully.

Barbra and her team, led by her selfless champion of a personal manager Marty Erlichman, had worked tirelessly to get her that lead in *Funny Girl*, but once she finally landed the opportunity to play Judy's old costar Fanny Brice there were many problems in rehearsal. Her director Garson Kanin was of so little help to her that Barbra was forced to look to her old acting teacher Alan Miller, who agreed to work with her on the role. Barbra got her friend Peter Daniels a job as a musical director on *Funny Girl*, and she was not happy when she found out that Daniels was having an affair with her understudy Lainie Kazan.

There was often more drama during the *Funny Girl* rehearsals than there was onstage, but Barbra kept her eye on the prize through it all. Finally director and choreographer Jerome Robbins was brought back to the project to get it into shape for the Broadway opening, and Barbra responded immediately to Robbins and loved working on new scenes every night.

Barbra was tough. When she felt bullied by Kanin or by Ray Stark, the producer who was married to Brice's daughter Fran, she was capable of saying "Fuck you" in her dressing room to both of them because she knew her worth. She was very young and not too experienced, and these were seasoned older show business guys, but this did not matter. Barbra never showed the dimmest respect to her elders. Nothing could throw her, and she even thrived on the chaos of this production.

Diana went to see her daughter open in Philadelphia. "Roslyn and I had seats in the first row, center—seats anyone would have loved," she said. "But I was so nervous before the show—I seemed to feel everything that I knew Barbra was going through. I was so overwhelmed that I just couldn't sit still. I had to leave my first-row seat, and stand in the back of the theater. As I heard Barbra singing, I got emotional. She was so terrific it upset my balance—my feelings just welled up in me. I felt fearful for her and excited and proud—all at the same time."

When *Funny Girl* opened on Broadway, Barbra was everything she needed to be, giving a performance that wowed the whole town and the whole industry. She displayed all of her talents here, both comic and dramatic, and she sang with that huge and distinctive voice—this was Making It Big and being noticed in the biggest way. Though she was still in her early twenties, Barbra had been working toward this goal since she was sixteen years old, and that's a time in life when every day feels like an eternity.

A lengthy *Life* magazine profile of Barbra after her triumph on Broadway claimed that Frank sent her a letter that read, "You were magnificent. I love you." The magazine said that she was "a born loser," but now she was supposedly Cinderella. "Ugly duckling sang her way to wealth," read the crude cover line of an Australian women's magazine. She was the American dream. Kay Medford, who played Fanny's mother in *Funny Girl*, spoke of the difference between Judy and Barbra. "Judy, you felt sorry for," Medford said. "This one, you stand back in awe."

The cast album of *Funny Girl*, which was recorded shortly after the show opened, features plodding tempos for the now well-known songs, something that Barbra rightly complained about. The song "Who Taught Her Everything?" has Fanny's friends and family members afraid that they will be abandoned after Fanny has become a Ziegfeld star onstage, and this relates directly to the way Barbra herself no longer needed some people who had helped her on the way up. There were personal reasons for cutting off her first boyfriend Barry Dennen, but Robert Schulenberg and Terry Leong found themselves similarly edged out of her social circle.

Her album *People* (1964), which features the hit ballad from *Funny Girl*, is all show-off stuff, and bombastic if you will, but almost all of it is glorious, especially a "How Does the Wine Taste?" with castanet backing. The one misstep is Irving Berlin's "Supper Time," which Judy had tried on her TV show; shorn of its racial context, it is just a dramatic number that is not suited to either of them in any way. Barbra does "Will He Like Me?" from *She Loves Me*, which was originated by soprano Barbara Cook, a great singer who said late in life that she found Barbra's singing "too studied."

Barbra already had her detractors, and Frank was not actually a fan of Barbra at first. His valet George Jacobs wrote that Barbra's singing "drove him completely around the bend" and that Frank thought that Barbra was "too phony, too forced, too theatrical, rubbing her Brooklyn-ness in your face," whereas Frank took pains never to sound like Hoboken when he sang.

Her manager Marty Erlichman spoke about a party where Barbra was about to be introduced to Frank and how nervous she was: "What will I say to him?" Barbra asked. She was brought over to Frank, and they spoke briefly, and Frank sat her down as if they were going to talk, but then he went away for a moment, and when he returned, Barbra stood up, and it was all very awkward. "I think I goofed," Barbra told Erlichman.

Truman Capote started out as a fan of her early club performances, but he eventually spoke out about Barbra's larger-than-life excessiveness in regard to his song "A Sleepin' Bee," which he wrote the lyrics for. "Streisand's great fault as a singer, as far as I'm concerned, is that she takes every ballad and turns it into a three-act opera. She simply cannot leave a song alone."

A superstar now, Barbra took a swanky apartment that overlooked Central Park. As an older woman, Barbra said that Judy came to see her sometimes in this period of her first major success. Barbra did her best to avoid the small-minded negativity of her own mother Diana but she often sought out or welcomed mother figures in her life, most notably her best friend Cis Corman.

"She used to visit me and give me advice," Barbra said of Judy. "She'd come to my apartment in New York, and she said to me, 'Don't let them do to you what they did to me.' I didn't know what she meant then. I was just getting started."

32

Ella and Frank

ELLA FINALLY LANDED herself a real part in a movie called *Let No Man Write My Epitaph* (1960), an ensemble picture in which she plays Flora, a saloon singer and pianist who becomes a drug addict. The camera loves Ella's sweet and sad face, and she rises to her Big Scene where drug kingpin Ricardo Montalbán roughs her up because she doesn't want to be a pusher of narcotics. Ella doesn't try to "act" in this scene but simply puts herself into the situation and lets genuine emotions of hurt and fear come to the surface.

Ella appeared on Edward R. Murrow's noted interview program *Person to Person* and seemed very nervous but soldierlike as she showed off some of her autograph collection, including one from Frank that read, "Ella, thanks for waiting so long for this." Norman Granz sent her out on a European tour and recorded a live set in Berlin in 1960, which was when Ella tried out "Mack the Knife" and forgot the words and then winningly came up with some of her own on the spot: "You won't recognize it / It's a surprise, it!" This daredevil save of a performance was released as a single and it became an unlikely hit for Ella, and so "Mack the Knife" was a tune that was added to her shows from then on as a surefire crowd-pleaser.

In 1961 Ella did a two-volume Harold Arlen songbook with Billy May as her arranger, and she went all out on a lusty seven-minute version of "Blues in the Night," coming as close to belting as she ever would on record. Ella is extremely stimulated on this set by May's brassy horn

Ella in *Let No Man Write My Epitaph* (1960).

excursions and also by these Arlen melodies; this is one of the jazzier songbooks, and she sounds like she's having the time of her life. Best of all, Ella was born to sing the Arlen and Mercer "Ac-Cent-Tchu-Ate the Positive," which goes some way toward wiping out the sting of Bing's original.

Ella also tackled three Judy songs here: "Get Happy," which of course suits her perfectly; "The Man That Got Away," which she manages to make her own; and "Over the Rainbow," which she didn't want to sing because it was too associated with Judy. Ella finally agreed to do it, but she was unhappy about it, and yet of course it's an ideal song for her, too, and she fills it with childlike yearning and a touch of pain, plus a tiny bit of vibrato for the last note that could be taken as a kind of calling out to Judy.

Ella had become involved with a younger Danish man in 1961, and this worked out happily for her for a time; she took an apartment in Copenhagen and he was her live-in boyfriend. Perhaps inspired by this new lover, Ella recorded a very sexy and intimate album called *Clap Hands, Here Comes Charlie!* with a jazz quartet led by Lou Levy, and she really commits to "You're My Thrill" and "My Reverie," sings in a very high register on "Stella by Starlight," and ends a tune called "Signing Off" with a very long sustained note with no vibrato. She does Billie's "Good Morning Heartache" on this record with simple yearning, for Ella does know about heartbreak, but she treats it lightly.

In a recording of her act at the Crescendo club in Hollywood in 1961, Ella asks, "Can I have a sexy light for this one?" and then she says, "It doesn't help, but anyway . . ." This is a rare instance of Ella revealing her insecurities in performance, but she was sexy for anyone who cared to look deeply at who she was, as Louis did when he called her his "buxom belle" when they sang together.

The five hours or so of these concerts in Hollywood show that Ella's repertoire was so capacious that she could do show after show and she didn't need to repeat songs; how did she remember all of them? Ella references Frank a lot here, both in her patter and in lyrics, and before she does "Good Morning Heartache" she says it was "made popular by the late Miss Billie Holiday." It was as if Ella had become a one-person museum of song and singers, an institution, a sumptuous library of popular music that you can spend all day in.

Ella recorded two albums with Nelson Riddle in 1962, and they both feature Ella the Technician, the impersonal Ella that people sometimes complain about, keeping herself interested in songs she had done before with slight rhythmic variations in the phrasing. Norman Granz came to a session for their second album and said, "Ella's singing so badly tonight she's about ready to record with Sinatra."

But in 1963 Ella recorded one of her best albums with Riddle, a Jerome Kern songbook on which they outdo themselves for a stealthy, building "All the Things You Are" that stands with "Blue Skies" on her Irving Berlin songbook as perhaps the finest single track Ella ever recorded; particularly thrilling is the way Ella holds back on the words "some day" while also somehow making them swell hopefully, and then the nearly masculine swagger she brings to her last "some day." Kern was the premier melodist among American songwriters of his time, and Ella was ready to lavish all of her mature artistry on some of the best Kern melodies, especially on her very soulful "Why Was I Born?"

The reality of segregation in America began to make things difficult for Ella as she kept up her constant round of live performances. She had been touring in Europe, and Ella kept getting asked questions about the civil rights movement and what was happening in the South, so many questions and so often that she finally felt moved to speak on this subject to interviewer Fred Robbins, calling the racial situation in America "really pitiful."

"Maybe I'm stepping out, but I have to say it because it's in my heart," Ella told Robbins. "It makes you feel so bad that we can't go down through certain parts of the South and give a concert like we do overseas and have everybody just come to hear the music, enjoy the music, because of the prejudice thing that's going on. I used to always clam up, because you say, 'Gee, show people should stay out of politics,' but we have traveled so much and been embarrassed so much, they don't understand why you don't play in Alabama, why can't you have a concert. Music is music."

Speaking of the generational divide among white bigots, Ella said, "The die-hards, they're going to just die hard, they're never going to give in. You've got to try to convince the younger ones. They're the ones who've got to make the future, and they're the ones we have to worry about, not those die-hards." She stopped talking then and cried, "I really ran my mouth now! You think they're going to break my records?" The interview, which was meant for radio, never aired in 1963, but it has survived. Speaking to her colleague Tony Bennett about racial prejudice in America, she said simply, "Tony, we're all here."

An album called *These Are the Blues* (1963) proved that though Ella had a right to sing the blues, they just weren't her thing. By the time she did a record called *Hello, Dolly!* (1964), Ella was eyeing the changing market for pop with a cover of the Beatles song "Can't Buy Me Love." That same year, Ella and Nelson Riddle did a Johnny Mercer album, which was her last official songbook, partly because the market for this kind of album was beginning to close down.

Ella really digs into Mercer's very elaborate and extreme wording here, Billie-style, and this pays off especially on "Midnight Sun," where she weighs each of the many fancy words like "alabaster palace" and "aurora borealis" and places them perfectly, with Riddle's vibraphone notes descending behind her like the stars she sings of. Best of all on this record is a very deeply felt "I Remember You" with verse, a worthy tribute to the stormy love between Mercer and Judy that inspired it. Ella was not only a museum of song but also of singers, and in this period she did a lot of melodic talking to both the lost Billie and the broken Judy.

"For Sidney Poitier I whistle and stamp!" Ella sings on "The Lady Is a Tramp" in her 1964 concert in Juan-les-Pins, France, where the noise of crickets amuses her greatly and even inspires her to sing an impromptu song to them. "When I stop, they stop, that's what's funny!" she cries, but Ella could handle any audience reaction, even insect. She did sometimes get annoyed by Roy Eldridge and his star trumpeter solos behind her, which did not fit smoothly into her act, but Norman Granz had hired him and so she felt she had to put up with it.

Ella's closest rival Frank was seeking more control of his recording career by 1960. When Capitol wouldn't give him the financial deal he wanted to produce his own records, Frank set about finishing off his contract with them so that he could start his own company, Reprise. He collaborated with Nelson Riddle on *Nice 'n' Easy* (1960), on which he was in great voice and had some songs that very much suited him like "That Old Feeling" and "How Deep Is the Ocean?" But he rushed through *Sinatra's Swingin' Session!!!* (1961) with Riddle so that most of the tracks were just over two minutes or under, and Riddle later called it "a disaster" because Frank took all the tunes twice as fast as they were written just to screw over Capitol Records.

When Elvis came out of the army, Frank grudgingly had the younger singer on his TV show, and he looked like a square next to Elvis—the past, corny—so that he was fighting for continued relevance on all fronts. Rock 'n' roll was a threat to his eminence, but Frank had his mind on many other things. He and Judy both went to meet Nikita Khrushchev when the Russian leader visited Hollywood in 1960, but Bing pointedly did not.

Frank was now set on securing political power, and so he focused on aiding the presidential campaign of John F. Kennedy, who was eager to meet as many beautiful women as Frank could find for him. Among these was Judith Campbell, a party girl who spent time with Frank, JFK, and Sam Giancana, the head of the Chicago mob and a psychopathic killer who was always an honored guest for Frank.

There was a party in November of 1960 at Frank's place in Palm Springs that JFK attended that sounds like an orgy of sorts, the sort of event that was a specialty of Frank's songwriter right-hand man Jimmy Van Heusen. Meanwhile JFK's brother Bobby Kennedy was going after the mob, and in hearings on TV Bobby openly mocked Giancana. So Frank was playing a dangerous game here with these powerful figures, and he was really playing with fire with Giancana, who could have easily had him killed.

Peter Lawford, the snaky brother-in-law of JFK, was now a member of the Rat Pack who was liked by no one but kept around for the family connection. Key Rat Pack member Sammy Davis Jr. idolized Frank, and he loved and he hated him, and he hated him. Davis happily campaigned for Kennedy, and Ella attended an important fundraiser for JFK that Frank organized, and Judy was also out there campaigning for the youngish presidential hopeful, who had most of the best of show business on his side. When Mississippi delegates booed Davis at another JFK fundraiser, Frank took him aside and gave him a pep talk, but being Davis in the Rat Pack was never going to be easy.

Norman Granz made it known that he thought Frank didn't push back hard enough over racism in Las Vegas, where Davis and Ella and Lena Horne and other Black artists weren't allowed to eat in the restaurants where they performed, or stay in the hotels. Davis wasn't even allowed in the steam room at the Sands Hotel, which Frank had a financial interest in.

On the night of the presidential election, Frank was very much Dolly's son, trying to get Nixon on the phone to get him to concede. After JFK won, Frank put together a top-of-the-line entertainment for the inauguration, and he flew Ella in from Australia for the event, where she was to sing "Too Close for Comfort." This was meant to be a reference to the close election results, which had been secured by Giancana's influence in Chicago.

Davis was disinvited from the inaugural because he had married a white actress named May Britt, and the Kennedy campaign, led by JFK's openly racist father Joe, did not want it to seem as if the new president approved of interracial marriage. Some of the Black musicians like Buddy Collette and Joe Comfort were put up in a motel in Maryland.

No amount of access or success could appease Frank's insecurities, or the disapproving way that Bobby Kennedy and Jacqueline Kennedy looked at him. After a drunken argument with Desi Arnaz about the TV show *The Untouchables*, which Arnaz produced and which Frank felt made Italians look bad, Frank spiraled out of control.

At 4:00 AM, when he arrived at Jimmy Van Heusen's house, Frank took a carving knife from the kitchen and slashed a Norman Rockwell painting of Van Heusen that the songwriter particularly loved. "If you try to fix that or put it back, I will come and blow the fucking wall off," Frank told him. There were two women there, and one of them tried to defuse the situation by complimenting Frank's records. "Why don't you go slash your wrists," he told her, still ashamed that Van Heusen had saved him after his most serious suicide attempt. Like all members of Frank's entourage, Van Heusen put up with the abuse and the drama because of what it meant for his career.

Far worse was to come. On the night of June 30, 1962, at Cal-Neva, a lodge and casino Frank had a financial interest in, a deputy sheriff named Richard Anderson stopped by to pick up his wife Toni. Frank had been involved with Toni, who worked at Cal-Neva, and he got into a fight with Anderson, who punched Frank so hard that he was not able to perform for several days afterward. Frank had Anderson suspended from the police force.

On July 17, Richard and Toni Anderson were driving to dinner when a car coming at high speed forced them off the road and their own car smashed into a tree. Richard was killed instantly, and Toni suffered multiple injuries. The other car didn't stop, and it was never traced. Frank liked to throw his weight around in an "I have friends and you'll sleep with the fishes" way, but it was usually just talk. What actually happened in this situation with Richard and Toni Anderson cannot be known for certain, but it doesn't look good.

Frank was really spreading himself thin as a vocalist. Gone were the days when he would spend eight months trying to get his string quartet record *Close to You* (1958) just right; now he was tossing out album after album for Reprise and trying to finish up what he needed to do for Capitol. Frank slammed through all sorts of strident up-tempo numbers with strained high-note finishes, and the market was soon glutted with Sinatra records, including compilations of old tracks from Capitol.

His old arranger Axel Stordahl was excited to work with Frank again on *Point of No Return* (1962), but since this was Frank's last obligation to Capitol he didn't care about it, which shows especially on an embarrassingly listless and on-the-beat "These Foolish Things." Yet the first eight tracks are very pretty, especially a vulnerable version of Noël Coward's "I'll See You Again" and a "September Song" that features a Billie-ish dying fall on the word "November."

Frank got back in the zone creatively for the all-ballad *Sinatra & Strings* (1962) with arranger Don Costa for Reprise, where he offered his best-ever "Night and Day," relentless yet thoughtful and reflective. He also did a new "All or Nothing at All" with his huge high-note finish from 1939, but this time it is maturely connected vocally rather than the chance-taking of a kid wanting to be noticed. The underrated Costa has a sense of drama that suits Frank very well, and Costa gives an impressive amount of ominous grandeur to "Yesterdays" and Russ Columbo's old signature hit "Prisoner of Love."

There were four other Sinatra albums released on Reprise in 1962, including a program of songs recorded in England after a long tour that he barely got through because his fragile voice was so exhausted, and his three packs of unfiltered Camel cigarettes a day didn't help. On a date with Count Basie, Frank proved totally incapable of playing with rhythm or time like near-effortless Ella.

But he also did one of his best movies, *The Manchurian Candidate* (1962), a vivid and clever political thriller about a presidential assassination in which he plays a brainwashed ex-soldier who sweats and suffers a lot. Frank is vividly himself here, fully involved and in the moment, which is partly why he didn't want to do more than one take of his scenes; he couldn't repeat his effects the way a trained theater actor could. He blinks a lot on-screen, which is especially noticeable when he is listening closely to a scene partner, and this gets across the mental turmoil of his character.

Frank kept sending gifts to JFK, but they were returned, politely and formally. Yet the president was set to make an official visit to Frank's place in Palm Springs on a weekend in March of 1962, and Frank was hugely enthused about this visit, spending all his time planning parties and making sure that everything on his property was perfect and inviting. This was it, this was his entry to real power and influence. This was his very own president.

But then a call came through from Peter Lawford. The president would not be coming. At first Frank thought that the trip had been canceled, but Lawford told him that JFK was still coming to Palm Springs but he wouldn't be staying with Frank. Lawford tried to blame the Secret Service at first, but he finally admitted that Bobby Kennedy was behind it and that Bobby didn't want his brother associating with Frank anymore. Frank smashed the phone he was holding, and then he got Bobby on another phone. When he was done talking to Bobby, Frank smashed that phone as well.

Frank's valet George Jacobs remembered him being "like a little kid" and "nearly in tears." Frank called Lawford again, desperate for a way to somehow fix this or somehow allow himself to at least save face. But then Lawford told Frank that JFK had already secured another place to stay for his trip. "So why didn't you tell me this on the first call?" Frank asked, his face getting redder. Lawford tried to say that Frank had cut him off without giving him a chance. "So where, where?" Frank asked. There was a silence on the other end. And then Lawford said, "He's staying with Bing Crosby."

Jacobs saw Frank drop the phone on the floor. Frank couldn't speak for a while, and he just stared out at the desert and looked like he had been told about a death. Finally Frank told Jacobs what had happened, and his anger started to build, and he started to rant and lose all control. At last he told Jacobs that they were treating him "like a fucking n****r."

Frank had made that tour in the mid-1940s to talk to kids and tell them to stop using words like that, but he himself never stopped using racial slurs. Neither did his mother Dolly, and neither did anyone in his immediate circle. And now he was telling his African American right-hand man George Jacobs that the Irish Bing and the Irish JFK were putting the Italian in his place, just like they used to do in Hoboken. Frank was very aware of the hierarchy of how people looked down on each other, and he hated it, but he also participated in it. His own racism was tied to his capacity for vengeance, and at this moment of high stress, it revealed itself in all its ugliness.

Just how aware Bing was of the full extent of this situation is an open question. He was a Republican by this point, but surely he was happy to welcome a young Irish president, even if it meant Frank was humiliated in the press. What makes this all even more intriguing is that it was during this presidential visit at Bing's ranch in Palm Desert that Frank's former lover Marilyn Monroe spent the night with JFK for the first time. What did staunch Catholic and family man Bing make of this?

Ten years prior Frank had overtaken Bing as the major male American pop singer, and Bing had accepted that gracefully. But when push came to shove socially, Bing was still king. Maybe he was no longer the most admired entertainer in America, but he was still one of the most admired, even if that didn't keep Bing in the steady work that he would have liked.

Bing recorded a disappointing album with Louis in 1960 with a corny vocal chorus, and he starred in another college movie called *High Time* for Blake Edwards, who put Bing into several situations where he was physically tested or might have been physically harmed. In one scene here Bing dresses in female drag for a frat initiation, and the fascinating thing is that he is secure enough in his own masculinity to uninhibitedly explore what it might be like to be an older woman instead of an older man, something Frank could never have done.

Bing really sang out on a Latin-flavored album called *El Señor Bing* (1960), where he was bolstered by some heavy beats behind him courtesy of Billy May, and he did a sing-along album of parlor songs and another Hawaiian album called *Return to Paradise Islands* (1963), which has Nelson Riddle backing and is very pleasing, if nowhere near the artistry of Frank's Riddle albums of the 1950s. Bing even recorded a

country album in 1963, and his aloofness was suited to the lonely songs
he picked for it. Bing was not innovating, but he was holding his place.

A wounded Frank was getting more blunt and impatient on his own
records. When he teamed with Riddle and a very large orchestra for
The Concert Sinatra (1963), his style was bombastic, and he hit some
off-key notes, or what he called "clams," something that Bing and Ella
had put behind them decades before. His version of "Ol' Man River"
with dialect is embarrassing, even worse than his earlier versions, and
particularly unfortunate given Judy's triumphantly empathetic version
of it on her TV show.

On an album dedicated to tunes that had won the Academy Award
for best song, Frank's version of Bing's hit "In the Cool, Cool, Cool
of the Evening" is anything but cool. But he rescued a gorgeous album
recorded in 1961 by Rosemary Clooney and Nelson Riddle in the midst
of a painful affair and put it out on his Reprise label and called it *Love*,
and it is one of the most emotional and romantic records of this time
period.

Frank was seeing dancer Juliet Prowse but still pining for Ava, and
she still pined for him. Ava's friend Claude Terrail remembered hanging
out with her at this time and how she would bring her Frank albums
out: "She would put one of his records on and have a private talk with
him, as he was singing. She would sit and listen and say, 'Yes, yes, I
know . . .' or 'No, don't say that . . . you must forget . . .'"

In mid-1963, Frank and Ava got to talking on the phone and feeling
nostalgic, so much so that she even moved some of her things into his
apartment in New York. But the presence of Sam Giancana in Frank's
life quickly soured Ava on the idea of a reunion. Giancana's longtime
mistress Phyllis McGuire was on an episode of *The Ed Sullivan Show*
that Barbra also made an appearance on, the wholesome-seeming moll
set up against the "kook" from Brooklyn with the stratospheric voice.

In September of 1963, Frank pulled Judy up onstage to sing "The
Birth of the Blues" with members of the Pack at Cal-Neva, but he had to
relinquish his financial interest in that casino after an altercation involving
Sam Giancana in the hotel area made the papers. This was the point when
Frank finally dropped Giancana just as he had been dropped by JFK.

Frank was signing other artists to his Reprise label; resistant to modern pop, he refused to sign rock acts at first and stuck to singers he admired like Jo Stafford, Rosemary Clooney, and some of the Rat Pack. He wanted very much to sign Bing, and he did get Bing to sing on some Broadway musical albums that Reprise put out, but Bing wasn't about to sign just with Frank. He would make lofty guest appearances only.

For a Rat Pack movie called *Robin and the 7 Hoods* (1964), Bing was engaged to play a "special appearance" sort of role, which might have been perceived as a comedown, yet he managed to walk right off with the whole thing. Frank had stopped caring about his movies, and so Bing was happy to pick up the slack, mugging a bit and dispensing tasty vocabulary words like "amanuensis."

It was while they were shooting this picture that John F. Kennedy was assassinated in Dallas. When everyone returned to the set of *Robin and the 7 Hoods*, they shot a number called "Style" with Frank, Dean, and Bing, who doesn't have the high notes for this song but somehow fakes his way through and steals the number just as he steals the movie itself from the vacationing Rat Packers.

In the wake of the Kennedy assassination, Frank hastily put together a patriotic album for Reprise on which he engaged his idol/rival/nemesis Bing to croon as well. Bing does an Irving Berlin song in which he sings, "Take a look in your history book and you'll see why we should be proud," not a line anyone could confidently sing today.

This Frank and Bing record might have made sense in the moment, but it's a real lemon; it was Frank's idea, and Frank was creatively floundering while Bing still coolly had his eye on the ball. They sing a Cahn and Van Heusen song together called "You Never Had It So Good," very insistently but unconvincingly.

The constant drama in Frank's personal life reached another peak when his son Frank Jr. was kidnapped. Frank Jr. had been trying to make a small career of his own as a singer, and he idolized his father, but Frank had never been close to his son, so there was a lot of guilt mixed up in his reaction. Frank Jr. finally managed to escape, and things got more awkward when the press started to suggest that he faked the kidnapping for publicity, which wasn't true.

By the summer of 1964, Frank began to put on weight, and this made him look less vulnerable and more thuggish. He still had photos of Ava all over his house—in the bathroom, in the kitchen, even over his bed—but a very young Mia Farrow was pursuing him. When Frank's Rat Pack compadre Dean Martin hosted an episode of *The Hollywood Palace* on which the Rolling Stones appeared, Martin outright mocked them and rolled his eyes after they performed, but rock 'n' roll was clearly more than a fad now.

In a splashy cover story for *Life* magazine in April of 1965, Frank offered an essay titled "Me and My Music." First he takes on Bing, saying that he imitated Bing initially but then determined to be his own kind of singer, and he speaks of his early youthful fan base. "And he (Bing), strangely enough, had appealed primarily to older people, middle-aged people."

There is a section about how he liked to subtly use a microphone: "Many years ago I found that I could take the mike off the stand and move around with it. That's a boon, and so many singers don't take advantage of it." This is when Frank starts in on Ella. "Ella Fitzgerald, poor girl, still doesn't. They set up a mike for her and she never touches it. You can't even see her face."

Frank praises Tony Bennett, condemns Lena Horne as "mechanical," and then moves in for the kill on both Ella and Judy and their bad habit, he felt, of taking a breath in the middle of a phrase. "Technically two of the worst singers in the business," he concludes of Ella and Judy, and this is made worse by a large pull quote on the page that reemphasizes his slam: "Judy and Ella are technically terrible," it reads in large italicized letters.

Whatever Billie happened to be thinking and feeling about Ella in the 1930s and '40s, she never blasted her in print like this. But Ella was now Frank's nearest rival as the finest popular singer of the time, and so attacking her on a point of technique was his way to try to knock her down a notch.

Ella does sometimes take an unnecessary breath during a phrase if she is paying more attention to the melody than the words, which was something that Frank's mentor Billie herself would have scorned. But Ella was recording an enormous amount of material during her Verve period, and so some missteps here and there were inevitable. To attack

Ella's achievement to this point as a whole was unfair of Frank, and attacking Judy at the same time was more than cruel.

Judy had been his lover, and she had sometimes relied on him too much for consolation. She had made a storied comeback at Carnegie Hall and was singing better than she ever had on her TV show, but that series was canceled, and it was looked on as another failure for her then. So Frank was kicking Judy when she was down. Whatever his thoughts on singing correctly, this piece also feels like it partly sprang from Frank's need for vengeance, professional in Ella's case and both personal and professional in Judy's.

Surely Ella read or heard about what Frank had said about her singing in *Life* magazine, and it is easy to imagine the reaction of Norman Granz, who couldn't stand Frank as a person or as a singer. Granz was always wrangling with Frank when he sang with Ella, and Frank had been furious when a deal to buy Granz's Verve Records had fallen through. So in attacking Ella, Frank was also getting back at Granz.

Frank knocks Barbra's song "People" in this *Life* article but refrains from saying anything on what he thought of her singing, which in retrospect was a smart move. Writing of Sarah Vaughan and her extravagant instrument, Frank says he had been "irritated" by her "experimenting" but likes her recent work better, yet he puts his praise curiously: "Sassy is so good now that when I listen to her I want to cut my wrists with a dull razor." He says that he will quit singing himself when "the vibrato starts to widen and the breath starts to give out."

For all his emphasis on technique, Frank was of course capable of technical lapses himself, and he was hitting off-key clams on records even in his prime. His voice is often shaky on *September of My Years* (1965), an "I'm fifty" album done with Gordon Jenkins, and even though Frank is really feeling the schmaltz on this commemorative record, it doesn't matter because the songs are not first-rate schmaltz from his team. He is very specific about the images and people he sings about on the stiff and presentational "It Was a Very Good Year," like a method actor, and the self-pity gets thick.

On a 1965 TV special where Frank is interviewed by Walter Cronkite, Bing turns up to offer some light and lightly undermining comments, the self-deprecating master looking askance at his younger rival. "I think he sings a good deal better than I ever did," Bing claims. When asked about all Frank's public turmoil, Bing says airily, "Yes, I've heard rumors Frank's had a few beefs with the gentlemen of the press. As we all have, you know. Maybe Frank's are a little more spectacular because he's more of a spectacular fellow, and he's Italian, and probably has a little quicker fuse than most of us, particularly myself. I'm lethargic. . . . Sometimes I get a little irked about things I read about myself or about my family; it rolls off my back. Little Frank is not built that way. He's a little more demonstrative."

In early April 1965, right before Frank's *Life* magazine broadside against her was published, Ella almost collapsed onstage in Munich due to a relentless schedule where she did two shows a night in different cities. "I just went berserk," Ella said. "My drummer had to grab me and take me off. The people guessed something was wrong, but they applauded and wouldn't leave the hall."

Ella eventually went out and finished the concert, but she had to cancel a few others to get some rest. Her own frustration with Granz became apparent when Ella released a statement: "A concert artist would never agree to do as we do. It's too much hassle. You're afraid that if you say no, people will say you don't appreciate what they've done for you. Some people get very angry when you're ill."

Ella recovered, and she responded by recording one of her greatest albums, *Ella at Duke's Place* (1965), where she gave her whole all-embracing heart over to the four tunes with Billy Strayhorn lyrics, so much so that this album might have also been called *Ella and Strayhorn*. She is fully in the zone here, sweeping up and caressing the Strayhorn words to "A Flower Is a Lovesome Thing," setting a mood of slowly unfolding sensuality and sustaining it. The way Ella sings the words "I like the sunrise . . . I hope it likes poor me" on "I Like the Sunrise" wipes away circa-1965 Frank and his vendetta and his maudlin striving.

Best of all on this album is "Imagine My Frustration," a Strayhorn lyric about a wallflower at a dance that Ella sings in the spirit of defiance, as if she is somehow *exhilarated* by her own loneliness and neglect partly because she sees it so objectively and so clearly and also because she has the driving forward rhythm of Ellington's band pushing her to incongruously celebrate her own isolation. That's what great art can be.

Ella at Duke's Place was a very happy album for her, with none of the pressure of the Ellington songbook from 1957. The band was well prepared, and the courtly Ellington was so enthused by her performance that he did a soft-shoe dance with her in between takes of "Brown-Skin Gal (in the Calico Gown)," to the delight of everyone. Ella gave a party at her swanky home after this album was finished. It stands as a peak of her mature creativity.

33

Judy: After You've Gone

IN MAY OF 1964, Judy did a tour of Australia that ended in disaster after customs confiscated her pills. She was in the outer limits of pill addiction, but the main seesaw for her was amphetamines versus barbiturates in very large quantities, and she could barely function without these pills, let alone sing. Judy wound up getting booed off the stage in Melbourne after two successful shows in Sydney, and then there was a serious suicide attempt with pills in Hong Kong during a typhoon where her new companion Mark Herron had to fight to keep Judy alive. Her vocal cords were badly damaged after her stomach was pumped in the hospital, and she was warned not to sing for a year. But Judy never did what she was told to do post-MGM.

Judy's daughter Liza was beginning to make a singing career of her own and get some attention, and she had to weather comparisons not just to her mother but to Barbra as well. In an interview done in Australia, Judy said that Liza was going to understudy Barbra in a Broadway show, and she also said that Liza was getting her own Broadway show written for her.

On her early records Liza worked with Peter Matz, who arranged Barbra's albums, and so Liza was being positioned as a new star in the Barbra mold: extreme, brash, and idiosyncratic. Judy asked Liza to do a concert with her in London at the Palladium, and Liza gently declined, saying she didn't think it was a good idea, but then Judy announced the concert in the press, which meant that Liza would have to accept.

When Judy did another interview with Jack Paar on the stage of the Palladium in late 1964, she was clearly a changed person, and part of this comes from a hard-looking and indifferent makeup job, but Judy's eyes are lifeless underneath the false eyelashes. Her instinct for mockery is at its most lethal here. She tells a story about Marlene Dietrich playing records of only applause from a concert tour, and she says, "Marlene isn't one of our better singers, but she looks so marvelous."

In the concert with Liza at the Palladium, Judy's voice is very ragged. She had been in the best voice of her life on her TV show in late 1963 and early 1964, and yet by the end of 1964 the strength and clarity of that voice was gone, the tone was crushed, and there was vocal-damage gravel on the staircase of her vibrato. It felt as if Judy had sung her heart out and sung too much and with too much abandon in the early 1960s, and now the price finally had to be paid. Judy hits a very off-key note on "Just in Time" on the second night of their concert at the Palladium, which was filmed, and she knows her voice isn't where it needs to be, and so eighteen-year-old Liza picks up the slack, ready to work that audience herself if necessary.

It is clear that Liza adores her mother and does not want to compete with her, but Judy is in a foul mood during a lot of this filmed concert, and she keeps pushing Liza's microphone up in a maternal way that is aggressive and unhelpful. They do the medley that Barbra and Judy had done on *The Judy Garland Show*, which is unfair to Liza because once again it sets her up for an impossible double comparison.

"My high notes won't come out tonight," Judy says, murderously, as she sits on the stage and sets herself up for a comparison to Barbra by doing "The Music That Makes Me Dance" from *Funny Girl*, and she loses that contest, though she might not have if she had done the song earlier in the year.

Judy even attempts to do a duet of "Don't Rain on My Parade" with Liza at the Palladium, but she warns her audience first. "This next song is a song that's im*poss*ible to learn, and I haven't! It's really agony . . . I don't know one *word* of the next song, and it's really a tongue-twister," she insists before they stumble through it, and Liza supplies some of the words Judy misses; this shaky duet was not included in the film of the concert or the album version. The following year Ella tried "Don't Rain on My Parade" during a London concert, and she swings the melody very hard and enjoyably, but the densely packed words screw her up, and this all signaled that one of Barbra's signature songs was maybe not of the highest quality. Its lyricist Bob Merrill had written Patti Page's 1952 novelty hit "(How Much Is) That Doggie in the Window?," a ditty that Billie was particularly scornful of.

"How can I follow that?" Liza asks after Judy finishes one number in their joint concert, and Judy quietly replies, "You can follow it just by hitting better notes," and the mortified way she says this makes it especially apparent that she knows her singing voice is in bad shape. Judy warms up slightly only when she gets to be waspishly funny, wondering why Jeanette MacDonald refuses now to talk to her, and saying, "We'll do them all, we really will, we'll be here for days, you're a *greedy* audience." In the end credits to this filmed concert it says, "Produced and staged by Mark Herron," and Judy married the younger and gay Herron in 1965.

Judy's voice was somewhat improved when she appeared on *The Hollywood Palace* in 1965, but bum notes crept in again when she appeared on this show in 1966; she does "By Myself" with its big unaccompanied finish, and her voice just isn't up to it, but the audience applauds to encourage her and bolster her. She was signed to play Jean Harlow's stage mother Mama Jean in *Harlow* (1965) opposite Carol Lynley but abruptly dropped out of this project ten days before shooting was to start.

There are conflicting stories about Judy's brief stint playing Broadway monster Helen Lawson in *Valley of the Dolls* (1967) before she got fired, but Judy was all wrong for that Merman-like part, and she knew it, and so it is likely that she deliberately got herself out of it because she didn't want to play it. "I don't want to be a harridan on the screen, and I don't think people want me to be," Judy said.

Judy was developing an unhealthy relationship with her audience now, and this was really manifested in 1967 when she did another comeback concert at the Palace and her fans went wild when she managed to hit a note they remembered, but there were a lot of notes that Judy couldn't hit anymore. "Sympathy is my business" was how Judy described her star persona to her daughter Liza and to Sid Luft, and Judy put it another way after the successful Palace opening when she told her friend Paul Millard she was happy and then remarked, "Who needs a happy Judy Garland?" in a low, satirical voice.

Her off-screen life was an ever-worsening nightmare, partly because Judy had become a pyromaniac, often setting rooms and herself on fire. She had no money at all a lot of the time because David Begelman had stolen most of her large fees, and so her most basic bills were sometimes paid by her servants or by loyal fans. At a concert in New Jersey in June of 1968, she had an arrangement made of "Free Again," which Barbra had recorded on her French album *Je m'appelle Barbra* (1966), but only sang it once. "I'll never sing it as good as she does," Judy said.

Judy had been recording tapes for a prospective memoir, and they make for painful listening. Her speaking voice when she isn't "on" for an audience is lower and more solemn, though there does seem to be something wrong with the tape speed at times. This is the voice of a broken, defensive, and very sick person whose mind is in considerable disarray, tormenting her with justifications and rage at those who have exploited her. "I don't really care about anybody but me!" Judy admits at one point on the tapes, trapped in a hell of poisonous ego.

Judy bemoaned the loss of "that beautiful voice" and would uninhibitedly talk about being a great star to her friends, whereas toward the end of her own life Billie modestly said in a radio interview that she was expert "in my little way," and of course Bing made a career of modesty. Judy knew that she was Judy and she thought about it too much, and this is partly what caused her to behave in such ghastly and unacceptable ways.

Liza kept a stomach pump for whenever she had to rescue her mother from another suicide attempt, and she once held her mother's feet when Judy tried to jump out of a window. Much as she loved Judy, the very good-hearted Liza finally couldn't stand to be around her sickness anymore, and she understandably began to distance herself so that she could get on with her own life, but not before Judy set her daughter up with a gay husband of her own, entertainer Peter Allen, who had been involved with Mark Herron.

Judy's housekeeper Alma Cousteline said that when Liza could no longer return calls from her mother that Judy said "ugly things" about her daughter, and it is a great sadness if she did sink to this level. Worse even than this, Judy turned into her own mother Ethel Gumm when she saw her daughter Lorna in a school play and told her friend Doug Kelly, "Fuck Liza! This one's going to pay my rent!"

Judy in her madness had developed a taste for physical fights, and she was always throwing things at people and getting into brawls, and there came a point when her children Lorna and Joey had to get away from this and stay with their father. Judy was a menace to herself and to others, and she could only find some sanctuary finally with a small group of gay men who would take her in and try to keep her alive, notably John Carlyle, who sometimes tried to be her lover, Tucker Fleming, and Charles Williamson.

A friend named John Meyer got Judy a gig at a piano bar in Manhattan where she would come in after midnight and sing a few songs and they'd give her a hundred bucks in cash—it had come to that. There is a lively and very drunken recording of Judy singing around the piano after one of these gigs just for fun where at one point she says, "I'm the Ella Fitzgerald of the sad song." And then, far more cuttingly, she says, "Somebody told me that Ella Fitzgerald was the Helen Hayes of jazz!"

Meyer also got her a gig at the Talk of the Town nightclub in London in 1969, and Judy brought along a young pianist named Mickey Deans, a quasi-Sid who thought some money might still be made off her. When Judy was late to one show, she was pelted by the disgruntled audience with breadsticks and cigarette packets.

Judy divorced Herron, and Deans became the new husband, but only flamboyant singer Johnnie Ray came to this wedding. In a short documentary made of her engagement in London, Judy looks painfully thin, and in a close-up where she is trying to sing with Ray's piano accompaniment, her face is so open and so horribly lost that it looks like there has been a lot of damage done to her mind. The camera catches her doing a last heartfelt "Over the Rainbow."

Judy and her husband went to New York, where they stayed with Charles Cochran and jazz singer Anita O'Day, who had recently kicked her heroin habit. "Judy just never seemed to have an hour when she wasn't taking something," O'Day said. "That doesn't mean there weren't laughs. She had a wild, self-mocking sense of humor that was wonderful. Even so, I worried about her being so thin—74 or 84 pounds—and I never saw her eating."

Hard-boiled O'Day was taking Dolophine pills whenever she got the urge to fix, and one day she found her pill bottle empty, which cooled things between her and Judy for a bit. Liza came to visit her mother at Cochran's apartment, and she thought that Judy didn't seem like herself, as if she were winding down.

When Judy found out that O'Day was playing at a club downtown called the Half Note, she insisted on going to see her but then kept putting it off until one night when she finally said she was ready. Judy went to make up, and about a half hour later O'Day went into Judy's room and saw that she had only drawn one line on her eyelid. "She had no idea of time—which is what happens to you," O'Day said. To O'Day, Judy seemed like "one of the walking dead."

Judy made it to the Half Note and took in O'Day's song stylings before getting up, kicking off her shoes, and singing "Over the Rainbow" for the jazz audience. There is a recording at a party afterward of Judy singing Irving Berlin's "I Love a Piano" in a high, girlish voice just for her own pleasure. She traveled with Deans back to London shortly thereafter.

Judy was forty-seven years old when she died from an overdose of barbiturates on June 22, 1969. She was deeply in debt, and so in one final act of largesse Frank helped to pay for her funeral, at which both Frank and Bing were in attendance.

34

Barbra at the Top

Louise Lasser was Barbra's understudy in *I Can Get It for You Wholesale*, and many years later she spoke about the first time she heard Barbra sing. "In 1961, Woody (Allen) and I had gone to the Bon Soir to see Felicia Sanders," Lasser said in 2006, "but Barbra came on stage first, and—what is that feeling you get? I can't even explain it. She opened her mouth, and never was my life the same after that. She was a life-altering presence. It makes me want to cry just talking about it."

Lasser was not the only one whose life was altered when they heard Barbra's voice. Barbra's young gay male entourage knew what she meant and what her voice represented, and so did sensitive women like Lasser, and this would be Barbra's core audience. For those who responded to her, it felt as if they could finally breathe for the first time in their lives. What this core audience got from Barbra was the sense that the exceptional and the otherworldly could somehow pour out of someone who was viewed as an outcast, and the people who heard it were stunned and changed, and her attitude said that they should have known better all along. They should *not* have underestimated her.

This was vengeance on a grand fantasy scale that no one could have expected or conceived before, so much so that even the squares and the jocks and so forth would be dazed from it and slack-jawed out in the dark of the audience, and they would have to admit they had been wrong, and they would basically have to submit.

While she played out her long run onstage in *Funny Girl*, Barbra shot her first TV special, *My Name Is Barbra* (1965), which features no guest stars. This show is shot in lustrous black and white, and the twenty-three-year-old Barbra is in probably the best voice of her life here, able to dominate a whole hour of screen time mainly with her singing just as Judy does on the last episodes of *The Judy Garland Show*.

A childhood pic of Barbra dissolves into a shot of her performing the title song, which was written by Leonard Bernstein, and she goes on to sing a sensual, lingering "Make Believe" that blows Bing's early version of this tune out of the water. Barbra presents her long nose to the camera in profile as she sings it, and she is intense, dramatic, commanding, with beautiful clear skin. We hear children's voices cry, "Crazy Barbra!" at her, and she returns to a childhood state for the next section, for Barbra has a Gatsby-ish need to return to her past in order to somehow change it.

In the next segment Barbra is found sitting on a drum and singing a parody "blues" song before shrugging it off to tell a comic story centered around her finds in thrift stores, and this leads into a medley of Depression-era songs set against her prancing around the Bergdorf Goodman department store in Manhattan, a place where she couldn't get served before she became a star in *Funny Girl*.

Audience laughter keeps building at her audacity as Barbra moves from "Nobody Knows You When You're Down and Out" to Bing's "Brother, Can You Spare a Dime?," which she does in a camp style that puts economic despair entirely aside and insists on upward mobility. Her huge conquering high notes at the end of "Any Place I Hang My Hat Is Home" are particularly overwhelming, and she finishes with a camp-exultant "The Best Things in Life Are Free."

The last part of *My Name Is Barbra* is a straight concert, and Barbra offers her best-ever versions of songs she had been perfecting for years in her nightclub act: a growling, enraged "When the Sun Comes Out" and a thrill-ride up-tempo "Lover, Come Back to Me," and she does "My Man" as a power ballad and moves as far away from Billie's beaten-down version as it is possible to go. The young Barbra presents an image of strength and power, all vulnerability a distant memory that she uses only as a spur to move forward.

In the rush of all the Barbra publicity, a radio show played the record that Diana had made with her daughter, and Diana received some offers to sing on TV. "Somebody wrote that I was trying to compete with my daughter, which is silly," Diana said. "I don't sing like Barbra. I sing a melody simply. I'm too busy working and raising my younger daughter to want to pursue a singing career now. But it's nice to know that someone wants me to. I could never appear before many people, but recording in a quiet room, I think I could do that. Anyway, it's in the back of my mind. Maybe I'll do it someday, who knows!"

Louis Kind even talked briefly about his stepdaughter for an interview. "It took Barbra a little while to accept me, even though she had no remembrance of her own father," Kind said. "But she was a sensitive child and I imagine she thought she would be disloyal if she called me 'Daddy.' She never did. She called me 'Louis,' just as her mother did. I had to be satisfied with this." Unmentioned was the time Barbra had humiliated herself and called him Daddy and he had ignored her.

"She was a shy little girl and sometimes moody, but terribly smart and loving, once you won her confidence," Kind said. "I'm sure she didn't like being uprooted from her grandparents' home. To ease the tensions at this time, we sent Barbra to visit them often. She loved them dearly. Sometimes Barbra and I would get along fine—sometimes she'd seem remote. She loved playing games with me, especially patty-cake. And she loved the ice-cream treats I bought her. I let her mother do all the disciplining and I tried to provide the fun." The full story of his denial of "ice cream treats" for her went untold until Barbra spoke of it.

Her career in overdrive, Barbra put out two albums related to *My Name Is Barbra* in 1965 with songs that had not made it on to the special itself; her voice soars on all the tracks, high and higher and then higher still, no limit. The first album was done very fast. She recorded all the songs and a week later the record was in stores and the second album came out six months later, around the time *My Name Is Barbra* aired a second time on CBS.

Barbra sings "My Pa" as a tribute to her lost father on the first record, and when she does a delightful up-tempo "I've Got No Strings" from *Pinocchio* (1940) it feels very true, for that voice of hers has nothing human holding it back or down to earth. For these records Barbra was still excavating old forgotten songs like "If You Were the Only Boy in the World," which Bing's onetime rival Rudy Vallée had sung in *The Vagabond Lover* (1929).

Ladies' man Vallée had crossed paths with the young Barbra and had told her that she'd never make it on *The Joe Franklin Show*, but it was his crooning that was forgotten by 1965. Barbra was of a different generation—not quite a baby boomer but close. She was sure of herself to the point of arrogance, and not too concerned with being a "nice person" because she saw how phony that was with many people, particularly in show business.

Barbra picked a few obscure Rodgers and Hart songs for these records and gave them vibrant life, and her version of "He Touched Me" reaches a climax but then reaches a climax beyond that and then another climax beyond that, so that her frenzy on the words "nothing, nothing" is up there somewhere that no popular singer had been before. What *is* this voice? Something from another planet? These records show enormous gains in control over her first two albums, especially in regard to low notes, never her forte but far more supported now.

Barbra had won herself a very devoted fan base made up of young boys and girls who felt like outsiders, and they followed her around, and she was very ambivalent about them. The kind of adulation they were giving her didn't feel earned to her, and these fans would applaud and cheer before she had even done anything onstage in *Funny Girl*. Barbra was not impressed by all the famous people coming backstage to tell her how great she was, and she was getting increasingly alienated and uncomfortable—and unsatisfied.

This feeling of dissatisfaction is particularly apparent in some of her reactions to the audience on her second TV special *Color Me Barbra* (1966), which was filmed in color. If anything, the Voice is even more resplendent and otherworldly here, but the owner of it is a narrowly focused and inexperienced young girl who sometimes looks like she is apprehensively peeping out from underneath it. Speaking to *Life* magazine as she shot this special, Barbra said that she was afraid that some people were waiting for her to bomb after the success of *Funny Girl* and *My Name Is Barbra*.

Shooting at the Philadelphia Museum of Art, there were problems with the color cameras that caused delays, and director Dwight Hemion was very impressed by Barbra's professionalism. "Barbra stayed up for twenty-four hours," Hemion said. "She lay down on the floor of a hallway of the Philadelphia Museum, I'll never forget it. There was nothing comfortable about any part of this. She slept for probably six hours in the hallway, and eventually the camera was ready. I mean, a lot of people could have said, 'The heck with this,' and moved on . . . (she was) not making a big deal of it, which she could have."

When Barbra performs the semi-operatic "One Kiss," which was the song her mother Diana used to sing, she pushes her voice to go superhigh, and you can see her willing the pure sheets of sound to come out with no vibrato. On the set of *Color Me Barbra*, Diana told a reporter for *Look* magazine that she had once made a record of "One Kiss" and sang a few bars for him after saying, "Of course, we sing it our own way."

Dressed as an Egyptian princess for "Where or When," Barbra produces a crazily ultra-high last note that sounds like some message from beyond our space-time continuum. But in the last concert section of this special, after she finishes "Any Place I Hang My Hat Is Home," Barbra's reaction to the over-the-top applause and cheering of her fans is so uncomfortable as to seem contemptuous, and this is very different from her seemingly sincere expression of appreciation for the applause at the end of *My Name Is Barbra*. "I hate them, I hate them," Barbra told her manager Marty Erlichman, and when some numbers needed to be redone Barbra wanted the audience to leave. It took a half hour before Erlichman and her director could convince her that they needed to be there.

It's as if Barbra feels their adulation is false, whipped up, and somehow unconnected to her, and she can't stand that. Consequently, live performing was something that she was looking to put behind her as soon as she could. As an older woman, Barbra understood this reaction to her fans differently. "When I was young, there was a bit of self-hatred," she said. "And then you kind of don't like people who like you, you know?"

Some executives at Columbia spoke to Barbra about expanding her popularity in Europe, and so Barbra collaborated with Michel Legrand on her Gallic-flavored album *Je m'appelle Barbra* (1966), where she sang some of the verse to "Autumn Leaves" in French. Legrand told a story about how Barbra did twenty-eight takes of this song until he took her aside and said that the first take was the best, and she replied that she knew that. Legrand asked why she kept on singing it, and Barbra told him, "Just for the pleasure of it," which he loved.

Barbra was pregnant with her son Jason when she was finishing this record in the fall of 1966, and she wrote a pretty melody of her own for it called "Ma Première Chanson," but an up-tempo "I Wish You Love" doesn't work at all, as Frank had found out when he tried taking that song fast on an album in 1964. There are a lot of ideas on *Je m'appelle Barbra*, but most of them aren't good ideas, and the wistful songs don't really suit Barbra, who isn't much for regret and longing. It's somewhat like her own *Close to You*, a labored-over noble failure, but part of a period where everything she touched turned to gold and she was pledged to creative adventurousness.

Ray Ellis arranged for her discreetly on *Simply Streisand* (1967), giving her a melancholy opening for "My Funny Valentine," which she sings tenderly and sincerely. Barbra is very focused here, lavishing her attention on some of our most beautiful ballads, like "The Nearness of You," "All the Things You Are," which she sings with the verse to a light samba beat, and a rather lustful "More Than You Know."

"I hired Ray Ellis because I had fallen in love at sixteen years old, I found records at an A&P that were on sale for $1.69, there was this album called *Lady in Satin*," Barbra said. "Billie Holiday, and my God, I just loved that album, played it to death, and I saw that Ray Ellis arranged the songs for her, and I thought, boy, if he's good enough for Billie Holiday he's sure good enough for me."

Barbra does Billie's "Lover Man" as a kind of remembrance of such hunger, steering clear of Billie's abjection as if to say, "I've had this, and I'm going to have more," and she recorded Judy's "The Boy Next Door" when Judy was still alive to hear it. Barbra's persona on this record, which stands as one of her best, is one of horny determination, and Judy was like that in real life, but it was never part of her performing image, so this is progress on several fronts. *Simply Streisand* ends with a nice campy

"Stout-Hearted Men," which Barbra treats to some funny pauses that flag Mae West as one of her key inspirations.

Young Barbra was often very funny in her front-stoop Brooklyn way, and this is apparent on her comically fast-paced version of "Jingle Bells," the first song Judy ever sang onstage, on *A Christmas Album* (1967). Barbra had a cold when she recorded this record, and it gives her a slightly huskier tone. As if to make up for this, she overembroiders "Have Yourself a Merry Little Christmas" with vocal mannerisms, so that this is still safely Judy's song.

She does the verse about being in Beverly Hills for Bing's "White Christmas," and this signals what is so enjoyable about this album, which is that Barbra doesn't take these songs all that seriously; this is one woman who isn't dreaming of a white Christmas, for she's having far too much fun for herself in Beverly Hills. Barbra offers some rolled *r*'s on "Ave Maria," and her "Silent Night" is not gold being poured out of a cup but butter for an oven-fresh roll. There is some oversinging on *A Christmas Album*, but no one listening to Barbra is looking for restraint.

Her third TV special *The Belle of 14th Street* (1967) has guest stars and a lot of ideas that don't quite work, but this is an underrated program with several offbeat concepts that showcase Barbra's talent and intensity. It was meant to pay tribute to the spirit of vaudeville, and so Barbra camps the very old song "Alice Blue Gown," which turns into a striptease, a first signal that she very much enjoys showing off her curvaceous body.

Marty Erlichman got Barbra a vocal coach named Maurice Jampol because after her pregnancy Barbra felt that her voice was somehow different or diminished. "Streisand lost her voice when she had her baby," Jampol told the *Pittsburgh Press*. "So her manager dug me up to help get her voice back into shape quickly. She had lost the top and bottom parts of her voice. I don't know exactly how it happened. But I figured she might have lost some of the tension in her belly. We had to rebuild that part of her voice that she lost, and I thought she did the job for CBS beautifully." No strain is evident on the program itself, but this showed that Barbra's voice wasn't always this magic thing she could switch on and off at will.

There is a section of *The Belle of 14th Street* where Barbra assumes the role of an aged German soprano, and this is a very pointed characterization from the in-your-face Jewish star in which she satirizes the sort of Teutonic musical chauvinist who cries, "Brahms, Beethoven, all German!" and also announces, "We shall march all over your country!" We even get to see Barbra do some Shakespeare when she plays Ariel in "a taste of *The Tempest*," a reminder that she wanted to play Medea and Hamlet when she started out.

The Belle of 14th Street ends with another concert, this time against an art nouveau background, where Barbra caresses "My Melancholy Baby" and sings "I'm Always Chasing Rainbows" in a way that lets us know that if *she* chases a rainbow, she will get it and she will get over it, it's no problem. When Barbra does Irving Berlin's "How About Me?" here, which Judy said was such a sad song that it was "mean," she is as sad as she can be, which isn't too sad, and this is a relief after Billie and Judy. What makes the difference is that the young Barbra was living her life like a dynamic man would live his life, and she was never tempted by the sexist traps that snared Billie and Judy into bad relationships with men who took more than they gave.

Her fourth TV special was *A Happening in Central Park*, a live concert done in front of 125,000 people on a very humid night. This was a nerve-wracking experience for Barbra because there had been death threats against her, and so she did her best to move a lot so as to be a moving target. Because of her understandable anxiety, Barbra forgot the words to several of her songs, completely blanking on them, and this bolstered her determination to quit live performing.

Yet this concert is one of her greatest achievements. Barbra is a very rare kind of butterfly here in her flowing outfits with bat sleeves, her Cleopatra eyeliner, and her towering beehive of hair. She does sensual little riffs for her amatory "The Nearness of You" under the opening credits of the special, and Judy's magic man Mort Lindsey is conducting for Barbra here, even bringing her some tea in between some of her "in a rage" numbers like "Cry Me a River" and "Down with Love," where she uses her own tension and fear to really make them land. Barbra's anger is forthright and cleansing, whereas Frank's is twisted and destructive.

Barbra is also very likably zany in this concert, mocking *The Sound of Music* and crying "Santa Claus is dead!" There are close-ups of audience reactions throughout the program that show young men and women who are often wearing glasses, and they look like misfit theater kids and artsy outcasts. These fans appear smart and intense and cool in their own way, and for these people Barbra is a queen and an example that being different can pay. There is a shot of a cute African American guy holding up a sign that says I LOVE YOU that is particularly winning.

Ray Stark had planted an item with columnist Dorothy Kilgallen that Shirley MacLaine wanted to do a movie of *Funny Girl* with Frank, and David Begelman, who was still acting as Barbra's agent then, had to reassure her about this. "I only wanted to do *Funny Girl*, and Ray refused to give it to me unless I signed a four-picture deal," Barbra said. "I remember my agent saying to me, 'Look, if you're prepared to lose it, then we can say, sorry, we'll sign only one picture at a time.' I was not prepared to lose it."

Barbra wanted to be a movie star, and the plush film version of *Funny Girl* (1968) was set to be the vehicle of all time for her, with the prestigious William Wyler as director and Herbert Ross to direct the all-important musical numbers. Stark and Barbra had first spoken to Sidney Lumet about directing, and he thought that Sean Connery might play Nicky Arnstein. Lumet put in six months of work on the project before being given the gate by Stark, Barbra, and Marty Erlichman.

Most important to Barbra was her cameraman Harry Stradling. "When I arrived in Hollywood, I didn't have the usual qualifications for a movie star," Barbra said. "I have a strange face, very different from each side. People who are easy to photograph typically have very symmetrical faces, big heads, big eyes. I have a small head, a very odd nose, my mouth is too big and my eyes are too small. But Harry enjoyed the challenge and we became fast friends. We spent hours experimenting with the light, hard lights, eye lights . . . Harry even rigged up what he called a 'Strei-light' held by a best boy who followed me around when I moved. It was fantastic."

According to Jule Styne, Frank was interested in working with Barbra. "Sinatra as Nicky Arnstein opposite Streisand, that would have been the collector's item of all time," said Styne. "Imagine having four songs in that score sung by Sinatra, imagine a duet by these two great people. He wanted to do it, but Ray Stark said he was too old. He would have been sensational!" Even if Stark had approved, this idea of Frank playing Nicky Arnstein with Barbra in *Funny Girl* would have required new songs for him, and the focus was to be on putting Barbra over on-screen.

Paul Newman was approached, but he turned it down, citing his lack of any musical aptitude. Finally Stark had Barbra meet with Omar Sharif, and she was very taken with him after he kissed her hand and said some flattering words, and so Sharif it was. Sharif is a wet blanket in *Funny Girl*, but he does kiss her passionately at least, and he gives the impression, like George Brent used to, that he is better off-screen than on.

Wyler was patient with Barbra and let Herbert Ross do a lot of the work, restricting himself to simple requests like "Tone it down," which she accepted. "She's not the most relaxed person, but neither am I," Wyler said. "She worries about everything. I think that's fine. Lots of people don't worry about anything, but I'd rather have her worry too much than too little." Wyler was famous for ordering many takes of scenes, and obsessive Barbra was happy with this and offered up something new for each one of them.

Her on-the-spot behavioral improvisations enriched the film, as when she decided to cough at the smoke after Fanny strikes glamorous Garbo-esque poses by a train for photographers. But Barbra got a bad reputation in an envious Hollywood right away because she was honest to the point of unconscious rudeness, she wanted to do things her way, and she was a complainer who didn't like the hours of moviemaking and the early rising any more than Judy did.

Funny Girl is as close to a one-woman show as a movie gets. Judy's *A Star Is Born* was also a movie meant to showcase her, but James Mason played a key role in that along with several strong character actors like Jack Carson and Charles Bickford, whereas Barbra's movie debut is all her all the time. An unusual number of lines sound post-dubbed, and there is some tricky editing, as if scenes were always being improved or changed.

Anne Francis admitted in 2002 that her publicist planted an item about Barbra insisting that Francis be almost totally cut out of *Funny*

Girl, and she apologized for this false story, but the damage had been done. The legend of Barbra as some monstrous diva who must be obeyed started when she was shooting her first movie in Hollywood, and it has followed her ever since.

Funny Girl is a film very clearly shot on studio sets, which is why the tugboat conclusion of her showstopper "Don't Rain on My Parade" is so effective, because it is a real boat on real water, and Barbra's agony as she runs with the suitcases was real; this was one scene she didn't want to keep on doing. "She's not the athletic type," said Ross before trying to mollify her into doing one more take of this run to the tugboat.

The story of *Funny Girl* is basically the same story as *A Star Is Born*: the woman rising and the man falling. Barbra raises the stakes of this narrative very high for Fanny, making us feel that Nick is her first love and that there will never be another, which is why her rendition of "My Man" at the end of the two-and-a-half-hour runtime packs such a wallop, because it has all of her carefully built feeling of passion for this one man behind it.

Barbra had a fling with Sharif while she was making *Funny Girl*, and she and Wyler had him sent for to play the last scene between Fanny and Nick right before she went out to sing "My Man" so that she could use her own feelings about their parting. Sharif said that she was particularly moved when he would say to her, "You are beautiful," and he did this around ten times for her as they shot take after take to get it right. Her husband Elliott Gould was there that day on the soundstage, according to columnist Joyce Haber.

For this crucial and highly dramatic "My Man," which is the emotional climax of the film, Barbra starts speaking the lyrics as if she is too overcome to sing them, and then some drums come in and Barbra starts lip-synching to her own enormously powerful vocal of this ultimate torch song, deploying her growl effect on the word "difference," which gets across that Fanny has been indelibly marked by this first love, but she will go on.

The transition between her first tentative verse of "My Man" in tears done live to the great surge in volume on the recorded track is so moving because it dramatizes that shocking moment when everyone first heard

Barbra sings "My Man" at the end of *Funny Girl* (1968).

Barbra sing, the way she looked like the wallflower at the dance but was actually a queen on top of some mountain only she had scaled.

Judy was one of the most convincing lip-synchers of all time in her movies, whereas Barbra never liked to lip-synch and avoided it whenever she could, but the switch from a live performance to a controlled lip-synch of the second verse of "My Man" makes its full impact even seen in isolation on YouTube, let alone as the finish of a two-and-a-half-hour movie.

Barbra was nominated for the best actress Oscar for *Funny Girl* against very stiff competition, and she looked very nervous in the audience as Frank came out to sing the song "Star" at the top of the show. She had been asked to become a member of the Academy even though she had only one credit (the rule was you had to have three), and so when Ingrid Bergman announced that Barbra had tied with Katharine Hepburn for *The Lion in Winter* it became apparent that her vote was the vote that secured this if we safely presume that Barbra voted for herself.

This was the height of success, but what followed were two missteps. Clive Davis, the new head of Columbia, told Barbra to sing more rock-oriented songs after *Simply Streisand* didn't sell as many copies as the company would have liked, which led to *What About Today?* (1969), an attempt to give Barbra more contemporary material to sing, and the result was so incongruous that this recording is almost enjoyably bad.

Barbra didn't know how to handle songs by the Beatles or Paul Simon, and nothing on *What About Today?* suits her. It isn't just a question of her soaring voice not fitting the new sounds of the moment, but the sentiments of the songs are also alien to her. "With a Little Help from My Friends" has an entirely different and unflattering meaning when she sings it, and when she oversings Buffy Sainte-Marie's "Until It's Time for You to Go," it's certain that she is not a willow and that she will never bend.

Carol Channing had won the Tony for *Hello, Dolly!* the year that Barbra was up for *Funny Girl*, and now Barbra was given Channing's role in the expensive movie version of *Hello, Dolly!* (1969) even though she was in her midtwenties and Dolly Levi is supposed to be a middle-aged widow. This is a part for Doris Day, or maybe a comeback part for Betty Grable, not a young Barbra at her peak.

"I really didn't respond to the Broadway show—a piece of fluff," Barbra said. "It's not the kind of thing I'm interested in. I'm interested in real life, real people, and in playing Medea. *Dolly* takes place in an age before people realized they hated their mothers—the whole Freudian thing. So it wasn't something I could delve psychologically into too deeply." Yet she perversely accepted the role partly because she knew some people thought she shouldn't do it.

Her introductory star close-up in *Hello, Dolly!* is very campy, as if she is saying, "Yes, I'm miscast, but I'm going to sing the hell out of this score anyway." She charges ahead here mechanically amid very ugly color, some unfortunate "musical comedy acting" from a few of the young supporting players, and a leading man, Walter Matthau, who couldn't stand Barbra on-screen or off. Barbra had ideas, and Matthau and her director Gene Kelly would not listen to them, which made this an unpleasant experience for everyone. The dislike between Matthau and Barbra is so palpable that it throws her off in their scenes, as if she is afraid to interact with him.

"One day I had an idea about something I thought would be funny involving a scene in a wagon," Barbra said. "I said, 'What do you think of this?' and people started to laugh. But all of a sudden Walter Matthau closed his eyes and started screaming: 'Who does she think she is? I've been in thirty movies and this is only her second, the first one hasn't even come out yet, and she thinks she's directing? Who the hell does she think she is?' I couldn't believe it. I had no defense. I stood there and I was so humiliated I started to cry, and then I ran away."

Matthau was a difficult and competitive actor, and *Hello, Dolly!* was shot during a very hot summer in heavy period costumes, and Bobby Kennedy had just been shot on the day of Matthau's big blowup at Barbra, so he was in a particularly bad mood. Stories about their conflict got repeated over and over again and embellished through the years and once again unfairly added to Barbra's reputation for being tough or exacting to work with.

In 1964 Louis had a number-one hit with a recording of "Hello, Dolly!" and so he was hired to sing part of this title song with Barbra on-screen. It's easy to imagine Louis playing Matthau's part with Pearl Bailey in their own movie of this material, but he was still being restricted to star cameo parts as late as 1969. The year previously, Louis had remarked, "Madame Streisand . . . she's trying to out-sing everybody this year!"

Louis had played Cicely Tyson's grandfather in *A Man Called Adam* (1966), a vehicle for Sammy Davis Jr., and there are several close-ups in that movie that show the weariness of his face when it is not smiling brightly, but he smiles brightly for Barbra in *Hello, Dolly!*, and she treats him tentatively, as if not fully cognizant of just who he is and what he represents, yet moved to show respect, which is a rare mode for her.

Louis and Barbra interact in *Hello, Dolly!* (1969).

Barbra worked with Judy's second husband Vincente Minnelli for *On a Clear Day You Can See Forever* (1970), another Broadway musical adaptation, and she rejected Neal Hefti and insisted on Frank's key collaborator Nelson Riddle to do the arrangements of her songs. "She was trouble," said producer Howard W. Koch. "Nothing was good enough for her. But she and Nelson were like a team from the time we switched."

Before shooting began, Paramount threw a reincarnation ball where guests were supposed to come as the person from a past life they would most like to be, and Barbra came as the great French writer Colette while Minnelli came as the Italian revolutionary Garibaldi. This was a sumptuous and expensive production all around, and Barbra got a dressing room with Regency furniture and silk wallpaper that cost $40,000.

In *On a Clear Day You Can See Forever* she is back to playing Kooky Barbra as Daisy Gamble, a girl who wants to quit smoking and discovers a past life, and this feels like a regression for her as a performer. There are flashback scenes where Barbra plays a titled lady and is dressed in outlandish getups by Cecil Beaton. In the most notable of the flashbacks, she wears a turban with egg-like designs on it and stares lasciviously at a beautiful blond man (John Richardson) while her soaring vocal for "Love with All the Trimmings" plays on the soundtrack. This is Barbra at her most daring and insecure, nestling a glass in her bosom and trying to be a goddess like Greta Garbo or Marlene Dietrich, and Minnelli doesn't protect her here the way he protected and guided Judy in *Meet Me in St. Louis* and *The Clock*, for he is older now, and not so intimately involved with his star.

Minnelli's third marriage was breaking up as he shot this movie, and Judy died during production of it, so his mind was often elsewhere. He gracefully accepted Barbra's need to question every aspect of the project. "I have no ego about such things," he said. "The important thing is to make the picture. Consequently, I listened to what Barbra suggested, and implemented some of her suggestions. I found her creative and bright, and we got along beautifully."

Paramount lost faith in the movie and cut it from Minnelli's 143-minute version down to 129 minutes. Unlike Barbra's first two films, it was not sent out as a special roadshow picture but was given a general release. Big-budget musicals like this were going out of fashion on-screen, which meant that Barbra would have to change and adapt going forward into the 1970s.

"In a way, Barbra is fulfilling an old dream of mine," Diana said in an interview at this time. "I wanted to be a singer when I was a kid, but in my family, my father wouldn't hear of it—although he occasionally sang as a substitute cantor in our temple. It was my frustration, too—not becoming a singer. But I was very shy—much too shy to push. Barbra was shy, too, but her desires were stronger than her shyness." Diana smiled. "It's nice to think that dreams can be handed on, isn't it?" She was taking singing lessons twice a week now and had thoughts of maybe doing some singing herself, just like her daughters Barbra and Roslyn. "Anything's possible," Diana said.

35

Frank and Ella at the Crossroads

IN 1965 FRANK released his own retrospective album, *Sinatra: A Man and His Music*, with a TV special to go with it. This look-back recording follows the pattern of Bing's own musical autobiography project from 1954, even down to the patter in between songs, though Frank's reminiscing is often less than inviting. Most notable here is that Frank finally nails "Soliloquy" from *Carousel*, achieving the semi-operatic sound he wants through sheer force of will.

Frank next did a pretty moon-themed album with Nelson Riddle called *Moonlight Sinatra* (1966), on which he performs Bing's "Moonlight Becomes You" and an "I Wished on the Moon" with verse done slow and sexy. His daughter Nancy had a hit single with "These Boots Are Made for Walkin'," which has lyrics like "You keep lyin' when you ought to be truthin'," and Frank had his own hit with "Strangers in the Night," a song he hated.

Frank married the much younger and very calculating Mia Farrow after prodding from his Hollywood society friends like Edie Goetz and Rosalind Russell, and this was a midlife crisis moment for him that was marked by a hit single called "That's Life," which he did in a very angry way because he wanted to be done with it so that he could go off to dinner and drinks. There was another hit single at this time in "Summer Wind," which has evocative Johnny Mercer lyrics and even more evocative Nelson Riddle backing with electronic organ.

In this hectic period, Frank also recorded a rare live album of his act at the Sands with the Count Basie orchestra, cracking the whip in an intimate setting with his virile and grabby phrasing and insisting that the audience endure a lengthy comedy monologue in a way that said, "Laugh, or else!" His voice is a little ragged sometimes here, but he does an impressive high-note finish with no vibrato on "You Make Me Feel So Young."

In June of 1966, there was a celebration for Dean Martin's birthday at the Polo Lounge at the Beverly Hills Hotel. The Sinatra and Martin party got rowdy, and this noise bothered two men sitting near them, Frederick Weisman, the president of Hunt Foods, and Franklin Fox, a businessman from Boston.

Weisman asked the group to quiet down, which Frank took exception to. According to Fox, Frank also made an anti-Semitic remark, and things escalated, and Frank started to vent his fury at Weisman. In the ensuing fight, both Fox and Martin's wife Jeanne said that Frank threw a phone at Weisman, though George Jacobs wrote that it was Frank's other right-hand man Jilly Rizzo who hit Weisman on the head with the phone. Weisman's skull was fractured, and he was taken unconscious out of the Polo Lounge to an ambulance.

For two weeks Weisman was in the hospital in critical condition. "That's the only time I think I ever saw that man scared," said Frank's friend Corinne Entratter of Frank. "If this guy croaks, I'm fucking finished," Frank said, guilt-ridden and in despair. He got into an argument with Farrow when she said that what had happened was probably not his fault, which only made him feel worse. Weisman finally recovered, and he did not press criminal charges, though Jacobs wrote that Frank paid him off big time.

In September of 1966, Ella appeared with Frank at a fundraiser he hosted, and since Frank almost never apologized to anyone in his life, his attack on Ella's singing in *Life* magazine likely went unmentioned between them. Ella was the better person, of course, and could rise above this, and she could also sing him under the table, and he knew it.

"Not only does she sing better, but she's funnier too!" Frank said of Ella when she appeared with him on a TV special in 1967. Ella always spoke very highly of Frank in the press and to her intimates, and yet there is sometimes a very slight edge in her manner on this special, that same edge that came out when she would say her "All right" to an unruly audience. According to pianist Paul Smith, Frank gave Ella his dressing room and couldn't do enough for her, and so he was trying to make amends in his hyper, adolescent way.

Ella and Frank try a few current pop tunes on a medley together, and both look like they know how unsuitable these songs are for them. When they do "The Lady Is a Tramp" together, Frank tries very hard to swing, but he looks and sounds pretty square by Ella's standards. Shortly after this special, Ella and Frank spent three days rehearsing for an album together with Nelson Riddle, but that was dropped after Norman Granz got into an argument with Frank about which songs to sing with Ella.

In early 1967 Frank recorded one of his best albums, *Francis Albert Sinatra & Antônio Carlos Jobim*, a collaboration with the Brazilian composer on which he is at his most delicate, creating perfect hushed make-out music and even sounding boyish again rather than coarse. This is the last we hear of the enchanting Frankie from the 1940s, and it was proof that the Monster still had this in him. But he has lower notes now that Frankie didn't have: "What is the evening . . . without you . . . it's nothing," he sings on "If You Never Come to Me," hitting a bass note on "nothing."

Coarseness unfortunately held sway in a series of movies that Frank made at this time where he played a conservative and disgusted detective. *Tony Rome* (1967) features a swinging theme song sung by his daughter Nancy about how fathers need to lock up their daughters when Frank's Tony is around, an uneasy concept that was amplified by their hit father-daughter love single from 1967 called "Somethin' Stupid."

There's more than a little misogyny in *Tony Rome*, a contempt for women and for weakening standards that led to the homophobia of the extraordinarily unpleasant *The Detective* (1968), a very conflicted movie in which Frank tries to be both right-wing and left-wing at once, and what results is an often-ugly mess of attitudes. This move toward the right politically was part of Frank's anti-rock and anti-hippie stance, and in *The Detective* his character warns against "this sick world" and even the sick psychiatrists who are urging us to accept it, yet he also says that African Americans are right to riot about poor housing conditions.

But then some outright hostility with no leavening came into the open for *Lady in Cement* (1968), a sequel to *Tony Rome* in which Frank has a very nasty encounter with a gay club owner and openly mocks his lisping way of speaking; this is followed not long after by a scene in which Frank again lisps to mock a gay funeral director. Such brazen hatred of gay people is matched by the dismissive hatred of women on display here, and these are two sides of the same coin. The worst thing about the prejudice in *Lady in Cement* is that it is supposed to be funny, and of course Frank is never funny.

Frank's bad behavior was at its most out of control in this period, especially when he was lording around as the king of Las Vegas. Comedian Jackie Mason was shot at and punched for telling Sinatra jokes, and comic Shecky Greene took his life into his own hands when he joked, "Frank Sinatra saved my life once. These guys were beating me up, and Frank said, 'OK boys, he's had enough.'"

Frank had other people do his dirty work for him, and bearlike bar owner Jilly Rizzo was the member of his entourage most often called on to threaten or commit violence on his behalf. "I saw him have Jilly kick people," Greene said. "Once we went downstairs to the Fontainebleau coffee shop. It was four or five o'clock in the morning. Sinatra liked these hot brown rolls they had, so we went down there to see if they were done yet, and they weren't done. And Frank got mad, and he said something to Jilly, and Jilly kicked the baker and broke his ankle."

"Light My Fire," a hit single by the Doors, seemed to be everywhere now, and this was among many things that drove Frank crazy. He got into a brawl with Las Vegas casino manager Carl Cohen and threatened to have him killed, huffing and puffing and calling Cohen names, but when Frank pulled out his worst and cried, "You kike!" the burly Cohen immediately got up and punched Frank in the mouth and knocked him to the floor, smashing the caps off his two front teeth. Frank got up and tried to throw a chair, and he yelled to his enforcer, "Get him, Jilly! Get him!" But Jilly was not going to take on the powerful Cohen, who was six foot three and weighed 250 pounds.

As Frank went on these rampages, Ella was coming to the end of her tenure at Verve Records. While she was touring with the Duke Ellington band in July of 1966, Ella received word that her half sister Frances had died, and she flew to the funeral, which caused her to miss a concert date. When Ella returned to the tour just a few days later, she was in no emotional condition to perform, but she felt she had to go ahead because Norman Granz was filming a concert on July 27. During this performance, Ella kept breaking down crying in between songs, and when Ellington saw what was happening, he shortened the first part of the concert in order to spare her.

As Ellington went out to play his final set, he assumed that Ella would not be performing anymore that night, but when the band started to play Granz started shouting to bring Ella on. Ellington ignored this and just played louder, and afterward Ellington and Granz had a fight that resulted in Ellington parting ways from Granz for the time being. Ellington was very angry about Granz's insensitivity toward Ella and the way he was treating her more like a music machine than a person, and so he stood up for her.

Ella was nearing fifty years old, and she had been swinging hard for over thirty years. On the live concert album *Ella and Duke at the Cote D'Azur*, which was released in 1967, she still has her full voice and control, her pure sustained notes, her high notes, the works, and when she did two albums of religious music for Capitol in 1967, Ella was feeling it, and her voice was still at its peak.

But by spring of 1968, when she recorded an album of medleys for Capitol called *30 by Ella*, there was a marked change in her voice. Just as with Judy, within the space of a year Ella's singing voice declined and acquired a wobble that didn't let her move smoothly through her vocal range or sustain notes in the same way. Vibrato had always been a choice for her, a way of making certain notes prettier, but now this vibrato was creeping in whether she wanted it there or not.

A young Aretha Franklin had begun recording standards for Columbia Records with John Hammond as her producer, and she was singing Judy songs: "Over the Rainbow," "You Made Me Love You," and even "Rock-a-Bye Your Baby with a Dixie Melody." Franklin herself was a big Judy fan and always spoke about her reverently throughout her career. "Judy Garland is a singer with a capital S," Franklin said. "And talk about soul. This woman was soul personified. Judy Garland is a class by herself."

Franklin was even singing Bing songs like "I Surrender Dear" and "I Apologize" at the beginning of her recording career, and it became especially clear that these standards were confining her after she made her breakthrough R&B album *I Never Loved a Man the Way I Love You* in 1967 for Atlantic Records. Over the next few years at Atlantic, the versatile, set-apart, singular Franklin could do no wrong, and her sound felt like a liberation. Frank introduced Aretha for the 1968 Oscars, where she sang Barbra's song "Funny Girl."

Ella made an attempt to be hip and contemporary with *Sunshine of Your Love* (1969) and *Ella* (1969), but Ella wasn't Aretha, and she knew it, and several of the new songs she was doing in this period are so poor and unsuitable, like "This Gun Don't Care" and "Yellow Man," that they make her novelty songs of the late 1930s and early '40s sound far better by comparison. And Burt Bacharach's melodies don't sound too challenging after all the great melodies from Kern, Porter, and Berlin and so many others that Ella had feasted on for decades.

Frank was similarly adrift at this time when it came to records. When he sings Joni Mitchell's "Both Sides Now" on *Cycles* (1968), he doesn't seem to understand the song at all, even though aspects of it should suit him. A brainy, confident, and independent woman like Joni Mitchell was alien to his worldview, and it was this above all that left him looking like a throwback. "Both Sides Now" is a flowery, high-flown, objective Billie song, but she was no longer around to sing it.

Frank served Mia Farrow with divorce papers on the set of *Rosemary's Baby* (1968) after he saw photos of her dancing with Bobby Kennedy at a benefit fashion show at which both Ava and Barbra were also present. Appalled by what he was seeing of the protests of the youthful radical left on college campuses, and chagrined after a humiliating meeting with President Lyndon Johnson in which Johnson condescended to him just as FDR had, Frank continued to move to the right politically.

Though he didn't like Paul Anka's lyrics to "My Way," Frank knew immediately that it would be a hit for him, and it was indeed a defiant hit on the radio, beloved of self-pitying jerky men everywhere, the guys at the end of bars that no one wants to talk to. At this point Frank began to be pursued in a highly dedicated way by Barbara Marx, a former showgirl, and he couldn't stand her at first, but she had a forever-upbeat attitude and she was always around.

There was a moment when Frank was seeing more and more of his society hostess friend Edie Goetz after the death of her husband, and she enjoyed his attentions. Goetz was the daughter of Frank's old MGM boss Louis B. Mayer, and she was still tops socially and the ultimate in class to Frank. One night, overcome with emotion as he tended to be, Frank impulsively proposed to Goetz, who was surprised. "Why, Frank, I couldn't marry you," Goetz told him. "Why . . . why . . . you're nothing but a hoodlum." Frank took this in, walked out of the room, and never spoke to her again.

Frank talked of wanting to a do a musical version of *Born Yesterday* with Barbra, which was a good idea, but nothing came of it. Instead he recorded one of his worst albums, *A Man Alone* (1969), which consists of songs with lyrics by popular poet Rod McKuen, whose books were selling like hotcakes for Frank's publisher friend Bennett Cerf. Frank even did some spoken word recitations here, so seriously that the result verges on camp.

Totally lost, Frank also tried a concept album written by Bob Gaudio and Jake Holmes called *Watertown* (1970), which tells a kind of musical story about a very traditional sort of man abandoned by his wife who is left to raise their two young sons. Frank tries to play a role here that is very far from his own swaggering persona, and so this record is in the brave experiment / noble failure category. It was on *Watertown* that it became apparent that Frank in his midfifties was beginning to become afflicted by the same problem that Ella was having: shaky vibrato where none is intended.

Frank was particularly taken by a song Gaudio and Holmes had written for *Watertown* called "Lady Day," which was supposed to be about the wife and how her dreams had destroyed her. Frank saved it and included it on a 1971 album as a tribute to his lost mentor Billie. "Lady Day" features a soaring and very melancholy Don Costa backing, and Frank really outdoes himself here, making words like "breezes" and "pain" sound like exactly what they are meant to convey, and no one else could sing the word "bitter" so expressively.

Frank sang so many songs to Ava, but this song for Billie is the real killer in his catalog. Billie was the woman he idolized and the woman he was too scared to try to love, and she was the woman who had influenced his style more than anyone else. There is no great run of albums in the 1950s for Frank without Billie, and he knew it, and it pained him greatly that she was gone and that she had suffered so much. Frank was a monster, but he was capable of love on this abstract plane, and he is reaching out to Billie here with all his strength and tenderness, and this isn't the self-pity of "My Way." This is Frank at his best, and he is at the end of his tether himself creatively, which makes this performance even more naked and empathetic.

36

Bing in Winter

BING'S CAREER WAS winding down, and so he focused more on family life with his second wife Kathryn and their three children, Harry, Mary, and Nathaniel. When Bing did work, the children would travel with him, and Kathryn would tutor them. His sons from his first marriage were still getting into trouble all the time in the 1960s, and so Bing dealt with that as best he could while trying to do better with this second chance at fatherhood.

He tried a sitcom in the mid-1960s, but that was short lived. On record Bing went fairly seamlessly with the times and was suited to songs like the druggy "Up, Up and Away," for he always did have a drop-out side. But more than that, it was his absorbent Bing-ness that could handle practically any type of music and make it his own, even if he did finally founder in his duet with the Temptations on "My Girl" for *The Hollywood Palace*.

While Barbra, Frank, and Ella struggled with the new easygoing, quirky, atmospheric pop music, Bing took it in his stride. His version of Joni Mitchell's "Both Sides Now" is sensitive and touching from his own slightly aloof perspective. The words "If you care, don't let them know, don't give yourself away" have a new resonance when Bing sings them.

Bing was never going to be an openly affectionate guy with his intimates, but he was mellowing slightly. When he sings "Basin Street Blues" on TV with Louis in 1959, there is a moment where Bing thinks of putting his hand on Louis's shoulder, but then he thinks better of it,

287

afraid of that sort of intimacy. But by 1965, when he sings with Louis on *The Hollywood Palace*, Bing puts his hand on his friend's shoulder with all his affection for this man that he loved.

In an interview with *Ebony* magazine, Louis said, "I've never been invited to the home of a movie star—not even Bing's. You don't have to be in people's faces to appreciate the warmth they have for you. We all appreciate each other's talents. Do I think any of them have any lingering prejudice? If they do, they don't show it. They must be damn good actors. I'd feel chilliness in a minute."

When asked about this Louis interview by Gary Giddins, Bing put on his cool and unflappable mask as he replied, "I heard Pops said that. But you know Louis and Lucille never invited me to their home." Yet there might have been some regret from his side based on Bing's correspondence with Louis toward the end.

Louis was in bad health by the early 1970s, but he insisted on still performing, doing a two-week engagement at the Waldorf-Astoria's Empire Room in March of 1971 against the advice of his doctors. He had a heart attack and was hospitalized, but he kept up his trumpet playing and dreamed of going back out on the road.

Louis received a letter from Bing while he was still in the hospital. "I think of you often," Bing wrote, "and I always recall, with pleasure, the times when we get together for an appearance, or a visit. They're too infrequent, it seems to me, and when you get back to work, we'll have to change all this."

When Louis died in his sleep of a second heart attack in July of 1971, Bing, Ella, and Frank were all pallbearers at his funeral. Ella was wearing dark glasses, and when George Wein asked her if she was going to sing, Ella told him, "I'm here to mourn." Bing wrote Louis's widow Lucille, "I know of no man for whom I had more admiration and respect."

The same year Louis died, Bing took his last acting role in a thriller for television called *Dr. Cook's Garden*, in which he plays a doctor who euthanizes his patients without their consent. This last movie discovered that Bing's smooth bass voice could be menacing, for it is such an all-encompassing and near-hollow sound that it could be taken to mean anything.

The character of Dr. Cook is Bing's only on-screen villain, and he is quite convincingly evil as that "gold poured out of a cup" voice says chilling things. There is a rather strenuous physical fight scene for him late in this picture, and it's surprising that Bing would want to play such a taxing role when there was so much golf to be played, yet he always knew just when to take his public off guard.

This plunge into smart horror didn't mean Bing was ready for anything. When he guested on Carol Burnett's TV show, she effusively kissed him on the neck, and he reacted with near-horror and distaste, unable to handle her warmth. He was in ill health for a bit before he recorded a pet project called *A Southern Memoir* (1975), which he paid for himself. Aside from some "groovy" saxophone and tambourine backing here and there, this is a solid album that features some fine late singing from the Old Groaner, with some jazzy accents reminiscent of his youth.

Bing did an album with Fred Astaire, and he continued a steady stream of TV specials on which his family often appeared with him, and his two sons with Kathryn are cute and appealing, whereas the four Dixie sons had always been mean minded and competitive. He wanted to do some live singing again, and so he was booked into the London Palladium in the summer of 1976 for a charming retrospective concert that was recorded. Bing explains the context of Stephen Sondheim's "Send in the Clowns" for his audience very articulately and then says that he enjoys Sondheim's "oblique" lyrics.

Bing can do a Carole King number like "You've Got a Friend" and make it work for him because it is the offspring of a soothing 1930s song like his "Pennies from Heaven." His children with Kathryn can't sing on key here, but Bing's performing with them is charming, whereas when he sang with his first set of sons, the results were always tense. He "picks a few old chestnuts out of the ashes" for a lengthy medley starting with his first real hit "I Surrender Dear," and the audience joins him on "Pennies from Heaven." Bing had so many hits that he doesn't even do "Out of Nowhere" or "Mexicali Rose," and they are missed.

Rosemary Clooney, who played in this concert with Bing, saw him mouth the words "I love you" to the audience, and this was a big deal for a guy so reserved that he told Barbara Walters he could never do anything so "flamboyant" as to say "I love you" to his wife and children. When Clooney had a nervous breakdown in the late 1960s and was in the hospital, Bing had sent her a telegram that read, "Is it a boy or a girl? Love, Bing." This made Clooney laugh and lifted her spirits, and now Bing was helping get her career back together.

Bing wasn't happy that they didn't sell as many tickets as he would have liked when the show played in New York, but he took it with his usual calm. When his daughter Mary saw him casually reading a paper before a show, she asked him, "Dad, aren't you nervous?" Bing looked over his paper at her and said, "Nervous? What's there to be nervous about?"

When Bing was taping a special to commemorate his fiftieth year in show business in March of 1977, he took a very bad fall. "Bing said farewell from the center of the stage, while the section behind him, which held the Joey Bushkin Quartet, silently descended twenty-five feet into the basement," said Kathryn. "Bing bowed, stepped backwards out of the lights, and disappeared into the void. Whirling in midair, he grasped a handful of drapery, which ripped free, but slowed and deflected his fall. Just missing the quartet's drums, which would have cut him in two, he landed on his left hip on the concrete floor. . . . Medics arrived with a stretcher. As we left the auditorium, Bing began humming, 'Off we go, into the wild blue yonder. . . .'" As always, he took a setback like this calmly, and he recovered and returned to performing, playing the Palladium again.

Bing did a TV special with his family on which David Bowie made a guest appearance. Larry Grossman, who was a writer on this special, remembered that Bowie refused to sing "The Little Drummer Boy" and said, "I hate that song. If I have to sing that song I can't do the show. I'm doing the show because my mother loves Bing Crosby."

Bing's writers came up with a counterpoint duet for Bing and Bowie, and the result on-screen is one of the strangest juxtapositions of performers imaginable, made even stranger later in the special when Bing and his family are chatting and this is intercut with Bowie doing a very sexy and narcissistic version of "Heroes" where we see him embracing himself from behind in ultra-tight pants as two other Bowies look on, a contrast so jarring that it feels hallucinatory.

Bing did his old hit "June in January" with verse on an album called *Seasons* (1977), where he also offered a reflective and urgent "September Song." The last track on this recording is Charles Aznavour's "Yesterday When I Was Young," which Bing fully understands and delivers with admirable dryness.

On some outtakes, Bing is heard reminiscing and joking with the musicians. "I have nowhere to go . . . pub don't open until noon!" he says. Speaking of the change in popular music, Bing says, "You know, when they first came around, these rock and roll groups, I'm talking about fifteen years ago, they were *awful,* the harmony they used, but now there's a lot of good musicians."

Bing also speaks here about what happened to his voice in the 1940s. "I lost my high notes," he says, a touch mournfully. "I used to have a lovely falsetto—I used to get grand mail, marvelous mail I got in those days," the tone of his voice lightening very humorously in a sophisticated Judy-ish way.

In October of 1977, Bing flew to Spain to play some golf. On October 14, he played eighteen holes with World Cup champion Manuel Piñero, and he was in fine fettle. A few construction workers asked him for a song, and Bing obliged with Frank's hit "Strangers in the Night." They finished, and Bing said, "That was a great game of golf, fellas. Let's go have a Coca-Cola." As he walked to the clubhouse, Bing collapsed and died instantly of a heart attack. There was a modest funeral, no fuss.

Ella was rhapsodic about his sound when she was interviewed for a TV special in Bing's honor in 1978: "And when he hit those low notes . . . oh!" Ella said, as if overcome. "I just used to wait for those low notes! They'd be so deep, and so clear."

All-American Bing went out in a gentle flicker of glory, the voice much the same as ever, ever-renewing, omnipresent, a balm in times of great trouble, a voice that said "stop crying," a voice that would never go back to his nowhere, a voice always coming back to us some sunny day.

37

Movie Star Barbra and Frank and Ella on the Road

BARBRA TOOK A plunge into full-on 1970s grittiness in *The Owl and the Pussycat* (1970), an adaptation of a two-hander play in which she plays an aspiring actress and dilettante prostitute named Doris who crosses swords with a struggling novelist and bookstore employee named Felix (George Segal). Both loudmouth Doris and pedantic Felix are fringe New York types, and they are both losers; his short stories sound pretentious, while she has done a porno called *Cycle Sluts*. This picture doesn't depict a Hollywood version of New York but is shot on location on the real streets of run-down 1970 Manhattan, and it has guts and nerve to spare.

Producer Ray Stark at first told the press that Barbra would be singing in *The Owl and the Pussycat* and that Doris was going to be reimagined as a folk singer, but Barbra reacted against this and determined that she was only going to play straight roles in her next few movies. She was always bridling now about being under contract to Stark. "I was pushed around," Barbra told *Newsday*, referring to how Stark wanted her to sing as Doris. "Made to feel like I was a bad little girl or something. There was no reason for that."

Doris is very aggressive and manipulative but also vulnerable, and so this is a perfect role for Barbra, who doesn't sing a note and doesn't need to. She attacks the part of Doris with zeal and inventiveness, and Segal is a strong scene partner for her, and a very high energy level is maintained by director Herbert Ross, who expertly controls the pace and timing of the material. Times had changed drastically, so much so that MGM-bred Judy is unthinkable in the part of Doris, though Billie might have been good in it. (The role of Doris had not been written as African American, but she was first played onstage by the gifted Diana Sands opposite Alan Alda. Stark had wanted Sidney Poitier for the role of Felix, but Poitier turned the role down.)

In the first scenes Doris repeatedly calls Felix a "fag," and this makes her seem more unsympathetic now than she is intended to be, but the chemistry between Barbra and Segal eventually smooths that over. The plot of *The Owl and the Pussycat* is a screwball comedy setup in its way, with a free-spirited woman encouraging an inhibited male to go wild, yet it works both ways here with Felix as a kind of Barry Dennen–like mentor to Doris, who enjoys learning new vocabulary words. But Doris does not have Barbra's freak singing voice, which was always her trump card, and so this mentorship can only go so far.

The Owl and the Pussycat proves that the driven Barbra could have made it just on her acting talent and comic timing, for she excels as this uncouth and not very bright and fairly uncensored woman, and she is especially encouraged by Doris's horniness, which lets her not worry so much about being beautiful and allows her simply to be sexy. Barbra did a topless scene for this movie, but in the end she demurred and had it cut out.

"What will my mother think?" Barbra asked Herbert Ross before they shot this nude scene, and she was embarrassed when Diana made a visit to the set and saw her in a scanty outfit. Some outtake photos did wind up in magazines, and she sued one called *High Society*, but the situation left her ambivalent, for she did have an exhibitionist side that would come out in later films.

Barbra fully surrendered to modern pop for the album *Stoney End* (1971), and it was a commercial hit, but the songs were all alien to her sensibility because they were not about character but were snapshots of moods and atmospheres, and with ambient electric rock fuzz around her pure voice. Richard Perry, the producer of the record, wanted Barbra to sing on the beat, which she found very difficult to do. A similar follow-up for Perry called *Barbra Joan Streisand* (1971) only emphasized her disconnect from the pop musical zeitgeist of this period. When Barbra sings Carole King's "You've Got a Friend," surely we don't think that *she'll* come running if we call for her.

Her attempts at being funky and soulful and relatable only emphasized her apartness, and her grandeur. Barbra self-consciously smoked a joint—or pretended to—on a live concert recording in 1972 that was meant to raise funds for presidential candidate George McGovern, asking, "It's still illegal?" but still coming off as a square. She sings "My Man" again here with some of the narrative section, but Barbra never sang the lyric "he beats me too" as Billie and Ella did.

Barbra was not pleased with the script of *What's Up, Doc?* (1972), which was an outright screwball comedy and tribute to that 1930s genre by cinephile director Peter Bogdanovich. "It's not funny, it's not funny, and I know funny," she told her costar Ryan O'Neal, with whom she had a fling following her divorce from Elliott Gould. After a first read-through of the script where Madeline Kahn got a laugh on every single line, Bogdanovich found Barbra crying in her dressing room and saying, "I'm an extra in this picture, I'm an extra."

But her misgivings are not apparent on-screen, and the material suits Barbra just as much as the Cole Porter song "You're the Top," which she soars through under the opening credits. Her Judy Maxwell is a disruptive element in any situation, blithely leaving chaos wherever she goes, and Barbra emphasizes the lust that Judy feels when she first sees bespectacled hunk Howard Bannister (O'Neal), lingering over the word "hot" when Judy first sees him as she is ordering a hot fudge sundae.

Yet Barbra had reason to worry about Kahn, who really does manage to steal the film as Howard's adenoidal fiancée Eunice Burns. Kahn is so comically extreme and yet so believable at the same time that she gets huge laughs just by repeating Howard's name in a censorious way, and Barbra only wins the film back in a sequence where Judy is randomly found under a drop cloth on a piano and sings "As Time Goes By" in a luscious and caressing sort of way.

What's Up, Doc? is a farce that is somewhat in the vein of the meta Bing and Bob Hope *Road* pictures because it isn't concerned with believability, and it was a hit, which surprised Barbra, who was convinced it would be a failure. Unsatisfied with this success, Barbra produced and starred in a small mood piece called *Up the Sandbox* (1972), a feminist movie in which she plays a housewife and mother who has fantasies that play out very realistically on-screen. Whereas *What's Up, Doc?* is very old fashioned, *Up the Sandbox* is a very up-to-the-minute and exploratory examination of one woman's psyche and its contradictions and anxieties, and it is sometimes obscure, but it has bold moments.

Barbra's Margaret Reynolds lives on the Upper West Side, which had become run down and crime-ridden by the early 1970s. In one fantasy sequence, Margaret joins a group of African American militants to perform a terrorist action at the Statue of Liberty, and so we have a cossetted, fairly happy female character here who is fantasizing in order to address the problems of an entire culture. *Up the Sandbox* is a political picture in its way about a woman who likes her life but is uneasy with the racial injustice and unrest she sees around her.

"This man in the fantasy, I thought they should be lovers," Barbra said. "This guy who's in the fantasy is in the party scene as my friend's husband. My Black friend in the park. So, there's probably a sexual attraction somewhere in her mind. And she puts this together so that he becomes her fantasy lover—that's why she's part of this group. Unfortunately, the studio made us cut out the kiss at the end. It was, at the time, very shocking, I suppose. A white woman kissing a Black man—I didn't think it was shocking. But he was a very attractive, very nice guy."

In their public comments about this picture, director Irvin Kershner and cinematographer Gordon Willis placed an emphasis on how much time was spent on the way Barbra would look on-screen. "Before we started, I took dozens of photographs of Barbra," said Kershner, "different lighting conditions, different angles, trying to find where she looked glamorous, where she looked 'house-wifely,' where she looked like a love object, where she looked like a mother who'd been up all night with her babies. Well, I think we found it. . . . [Gordon Willis] loved the story, he was just afraid of Barbra. Well, I showed him all the photographs I had taken, introduced them. He liked her, of course, because she has a great personality—and she made him laugh, which he of course enjoyed—and he finally said he would do it."

"She likes to talk about lighting," Willis told *American Cinematographer*. "She had a 'left-side, right-side' kind of concept about herself. I said, 'Are you going to go through this while moving left-to-right, Barbra? Aren't you ever going to go right-to-left?' The truth of the matter is that she looks good from both sides, but she thinks she only looks good from one side. Well, if that's on her mind, that's on her mind, and you have to deal with it."

Up the Sandbox is a movie in which Barbra deals with her most controlling and unpleasant on-screen mother (Jane Hoffman), who is portrayed as a snooty racist, and their conflict ends up with a very satisfying fantasy physical brawl at a family dinner. Barbra said that this scene was her idea. "It was based on the last time my family had a reunion," she said. "It was the first time I ever used real situations from my life put into a movie. Before that I was probably scared to, like how could I do that? It wasn't important enough."

The feelings generated by *Up the Sandbox* are complex and unresolved, and it was not a commercial success. "I don't think people wanted to see me play a housewife who wasn't funny," Barbra said. "It was very discouraging. I remember taking a friend to the theater in Westwood and there were four people there. It sure made me feel bad."

Louis McKay was credited as a technical advisor on *Lady Sings the Blues* (1972), a fictionalized biopic of Billie's life that served as a star vehicle for Diana Ross, and so that explains why McKay himself is portrayed by the beautiful Billy Dee Williams as the sweetest, most attractive, and most loyal boyfriend a junkie singer could ever have. Ross gives a performance filled with uninhibited, charismatic behavior and makes her Billie a vulnerable, lost child torn by feelings of ambivalence toward her mother Sadie, who is played by Virginia Capers as a nice but clueless woman unaware of the problems in her daughter's life. Ross's sparrow-like Billie could never administer a beatdown to anyone; she looks like a strong wind could carry her away.

Ross was nominated for an Oscar for *Lady Sings the Blues*, but she lost to Judy's daughter Liza Minnelli in Bob Fosse's *Cabaret* (1972), a musical adaptation of Christopher Isherwood's *The Berlin Stories* in which Minnelli plays the madcap bohemian Sally Bowles, a girl who wears green nail polish and gets herself involved with a mainly gay guy (Michael York). Comparisons to Judy were made, of course, but Minnelli's persona is far more upbeat and hedonistic, and she made far simpler pleas for the love of her audience.

Bette Midler also put out her debut record in 1972, so Barbra had some competition by this point, even though she was still very much at the top. She did a final TV special in 1973 called *Barbra Streisand and Other Musical Instruments* that was filled with ideas about music and what sounds can convey, and it was also filled with standards rather than the pop music she had been recording. This program was shot over ten weeks, mainly in London, and there was a lot of stopping and starting due to the schedules of everyone involved.

Barbra worked long hours with intense dedication, so much so that she was annoyed to have to give an interview to *Cosmopolitan*. "Because you're here I'm not having lunch with the director, the producer," she said. "I'm not discussing the shots and angles we'll be working on for the next seven or eight hours. Yet what goes into those hours is forever, for posterity, that's my show and a part of my life. But what am I going to get out of an interview? It doesn't help the work to do an interview." This kind of honesty and tactlessness was partly what got her such bad press. MGM-trained Judy would never have spoken this way to a journalist.

This TV special has a section devoted to percussion where Barbra sings, "People who got rhythm are the luckiest people in the world," and if that is so then she is not among those lucky people. Ella had the best time ever, Billie played around with it, Bing was a rhythm singer among other things, and Judy could swing acceptably when she was young, but Frank was hopeless with a rhythm number while Barbra has no discernible sense of rhythm at all.

In another segment of this 1973 special focused on world music, Barbra dresses in various costumes, and one of these outfits comes perilously close to blackface. Ray Charles is her guest star here, and Barbra looks and sounds awfully square next to him, just as she looks square compared to the fluidity of Diana Ross, who had actually recorded an album of songs from *Funny Girl*, and the camp edginess of Bette Midler.

But that same year, Barbra got her best screen role in *The Way We Were* as Katie Morosky, a left-wing political activist of the 1930s and '40s who falls deeply in love with a WASP golden boy named Hubbell Gardiner (Robert Redford). This part was written for her by Arthur Laurents, a waspish gay playwright who had been a kind of mentor to her ever since he had directed her breakthrough musical *I Can Get It for You Wholesale*.

Laurents based the character of Katie on a girl he knew in college named Fanny Price, who was always agitating for left-wing political causes, and the character of Hubbell was partly based on the screenwriter Peter Viertel, who informed on his own wife Jigee Viertel during the McCarthy-era Communist witch hunt in Hollywood in the late 1940s, which Laurents had experienced firsthand.

The attraction between outcast Katie and school star Hubbell at college in the 1930s is a movie fantasy on one level, but Laurents provides it with just enough realistic detail to make it seem believable. Director Sydney Pollack fetishizes Redford's looks and "in the moment" mannerisms to make them feel particularly seductive to both Katie and Barbra, and it is made convincing that Hubbell himself is seduced by Katie's passion and conviction, which as a cynic he lacks.

A post-college Katie takes a drunken Hubbell home with her after she encounters him again at a bar during World War II, and he does not recognize Katie in his stupor before passing out in her bed. Katie boldly takes off her clothes and gets into bed with her dream man Hubbell, and Barbra plays this very difficult scene well, and with lots of conflict. There is "I can't believe this" pleasure as Katie closes her eyes, and then she looks up as if to place this moment on a higher plane, but this is followed by some moral misgivings about what she is doing, for this is Katie Morosky, and as Barbra plays her Katie Morosky always wants to be in the right.

Hubbell rolls over on top of her, and a tear falls from her left eye after she says, "Hubbell, it's Katie." When he passes out, she is desolate when she says, "You didn't know it was Katie." The very deep level of hurt that Barbra excavates for this moment is the most vulnerable she has ever let herself be on-screen.

Laurents had a lot of trouble with Pollack and Redford on *The Way We Were*, and in his more-than-frank memoir *Original Story By* (2000) he details why certain political and character points he was trying for got blunted because both the director and the male star wanted to make Hubbell as attractive and sympathetic as possible. Laurents's material about the Hollywood blacklist of the late 1940s was very personal to him, and it was rewritten and rewritten again by many other writers before shooting began, but Barbra fought for Katie and kept bringing back parts of Laurents's original script.

"The set was an unacknowledged battlefield," Laurents writes. "Sydney and Redford on one side, me on the other, Barbra in between for more than obvious reasons: she was infatuated with Redford. That itself was obvious to everyone on the picture, not excluding Redford who handled it well, neither encouraging her nor using her crush to his advantage."

Katie's politics in *The Way We Were* are dramatized with some complexity. She has good intentions always; she wants to get the way African Americans are treated in the army on to a radio broadcast, but she has a poster of Stalin on the wall of her apartment near a poster of Roosevelt, and the show trials in Russia had been widely reported by the late 1930s. Katie has her curly hair ironed in Harlem, and she says, "I actually have friends in Harlem" to Hubbell's WASPy friends in a proud, defiant way that edges into an unattractive area of moral self-satisfaction.

Laurents offers Barbra that most old-fashioned of diva set pieces, a monologue conducted on the telephone where Katie plays the pity card with Hubbell after a breakup, a card that can never be played again. Laurents felt that Barbra shouldn't have kept putting her hand in front of her face as she played this scene, but it feels psychologically accurate. Katie gets Hubbell back by being very manipulative here, and when they reconcile that poster of Stalin is directly behind her.

In the Hollywood scenes, Stalinist Katie winds up fighting for free speech, which Hubbell insists "we will never have in this country," and the ironies begin to pile up. *The Way We Were* is obviously missing scenes, and certain characters could benefit from being fleshed out, whereas Lois

Katie watches Hubbell walk away at the end of *The Way We Were* (1973).

Chiles's waiting girlfriend from college on the sidelines is given far too much screen time. But the main romantic charge of Laurents's initial idea comes through all compromises forced by Pollack and Redford, particularly in the last sequence, where Barbra's Katie meets Hubbell again years later and has resigned herself to being a semi–good loser.

Some of the key deleted scenes from *The Way We Were* were included on a 2008 DVD of the film, and they serve to emphasize the profound sexual connection between Katie and Hubbell in the midsection of the movie when they have reconnected during the war and also Hubbell's betrayal of Katie when the Hollywood studio that employs him wants her to inform on her friends.

These scenes, which are in fairly good visual condition, drastically strengthen *The Way We Were*, but they were cut because they would have made certain members of the audience uncomfortable, and Pollack wanted a hit, which he got by betraying his characters and Laurents's full conception. Surely Katie Morosky would have sneered at the neutering of her own movie, and Barbra herself took this as a need for more creative control in the future.

Katie is informed on by the worm-like Frankie McVeigh, who was played by James Woods, a young actor who instinctively knew how to handle Barbra. "On *The Way We Were* we hadn't been introduced yet," Woods said, "and I'm standing there and she turns and says, 'Are you afraid of me?' I said, 'Fuck no!' just like that. I said, 'Honey, you can sing, but when they say action, it's every man for himself and you're in second place!' For a moment I thought, 'I'm fired,' and then she said, 'Kid, we're going to be friends for life.'"

Barbra showed her creative chutzpah and keen curiosity in this period when she recorded an album of songs by composers like Debussy, Hugo Wolf, and Gabriel Fauré. It was as if she thought she could will herself into being a soprano with heavenly legato like Elisabeth Schwarzkopf, but a singer needs to train their voice extensively before they can sing classical songs like this properly, let alone well, and Barbra is fairly lost here, sounding muffled and tentative, like she knows this is a mistake but she wants to try anyway. Low notes are a particular problem, and Barbra sounds best on a Handel song because she can stay up in her highest register.

The album was held back a few years and finally released as *Classical Barbra* (1976), and she secured endorsements from Leonard Bernstein and Glenn Gould, which must have finally impressed Diana, at least. Gould called her voice one of the "natural wonders of the age, an instrument of infinite diversity and timbral resource" in a wide-ranging and eccentric article for *High Fidelity* in which he directly compares her to Schwarzkopf: "Like Schwarzkopf, Streisand is one of the great italicizers; no phrase is left solely to its own devices." Barbra was only sheepish about this effort afterward. "I was going to write on the album, 'a work in progress,'" she said. "But they talked me out of it."

Barbra turned down an Ingmar Bergman film of the operetta *The Merry Widow* because she wanted him to rewrite the second half of his script for her and he refused. But she fulfilled a lifelong dream at this time when she did a scene from *Romeo and Juliet* at the Actors Studio for method guru Lee Strasberg and played Juliet as a horny spoiled brat with Sally Kirkland, who had been in *The Way We Were*, as the Nurse. Her interpretation was received favorably by Strasberg, and an excited Barbra sought to play Juliet in a full production of this Shakespeare play on television, but the networks stymied her with questions like, "Will you sing?" and "What male star will play Romeo with you?" and the idea was finally dropped.

Barbra's extreme power had its limits, and Frank's power was ebbing, but not his taste for upsetting and humiliating encounters. In the summer of 1970 at Caesars Palace, he got into trouble for not paying back his markers, which had been his custom as the king of Vegas, and there was a scuffle in which a gun was pointed at his head by casino boss Sandy Waterman after they exchanged some racial epithets, a very dramatic scene witnessed by a large group of people.

In spite of the fact that Frank was the obvious basis for the character of singer Johnny Fontane in *The Godfather*, Frank toyed with the idea of playing Don Corleone himself in the film version, telling Francis Ford Coppola that he would be interested in portraying the mob boss even after he told off author Mario Puzo in public for writing the Johnny Fontane character. Like Billie, Frank felt different ways at different times and made no apologies for that, or for anything else.

Frank began to talk about retiring from show business, for he had lost all interest in making movies and he no longer knew what to record. Finally he announced for certain that he was quitting in 1971, and his final concert was to be a fundraiser for the Motion Picture and Television Relief Fund, at which Barbra would also be performing.

When Barbra finished her five-song set, Rosalind Russell came out and made a grand and emotional speech about Frank retiring, and called him "the greatest entertainer of the twentieth century," after which Frank entered to do some of his signature songs with Nelson Riddle conducting. Most notably, he does "Ol' Man River" with empathetic power and emotion and with some of his lowest notes and his most rigorous breath control, so that it is at least competitive with Judy's great TV version. Frank finishes with "Angel Eyes," vanishing after he sings, "Scuse me, while I disappear . . ." before briefly coming back out to say goodbye to his audience.

It was a showman-like exit, but Frank got bored doing nothing real fast, and more so after Bing wrote him a letter: "I can't believe you're going to remain supine for long. You're at the peak of your form and you still have so much to give." Urged on by his old idol like this, Frank made a comeback in 1973, doing an album called *Ol' Blue Eyes Is Back* on which he takes a stab at "Send in the Clowns." Frank began playing to large audiences now at stadiums like Madison Square Garden, and he was regarded as a big-money nostalgia act, the voice still sharp but raspier with time.

It was at this point that Frank became the menacing yet somehow empty older singer parodied by comics like Mel Brooks, Phil Hartman, and many others, a vessel of negative energy, his status as the Chairman of Humiliation dimmed. Frank was prescribed an antidepressant called Elavil that he took regularly, and this served to keep his worst impulses in check.

Frank married a fourth time in 1976 when he finally gave in to Barbara Marx, who was disliked by his children. His daughter Tina called Barbara "a relentless strategist," and Barbara did her best to drive an even deeper wedge between Frank and his kids. His mother Dolly couldn't stand Barbara and minced no words, calling her a whore, but Frank did his best to stay above his family's infighting, which he hated. The seemingly unsinkable Dolly died in a plane crash in 1977, but she still remained very alive as a figure of fear for Frank as he aged.

In 1980 Frank did an ill-advised three-album set called *Trilogy*, the third record of which was an embarrassing sort of song cycle by Gordon Jenkins set in space. Some of this is so bad that it sounds like a put-on, but of course Frank's idea of humor was almost always gruesome: "Uranus is heaven!" he sings at one point. Billy May and Don Costa did the first two records for *Trilogy*, but Nelson Riddle refused to participate.

Ella gradually began to phase out most of the "now sound" contemporary songs in her act to focus again on standards, and she had total recall of them. When Ella spotted Benny Goodman in her audience at a performance in midsummer 1971, she told her band to play a song she had cut with him in 1936 called "Goodnight My Love" and remembered all of it while her musicians did their best to keep up with her.

Ella began having trouble with her sight due to diabetes, but this did not slow her down. Finding contact lenses uncomfortable, she started wearing large glasses onstage, which she didn't like at all but soon accepted. Norman Granz was still overseeing her career, and he created a new label for her called Pablo that was named after his favorite artist Pablo Picasso, and Ella recorded a new album of Cole Porter tunes in 1972 with Nelson Riddle that was later released as *Dream Dancing*.

Riddle's intro to "My Heart Belongs to Daddy" sounds like the theme song to a 1970s cop show (he was taking TV work at this point). Ella could still be in form on her up-tempo tunes in concert, but the slow ballads on this Porter record show how much her voice was plagued now by a vibrato that screwed up everything for her: pitch, intonation, breath control. And she knew it. "Now I'm Mary McQuiver," Ella told her accompanist Paul Smith while listening to this second Porter album, but she went on regardless. Ella herself wrote some lyrics to a Porter melody and called it "Without Love," in which she says that a woman without love is like "a zero in the void."

Though she did not sing at Louis's funeral, Ella did sing "Solitude" and "Just a Closer Walk with Thee" at the funeral of Duke Ellington in May of 1974, and at one point she froze, even though she had the words to the second song in front of her. After the service, Ella couldn't remember if she had sung the words correctly.

In June of that year Ella appeared with Frank in the midst of his comeback at Caesars Palace, and they would always get a standing ovation for their duet of "The Lady Is a Tramp." Frank was so enthused by the response that they played their show together with Count Basie in New York in September of 1975, for they were united now as ambassadors for the American songbook.

Yet Norman Granz felt that Frank was still being competitive with Ella, and he wrote an angry letter to the *New York Times* saying that Frank had bullied Ella and Basie into accepting changes in their program. "He also switched closing numbers with Fitzgerald, while trimming the band's portion of the program," said Granz biographer Tad Hershorn. "Granz knew that Ella and Basie were loath to make waves with Sinatra on such matters."

Ella did several albums just with Joe Pass's guitar as accompaniment, letting her wobbly older voice be heard naked and without the cushion of a band, and these recordings are often rugged experiences. Some of her live albums show that she could still be very inventive on fast scat numbers, and she enjoyed bringing out old Billie songs or old Bing songs as if she were looking through a family album. In an interview she did with Brian Linehan for Canadian TV in 1974, Ella looks delighted when he brings up her sexy quality as a performer, which moves her to say, "Sometimes I'd like to write a book and hope that people might see the other side of me."

As these shows and records went by, it became apparent that Billie was on Ella's mind. She did Billie's "Fine and Mellow" for an album, and when she performed "My Man" she included the "he beats me too" line that Barbra never sang. On a live album with Count Basie from 1979, Ella even attempts "Some Other Spring" and introduces it by saying it is "a song made popular by the one and only . . . the great Miss Billie Holiday. . . . We'd like to try and sing it for you." Ella's curation of songs has no limit, so much so that she even does a bit of "Dixie" here during "Honeysuckle Rose."

As the First Lady of Song, even in vocal decline, she was going to claim and reclaim everything, but Granz did continue to exert some control; he hated Stephen Sondheim and refused to let Ella do his numbers. There is newsreel footage from this time where Granz tries to affectionately kiss Ella's cheek and she flinches. She was always on her guard, but it also shows her mixed feelings for Granz.

By the mid-1970s Barbra was stuck between the past and present musically. She had two albums out called *The Way We Were* in 1974. One was a soundtrack that included her theme song and instrumentals of standards like Bing's "Red Sails in the Sunset" and "Wrap Your Troubles in Dreams," and the other featured a cover on which she looks like "an Iranian kindergarten teacher" according to sharp-witted writer Ethan Mordden, and this was made up of mainly contemporary material.

It was in 1974 that Barbra started to cash in and really tried to join the mainstream, and this was when she made a crucial mistake professionally. She had accepted a poor comedy script called *For Pete's Sake*, and she needed someone to create a short wig for her, which is how she met lothario hairdresser Jon Peters, who saw his opportunity with her and went right for the kill.

Peters yelled at Barbra for being late to their first meeting, when being late was one of the things about herself that Barbra disliked but couldn't seem to change, and then he softened and paid her a compliment. "You have a great ass," Peters told her, and whether consciously or not he had hit on her Achilles' heel: her desire to be seen as sexy and attractive.

Peters was sexy himself and exciting in his way, a mythmaker, a go-getter, and an idiot. Under his influence, Barbra recorded what she came to regard as her worst album, *ButterFly* (1974), which was masterminded by Peters, who kept referring to Barbra as "my woman." The cover features a stick of butter with a housefly on it, one of Peters's bright ideas, and Barbra attempts to get funky on this record and brags of sexual liberation. The nadir here is a version of David Bowie's "Life on Mars" that Bowie himself publicly called "bloody awful" and "atrocious" in *Playboy*, which meant that rock stars weren't going to be as polite with Barbra as classical musicians.

For Pete's Sake is just as bad or even worse, so low level in its search for laughs that don't come that it sometimes even winds up being offensive, but Barbra was fatally distracted now. Peters's wig for her is attractive at least; if only he had stuck to hair and the bedroom rather than the movie set and the boardroom. Unlike Judy, Barbra kept control over her finances and didn't let Peters meddle with them, which caused some friction between them. Peters and Barbra's agent Sue Mengers pressured her into firing Marty Erlichman as her manager, and she let Peters attempt to handle her career.

Ray Stark still had Barbra under contract for one more movie, and he insisted on a sequel to *Funny Girl* called *Funny Lady* (1975), which featured biting songs by John Kander and Fred Ebb, who had made Liza Minnelli into a star. At first Barbra told Stark that he would have to drag her into court to get her to do this movie, and so he only had her services here under extreme duress. Consequently, Kander and Ebb found her less than congenial. "You feel you're working for her, not with her," Kander said.

Cinematographer Vilmos Zsigmond was fired when the film he shot looked too dark to everyone. This was a particular problem on the "(It's Gonna Be a) Great Day" number, which featured forty African American dancers who could barely be seen in the Zsigmond footage, and so veteran Hollywood cameraman James Wong Howe took over on short notice. Harry Stradling had used a diffusion lens for his close-ups of Barbra in her first movies, but Howe refused to put this lens on his own camera and told Barbra he could get the same effect with lighting.

Ben Vereen was cast as a character called Bert Robbins, an entertainer who is seen in two numbers, an ill-advised parody of *Uncle Tom's Cabin* that was cut down to just a few moments in the movie, and a solo routine in which he was made to wear a watermelon suit. When Vereen made a screen test for the *Uncle Tom* section, he was actually asked to put on blackface, and he did, but thankfully it was not used for the movie.

Barbra's Fanny in *Funny Lady* has become cold and elegant and very unlikable, and she meets a Jon Peters–like figure in James Caan's Billy Rose, but with a difference, for Rose was at least capable of writing the lyrics to songs like "More Than You Know" and "Paper Moon." This Fanny has moved from the mad first love of Nicky Arnstein to the expedient show business connection of Caan's Billy Rose, and the result, even if realistic, is unpleasant, depressing, and unnecessary.

But Barbra is at least in resplendent voice here on "(It's Gonna Be a) Great Day" and on a very angry Kander and Ebb number called "How Lucky Can You Get." It might be argued that her singing voice in 1975 was even stronger technically than in 1965, though she was creatively lost now.

This became particularly apparent with her remake of *A Star Is Born* (1976) set in the rock world, on which Peters was listed as a producer after he tried to push his way in as her director or her costar or both. Kris Kristofferson was enlisted to play the fading rock star John Norman Howard after Elvis Presley and Mick Jagger had been approached, and he sings in a rough and toneless voice.

Kristofferson's John compliments Barbra's aspiring singer Esther Hoffman almost at once: "You've got a great ass," he tells her, just as Peters had, and the camera stares at her ass, and a roadie slaps her ass, at which point this begins to seem like it is going to be a movie solely about Barbra's behind, and this isn't far off. "You're a charmer, you got a sweet little ass," John tells her later in the film as she bends over for the camera in white short shorts.

Esther becomes a star when John pushes her out to sing at one of his concerts, and it is not remotely believable that his rock audience would respond to her sound so positively. *A Star Is Born* portrays music fans and music press as openly hostile and envious, and Kristofferson's John is seen as a pure victim far removed from the magnetic and very flawed Norman Maine played by James Mason in Judy's version of this story.

Barbra's Esther puts makeup on John and tells him he's pretty, and this is an insight into her point of view, for putting on makeup is seen by her as an act of love. The only saving grace here is two songs: "Evergreen," which Barbra wrote the very pretty melody for, and the moody "Lost Inside of You."

A Star Is Born got very bad reviews and there was bad feeling all around, with its director Frank Pierson even attacking both Barbra and Peters in print in an article called "My Battles with Barbra and Jon" before the movie came out—but it made a mint. Pierson is unsparing in his article about the foolishness of Peters, and he is unkind about Barbra and all her questioning and her need to feel loved, her immaturity, her aloneness, and her fears.

In a wide-ranging interview she did with Lawrence Grobel for *Playboy*, Barbra attempted to defend herself and her indefensible boyfriend, and honestly addressed her own tactlessness: "I am not a mean person. I don't like meanness in anyone around me. Maybe I'm rude without being aware of it—that's possible." She called her problem with always being late "a terrible psychological fault."

Speaking of singers she admired, Barbra mentioned Aretha Franklin and her high notes, which she envied, and Joni Mitchell, and Billie, and she showed her earlier education in more obscure worthy names by praising the ghostly-sexy song stylist Lee Wiley. She said she saw Judy's version of *A Star Is Born* several times and admired how "all that emotion was so real."

Barbra took the glamour of being a movie star in the classic Hollywood sense seriously. "One of the reasons I care about being a movie actress is to be remembered, to be slightly immortal," Barbra said, "because I think life is so short that by the time we get to see things with some sense of reality and truth, it's all over. So I'm sure that's why I care so much about making movies. It prolongs your life."

Barbra was frank about how she felt about her Oscar win and loss for acting. "The year I got the Oscar with Katharine Hepburn, I was embarrassed to get that award," Barbra said. "Because there were five great performances that year and I felt that, first of all, it's all unfair, because one year there might be two good performances, one year there might be none. One year there might be seven. Why is it limited to five? Art doesn't have those kinds of limits. And I thought each one of those performances was extraordinary. Now, the year I was nominated for *The Way We Were*, I felt I deserved that award. I felt I was the best of those five for the year."

Barbra read all the slams of *A Star Is Born* and took them personally. "I wish I could be like Shaw, who once read a bad review of one of his plays, called the critic and said, 'I have your review in front of me and soon it will be behind me,'" she said. "I wish I could be above it all like he was." Characteristically, Barbra tried to relate her image problem to a bad memory from childhood. "When I was nine years old, sometimes the girls would gang up on me in my neighborhood, make a circle around me, make fun of me, and I'd start to cry and then run away," she said. "I'm still trying to find out why. It has nothing to do with being a star. What did I do? What did I vibrate? What made them angry at me?"

Yet she was popular and commercially successful at this time in spite of the controversy about Peters and the bad notices. Barbra's posterior was once again the star of *The Main Event* (1979), in which she plays a perfumer turned boxing promoter and actually bends over in front of the camera during the credits so that "A Jon Peters Production" can be printed over her behind.

As long as Barbra sang contemporary pop of some kind in this period, it sold, but there is very little of value on any of her late-1970s albums. She did eight-odd minutes of disco with Donna Summer for a single called "No More Tears," and a shortened version got lots of radio play. Barbra manages to bulldoze Summer here—even though Summer was the undisputed queen of this genre—with her "I never need to breathe" high notes.

Guilty (1980) was a big-selling album for Barbra where she collaborated with Barry Gibb of the Bee Gees, who wrote all the tracks and gave her several hit singles. Once again, Barbra had trouble singing on the beat. Producer Karl Richardson spoke of having to do a lot of tinkering with the tracks in order to lock free-form Barbra into strict rhythms and even pitches that were not scooped into.

The songs on this record epitomize the modern pop of 1980 in that they are tasty and disposable and so tied to their original performers that no one else could cover them without sounding like they were doing karaoke. The lyrics for *Guilty* are cryptic; why is being a woman in love a "right" Barbra has to "defend again and again"? Barbra herself questioned this, but it didn't matter. It was dramatic, and Barbra was famously dramatic, and that was enough. This was car radio music, a fleeting mood for traveling down the road and then on to the next, whereas when Frank sang about Ava there was a sense that it was official, and that the feelings were permanent.

In their old age, Frank and Ava were still thinking about each other. He sent her flowers every year on her birthday, and she would keep them in a vase and look at the dead flowers all year until another bouquet came on the next birthday. When his wife Barbara told him that his relationship with Ava never could have worked, Frank plaintively asked, "Why?" as if he needed an answer. "Too much hurt," Barbara told him, and according to her Frank took this in and finally agreed with her, but this comes from a self-serving memoir in which Barbara's phoniness is so one hundred percent that it's impossible to even read between the lines of anything she says.

According to Barbara, Frank had mellowed quite a bit in his old age. He wouldn't even let anyone kill a bug in his presence and would say, "Don't kill the little fella, that's a pal of mine." She also wrote that when Frank would go into a rage as an older man he didn't really mean it to be taken seriously. Frank wasn't funny himself, but he loved to laugh, and his anger could always be defused now if he could see the humor of a situation. Yet he would carry a pistol onstage with him, either in his boot or in the small of his back.

On his album *She Shot Me Down* (1981), which is his best late effort, Frank covers a Judy song and sings of "a long-lost loser lookin' for his gal that got away." Gordon Jenkins and Don Costa and other old standbys did the arrangements here, and there was no attempt to sound contemporary, but Quincy Jones brought in some synthesizers for Frank on the far less impressive *L.A. Is My Lady* (1984). Still performing live, Frank would often end his concerts by saying, "May you live to be 105 and may the last voice you hear be mine."

The late 1970s and the '80s were a tear-down time for icons of the '30s and '40s. The publication of Christina Crawford's *Mommie Dearest* in 1978 was so commercially successful that other children of stars wrote their own books, and Bing's reputation took a permanent hit when Gary Crosby's *Going My Own Way* was released in 1983.

According to Bing's daughter Mary, she had lunch with Gary shortly after his memoir came out, and Gary told her that his publishers had advised him that the worse he made Bing the more books they would sell, and so he took some creative license and lived to regret it. The image of Bing as a bad father was cemented when two of the sons from his first marriage committed suicide, Lindsay in 1989 and Dennis in 1991. Both of them shot themselves, Lindsay with a rifle and Dennis with a shotgun. Bing's second family could do nothing to mitigate or balance the way Bing was increasingly seen by the public.

Frank kept on going in the 1980s, but he was often very removed and distant. When Ava wound up in the hospital after a stroke in 1986, a phone would be held up to her ear and Frank would talk to her. "I love you, baby," he said. "It stinks getting old." He himself had some health problems, but he kept up the touring, at least partly because his fourth wife Barbara enjoyed buying jewelry so much. At age seventy, he was reading his lyrics off of large teleprompters and barking out the words of his songs. Frank would close the vowel now on certain notes of a song like "Luck Be a Lady" because it was easier to control them that way and vocal damage was less likely to occur.

In late 1988 he embarked on a tour with Sammy Davis Jr. and Liza Minnelli after Dean Martin proved unable to keep up with the pace in large arenas. At Barbara's suggestion, he had begun singing "New York, New York," a song that Liza had originated in the gritty 1977 Martin Scorsese picture of the same name, which was meant as both a tribute to and a deconstruction of the movies that had made Judy famous. Frank was reluctant at first, not wanting to steal a song from Liza, but his version became so popular that he had to keep doing it, and so they duetted on it for their concert.

Frank wandered the stage looking malevolent but spent while Davis and Liza pushed their energies into overdrive around him. Billed as "The

Ultimate Event," this Sinatra-Davis-Liza concert wasn't much for music, but it was a show. "For all the years they had known each other, Liza was not completely comfortable around Frank when they were not on stage," said his manager Eliot Weisman.

Ella took a page from Frank's songbook and tried an album devoted to Brazilian composer Antônio Carlos Jobim in 1981, and there was at least lots of music underneath her frayed voice here to cushion it. She worked with Nelson Riddle again on the optimistically titled *The Best Is Yet to Come* (1982), on which Ella sings Billie's "God Bless the Child" in her own way, and she was still singing Billie's "he beats me too" on "My Man" as late as 1986 on a record with Joe Pass. Ella did a series of lucrative commercials for Memorex, and she was still up for doing one-nighters all over the world. "Do you think they liked me?" she would ask her last manager after shows.

Her determination to keep performing was so great that she even got back on the road after open-heart surgery in 1986, and she was delighted when a rediscovered concert from 1958 called *Ella in Rome* was released for the first time and went to number one on the *Billboard* charts. In July of 1988, Ella took a fall at a concert at the Hollywood Bowl but saved it by crying, "It's OK, I'm OK, I'll just sing from down here!" Some of the audience left after this, assuming she would not continue, but after an interval Ella kept on singing for them seated and ad-libbed a few bars of "Since I Fell for You." She was the ultimate trouper.

In 1988 Ella was also presented with an award by the NAACP, and she was still keeping an eye on the music scene: "I'm so proud to be in class with all of these younger ones coming up. . . . They ain't going to leave me behind, I'm learning how to rap!" she cried. This got a big laugh, but surely a younger Ella could have mastered that genre as well.

Ella was an increasingly private person now, but her intimates enjoyed her company, and her focus on her art. Her last affair had been with a man in law enforcement in the Philadelphia area, according to Lou Levy, and this had been a long-term engagement that had brought her some pleasure. "She had a great sense of humor," said her accompanist Jimmy Rowles. "She loved to laugh, and she loved to talk about music and songs. That's the topmost subject she likes to talk about."

Ella accepts an NAACP award in 1988.

By the early 1980s Barbra was far less interested in singing and in music except for financial gain. She did a favor for her agent Sue Mengers when she agreed to appear in *All Night Long* (1981), which was directed by Menger's husband Jean-Claude Tramont, and she was paid $4 million to be second-billed to Gene Hackman and play a feathery blonde named Cheryl.

All Night Long is notable in that Barbra does a very soft-spoken, quasi–Marilyn Monroe characterization that is rather far from herself and her past screen persona, almost as if to prove that she still had the skill to do that. Instead of straining to be sexy as she had in her last few pictures, Barbra actually is sexy as Cheryl because she is acting it, with a different look and a different voice—that's the kind of freedom that acting can bring. Cheryl is a screwball comedy heroine who disrupts a male character's life for the better, and she writes all kinds of music: "Country, Hawaiian, gospel," she says, and when Cheryl tries to sing she can barely carry a tune, a nice joke.

Keeping her eye on Broadway, Barbra recorded "Memory" from *Cats* as a single, and this is most noteworthy for featuring perhaps her most supported and impressive low notes on the words "burnt-out ends of smoky days." And then she brought all her focus to a quixotic passion project that she would both direct and star in, *Yentl* (1983), which is at least far better directed than the last few movies she had been starring in. Both Sue Mengers and Peters told her that she shouldn't or couldn't do this movie, and so she finally fired Mengers and started to distance herself from Peters professionally and free herself from him personally. Their breakup would be slow and vague rather than decisive.

Barbra had wanted to play this role since 1969, when she was first sent the story by Isaac Bashevis Singer, and she tenaciously held out for it. After many years of false starts, *Yentl* was finally green-lit by Freddie Fields and David Begelman, the man who had embezzled so much of Judy's money.

Golden images from cinematographer David Watkin for *Yentl* allow Barbra to look younger than she is (high collars and bangs help) as a Jewish girl who passes as a boy in order to go on studying Talmud after the death of her beloved father. Barbra sings all the songs in *Yentl*, which were composed by Michel Legrand with lyrics by her standby couple Alan and Marilyn Bergman, and they are done usually as internal monologues, which makes the score like a song cycle or concept album.

As in all of her movies, Barbra is very physically playful with the man she is in love with (Mandy Patinkin), and as a director she carefully sets up a triangle between her character, Patinkin's Avigdor, and Amy Irving's compliant Hadass. The story of *Yentl* could be played as a farce, but Barbra presents it very earnestly. The attractions between Yentl, Avigdor, and Hadass would seem to open up stimulating questions about gender and sexuality, but Barbra firmly shuts this down toward the end.

Yentl is feminist by the standards of when it takes place, 1904, but it is conservative when it comes to sexuality, and this reveals that there was something of the prude and the traditionalist in Barbra. There are almost no laughs in *Yentl*, and this is disappointing because comedy is such a strength for her and the story seems made for comedy. Imagine imp-like, wild, anything-goes Judy in the part of Yentl and the film becomes much more exciting.

Barbra was not nominated for a best director Oscar for *Yentl*, which was generally well received and made money. Male movie stars like Warren Beatty and Robert Redford and later Kevin Costner and Mel

Gibson would be rewarded for their own similar efforts as directors, but Barbra was shut out at least in part because she was a woman and she had alienated many people in the industry with her lack of tact and her self-obsession. Add in her promotion of the outrageous Peters, who was beginning to climb the ladder to executive positions in Hollywood, and it became apparent why many thought she needed to be given a come-uppance of some kind.

Barbra still spoke of playing Chekhov, Ibsen, and Shakespeare, but she went with the times for one of her worst albums, *Emotion* (1984), which is filled with attempts at then-contemporary sounds with synthesizers and drum machines. To promote this stab at pop circa 1984, Barbra filmed two semi-comic music videos for singles from the album in which she wears fashionable clothes of this time, and this made it all seem even sillier.

"You know, you don't become Barbra Streisand and not be colorful and charming and witty and, you know, be able to get what you want from somebody," said John Mellencamp, who wrote one of the songs on *Emotion* for her. "And she was—of all the people I've ever met, she was the most—I guess the word could be manipulative, too. But I didn't mind, you know."

Barbra then made a creative comeback with *The Broadway Album* (1985), on which she finally returned to the sort of material that had made her a star to begin with and also first grappled with the most significant composer of musical theater at that time, Stephen Sondheim. And she was not afraid of asking Sondheim for lyric changes to make things clearer for her on his "Send in the Clowns." Chutzpah was still her middle name.

"I am a singing actress who likes to create little dramas," Barbra said. "And as an actress I didn't understand the last line, 'Well, maybe next year,' so I asked Steve how he would feel if I ended it with the line, 'Don't bother, they're here.' I didn't know how he would react, but he was so cute. He said a lot of people had asked him what the song meant—now they would understand it."

"Barbra Streisand has one of the two or three best voices in the world of singing songs," said the hard-to-please Sondheim. "It's not just her voice but her intensity, her passion and control. She has the meticulous attention to detail that makes a good artist. Frank Sinatra and Barbara Cook are the same way."

Sondheim was similar to Barbra in many ways. He was a mass of contradictions, a warmhearted grouch, a negative optimist, and he was an earthy Jewish man who had to deal with an unloving mother. His attention to detail also matched hers. They would seem to be meant for each other. Yet Sondheim's instincts were often much darker than anything Barbra could countenance, and these instincts sometimes edged into morbidity, which Billie and Judy would have welcomed, but not Barbra. Sondheim and Barbra do share a certain impersonal quality that comes out in their obsessive tinkering with their work, and this excites their fans and angers their detractors. So they have more in common than not, most of the time.

Her Broadway album begins with the male voices of her former director Sydney Pollack, producer David Geffen, and actor Ken Sylk telling Barbra that she shouldn't be going back to show tunes: "Sweetheart, it's just not commercial!" says one voice, and then "It's not what's selling nowadays," and "Personally, I love it" but "Nobody's into this kind of material."

But the record buyers might be into this kind of material if Barbra was singing it, and that was the chance she was taking. Walter Yetnikoff, the head of CBS Records, gave Barbra and her people a hard time about recording this album, and the company said that this wouldn't count as one of her approved albums until it sold 2.5 million copies.

Linda Ronstadt had made two albums of standards with Nelson Riddle, one in 1983 and one in 1984, and they had sold well, so it was maybe feasible again for an established singer to record show music, old and new, rather than pop songs with synthesizer beats. After the success of these Ronstadt and Riddle records of standards, Frank reached out to Riddle to record another album, but Riddle was in ill health, and he died in 1985. Ella went to Riddle's funeral, but Frank did not.

As *Emotion* had proved, this was a point in time when it was wise to pull away from the sound of the moment if possible; so much of that sound is unlistenable now. Barbra sounds impassioned again on *The*

Broadway Album, though her voice had started to get a huskier quality by 1985, with a bit of air in the tone. She is well suited to the drama of the Sondheim numbers, doing a Judy-like gasp on "Something's Coming," an epic "Being Alive," and best of all a "Somewhere" that puts her in an electronic space background that exactly suits those celestial "not of this earth" high notes of hers.

Barbra embraced and gathered up Rodgers and Hammerstein songs with "If I Loved You" and three numbers from *The King and I* set to a sexy background, and her repertoire stretched back to *Show Boat* again for "Can't Help Lovin' Dat Man." She also did two songs from *Porgy and Bess*, and this was likely one of the last times a white singer would feel comfortable doing those songs. Barbra still had her pronunciation eccentricities, turning the word "dare" into "damn" on "Not While I'm Around" and "find" into "flind" on "Somewhere," as if she felt things so deeply that the conventional way those words are supposed to sound would not do.

She contacted Marty Erlichman to ask if he would manage her again, and he didn't respond at first because his feelings had been badly hurt, but he eventually went back to handling her career, and she began to see wider horizons for herself. After the success of *The Broadway Album*, Barbra made her first major move into political engagement when she did a benefit concert in her Malibu backyard called *One Voice* to raise money for six Democrats who were running for the Senate. The political results satisfied her (the Democrats took back the Senate), but the creative results were very cautious.

Barbra's helpers for this event, her then-current boyfriend Richard Baskin among them, played a practical joke on her when they were fine-tuning the recording of *One Voice* where they added the sound of a man snoring during her rendition of "Send in the Clowns." The guys all thought it was hilarious, but Barbra did not, and she wanted to know who had initiated this joke so that he could pay for the twenty minutes that she felt had been wasted. Looked at one way, this story says that Barbra is no fun to work with, but looked at another way maybe this sort of frat-house-like Frank fun was just not for her.

Barbra chose to sing two Judy songs for the *One Voice* concert, including "Over the Rainbow," and she had misgivings about this at first. "I thought, I couldn't sing it, because it's identified with one of the greatest singers who ever lived," Barbra said grandly, and she called Judy "a wonderful woman" who "touched me so deeply," and that she had "the privilege of working with her." Barbra looks around before she starts Judy's signature song and says, "Who knows? She may even be listening."

Barbra has surprisingly little access to the anger she needs for *Nuts* (1987), a vehicle based on a play in which she plays a prostitute on trial for murder who is judged mentally unstable. Once again, Barbra seems to have stubbornly taken a part after being told she was wrong for it, this time by director Martin Ritt, who had been hired by Warner Brothers. On-screen she holds back, overemphasizing her own emotional delicacy and childlike quality at the expense of the rage that is supposedly alienating all the authority figures in the movie.

Ritt and Barbra had fights all the time on the set, which Ritt spoke about to the press, and this seems to have been one time when Barbra lived up to the worst of her press reputation as a self-absorbed egomaniac. She really wasn't right for this part, which had been intended for Debra Winger and director Mark Rydell before she signaled her interest in it.

Rydell had tried to work with Barbra on *Nuts* but soon departed. When he was interviewed by Stephen Rebello, Rydell was unsparing about what he thought of the result, saying that *Nuts* got "sacrificed on the altar of Barbra's narcissism. A picture that could have meant something was glamorized to a point where hairdos were more important than reality."

"What Barbra is is definite," said her costar Richard Dreyfuss. "And because she's a woman we take issue with that in a greater degree than if she were a man. If she were a producer-star-director of the male gender, we would accept all of her eccentricities in a much more forgiving, normal, unquestioning way. The fact that she is a woman brings all those things out in very sharp relief. . . . That doesn't mean I forgive her eccentricities, by the way, it just means that's the phenomenon we're discussing."

Barbra made some recordings in early 1988 for a sequel to *The Broadway Album*, but they were abandoned. Most notable of these orphaned tracks is her filmed performance of "Make Our Garden Grow" from the musical

Candide, which ends with a twenty-second-long belted high note on the word "grow" that seems to take even her by surprise at the very end, when she widens her eyes as if coming out of some held-note coma.

The only comparable feat of this kind in length and volume and emotional intensity is the twenty-eight-second note held by her favorite singer Johnny Mathis during his performance of "Pieces of Dreams" on *The Tonight Show* in 1978 on the word "home." Mathis not only sustains the pitch and tone and emotion of this note the whole time but even stops any hint of vibrato toward the very end of it, smoothing it out for a particularly "wow" finish.

Barbra is the show-off of all time, but Mathis had trained extensively to do a held note like this and he knows exactly what has been achieved afterward whereas Barbra was clearly surprised by her own note-that-might-never-end. In a moment like this, her own willpower is visibly what is motoring her talent, not just technique.

Her love life once again led her to questionable creative results on her album *Till I Loved You* (1988), on which she duetted with her new boyfriend Don Johnson and also took on another corny song from the reigning musical theater composer of the 1980s, Andrew Lloyd Webber, with his quasi-operatic melodies and the flowery lyrics by others that went with them.

Barbra was in attendance in April of 1989 when Ella received an award named after her from the Society of Singers. In December of 1990 Ella herself presented this annual Ella award to Frank, performing for him and also doing their "The Lady Is a Tramp" duet with him, and her sense of time, at least, was still intact. Jo Stafford came out of retirement to sing for Frank at this award ceremony, and it was as if the support to her once-perfect tone had been blasted away, with only the shell of a memory of her silvery voice still there standing, like a ruined cathedral. Ava had died in January of 1990, and with her went Frank's deepest longing for pain and excitement.

Due to her health problems, Ella's appearances narrowed down to three concerts a month, and then one concert a month. Her last live performance was in the autumn of 1992, and this was after she had lost several toes to diabetes, so she sang seated. In 1993 both of her legs had to be amputated below the knee, which was what finally stopped her from performing for good.

"How's Ella doing?" Frank asked producer Phil Ramone when he was considering a project being pushed by his manager and his wife Barbara: an album of duets with some singers old and new. Ella was too ill now to record with him, but Barbra was asked to sing "I've Got a Crush on You" with Frank, and she accepted. They would not be in the same studio but would be recorded separately, a concession to Frank's age and also to his reluctance to do the album, which he thought was a bad idea.

As described in his wife Barbara's memoir and the memoir of his manager Eliot Weisman, the recording of *Duets* in 1993 sounds more like elder abuse than anything else, with Frank basically being forced to sing when he didn't want to because Barbara wanted her own lucrative album opportunity that had nothing to do with his children, who would be getting the royalties for the older recordings he owned after he died.

"This whole idea sucks," Frank told Weisman, and he also said "This is a dumb idea" and "This is bullshit." He wanted Weisman to just use old tracks and said he couldn't sing anymore, but Barbara wasn't about to let this go: "Are you a washed-up singer?" she asked Frank, and she bullied him into going through with it.

Only Aretha Franklin was able to make the best of a very bad and unnatural situation on her track with Frank, "What Now, My Love?" For the duet with Barbra on "I've Got a Crush on You," Frank sounds very weak and cannot sustain notes, whereas Barbra has much of her full voice still, and they don't meld well and probably never would have. Frank was pushed to record the line, "I have got a crush, my Barbra, on you," and she chimes in with, "You make me blush, my Francis," but their disconnection is total and literal within the sterile chambers of modern pop recording.

According to Eliot Weisman, Liza Minnelli did not sing "New York, New York" with Frank on *Duets* because she was starting to get annoyed about how his version of that song had superseded hers; they sang "I've Got the World on a String" together instead. At his anniversary concert in 1990, Frank had unexpectedly pulled Liza up onstage to sing "New York, New York," and she still had her purse on her shoulder and had to try to sing it in his key, and so some small pushback against Uncle Frank was finally in order.

Everybody bought *Duets* and nobody liked it, for it is like a graveyard for this kind of popular music. All that can be felt are huge egos out of place and struggling against a very bad concept; every track is a mess of one kind or another. A particular shame here is the use of Nelson Riddle's classic arrangement of "I've Got You Under My Skin" so that it can be destroyed by the toneless rock bleating of Bono under the horn solo, a vandalization of something that had been perfect. Frank had made bad albums in the late 1960s and early '70s, but *Duets* and its sequel *Duets II* are in a hellish category all their own.

Bono presented Frank with a special achievement award at the 1994 Grammys, and Frank tottered out to be revealed as a diminished and sentimental old man. "Do you love me?" he asks his wife Barbara from the stage, which was something he often asked her, but it sounds very sincere here. Five nights later, Frank collapsed onstage while singing "My Way," and so it was time for him to finally stop performing, one of the few things that Barbara and Frank's children could agree on.

This was the period when the voice of Whitney Houston was everywhere, her a cappella opening of "I Will Always Love You" a highly dramatic Barbra-like signal to pay attention and submit to the tensile beauty and strength of one extra-human voice, but the meaning of that voice was always ambiguous, either impersonal or somehow hidden. Houston didn't make too many records. She was always most impressive and virtuosic in live performance, particularly in her three-song medley at the 1994 American Music Awards, where she sails through "I Loves You, Porgy," "And I Am Telling You I'm Not Going" from the Broadway musical *Dreamgirls*, and her own hit "I Have Nothing." Houston barely got to touch standards or show music during her prime, and this is clearly a loss for us.

By the mid-1990s, Ella rested in her beautiful home in Beverly Hills, which had been paid for through ceaseless touring, one-nighters all over the world, and difficult travel. Her sight was bad, but Ella watched her soap operas on television, and sometimes she would be driven to the ocean to reflect on her life and all she had achieved. She also spent time with her son Ray Jr. and her granddaughter Alice.

"I just want to smell the air, listen to the birds, and hear Alice laugh," Ella said. Ray Jr. himself said that in this last period Ella had "grace like you've never seen before." She died on June 15, 1996, at age seventy-nine, and she was buried in a cemetery in Inglewood, California.

Frank's mind began to wander toward the end, and he would see his mother Dolly sitting in a chair: "I'm trying to get some rest, but she keeps hanging around," he said. When his manager Eliot Weisman visited, Frank told him, "Dying is corny." At the end, on May 14, 1998, when he was eighty-two years old, Frank was taken to the hospital, and Barbara did not arrive until after he was gone.

Barbara did not call Frank's children to the hospital, which caused much trouble and resentment later. In her memoir, Barbara wrote a farewell scene, and Frank's manager Tony Oppedisano remembered him saying, "I'm losing." This likely didn't happen, but it is true to his persona.

Ultimate winner Barbra was in a retrospective mood near the beginning of the 1990s. She released a four-album set of mainly older and unreleased material that included a version of Billie's "God Bless the Child," which is a song that she seems to deeply understand, and a rendition of Stephen Sondheim's "There Won't Be Trumpets" on which she does sound like a musical instrument herself. These songs had been meant for her *ButterFly* album but were discarded, and they show what she could have been recording in 1974. Barry Dennen was still holding on to the tapes he had of Barbra's early performances, and Marty Erlichman finally gave up on trying to get them from Dennen for the set.

Barbra eventually directed another movie, *The Prince of Tides* (1991), an adaptation of a Pat Conroy novel in which she plays Susan Lowenstein, a glamorous therapist tending to the emotional wounds of a blustery blond man (Nick Nolte). Jon Peters brought the picture to Columbia for her, and she settled in to exploring each and every option for the script and the way the story might be told. Lowenstein in the book is described as "breathtakingly beautiful," and so Barbra put an emphasis on making herself look like some golden goddess on-screen, and of course she got knocked in the press for this.

Blythe Danner, who played Nolte's wife, later said that she felt the very macho crew was testing Barbra a lot, and Barbra herself has spoken more recently about the trouble she had with her cameraman Stephen Goldblatt and his crew and her male assistant director, none of whom were as helpful or enthusiastic as they should have been for her. For all her reputation as a taskmaster, Barbra found it difficult to stand up for herself under these circumstances.

Though Nolte was nominated for the best actor Oscar, Barbra was once again snubbed for her direction. Most notable about this rather tentative picture is the casting of her son Jason as the son of her character; he is very appealing, and first seen against a leopard-print pillow that harks back to her own star entrance in *Funny Girl.* Jason gave Barbra a CD of Billie's *Lady in Satin* for her birthday, and this inspired her to sing "For All We Know" for the soundtrack album of the movie.

In an interview of this time, Barbra offered a theory about Judy's troubles in relation to the way Barbra was seeing women attacking other women. "Maybe it's because women are not taking their own power," she said. "They're not doing more to help themselves. So they are angry. So they have to denigrate another woman as an equalizer. I used to say that about Judy Garland, because she would try to commit suicide every once in a while—that was the equalizer in her life. So people could pity her and not hate her."

This maybe reveals more about how Barbra looks at things than what was happening with Judy. And yet . . . Sexism is not usually thought of as one of Judy's problems, but the lack of control she had over her life often had this as a basis. Near-total lack of control over her life and career in the 1940s is partly what made Judy sick. Barbra insisted on total control, sometimes to a fault, but if she made mistakes, at least they were her own.

Barbra's pipes were in good shape at fifty for *Back to Broadway* (1993), which featured four Sondheim songs and two by Frank Loesser, who was always a singer's best friend. Some of Sondheim's more masochistic material was not a natural fit for her because Barbra has always tried not to be a self-pitying "what might have been" type herself, but she kept trying with Sondheim because he was now the only game in town musical-theater-wise.

In his memoir about their early life together, Barry Dennen says that Barbra called him out of the blue in 1992, a quarter of a century after they had last seen each other, and their conversation was awkward at first before she asked him, "Why do people hate me?" Dennen writes that her voice sounded "hurt, confused, and a little resentful."

In this phone conversation with Dennen, Barbra told him that she thought of herself as a "nice person" and worried about her image, which had turned so many people off by the early 1990s. Dennen heard insecurity and vulnerability in Barbra's voice; she could be that way with him because he remembered where she had started. Barbra told Dennen that she thought she had been "beloved" by her public, but now they were turning on her.

These issues aside, Barbra was calling Dennen after so long, of course, because she wanted something from him. He had given her direction at the beginning, and now at this midpoint he offered direction again, telling her that she should return to live performing. She brushed it off at first, but he knew she was intrigued. Barbra had been telling him about cash-flow problems, and Dennen said that a concert tour would take care of that.

It was in 1993 that Barbra got what Frank had wanted his whole life: her very own president. Bill Clinton was elected in January of that year, and Barbra had been a key fundraiser for him, bringing in so much money that the starstruck Clinton took all her calls and even listened to her thoughts on the policies he should support. It helped that she was drawn to his mother Virginia and got friendly with her, for Barbra was always looking for a mother figure.

In footage of her comeback concert in 1994, Barbra has adjusted to the slight huskiness in her midrange and her high notes are as not-of-this-earth as ever, even better than ever at times, as she impressively sustains notes for long periods with no vibrato. Diana is seen looking very loving and excited in the audience, and there are many boldfaced names in that audience, for this was an event of its moment. The tour began with a performance at the MGM Grand Hotel and Casino, which was practically all that was left of Judy's alma mater.

Barbra circa 1994 is a big one for platitudes in her scripted patter about the inherent goodness of people, but she is skeptical enough to keep herself very much apart from her public on a white art deco set. All humor is gone at this point. If Barbra had her Groucho moments as a young performer, now she is a goddess-like Margaret Dumont in slimming black, her blonde tresses there to be brushed from her face just as Katie Morosky used to brush the bangs of Hubbell Gardiner. In her youth it was partly Barbra's contradictions that made her a star, the tension of her being an instinctively negative person who wanted more than anything else to be hopeful and positive, and that conflict is what won over her first fans and kept them loyal through the Jon Peters years.

Barbra is very cautious with her songs in this 1994 comeback concert, especially when she does "The Man That Got Away" and stays very much on the beat whereas Judy was always prowling away from it to explore her emotions and get exhilarated by them. (On the album version of this concert, Barbra says, "Liza, that was for your Mom" afterward.) Barbra does display a certain enclosed level of emotion on this song and several others, as if she has had to fight immense battles to keep that emotion from getting depleted or contaminated by all her success, sycophants, and that public that she thinks has turned on her.

When someone cries "I love you!" from the audience, Barbra says "I love you" back, but through gritted teeth. However much she speaks about the goodness of humanity here, inside Barbra knows that everything is a struggle and that this love from her public could easily turn to hate. Barbra has never depended on her audience in the way that Judy did, and that's partly why Barbra survived and Judy didn't.

Barbra would never make a deliberate "mistake" to get her the sympathy of her audience, as Judy constantly did onstage. Everything was planned in this concert down to the second. She stuck to her standards and show music, and so Barbra was one of the few performers who was keeping the American songbook alive. Barbra had to compromise a lot before she came back to these songs and this music, but she never entirely gave them up, not in her heart.

Yet she has rarely addressed this directly. Sondheim wrote a version of his song "I'm Still Here" for this concert in which he references Barbra's "hit songs with no tunes" and how her attempts at "funk" really "stunk," but she didn't sing these particular lyrics for the broadcast concert or on the album.

There is some propaganda for the Clinton administration here, of course, including an endorsement of his crime bill. But Barbra was at another vocal peak in this concert, and her held high notes really are technical marvels. She had obviously gotten herself into shape vocally for this event, and it paid off.

Barbra had been trying to get a movie made of Larry Kramer's play *The Normal Heart*, but when financing couldn't be worked out, she directed herself in a romantic comedy instead called *The Mirror Has Two Faces* (1996), where she cast Frank's ex-fiancée Lauren Bacall as her mother. George Segal was demoted here from being maybe her best male costar to doing a small character part after Dudley Moore was let go because he couldn't remember his lines.

Barbra plays Rose, a professor whose students comically idolize her every utterance, and since Barbra had been getting over-the-top adulation for over thirty years, this is to be expected. As in all Barbra movies, her heroine falls in love with her leading man (Jeff Bridges) by being physically playful with him, this time during a snowball fight.

Bridges's Gregory is a professor who only wants a platonic relationship, and so he is the lusted-after sex object here. Rose wants to show Gregory one of her favorite movies, the Bette Davis vehicle *Now, Voyager* (1942), which is about a mousy woman brutalized by her mother who emerges as a swan after extensive psychoanalysis, a fantasy dear to both Barbra's heart and the heart of Davis's gay audience.

The scene where Rose comes on to Gregory and gets rejected is very painful because it gets at Barbra's primal wound as a young woman: the way she felt betrayed by Barry Dennen. In a sense, there was nothing for Barbra after she became a star that she could creatively use, and so she was always returning to these first experiences to make them come out to her satisfaction.

Rose gets herself a makeover, just as Bette Davis's Charlotte Vale does in *Now, Voyager*, losing weight, dying her hair blonde, and dressing to impress. She gets a reaction from everyone around her not because Rose is suddenly a knockout but because the weight loss and the grooming are such a drastic change from her usual casual and messy presentation.

This could be seen as Rose giving in and cheapening herself, but the movie makes a crucial error by totally buying into it as a positive transformation. The overreach is particularly embarrassing when Rose talks to her frumpy friend Doris (Brenda Vaccaro), who tells her that she thought they would always be "in the same boat," and now they aren't. *The Mirror Has Two Faces* was widely mocked when it came out because of the way Barbra loses control of the material in the last third and succumbs to her longtime Achilles' heel of wanting to be seen as sexy and attractive, but it's solid until the makeover at least.

Barbra called Barry Dennen again in 1997 when his memoir about their life together was about to come out, and she thanked him, in her own way: "Living with you was like a touch of God, not only as a relationship, but it was such an amazing thing, that you had this collection of records, and good taste, and everything." Slightly worried about what he would say about her, Barbra got very queenly when she finally told him, "I think you're entitled to your memory of me."

She defended her title as Queen of the Belters on a single with Celine Dion, and it was no contest, for Dion had a comparable instrument but none of Barbra's passion, specificity, and sense of drama. It was at this time that Barbra met the actor James Brolin at a party, and Brolin had gotten a too-short buzz cut, so Barbra went right up to him, touched his head, and asked, "Who fucked up your hair?" Barbra's bluntness and lack of tact had gotten her into trouble all her life, but Brolin welcomed and liked it, and they began seriously dating.

In 1998 Barbra married Brolin, and this moved her to release an album called *A Love Like Ours* (1999), on which she sings what they thought of as "their song," an old George Gershwin tune called "Isn't It a Pity?" about a loving couple who didn't meet until they were middle-aged. For this milestone in her personal life, Barbra turned not to Carole King or to Barry Gibb but to Gershwin.

Coda

Barbra in the Twenty-First Century

BARBRA'S *TIMELESS* CONCERT from 1999–2000 functioned much the same way as Bing's *A Musical Autobiography* and Frank's *A Man and His Music*: as a retrospective of her career in music and a kind of summing up, but unlike Bing and Frank she did almost as much talking and explaining as singing. *Timeless* was a real show and extravaganza for which Barbra hired a young actress named Lauren Frost to play her as a young woman and staged her first recording of "You'll Never Know" with Diana.

After a Bon Soir emcee introduces her, Barbra herself sings "Cry Me a River" in a far cooler way than she did as a young woman without the big final high notes, and when Barbra does "Miss Marmelstein," this time she is old enough for the original conception of her secretary character. The pairing of songs here shows thought and sensitivity: "Something Wonderful" with "Being Alive," for instance, which displays an understanding of the genealogy of musical theater in her time.

The most intimate portion of this *Timeless* show comes when Barbra goes into a monologue about how she was sent a love letter that her father Emanuel had written many years ago. About the subject of her beloved lost father Barbra is never guarded, and even less so as an older woman. She is closing in on sixty here, and at one point she says, "What a great business, huh, you get to age publicly?"

329

Barbra offers bouquets to both Judy and Frank, calling Judy "not
only a great artist, but a generous, loving being" and Frank "the greatest
singer of his time, who also had the bluest eyes," and she fixes the *Duets*
problem by singing along with a track of Frank in his prime, not circa
1993. She does an outstanding "Somewhere" with choir at the end of
Timeless, for she had really made that into a signature song.

Barbra released a melancholy Christmas album in 2001 filled with
good and overlooked songs: a Frank Loesser, a rare Sondheim, and even a
neglected song by Frank's underrated arranger Don Costa. "I'm so glad I
didn't give in and sing 'Let It Snow,' 'Winter Wonderland,' and all those
other up-tempo ditties," Barbra said. "I was almost talked into it, but I'm
glad I didn't." Such up-tempo material was never her thing because it
requires an Ella-like love of rhythm for its own sake, and Barbra was still
Queen of the Ballad, coloring words and taking them where she wanted
them to go. She had stopped performing live for the moment to focus
on enjoying her marriage to Brolin, but Barbra still wanted to record. "I
think I will always sing as long as my voice holds up," she said.

The year 2001 also saw two significant attempts at reclamation and
understanding for Bing and Judy: Gary Giddins's biography *Bing Crosby:
A Pocketful of Dreams*, which covers his early years from 1903 to 1940,
and *Life with Judy Garland: Me and My Shadows*, a TV movie based on
the memoir by Judy's daughter Lorna Luft, in which Tammy Blanchard
plays Judy as a young girl and Judy Davis takes over from the time of
Meet Me in St. Louis onward.

There had been a TV movie about Judy's early years in 1978 called
Rainbow in which Andrea McArdle of *Annie* fame had played Judy and
had sung with her own loud musical theater voice, and that was most
notable for Piper Laurie's steely performance as Judy's mother Ethel and
the surprising decision to deal with her father's gayness directly.

Life with Judy Garland: Me and My Shadows is centered on an extraordinarily sensitive and strong-minded performance from Judy Davis, a
major actress who gets all the externals of Judy right but then dives much
deeper into her sickness and the self-indulgence that destroyed her. Davis
does judge the woman and artist she is playing, but in her own tough-love
way, and the result increases our understanding of Judy's talent, partly

because Davis doesn't do her own singing but lets Judy's own rippling mountaintop voice speak and scream for itself.

The actress playing Barbra's mother Diana in *Timeless* offers the audience food, and the real Diana was still alive in 2000, but in failing health. She died at age ninety-three in 2002, and from Barbra's perspective, the dementia Diana suffered from had at least dissolved her negativity. "She forgot to be angry," Barbra said. "She seems calmer and more loving. So there's a curse and there's a blessing."

The connection Barbra had at the end with her mother was musical. "The only thing she could remember was some of the tunes of her childhood," Barbra said of Diana. "And so in her last years, I couldn't communicate with her with words, but I would say, 'Do you remember, Mom, you once sang that song?' And she could hum that with me." Barbra remained obsessed with Diana and tied to her, just as Billie was to Sadie and Frank was to Dolly and Judy was to Ethel.

Barbra picked Charlie Chaplin's "Smile" to sing for *The Movie Album* (2003), and her version starts out girlishly, becomes powerful and motherly, and then goes back to vulnerability for the end, a real classic Barbra three-act-play sort of interpretation that is very different from Judy's "bird in a storm" version of this song. She rescues "Emily," a Johnny Mandel tune with a Johnny Mercer lyric, and does "Goodbye for Now," a song based around Sondheim's very plaintive main love theme for the movie *Reds* (1981).

Everything was carefully molded for *The Movie Album*, and Barbra picked her favorite lines from many different takes of songs for each track, which was standard music practice at this point. The days of a singer like Billie or Ella or Frank coming in and singing a song once from beginning to end and leaving it at that were over for most big-name studio singers.

But there were some things Barbra could not keep to her specifications. "I like that analog has a warmer sound, you could hear surrounding noises, I wanted to keep that," she said. "Digital recordings often sound too clean, it's unlike life, it's too cold. I had to go along with the times eventually, but I fought it for a while and had many things recorded analog anyway."

Barbra reiterated that she had no plans to stop singing as long as she still had a voice. "I'm so pleasantly surprised I still do, and I thank God," she said. "I never practice, I never warm-up, I never do scales. I'm talking all day and I'm dealing with lawyers and real estate, and I'm designing houses and clothes and things like that." About the design, texture, and forms around her she was adamant, and she was also against morbid Frank's favorite color: "I'm very particular. There's not an orange thing in my house or in my garden."

The Ella-like curation of fine neglected songs on her last two albums had shown exquisite taste, yet on-screen Barbra allowed herself to plunge into the gross-out humor of the 2000s for *Meet the Fockers* (2004), in which she is introduced bending over for the camera just as in *The Main Event* and plays a sex therapist for seniors named Roz. This picture, which made a lot of money, is a grotesque exploitation of Barbra's interest in sexuality. That same year, she splashed around in the ego bath of *Inside the Actors Studio* as the obsequious James Lipton read off a good number of her awards, small and large, and she reacted with royal hauteur to the more halting student questions.

Barbra had said she was retiring from live performing after her 2000 *Timeless* tour, but she wanted to make money for the causes she believed in, and so she did another tour in 2006, which is when the middle register of her singing voice was starting to give her serious trouble. The huskiness that she had negotiated began to shade into raspy vocal damage, and this is the sort of thing that Billie or Frank might have used expressively, but Barbra was known for purity of tone. Her manner was much more casual now, as if perfection could no longer be aspired to and so something more human had to be offered in its place, but Barbra was visually impressive here in black-and-gold outfits, at times looking like the art deco American Radiator Building on Fortieth Street in Manhattan.

When she spoke to Oprah Winfrey before this tour, Barbra said, "I rarely listen to music—unless it's Billie Holiday. Or Shirley Horn . . . Maria Callas . . . and Mahler, Symphony no. 10. Those are things I never get tired of." Still in her uphill-battle mode, Barbra would get very annoyed in this period when anyone mispronounced her name. It should be pronounced like sand on the beach, she would say, no *z* involved. After all, people don't say Judy Gar-LAND.

In 2009 Barbra released a two-album set called *Love Is the Answer* on which she sang a program of songs with orchestra and then more nakedly with a quartet so that her voice was unprotected, and this was a mistake. Barbra had worried about the quartet version of the songs, and she spoke about this with her arranger Johnny Mandel. "She had mixed feelings about it," Mandel said, "mostly over concern that just the sound of a quartet might be too spare for her sound." He reassured her, but she was correct about this.

Love Is the Answer is Barbra's first studio album where the vocal damage rasp on her middle range is very evident, and yet she is still attempting to belt in that range as if the change has not happened, which is particularly painful when she does "Smoke Gets in Your Eyes." It is telling that when Barbra was promoting the album during an interview with the *New York Times* that she seemed particularly concerned about that track and asked the interviewer if he liked it.

Frank had asked Alan and Marilyn Bergman for a "performance piece" during his later concert years. "So they got together with John Williams and wrote this four-section piece," said performer and song archivist Michael Feinstein. "When they finished, Sinatra told them to come to Palm Springs. There was Williams at the piano and Alan singing, and when they finished Sinatra was sobbing. He said, 'Jesus, how do you know so much about my life?'"

Frank kept saying he was going to learn it, but he never did. "The Same Hello, the Same Goodbye" was a song extracted from this piece meant for Frank by Barbra in 2011 for her album dedicated to the music of her friends the Bergmans, and it clearly has to do with a Frank-and-Ava-style relationship, so this is a kind of reaching out to Frank the self-destructive romantic.

Barbra was far less inclined to work as she approached age seventy, and so *The Guilt Trip* (2012) was filmed close to her Malibu home. In this modest but sensitive and closely observed two-hander, Barbra plays Joyce Brewster, an overbearing but sweet woman who leaves her house in Montclair, New Jersey, to go on a road trip with her son (Seth Rogen).

Joyce is an unworldly, very ordinary sort of person, and of course Barbra is one of the least ordinary people on earth, and yet she is convincing in this role, which proves again that she does have acting talent and skill.

This woman she is playing in *The Guilt Trip* is very far from the viperlike mother of *Up the Sandbox*, and she is not like Diana either, though Joyce does tell her son at one point, "Food is love." Surely the temptation was to make Joyce far worse for comic purposes, as in Jane Fonda's comeback movie *Monster-in-Law* (2005), but screenwriter Dan Fogelman based his script on his relationship with his own mother, and it is never exaggerated; it has the ring of truth, and a lot of heart. Barbra even did a drunk scene for this movie and said afterward that she herself had never been drunk in her life.

Barbra reached the greatest heights professionally because of the gift of her singing voice, and it has sometimes felt like that gift is leading her rather than the other way around. That voice and her drive set her apart, but there was maybe a smaller and even ordinary person there still inside her, and she tapped into some of that for her role in *The Guilt Trip*, which was not a commercial success like several of her broader and cruder comedies.

Barbra also taps here into her own deep emotions as a mother of her son Jason, and when Joyce gets her feelings hurt, it's as if Barbra knows that getting your feelings hurt is part of the job of being a parent. Jason himself spoke of how he loved the vulnerability she brought to this movie after he saw it. In the last scene, when Joyce's face fills with all the love she has for her son, Barbra at seventy has never been more beautiful in close-up because she is showing some of her soul for the camera.

Judy didn't have money for food or her phone bill toward the end, but Barbra purchased a Van Gogh and a Modigliani and supposedly had a mall of sorts under one of her houses, a piece of information that was spun into Jonathan Tolins's 2013 off-Broadway hit *Buyer & Cellar*, a one-man show that starred Michael Urie and went on to play all over the place with different actors. Barbra is a figure of legend in that play, aloof, mysterious, filled with appetite, and defined by impassioned discontent.

In 2014 Barbra did her own duets album called *Partners*, on which she sang with her son Jason, and which reached number one on the charts.

Barbra shows some of her soul for the camera in *The Guilt Trip* (2012).

There was another concert tour on which Barbra played Brooklyn and did parts of the score from *Gypsy*, which she was hoping to make into a movie where she would play ultimate stage mother Momma Rose, a typically quixotic idea at this point given her age.

Arthur Laurents, who wrote the book for *Gypsy*, told the *Hartford Courant* that he had a discussion with Barbra about doing a movie of *Gypsy* in which she tried to convince him. "Do you think I can do it?" Barbra asked him. Laurents told her, "No." Barbra asked, "Too old?" Laurents told her, "It has nothing to do with age. You play for sympathy."

But Barbra had a personal reason for wanting to play Momma Rose in *Gypsy* on film. "So we started a conversation and she started to talk about her mother," Laurents said. "The conversation went on for three hours. At one point she said, 'I have to pee. I'll call you back.' And she called me back and told me more about her mother—who was worse than Rose. I said, 'If you can do that . . .' That's when I believed she could do it." But Stephen Sondheim, who wrote the *Gypsy* lyrics, was not in favor of this idea, which she held on to very stubbornly for years.

Barbra's presentation in concert was very loose by 2014. Many of her live performances wound up on YouTube the day after they were done. "Are you filming my whole show?" Barbra asks with some bewilderment at one point at the Barclays Center in Brooklyn, as she looks down at audience members with their phones up. "People have to pay for that," she says quietly, her voice drifting off, as if Barbra knows that this battle is already lost.

But she finally conquered some key Sondheim material and some Sondheim deep cuts on another far more ambitious duets album called *Encore: Movie Partners Sing Broadway* (2016), her best latter-day record, which features old-school orchestral backing and old-school songs like "I'll Be Seeing You."

This album once again made number one on the charts, which meant that Barbra had scored number-one albums in each of the six decades she had been working. It was 2016 and not 1985, and so Barbra was able to bring a keen sense of regret to the two big Sondheim torch songs she had saved up for this record: "Not a Day Goes By" and "Losing My Mind," on which she manages to stay in the high register where she always sounds her best.

"Make it a little bit more dramatic," Barbra says as her makeup is being applied for a 2017 concert that played on Netflix, where she kills with "Losing My Mind" and contrives to have the orchestra protect some of her shakier notes. Barbra is having to dig deeper into her own back catalog here and even pulls out "How Lucky Can You Get" from *Funny Lady*, which she makes more emotionally specific than in the film, lacing it with little jolts of anger and hauteur. The cries of "I love you!" from her audience, which were a narcotic to Judy, are still just minor annoyances to Barbra, who has become a rare sort of sacred monster, a diva who seems to stand a thousand feet tall and might crush whole cities if let loose.

She did an ominous version of "Happy Days Are Here Again" that ends with a whimper and a sigh on an album called *Walls* (2018), which features several intense cris de coeur that Barbra cowrote as a protest of the sideshow-like presidential administration of that moment, and this record didn't sell, but it showed her chutzpah was still there. There is an attempt at a contemporary sound here with percussion, and her own voice has a rough, angry charge sometimes on some of the tracks.

Jon Peters was now mega-rich from nominal producing credits on lucrative superhero movies, and he revealed that he had voted for Donald Trump in a *Hollywood Reporter* interview in 2017. Peters also revealed in that interview that he was still driven to compliment Barbra on her appearance, calling her to say that she looked gorgeous showing off her legs on the cover of *W* magazine.

Judy and Billie are still alive as roles or opportunities for actresses, and these endeavors will at least lead people back to their music. They were both drug addicts, and so they are seen as victims, which makes for dramatic depictions in books, onstage, and on film. Renée Zellweger actually won a best actress Academy Award for playing Judy in a feature film in 2019, and she did her own singing but made no attempt to sound like Judy; her voice was semi-toneless, with no vibrato. The result was very discouraging. When asked to comment, Judy's daughter Liza had the best rejoinder to this: "I hope she had a good time making it," Liza said.

Audra McDonald won one of her many Tonys for playing Billie in a one-woman show in 2014, and it was a technically skilled impersonation but more an excuse for a virtuoso performance than anything else; particularly distasteful was a scene where McDonald's Billie came out onstage with a hypodermic needle hanging from her arm. Andra Day dug far deeper into Billie as a role in *The United States vs. Billie Holiday* (2021), for which she was nominated for a best actress Oscar but did not win. Day clearly loves and understands Billie, which isn't easy, and she tries very hard to get her on the screen, but the movie saddles her with a fictional love story with an FBI agent, and poor Sadie is depicted as a mean prostitute who sends a very young Billie out to work on the streets.

Bing's image has never recovered from the impact of his son Gary's memoir. When Bing's name is mentioned, people automatically call him a bad father and leave it at that. He lost his high notes early, but then he just sailed along on his solid low notes all the way up to his final performances: nothing to it, modesty prevails. Bing is the quintessential American show business figure of his time, but his ease has not quite lasted in our culture, except at Christmas. Bing's image said that life was good and could be better, and he even had a second chance at a do-over with family life to prove it, yet it is that first broken family that still defines him in the public eye, for now.

Ella was beloved in her time, and she is still beloved. Frank made his mark, and his voice and image linger, never comfortably, always restlessly, never satisfied, which is something he shares with Barbra, who was the last singer to make it big on standards, on Harold Arlen and Jerome Kern. Barbra has achieved everything possible in her profession, so why is it that as an older woman she sometimes stares out at us with such near-offended dissatisfaction?

Whitney Houston suffered the public humiliation of a voice that would not do anything she wanted it to in her last concert tour before her death in 2012 at age forty-eight. Australian audiences jeered at her just as they had jeered at Judy. "She had everything, beauty, a magnificent voice," Barbra said on the day Houston died. "How sad her gifts could not bring her the same happiness they brought us."

A singing voice is a fragile instrument. As Judy and Ella found out, it can decline and fall within the space of a year. Singers never know when they open their mouth if the sound will still be there, and that was always part of the drama of Frank's singing. He really bet all his chips on the fragility of the voice so that if it came out strong it could feel like a triumph that might sweep away all humiliation, but humiliation was always lurking for him, lying in wait.

The story ends with great strides forward for equality. King Louis and Papa Bing could be closer friends now if they wanted to, and that's better even than their music, and their music was out of this world. Billie singing "They Can't Take That Away from Me." Ella singing "Blue Skies." Frank singing "Laura." Judy singing "A Cottage for Sale." Bing singing "It's Been a Long, Long Time." Barbra singing "Any Place I Hang My Hat Is Home." These are the sounds of American elation and possibility, and agony seen with clarity. Here are the sounds that signal a wound that might be healed or a wound that will show that understanding has been reached and a mark has been made and pleasure and solace and ultimate meaning might be found on the higher and abstracted plane of music. And that's something that we should always, always keep the memory of.

Notes

1. Bing: Out of Nowhere

"Every night between their outfit": Gary Giddins, *Bing Crosby: A Pocketful of Dreams, The Early Years, 1903–1940* (Little, Brown, 2001), 234.

"Oh—Daddy Bing": Giddins, 236.

2. Bing: Just One More Chance

"Any form of history": Margo Jefferson, *CBS This Morning*, October 28, 2018.

"After one rehearsal Bing came over": Giddins, *Bing Crosby: A Pocketful of Dreams*, 94.

"We practically lived there": Giddins, 98.

"I was able to allay": Giddins, 97.

"Bing was always a fella": Giddins, 96.

"They know I'm there in the cause": Terry Teachout, *Pops: A Life of Louis Armstrong* (Houghton Mifflin, 2009), 10.

"I'm proud to acknowledge": Giddins, *Bing Crosby: A Pocketful of Dreams*, 152.

"makes you forget all the bad things": Teachout, *Pops*, 122.

"There were just as many colored people": Giddins, *Bing Crosby: A Pocketful of Dreams*, 181.

"I remember the first time a friend": Teachout, *Pops*, 141.

"Bing's voice has a mellow quality": Teachout, 142.

"for what seemed hours": Giddins, *Bing Crosby: A Pocketful of Dreams*, 202.

"He practically drove through": Giddins, 208.

"Only remotely": Giddins, 209.

"Nine colored boys": Giddins, 288.

3. Billie's Blues

"As far as I'm concerned, all the Fagans": Donald Clarke, *Billie Holiday: Wishing on the Moon* (Da Capo Press, 2000), 14.

"always down in the dumps": Clarke, 20.

"big noble-looking girl": Clarke, 27.

"Eleanora always like the sad ones": Clarke, 30.

"She was getting a meal, missing a meal": Clarke, 27.

"She must have liked the men beating on her": Clarke, 35.

"I heard a record Louis Armstrong made,": Teachout, *Pops*, 10.

"He was just a rhythm man": Donald Clarke, *Billie Holiday*, 43.

"a fat thing with big titties": Clarke, 45.

"She was doing everything that Louis Armstrong": Clarke, 47.

"That's the kind of club it was": Clarke, 49.

"We used to try to drink 24 hours a day": Clarke, 50.

"The only man I think she ever loved": Clarke, 51.

"She was the kind of woman that you": Clarke, 58.

"The thing that I found out about Billie": Clarke, 59–60.

"I used to love to watch Billie eat": Clarke, 60.

"I didn't know enough about their business": Clarke, 63.

"This was Mildred's way": Clarke, 62.

"Billie! Billie! Billie!": Clarke, 62.

brought the great British actor Charles Laughton: Clarke, 425.

"sounded like her feet hurt": Clarke, 209.

"She was quite a pretty girl": Clarke, 76.

4. Frank in Hoboken

"They just kind of ripped me out": James Kaplan, *Frank: The Voice* (Knopf, 2010), 5.

Bing had been arrested and jailed: Barbara Sinatra, *Lady Blue Eyes: My Life with Frank* (Crown Archetype, 2011), 211.

5. Ella: You're Going to Hear from Me

"Someday you're going to see": Stuart Nicholson, *Ella Fitzgerald: The Complete Biography* (Routledge, 2004), 5.

"She always knew she was going": Nicholson, 13.

"My mother brought home": Nicholson, 10.

"He wasn't taking good care": Nicholson, 14.

"She hated the place": Nicholson, 16.
"I can even visualize her handwriting": Nina Bernstein, *New York Times*, June 23, 1996.
"That girl sang her heart out": Bernstein, *New York Times*.

6. Baby Gumm

"He was accused of being": Gerald Clarke, *Get Happy: The Life of Judy Garland* (Random House, 2000), 14.
"I'm going to be a movie star": Clarke, 52.
giving Baby pep pills: Clarke, 32.
"a ghastly, dirty lie": Clarke, 43.

7. Diana's Dream

"When I was 17": *TV Radio Mirror*, 1965.
"a nice shape": Gary Collins, *Hour Magazine*, syndicated by Group W Productions, April 26, 1982.

8. Bing at the Top

"Kitty, he was my best friend": Giddins, *Bing Crosby: A Pocketful of Dreams*, 310.
"pretty socialistic": Giddins, 313–314.
He left a little money: Giddins, 319.
"the robot of romance": Giddins, 316.
"I was a serious singer": Giddins, 352.

9. Billie and Ella

"throughout her body of work": Angela Davis, *Blues and Black Feminism* (Vintage Books, 1998), 195.
"jumpy and unnerved": Nicholson, *Ella Fitzgerald*, 18.
"I was promised a week": Nicholson, 19.
"I did something then": "Quotes," Ella Fitzgerald official website, accessed January 6, 2023, https://www.ellafitzgerald.com/quotes/; see also Hannah Wong, "First Lady of Song," Library of Congress, August 1997, https://www.loc .gov/loc/lcib/9708/ella.html.
"Look at him, he's robbing the cradle!": Nicholson, *Ella Fitzgerald*, 35.
"If it hadn't been for the Italian girl": Nicholson, 35.
"I was so knocked out by her": Nicholson, 37–38.

Wilson said that he preferred Ella's singing: Nicholson, 43.
"a big coat on": Nicholson, 43.
"A great band like that with Ella": Nicholson, 43.

10. The Hoboken Four

"I'm Frank": *Major Bowes Amateur Hour*, NBC Radio, September 4, 1935.

11. Judy Swings

"I want to be a singer, Mr. Beery": *Shell Chateau*, NBC Radio, October 26, 1935.

12. Sweet Leilani and Mexicali Rose

"It was like wandering": Giddins, *Bing Crosby: A Pocketful of Dreams*, 480.
"One thing—how about accommodations": Giddins, 454.
"one happy family": Mike Wallace, *Night Beat*, November 8, 1956.
"I heard my mother humming": Giddins, *Bing Crosby: A Pocketful of Dreams*, 519.

13. Billie Swings Her Way and Ella Finds a Hit

"She enjoyed singing so much": Donald Clarke, *Billie Holiday*, 116.
"it wasn't the pneumonia": Clarke, 188.
"When I came out on stage": Clarke, 130.
"When she came up she was tough": Nicholson, *Ella Fitzgerald*, 46.
Ella was a great "personality": *DownBeat*, November 1937.
"When Ella sang she had the whole crowd": *DownBeat*, February 1938.
who wrote about this historic night: Norma Miller, *Swingin' at the Savoy: The Memoir of a Jazz Dancer* (Temple University Press, 1996).
"That was Ella's own thing": Nicholson, *Ella Fitzgerald*, 53.
they didn't go down as well: Nicholson, 55.
"shoes hanging across her shoulders": Nicholson, 56.
Billy Rose saw her talking: Nicholson, 58.
having trouble with "race prejudice": *New York Age*, February 2, 1939.
Hammond wanted her to be a blues singer: Donald Clarke, *Billie Holiday*, 134.
"I put in a couple of big words": Anne R. Newman, "Elizabeth Bishop's 'Songs for a Colored Singer,'" *World Literature Today* 51, no. 1 (Winter 1977).
"Fuck 'em": Donald Clarke, *Billie Holiday*, 161.
"Some guy's brought me a hell": Clarke, 164.
"My recollection is that the song": Clarke, 164.
Gabler asked her for a blues tune: Clarke, 169.

14. Band Canary Frank

"You want the singer, you take the name": Kaplan, *Frank*, 75.
"It was real, it was not a gimmick": Kaplan, 76.
"I sure knew this was something": Kaplan, 94.

15. Judy and Mickey and the Rainbow

"I've got this vibrato": Gerold Frank, *Judy* (Harper Collins, 1975), 127.

16. Bing: Minstrelsy and Father O'Malley

"I sang several melodies": James Kaplan, *Irving Berlin: New York Genius* (Yale University Press, 2019), 197–198.
"I hope so": Kaplan, 197–198.
"Did they save my tuxedo?": Lincoln Barnett, *Life*, June 18, 1945.

17. Billie and Ella Travel Light

"After Chick died": Nicholson, *Ella Fitzgerald*, 63.
"I told him he didn't phrase right": Donald Clarke, *Billie Holiday*, 225.
Billie would often bring white girls: Clarke, 176.
"Billie's attitude toward her was alternately": Clarke, 175.
"She could consume more stimulants": Clarke, 223.
"I want to know what the Negroes": Clarke, 229.
"She gave me that coat to hold": Clarke, 230.
"You go back to singing 'A-Tisket, A-Tasket'": Nicholson, *Ella Fitzgerald*, 68.

18. Frank: The Voice

"There's only one singer": Kaplan, *Frank*, 102.
"Frank really loved music": Kaplan, 96.
"You can sing a note and use half": Kaplan, 105–106.
"Very good, Tommy": Kaplan, 123.

19. Judy: The Girl Next Door

"They had us working": Judy Garland, *McCall's*, January 1964.
"Lana's nice, but talking to her": Gerald Clarke, *Get Happy*, 128.
"If we had married, she would have": Clarke, 124.
"So! My daughter's crazy!": Clarke, 186.
"I don't sleep, Mom!": Mary Astor, *Mary Astor: A Life on Film* (Delacorte, 1971), 175–176.

"There was never a harsh word": Gerald Clarke, *Get Happy*, 201.
"It's not that at all": Clarke, 210.

21. Bing: Homecoming and Feet of Clay

"Bing was a sucker for guitar": Bill DeMain, *Performing Songwriter*, September/
October 2005.
"hated what she had become": Gary Giddins, *Bing Crosby: Swinging on a Star, The War Years, 1940–1946* (Little, Brown, 2018), 545.
"I don't know whether we Crosbys": Giddins, 537.
"That's all right, let 'em see": Giddins, 553.
"had a little bit of ice water for blood": Giddins, 571.
"She confided to me that she desperately": Patricia Neal, *Patricia Neal: As I Am* (Simon & Schuster, 1988), 107.

22. Billie: Lover Man

"I'm only gonna do four tunes": Donald Clarke, *Billie Holiday*, 244, 246.
"She's a really cute maid": Clarke, 246–247.
"a hole in the screen": Clarke, 246–247.
"Billy and I are doing quite a bit": Teachout, *Pops*, 256.
"God bless Louis Armstrong": Teachout, 324.
"Has done singing and housework": Julia Blackburn, *With Billie: A New Look at the Unforgettable Lady Day* (Vintage Books, 2005), 183.
"gotten to the place where she was": Donald Clarke, *Billie Holiday*, 273.
"They came to see me fall on my ass": John Szwed, *Billie Holiday: The Musician and the Myth* (Penguin, 2015), 60–61.
"done much for the race": Donald Clarke, *Billie Holiday*, 287.
"so she sings good": Clarke, 307.
he heard a violent argument: Clarke, 288.
"He was all mouth": Clarke, 289.
"little colored prostitutes on drug charges": Clarke, 296.

23. Ella Bebop

"Bullshit, you know the girl can sing": Donald Clarke, *Billie Holiday*, 273.
"With a singer like Ella, when she sings": Clarke, 278.
her stories about Vaughan: Billie Holiday with William Dufty, *Lady Sings the Blues* (Doubleday, 1956).
"When the band would go out to jam": Nicholson, *Ella Fitzgerald*, 96.

"We would go into the towns": Nicholson, 97–98.
"Oh, Lady Day be good": Nicholson, 120.
"As far as the audience is concerned": Nicholson, 121.

24. Judy and Frank at MGM

Dorothy Ponedel told a funny story: Gerald Clarke, *Get Happy*, 217.
"I'm going to have a baby": Clarke, 221.
"Mac, imagine this guy": Kaplan, *Frank*, 226.
"I think Bing Crosby is going to win": Hugh Fordin, *The World of Entertainment! Hollywood's Greatest Musicals* (Doubleday, 1975), quoted in "Ziegfeld Follies of 1946," The Judy Room, accessed January 6, 2023, https://www.thejudyroom.com/filmography/ziegfeld-follies/.
"doing everything in her power": Gerald Clarke, *Get Happy*, 226.
"crazy about her": Clarke, 247.
"Listen, buster, you write 'em": Clarke, 238.
"great amount of happiness": Judy Garland to Frank Sinatra, c. 1949, via RR Auction, accessed January 18, 2023, https://www.rrauction.com/auctions/lot-detail/336683204887359/.
"I'll have to be honest with you": Frank, *Judy*, 245.
"couldn't stand kissing him": Kaplan, *Frank*, 342.
"It was one of the dumbest things": Kaplan, 737.
"transformed me into an unspoiled child": Kaplan, 364.
"I am an addict": Gerald Clarke, *Get Happy*, 260.
he knew Judy wasn't serious: Vincente Minnelli, *I Remember It Well* (Angus and Robertson, 1974), 248.
"I was in the trap again": Gerald Clarke, *Get Happy*, 264.
"Hey, did you hear about L.B.'s accident?": Kaplan, *Frank*, 424.
"one of the really classic mistakes": Gerald Clarke, *Get Happy*, 269.
"I wanted to black out the future": Joe Hyams, *Photoplay*, January 1957.
"She was standing in the wings": "Bing Crosby Rediscovered," *American Masters*, PBS, December 2, 2014.

25. Bing and Dixie

"He would put out the money": "Bing Crosby Rediscovered," *American Masters*.
Dixie's funeral was "a circus": "Bing Crosby Rediscovered," *American Masters*.
"Do you like them, Irving?": Kaplan, *Irving Berlin*, 287–289.

26. Billie's Clef Blues

"Now when you first saw her": Donald Clarke, *Billie Holiday*, 311.

"From now on, you belong to me!": Clarke, 313.

"Carl, if I had to live my life without drugs": Clarke, 318.

"Lady was an ironical person": Clarke, 323.

"I've been listening to her": Clarke, 334.

"I don't dig all this modern stuff": Clarke, 335.

"Billie was a great artist": Clarke, 336.

"No, she's not like that at all": Clarke, 339.

"Anybody that belonged to her": Clarke, 343–345.

"You want these bitches, Carl?": Clarke, 346.

"She laid waste to the audience": Clarke, 372.

"I didn't dig being put in that position": Clarke, 372.

27. Frank's Fall and Rise

"Frank was a guy": Kaplan, *Frank*, 425.

"the sorest winner I ever met": Charles L. Granata, *Sessions with Sinatra: Frank Sinatra and the Art of Recording* (Chicago Review Press, 1999), 72.

Shaw said that Ava told him: Kaplan, *Frank*, 416.

"Yes, Bing Crosby is the best singer": Kaplan, 433.

"You're not going to put me on television": Kaplan, 465.

"hit some clinkers": Kaplan, 535.

"a truly memorable exit line": Ava Gardner, *Ava: My Story* (Bantam, 1990), 171–172.

"Hey, Ava—come on!": Kaplan, 552.

"Ava, why don't you tell the governor": Kaplan, *Frank*, 748.

"Don't be too disappointed": Kaplan, 714.

"I ran into person after person": Kaplan, 715.

28. Judy on the Comeback Trail

"Judy has been selfish all her life": Gerald Clarke, *Get Happy*, 312.

"Why did you let your mother die": Clarke, 312.

"Those two alley cats can't make a picture": Clarke, 315.

"ruthless selfishness": Clarke, 318.

"There has to be a flash of something": Hugh Martin, *Hugh Martin: The Boy Next Door* (Trolley Press, 2010), 305.

29. Frank and Ella Make Album History

"When my husband and I broke up": Nicholson, *Ella Fitzgerald*, 142.

"It was serious": Nicholson, 145.

"I guess what everyone wants": Nicholson, 146.

"I ought to kill you": Nicholson, 150.

"They took us down": Nicholson, 151.

"We would never use John Trotter": Nicholson, 151.

"There were hardly any second takes": Nicholson, 159.

"What diction she has!": Nicholson, 159.

"She's self-conscious": Nicholson, 162.

"When she made the album with Louis": Nicholson, 164.

"Who's the broad?": Barbara Sinatra, *Lady Blue Eyes*, 131.

"I must say I never thought": Gerald Clarke, *Get Happy*, 329.

"You stole my arrangement!": Peter J. Levinson, *September in the Rain: The Life of Nelson Riddle* (Billboard Books, 2001), 171.

"With Gordon Jenkins, it's all so": Granata, *Sessions with Sinatra*, 132.

"I want to get married again": Nicholson, *Ella Fitzgerald*, 171.

"It was a panic scene": Nicholson, 166.

"We planned far in advance": Terry Teachout, *Duke: A Life of Duke Ellington* (Gotham Books, 2013), 11.

"Ella really was very upset": Teachout, 301.

"Now the people who've been calling": Teachout, *Pops*, 333.

"Frank's gonna blow it": Rosemary Clooney, *Girl Singer* (Doubleday, 1999), 161–162.

"It fosters almost totally negative": James Kaplan, *Sinatra: The Chairman* (Doubleday, 2015), 175.

"With Judy, I'd just lock the door": Granata, *Sessions with Sinatra*, 133.

"made major sexual demands": George Jacobs, *Mr. S: My Life with Frank Sinatra* (It Books, 2003), 153–154.

"Ella Fitzgerald is the only performer": Kaplan, *Sinatra*, 214.

"I have never been so socially insulted": Nicholson, *Ella Fitzgerald*, 182.

"Boy, would I see the entourage": Kaplan, *Sinatra*, 158.

30. Lady in Satin and Billie at the Met

"She seemed to worry a great deal": Donald Clarke, *Billie Holiday*, 378.

the way Ella used her *"instrument"* now: Clarke, 429.

"crazy about Ella and Louis": Via the Billie Holiday Experience, YouTube, April 9, 2016, https://www.youtube.com/watch?v=-kswBptkpK0.

expert "in my little way": Wallace, *Night Beat*.

"It takes a very bad woman": Donald Clarke, *Billie Holiday*, 454.

everybody does it "pretty": *The Complete Billie Holiday on Verve, 1945–1959*, Verve, 1992, CD set.

"Even if they get a white actress": Donald Clarke, *Billie Holiday*, 400.

"With few exceptions, every major pop singer": *Ebony*, July 1958.

"It would be like Ella Fitzgerald saying": Donald Clarke, *Billie Holiday*, 413.

"There were so many people flocking around": Clarke, 424.

"I wouldn't mind, but it don't swing": Clarke, 436.

"I may have showed you how to bend a note": Jacobs, *Mr. S*, 150–151.

"I've always been a religious bitch": Donald Clarke, *Billie Holiday*, 441.

"I had never seen him hurt so much": Jacobs, *Mr. S*, 151.

"One late night in Palm Springs": Kaplan, *Sinatra*, 591.

31. Judy and Barbra

Phillips's horrifying 2015 memoir: Stevie Phillips, *Judy & Liza & Robert & Freddie & David & Sue & Me . . . : A Memoir* (St. Martin's, 2015).

"Listen, you motherfucker": James Kaplan, *Vanity Fair*, May 2011.

"I think we're in good shape": Kaplan, *Vanity Fair*.

"Everybody loved Judy Garland": Kaplan, *Vanity Fair*.

"Jazz and Judy Garland are mutually exclusive": Ralph Gleason, syndicated column, October 7, 1961.

"I sometimes feel that the audience": Undated clipping, 1961, The Judy Room, https://www.thejudyroom.com/judy-garland-the-concert-years-1960-1965/#1961.

"How are things going today?": Gerald Clarke, *Get Happy*, 368.

"I can't take it anymore": Mayo Simon, *Stuff*, October 11, 2019.

"You'll miss me when I'm gone": Gerald Clarke, *Get Happy*, 369.

"I must have been pretty obnoxious": Lawrence Grobel, *Playboy*, October 1977.

little mordent at the end of "You'll Never Know": Barbra Streisand, *Just for the Record . . .*, Columbia, 1991, CD set.

"I didn't like the reality of my life": Grobel, *Playboy*.

"Bob was the artist": Elio Iannacci, *Toronto Star*, July 28, 2021.

"just the trifle bit jealous": William J. Mann, *Hello, Gorgeous: Becoming Barbra Streisand* (Houghton Mifflin, 2012), 85–86.

"too pinched and nasal": Mann, 166.

"She will be around 50 years from now": Robert Ruark, syndicated column, January 18, 1963.

"a little corrective schnoz bob": Mann, *Hello, Gorgeous*, 166.

"What's wrong with your nose?": Mann, 139.

"I scare you": Mann, 167, 172.

"nervous and anxious and jealous": Mann, 388.

"Fuck you": Mann, 468.

"Roslyn and I had seats": Carmel Berman, *Motion Picture Magazine*, February 1969.

"You were magnificent": Shana Alexander, *Life*, May 22, 1964.

"Ugly duckling sang her way": Cover, *Australian Women's Weekly*, June 2, 1965.

"Judy, you felt sorry for": Martha Weinman Lear, *New York Times Magazine*, July 4, 1965.

"too studied": Charles McNulty, *LA Times*, March 2015.

"too phony, too forced, too theatrical": Jacobs, *Mr. S*, 216.

"What will I say to him?": Lear, *New York Times Magazine*.

"Streisand's great fault as a singer": Lawrence Grobel, *Conversations with Truman Capote* (Dutton, 1985), 55.

"She used to visit me and give me advice": Ben Brantley, *New York Times*, August 3, 2016.

32. Ella and Frank

"Ella's singing so badly tonight": Levinson, *September*, 158.

the racial situation in America *"really pitiful"*: *Ella Fitzgerald: Just One of Those Things*, directed by Leslie Woodhead (Eagle Rock, 2019).

"Tony, we're all here": *Ella Fitzgerald*, directed by Woodhead.

"a disaster": Kaplan, *Sinatra*, 341.

"If you try to fix that or put it back": Kaplan, 387.

Richard and Toni Anderson: Kaplan, 466.

"like a little kid": Jacobs, *Mr. S*, 164.

"She would put one of his records on": Kaplan, *Sinatra*, 495.

"And he (Bing), strangely enough": Frank Sinatra, *Life*, April 1965, 99.

"Technically two of the worst singers": Sinatra, 102.

"I think he sings a good deal better": *Sinatra*, CBS, November 16, 1965.

"I just went berserk": *Houston Post*, April 3, 1965, quoted in Nicholson, *Ella Fitzgerald*, 205–206.

"A concert artist would never agree": Nicholson, 205–206

33. Judy: After You've Gone

"Marlene isn't one of our better singers": *The Jack Paar Program*, NBC, November 25, 1964.

"I don't want to be a harridan": Gerald Clarke, *Get Happy*, 390.

"Who needs a happy Judy Garland?": Frank, *Judy*, 589.

"I'll never sing it as good as she does": Undated news item, The Judy Room, https://www.thejudyroom.com/judy-garland-the-concert-years-1966-1969/.

"in my little way": Wallace, *Night Beat*.

"ugly things": Gerald Clarke, *Get Happy*, 407.

"Fuck Liza!": Clarke, 407.

"I'm the Ella Fitzgerald of the sad song": Audio recording, November 2, 1967, The Judy Room, https://www.thejudyroom.com/judy-garland-the-concert-years -1966-1969/.

"Judy just never seemed to have an hour": Anita O'Day, *High Times, Hard Times* (Limelight Editions, 1989), 279–281.

Judy singing Irving Berlin's "I Love a Piano": Audio recording, June 15, 1969, The Judy Room, https://www.thejudyroom.com/judy-garland-the-concert-years -1966-1969/.

34. Barbra at the Top

"In 1961, Woody (Allen) and I": Peter Filichia, *TheaterMania*, October 23, 2006.

"Somebody wrote that I was trying": *TV Radio Mirror*, 1965.

"It took Barbra a little while": *TV Radio Mirror*, 1965.

afraid that some people were waiting: Diana Lurie, *Life*, March 18, 1966.

"Barbra stayed up for twenty-four hours": Michael Rosen, Archive of American Television, July 9, 2001, via FoundationINTERVIEWS, YouTube, December 6, 2018, https://www.youtube.com/watch?v=X-uYiSvxNwY.

"Of course, we sing it": Thomas B. Morgan, *Look*, April 5, 1966.

"I hate them, I hate them": Lurie, *Life*, March 18, 1966.

"When I was young, there was a bit": Howard Reich, *Chicago Tribune*, November 5, 2006.

"Just for the pleasure of it": *The Music Never Ends: The Michel Legrand Story*, BBC Radio 2, May 2, 2003.

"I hired Ray Ellis because": Promotional materials for *Release Me* by Barbra Streisand, Columbia, 2012.

"Streisand lost her voice": Christopher Sharp, *Pittsburgh Press*, October 31, 1976.

"I only wanted to do Funny Girl": Grobel, *Playboy*.

"When I arrived in Hollywood": Pete Hammond, *Deadline*, February 16, 2015, https://deadline.com/2015/02/birdman-barbra-streisand-sarah-jones-asc -awards-1201374638/.

"Sinatra as Nicky Arnstein": *Focus on Film* 21 (July 1975).

"She's not the most relaxed person": Pete Hamill, *Cosmopolitan*, February, 1968.

"She's not the athletic type": Murray Schumach, *New York Times*, July 19, 1967.

"I really didn't respond to the Broadway show": *Look*, December 16, 1969.

"One day I had an idea about something": Joe Morgenstern, *Los Angeles Herald-Examiner*, November 1983.

"Madame Streisand . . . she's trying to out-sing": Teachout, *Pops*, 355.

"She was trouble": Levinson, *September*, 231.

"I have no ego about such things": Minnelli, *I Remember It Well*, 379.

"In a way, Barbra is fulfilling": Berman, *Motion Picture Magazine*.

"Anything's possible": Judy Klemesrud, *New York Times*, February 23, 1970.

35. Frank and Ella at the Crossroads

it was Frank's other right-hand man: Jacobs, *Mr. S*, 230.

"That's the only time I think": Kaplan, *Sinatra*, 678.

"I saw him have Jilly kick people": Kaplan, 705.

"Get him, Jilly!": Kaplan, 729–730.

"Judy Garland is a singer with a capital S": Liner notes to *Judy* by Judy Garland, 32 Records, 1998, CD set.

"Why, Frank, I couldn't marry you": Kaplan, *Sinatra*, 805.

36. Bing in Winter

"I've never been invited to the home": David Dachs, *Ebony*, May 1, 1961.

"I heard Pops said that": Gary Giddins, *Weather Bird: Jazz at the Dawn of Its Second Century* (Oxford University Press, 2004), 314.

a letter from Bing: Louis Armstrong Fellows, "The Professional Journeys of Louis Armstrong and Bing Crosby," *West End Blog*, November 6, 2020, https:// louisarmstrongfellowsblog.wordpress.com/2020/11/06/the-professional -journeys-of-louis-armstrong-and-bing-crosby/#more-1292.

"I'm here to mourn": Teachout, *Pops*, 380.

"Is it a boy or a girl?": "Bing Crosby Rediscovered," *American Masters*.

"Dad, aren't you nervous?": "Bing Crosby Rediscovered," *American Masters*.

"*Bing said farewell from the center*": Kathryn Crosby, *My Last Years with Bing* (Collage Books, 2002), 389.

"*I hate that song*": "Bing Crosby Rediscovered," *American Masters*.

"*I have nowhere to go*": *Bing Crosby: The Complete United Artists Sessions*, EMI, 1997, CD set.

"*That was a great game of golf*": Greg Van Beek, *BINGANG* (Club Crosby fan magazine), Summer 2001.

"*And when he hit those low notes*": *Bing Crosby: His Life and Legend* (TV special), ABC, May 25, 1978.

37. Movie Star Barbra and Frank and Ella on the Road

"*I was pushed around*": Joseph Gelmis, *Newsday*, January 21, 1973.

"*What will my mother think?*": Wayne Warga, *Los Angeles Times*, April 26, 1970.

"*It's not funny, it's not funny*": William Madison, *Madeline Kahn: Being the Music, A Life* (University Press of Mississippi, 2015), 75.

"*This man in the fantasy*": Commentary for *Up the Sandbox* (1972; Warner Home Video, 2003), DVD.

"*Before we started, I took*": Commentary for *Up the Sandbox*.

"*She likes to talk about lighting*": Gordon Willis, interview at the American Film Institute, *American Cinematographer*, October 1978.

"*It was based on the last time*": Commentary for *Up the Sandbox*.

"*I don't think people wanted to see*": Lawrence Grobel, *Long Island Newsday*, October 1977.

"*Because you're here I'm not having lunch*": Peter Evans, *Cosmopolitan*, February 1974.

"*The set was an unacknowledged battlefield*": Arthur Laurents, *Original Story By: A Memoir of Broadway and Hollywood* (Knopf, 2000), 276–277.

"*On The Way We Were we hadn't been introduced*": Brantley Bardin, *Premiere*, 2005.

"*I was going to write on the album*": Anthony Tommasini, *New York Times*, September 24, 2009.

"*the greatest entertainer of the twentieth century*": YouTube footage of the concert.

"*I can't believe you're going to remain*": Barbara Sinatra, *Lady Blue Eyes*, 121.

"*a relentless strategist*": Kaplan, *Sinatra*, 850.

"*Now I'm Mary McQuiver*": Levinson, *September*, 242.

"*He also switched closing numbers*": Marc Myers, *JazzWax*, October 5, 2011.

"*Sometimes I'd like to write a book*": Via Brian Linehan's City Lights, YouTube, June 6, 2016, https://www.youtube.com/watch?v=dunLgfk3XWI.

newsreel footage from this time: *Ella Fitzgerald: Just One of Those Things*, directed by Leslie Woodhead.

"an Iranian kindergarten teacher": Ethan Mordden, *On Streisand: An Opinionated Guide* (Oxford University Press, 2019), 65.

"bloody awful" and "atrocious": Cameron Crowe, *Playboy*, September 1976.

"You feel you're working for her": James Leve, *Kander and Ebb* (Yale University Press, 2009).

attacking both Barbra and Peters: *New West*, November 22, 1976.

"I am not a mean person": Grobel, *Playboy*.

"Too much hurt": Barbara Sinatra, *Lady Blue Eyes*, 163.

"Don't kill the little fella": Sinatra, 188.

"May you live to be 105": Eliot Weisman, *The Way It Was: My Life with Frank Sinatra* (Hachette Books, 2017), 193.

she had lunch with Gary: "Bing Crosby Rediscovered," *American Masters*.

"I love you, baby": Kaplan, *Sinatra*, 867.

"For all the years they had known": Weisman, *The Way It Was*, 138.

"Do you think they liked me?": *Ella Fitzgerald*, directed by Woodhead.

"It's OK, I'm OK": Nicholson, *Ella Fitzgerald*, 236.

"I'm so proud to be in class": *20th Annual NAACP Image Awards*, NBC, January 16, 1988.

"She had a great sense of humor": Nicholson, *Ella Fitzgerald*, 237.

"You know, you don't become Barbra": Karen Swenson, *Barbra: The Second Decade* (Citadel, 1986).

"I am a singing actress": Stephen Holden, *New York Times*, November 10, 1985.

"Barbra Streisand has one of the two": Holden, *New York Times*.

"sacrificed on the altar of Barbra's narcissism": Stephen Rebello, *Movieline*, December 1991.

"What Barbra is is definite": Swenson, *Barbra*.

"How's Ella doing?": Granata, *Sessions with Sinatra*, 205.

"This whole idea sucks": Weisman, *The Way It Was*, 240–242.

"I just want to smell the air": *Ella Fitzgerald: Just One of Those Things*, directed by Leslie Woodhead.

"I'm trying to get some rest": Kaplan, *Sinatra*, 876.

"Dying is corny": Weisman, *The Way It Was*, 277.

"I'm losing": Eoghan Lyng, *Far Out*, May 14, 2022, https://faroutmagazine
.co.uk/frank-sinatras-final-words/.

very macho crew was testing Barbra: Blythe Danner, speech at Chaplin Award ceremony for Barbra Streisand, Lincoln Center, New York, April 22, 2013; Barbra Streisand, interview by Robert Rodriguez, Tribeca Film Festival, 2018.

"Maybe it's because women are not": Paul Rosenfeld, *Ladies' Home Journal*, February 1992.

"Why do people hate me?": Barry Dennen, *My Life with Barbra: A Love Story* (Prometheus, 1997), 15–16.

"Living with you was like a touch": Dennen, 260, 269.

"Who fucked up your hair?": Emily Kirkpatrick, *Vanity Fair*, August 2021.

Coda: Barbra in the Twenty-First Century

"I'm so glad I didn't give in": Robert Hilburn, *Los Angeles Times*, November 3, 2001.

"I think I will always sing": Edna Gunderson, *USA Today*, December 12, 2001.

"She forgot to be angry": Mary Murphy, *TV Guide*, January 2000.

"The only thing she could remember": Anne Stockwell, *Advocate*, October 28, 2003.

"I like that analog has a warmer sound": Elio Iannacci, *Toronto Star*.

"I'm so pleasantly surprised I still do": Melinda Newman, *Billboard*, September 26, 2003.

"I'm very particular": Sara Davidson, *Reader's Digest*, October 2003.

"I rarely listen to music": Oprah Winfrey, *O: The Oprah Magazine*, October 2006.

"She had mixed feelings about it": Marc Myers, *JazzWax*, October 15, 2009.

she seemed particularly concerned: Tommasini, *New York Times*.

"So they got together with John Williams": "Michael Feinstein," Concord official website, accessed January 6, 2023, https://concord.com/artist/michael-feinstein/.

he loved the vulnerability she brought: Bryan Alexander, *USA Today*, December 18, 2012.

"Do you think I can do it?": Frank Rizzo, *Hartford Courant*, May 22, 2011.

"I hope she had a good time making it": Marc Malkin, *Variety*, February 4, 2020.

"She had everything": Barbra Streisand, Twitter, February 12, 2012, https://twitter.com/barbrastreisand/status/168622314169188352.

Index

Page numbers in *italics* denote images.
KEY TO INITIALS: BC = Bing Crosby; BH = Billie Holiday; BS = Barbra Streisand; EF = Ella Fitzgerald; FS = Frank Sinatra; JG = Judy Garland

Mason, James, 173

Mathis, Johnny, 320

Matthau, Walter, 275–276

Matz, Peter, 237, 257

Maxwell, Marilyn, 138

May, Billy, 203, 241, 304

Mayer, Louis B., 53, 102, 109, 136, 138, 141–142, 147, 148–149

McCambridge, Mercedes, 170

McDonald, Audra, 337

McDowall, Roddy, 218

McGuire, Don, 165, 191

McGuire, Phyllis, 251

McIntyre, Lani, 57

McKay, Louis, 158, 159–160, 210, 215, 297

McRae, Teddy, 48, 67, 91

Medford, Kay, 239

Meeropol, Abel, 70, 138

"Meet Me in St. Louis," 231

"Memory," 314–315

Mengers, Sue, 307, 315

Mercer, Johnny, 24, 58, 85, 104, 171, 172

Merman, Ethel, 169, 218, 233

Merrill, Bob, 259

Merry Macs, the, 83

"Mexicali Rose," 59–60

Meyer, John, 261

Midgett, Memry, 209

"Midnight Sun," 244–245

Miller, Ann, 30

Miller, Annette, 27

Miller, Mitch, 163

Miller, Norma, 46, 66–67

Milne, Ethel, 29

Minnelli, Liza, 147, 172, 257–261, 297–298, 312–313, 321–322, 337

Minnelli, Vincente, 109–110, 135–136, 140–141, 142, 147, 171, 205, 277

Minter, Mary Miles, 231

"Miss Brown to You," 43

"Miss Marmelstein," 227

"Miss Otis Regrets," 186

Monroe, Jimmy, 93, 94

Monroe, Marilyn, 184, 250

"Moonlight Becomes You," 84, 279

"Moonlight in Vermont," 206

Moore, Ethel, 19

"More Than You Know," 268

Moretti, Willie, 100

Morgenstern, Dan, 49, 119

Morrison, Dorothy Walsh, 30

Mortimer, Lee, 145, 164

Mound City Blue Blowers, 7

"Muddy Water," 9

Muse, Clarence, 116

"Music That Makes Me Dance, The," 258

Musicaladers, the, 6–7

Musso, Vido, 65

"My Baby Likes to Bebop," 130

"My Buddy," 69

"My Funny Valentine," 268

"My Heart Belongs to Daddy," 183, 304–305

"My Love," 38

"My Man," 65, 66, 96, 122, 171, 198, 264, 273–274, 306

"My Melancholy Baby," 192, 270

My Name Is Barbra (TV special), 264